Java from
the Beginning

INTERNATIONAL COMPUTER SCIENCE SERIES
Consulting Editor: **A D McGettrick** University of Strathclyde

SELECTED TITLES IN THE SERIES
Programming in Ada 95 (2nd edn)   *J G P Barnes*
Human–Computer Interaction   *J Preece et al.*
Fortran 90 Programming   *T M R Ellis, I R Philips and T M Lahey*
Principles of Object-Oriented Software Development   *A Eliens*
Object-Oriented Programming in Eiffel (2nd edn)   *P Thomas and R Weedon*
Miranda: The Craft of Functional Programming   *S Thompson*
Software Engineering (5th edn)   *I Sommerville*
Haskell: The Craft of Functional Programming (2nd edn)   *S Thompson*
Functional C   *P Hartel and H Muller*
Java Gently: Programming Principles Explained   *J Bishop*
Java Gently for Engineers and Scientists   *J Bishop*

OTHER RELATED ADDISON-WESLEY TITLES
The Java Programming Language   *K Arnold and J Gosling*
Java Essentials for C and C++ Programmers   *B Boone*
The Java Tutorial   *M Campione and K Walrath*
The Java Class Libraries   *P Chan and R Lee*
The Java Application Programming Interface
   J Gosling, F Yellin, and the Java Team
The Java Language Specification   *J Gosling, B Joy and G Steele*
The Concise SGML Companion   *N Bradley*
SGML and HTML Explained   *M Bryan*
HTML 4   *D Raggett, J Lam, I Alexander and M Kmiec*
JDBC Database Access with Java   *G Hamilton, R Cattell and M Fisher*
Concurrent Programming in Java   *D Lea*
Programming the Internet with Java   *D Ince and A Freeman*
Java Software Solutions   *J Lewis and W Loftus*

OTHER TITLES BY THE SAME AUTHOR
Ada from the Beginning (2nd edn)   *J Skansholm*
Ada 95 from the Beginning (3rd edn)   *J Skansholm*
C++ from the Beginning   *J Skansholm*

Java from the Beginning

Jan Skansholm

An imprint of **Pearson Education**

Harlow, England · London · New York · Reading, Massachusetts · San Francisco
Toronto · Don Mills, Ontario · Sydney · Tokyo · Singapore · Hong Kong · Seoul
Taipei · Cape Town · Madrid · Mexico City · Amsterdam · Munich · Paris · Milan

Pearson Education Limited
Edinburgh Gate
Harlow
Essex CM20 2JE
England

and Associated Companies around the world

Visit us on the World Wide Web at:
www.pearsoneduc.com

First published 2000

ISBN 0 201 39812 5

British Library Cataloguing-in-Publication Data
A catalogue record for this book can be obtained from the British Library

Library of Congress Cataloging-in-Publication Data
A catalog record for this book can be obtained from the Library of Congress

10 9 8 7 6 5 4 3 2 1
04 03 02 01 00

Translated by Arrow
Typeset by 43
Printed in Great Britain by Henry Ling Ltd., at the Dorset Press, Dorchester, Dorset

Contents

Contents

Contents

14 Communication 441

15 A bit of everything 475

Appendix A Reserved words and operators 521

Appendix B LATIN_1 codes 523

Index 525

Preface

This book is intended for the new generation of computer users for whom concepts such as windows, menus, web pages and the Internet are familiar and natural to use. People used to programs with a graphical user interface (GUI) and to programs that are able to communicate with other computers at a distance through a network will probably expect that a book on programming will demonstrate how such programs are constructed. Programs with GUIs and communication programs all too often become very complicated, and so they are not normally dealt with in the basic programming literature. With Java all this is different: we now have access to new techniques which allow us to construct programs in accordance with new principles. In this book, therefore, programs with graphical user interfaces are discussed right at the beginning, and the question of communication is dealt with in detail. With advanced examples we have been able to include concepts which would be impossible in a more traditional programming textbook for beginners.

The new techniques used in Java are based on object-oriented methods, where programs are divided into independent modules, objects. We can make an analogy with the building of a house. Houses used to be built with relatively simple components – bricks, planks, nails, etc. If we go far enough back in time, not even these simple components were so easily available. Whoever wanted to build a house had to cut a tree down himself and saw the necessary planks. Now, increasingly whole modules are available for our use. Entire walls are produced and only need to be joined together on the building site, which of course means that the house can be built more quickly. Programming techniques have undergone a similar transition. Programmers used to have to write the greater part of their programs themselves and even construct their own programming tools (for instance, compilers and editors). We now try to use pre-existing program components which can be combined into a workable program. This means that the work of programming now takes place at a higher level of abstraction than ever before. It is now possible to write very advanced programs in a short time, programs which previously required an inordinate amount of time and work to produce.

Java is not merely a programming language. It is also a comprehensive library of standard classes. These standard classes are described in this book, and we use them to create the program components, that is, objects, with which programs are constructed. (This book is based on *Java 2 Platform, Standard Edition, v 1.2.*)

However, the book does not only deal with pre-existing classes. It also describes "ordinary", traditional programming and shows the different program constructions – expressions and statements, for example – that a programmer must master. If we may return for a moment to our analogy on the building of a house, we will know that details are essential for a good finish; it is here that a good builder will demonstrate his skill. In the same way, it is important for a programmer to know his craft, so that he can expertly join and exploit pre-existing program components, while adapting them to his specific needs.

To give visual presentations of objects, classes, relations and interfaces the Unified Modeling Language, UML, is used. UML has become a de facto standard for modeling object-oriented concepts.

Beginners should be able to use this book, and previous experience of programming is not necessary although advantageous. It is useful if the reader has some experience of computing and, for example, knows how to use a web browser.

Presentation of the book

Chapter 1 gives the background to Java and discusses compilation and execution of programs. Our first examples of programs with graphical user interfaces (GUIs) are also shown here.

Chapter 2 discusses classes, objects and methods, as well as such basic concepts as variables and expressions.

Chapter 3 deals with reading and writing from text windows and text files. This can be done in two ways: either we can use Java's standard classes, or we can use help classes we have constructed ourselves.

Chapter 4 gives the general background to object-orientation and demonstrates how object-oriented relations are described in Java. The chapter also gives an introduction to UML (Unified Modeling Language), a notation for visual presentation of object-oriented concepts.

Chapter 5 describes the classes we use to construct graphical user interfaces.

Chapter 6 deals with texts and arrays. Our ambitions in Java are much higher than in other programming languages with regard to the handling of letters and characters from different alphabets.

Chapter 7 contains a complete discussion of inheritance mechanisms. Some of the concepts discussed here are dynamic binding, polymorphism, abstract classes and interfaces.

Chapter 8 deals with exception handling. This is a mechanism used in Java to signal different types of error.

Chapter 9 deals with active objects and describes the construction of programs where several activities, so-called threads, are executed in parallel. The first examples of programs with moving figures are given here.

Chapter 10 discusses event-driven programs. Various types of events, such as mouse clicking and key pressing, are dealt with here.

Chapter 11 complements Chapter 5 and deals with menus, windows and dialog boxes.

Chapter 12 deals with pictures and sound, and the methods for showing moving pictures.

Chapter 13 discusses streams and files. A stream is a mechanism used by Java for reading and writing data. There are many different standard classes for streams. This chapter contains both an overview and a number of reference sections. Direct access files and tools for working with files and folders are also discussed in this chapter.

Chapter 14 deals with communication. Here we discuss the concepts of ports and sockets, together with different forms of communication: datagrams, multicast, connected communication links and client–server techniques.

Chapter 15 has a varied content. Some of the things we study are language constructions not required in the earlier chapters. There is also a section on recursion. This chapter describes the new classes introduced in Java 2 Platform to form different collections of objects (lists, sets, and maps).

There are many examples in this book. In addition, every chapter concludes with a set of exercises which the reader can do.

Interspersed in the text are a good number of "fact boxes" containing synopses of the classes, language constructions and concepts that have just been dealt with. These boxes are meant to give the reader an opportunity for revision but they can also serve for quick reference. The fact boxes are highlighted in the subject index.

Addresses

There is a website where, for instance, program code can be found for a number of help classes used in the book. The website will also contain solutions to the exercises. The web address is `www.cs.chalmers.se/~skanshol/Java_eng`. Comments on the book can be sent by e-mail to: `skansholm@cs.chalmers.se`.

Trademark notice

The following are trademarks or registered trademarks of their respective companies: Apple and Mac are trademarks of Apple Computer, Inc.; Java, Java Workshop and Solaris are trademarks of Sun Microsystems, Inc.; JBuilder is a trademark of Borland International, Inc.; Linux is a trademark of Linus Torvalds; Motif is a trademark of The Open Group; MS-DOS, Visual J++, Windows 98 and Windows NT are trademarks of Microsoft Corporation; VisualCafé is a trademark of Symantec Corporation.

Getting started

In this first chapter, we will be discussing how Java programs can be written and run. This will be demonstrated with a few simple examples. We will be looking at both programs that write in a text window and ones which make use of a graphical user interface (GUI). GUI programs can be shaped either as ordinary, independent applications, or as *applets*.

We shall be looking at examples of both techniques. This chapter begins with a short description of the properties of Java and continues with a discussion of the concepts of compilation, execution and interpretation.

1.1 What is Java?

Java is a programming language, developed by Sun Microsystems. Java became generally available in 1995. At first, Java was probably best known as a programming language used on the Internet to create dazzling effects on websites. A website can contain applets, which are small programs written in Java. When a browser such as Internet Explorer or Netscape downloads and displays a website containing a program in Java, the program will be run. Java can then generate sounds and moving pictures, or permit the user to communicate with the program by using the mouse and keyboard. But Java really is a fully fledged programming language. By using Java, much as with C++, complete application programs can be created which by no means need to be run through a browser.

Java has several characteristics which make it especially interesting:

- Java is platform-independent. By *platform* we mean a kind of operating system which runs on a certain type of computer. For example, Windows 98 on a PC is a platform, and Solaris, the Unix variant, on a work station from Sun, is another. That Java is platform-independent means that Java programs can be run on different types of computer systems without having to be changed.

- Java is object-oriented. In its construction Java is based entirely on object-oriented principles. A Java program, therefore, consists of a number of *objects* which work in conjunction with each other and which are described with the help of *classes*.

- Java contains classes to generate graphical user interfaces (GUIs). *GUI programs* can be written with the help of Java, that is, programs communicating with the user through windows, menus, buttons, etc. Different platforms normally have different functions to generate GUIs. A program written, for example, in C++ and intended to be run under Windows 95/98 or Windows NT, cannot be directly moved to another platform, let us say, X under Unix. This is because all the calls for the graphic functions have to be rewritten. The graphic functions for different platforms are also very difficult to learn to use. Meanwhile, the best part of using Java's classes to create graphics is that they, like the Java language itself, are platform-independent. We don't have to be familiar with a platform's graphic functions. It suffices to learn how Java's graphic classes work, and then we can write GUI programs for all types of computer systems! It pays for a programmer, even for a beginner, to learn to use Java's classes for graphics, since the odds are that there will be plenty of opportunities to use this knowledge.

- Java makes it possible to write parallel programs, for it supports multi-threading. This means that a Java program can describe several activities going on at the same time. For example, a moving picture can be shown at the same time as a user is allowed to enter data into the program.

- Java can be used on the Internet. As mentioned in our introduction, this is done by allowing websites to contain applets. With applets, we can create graphics on a website; we can also download a new website, or read a file over the net. It is even possible to create programs which make use of client–server techniques.

Are there no disadvantages to using Java? Is it not extremely difficult to learn? Of course there are negative aspects, the greatest of these being the performance aspect. When a Java program is run, or *executed*, as we say, it will proceed more slowly than if the program had been written in a "normal" programming language such as C++ or Ada. This has to do with the fact that Java programs are interpreted. (We will be looking at the concept of interpreting later in this chapter.)

The question as to whether Java is difficult to learn can be answered with a yes and a no. The core of the language is relatively small. The syntax (rules of the language) is actually based on C++. A Java program looks very much like a C++ program, and anyone knowing some C++ will feel at home. In fact, the most difficult part of C++, the question of *pointers*, has been removed from Java, making it much easier to understand a Java program than one in C++. All this means that it is relatively easy to learn the language of Java itself. However, it is not enough to master the language and its syntax in order to be able to write Java programs. This is because we are not usually satisfied merely with writing simple programs which write and read text in a text window. We would like to construct GUI programs, if possible, with moving pictures and capable of communicating via the Internet. This is much more difficult! There are all the different standard classes for dealing with graphics, events, multi-threading and different ways of communicating, that have to be learnt. In this respect, Java is not a small language, and a good deal of work will be necessary to learn it.

Java was first introduced to the public in late 1995, when it quickly became a byword for its ability to run applets in browsers. It has quickly become accepted in the computer world and is available for all common platforms, for example Windows, Apple Mac and Unix. Sun's official definition of Java is now called *Java 2 Platform, Standard Edition* (*J2SE*). This description includes the definition of the *Java API* (Application Programming Interfaces) which is a collection of standard classes that could be used in all Java programs. The latest version of J2SE constitutes a de facto standard for Java. Sun has developed a software development kit containing the different programs and class libraries necessary to develop and run Java programs according to J2SE. This kit is called *Java 2 SDK, Standard Edition* (*J2SDK*). You could say that J2SDK is Sun's implementation of J2SE.[1] J2SDK is generally available free on the Internet. There is also a package called *Java 2 Runtime Environment, Standard Edition* (*J2RE*). J2RE contains the environment necessary to run ready-made Java programs written for the J2SE. J2RE is a part of J2SDK and could be downlodad instead of J2SDK if you have no intention to develop your own Java programs.

A *package* is a collection of classes that fit together logically. A package can also contain other packages, which in turn can contain classes and packages, and so on. The Java API is organized in the form of a package, and everything in the Java API has been placed in one big package with the name `java`. The package `java` in turn contains a number of other packages with names specific to the model `java.applet`, `java.awt`, `java.io`, `java.lang`, etc. Of special interest is the package `java.lang`, which contains resources of a general nature necessary to all Java programs. (The contents of the package `java.lang` are therefore accessible in all programs without having to be indicated.)

1.2 Where can we find information about Java?

Everything we need can be found on the Internet. The most important starting point is Sun's own homepage for Java: `www.javasoft.com`. The latest version of J2SDK can be

---

[1] J2SDK was previously called JDK (Java Development Kit). You can still see the name JDK 1.2, which is an alias for J2SDK, version 1.2.

found here, together with a mass of documentation. Sun also has a homepage of a more general character: `www.sun.com`.

Another excellent website containing news about Java is the homepage for the magazine *JavaWorld*: `www.javaworld.com` with links to other interesting websites.

The web pages `www.winfiles.com/apps/98/java.html` and `www.winfiles.com/apps/nt/java.html` might interest users of Windows 95/98 or Windows NT. These pages contain information about different program development systems for Java, together with demo versions or shareware products for downloading. The site `www.apple.com/java` is of special interest to Mac users.

Apart from compilers, interpreters and other programs, Sun's J2SDK also contains a great deal of documentation. Of special interest is the fact that *documentation for all the classes in the Java API are there, too*. With the Java API all the information needed for practical programming work can be accessed. In addition, this documentation exists in a form facilitating the use of a browser (Netscape or Microsoft Internet Explorer) to search and read documentation on a PC. Detailed information about all classes can be retrieved easily and quickly.

The full documentation for the Java API is considerable and it would require several hundred pages to print out on paper. Since all Java programmers have access to documentation in J2SDK, this book, therefore, dispenses with a thick appendix. If further details are required, more information can be retrieved from the computer. Another reason not to include the Java API documentation in the book is that Java is still being developed. Additions and adjustments are taking place all the time, and the most up-to-date information is always found in the latest version of Sun's J2SDK, while a printed book cannot be changed as often.

1.3   Traditional compiling, linking and execution

We shall now describe how programs are written and loaded into the computer so that they can be executed (run). In this section, we will begin by giving a general description of the procedure for traditional programming languages such as C++, Ada and Pascal; in the following section we shall look at the procedure for Java.

A program that is executed exists in the computer's main memory and consists of a number of connected memory cells. A memory cell, or a group of memory cells, contains an *instruction*. By combining parts of the memory cells in different ways, different instructions can be represented. A program consists of a series of *instructions* which tell the computer exactly what to do. An instruction in the program is made up of a particular combination of ones and zeros but these combinations may look different, depending on the type of computer. For the program to be run on the computer, it must be stored in the computer's main memory. We usually say that the program exists in the form of *machine code*. The machine code is a code which is very "user *un*friendly", i.e. it is difficult to read *and* write. In the infancy of computers, they had to be programmed directly in machine code. Luckily, things have progressed and programmers today do not normally have to worry about the computer's machine code. Programs are now written in a *programming language* (such as C++), a more "user-friendly" form than the computer's machine code. Special translation programs can be used to translate from programming language to machine code, so enabling the written program to be run on the computer.

When a program is written, it takes the form of normal text. In order to input the original *program text*, or *source code*, as it is called, the programmer can use a simple text editing program, a so-called *text editor*. (Examples of these are Notepad in Windows and Edit in MS-DOS.) Figure 1.1 illustrates how the text editor program is

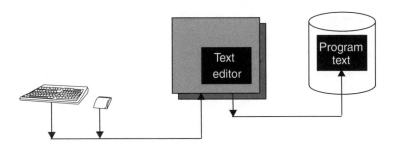

Figure 1.1

run. Written text is normally put into a file on the hard disk. Exactly how the text editor functions and which commands it understands will vary from system to system. A simple text editor will do nothing more than contain the text but more advanced text editors also "understand" the kinds of text they are processing. A text editor which knows that it is editing a C++ program can help the programmer by marking different program constructions with different styles or colours.

In the next step, the program texts are translated from normal text to machine code. This is done, as shown in Figure 1.2, with the help of a special translating program, a *compiler*. Every compiler is designed to take care of a particular programming language. To be able to translate a C++ program, access to a C++ compiler must be available. Similarly, to translate an Ada program, an Ada compiler must be used. A compiler can either be a separate program, or it can be a part of an integrated program

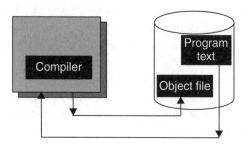

Figure 1.2

development system. Such a system contains all the tools needed, such as text editor, compiler and debugger.

For every programming language there are special rules for how different structures may appear (compare this with the rules for sentence construction in normal languages). We say that a language has a certain *syntax*. The compiler reads the program from the text file created earlier and checks first that the program is following the rules of the language, that is, is following the given syntax. If the compiler finds errors, error messages will appear on the screen. There may also be warnings for what may not be clear errors but may look doubtful to the compiler. Sometimes, the compiler will try to correct errors if they are not too serious, but compiling will usually stop when errors have been discovered. We then have to go back to the previous step and, with the help of the text editor, edit the program text and correct the errors. Once this has been done, a fresh attempt can be made to compile the program. This process often has to be repeated several times.

If the compiler does not discover errors, it goes on to translate the program from text to machine code. The compiler creates a file in which it saves the machine code generated. This file is then called an *object file*.

Since different types of computers have different machine codes, object files intended for one computer platform will not be suitable for another. Platforms must have different compilers. If we want to move a program developed on one kind of computer to another, we have to move the program text itself to the new computer and compile the program again there. This is easier if there are not too many details in the program dependent on one particular system. A program that can be moved easily from one computer platform to another is called a *portable* program. Even if programming languages are often standardized, the functions used by modern, GUI programs to generate windows, menus, buttons, etc., are different on different types of computer. This means, in practice, that GUI programs are far from portable. A great deal of work is necessary to move a program to another type of computer. (As mentioned earlier, these problems do not exist with Java. We shall soon come back to this point.)

Normally, a program consists of several program parts which have been compiled *separately* so we end up with several object files. Some object files (standard object files) may have been created previously, and these will also be a part of our program. Such standard object files may include functions for reading and writing data.

In order to put object files together into a program that can be executed, we run a special linking program, a *linker*; see Figure 1.3. The linker produces a complete unit, an *executable file*. Sometimes, a special suffix, for example exe, may be used in the file name to indicate that the file contains an executable program. The linker can be an independent program, or can be part of a program development system.

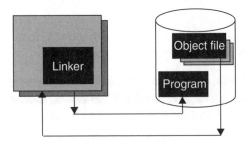

Figure 1.3

Linking can take place either *statically* or *dynamically*. In static linking, all the parts of the program are put into the executable file, while in the case of dynamic linking, references to the required object files are placed in the executable file. The object files themselves are not found in the executable file. When a dynamically linked program is run, the different object files will be automatically retrieved and stored in the main memory, if necessary. The advantage with dynamic linking is, of course, that it saves a lot of file space since different programs often contain common parts, input and output, for instance. These parts do not then need to be copied to all the executable files but can exist in only one edition, to which all the executable files will refer.

This leaves only the last step, that is to get the executable program into the main memory so that it can be run. But how does the computer know which program to run? For the answer, let us look at Figure 1.4.

In earlier diagrams, we have only shown one program at a time in the main memory, the program being executed. In fact, there are always parts of yet another program permanently stored. This is termed the *operating system*, shortened to OS. (Examples of common operating systems are Windows 98, MS-DOS and Linux.) The user can give

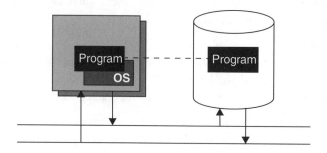

Figure 1.4

commands to the operating system through the keyboard, or can point and click with the mouse. A common command is to request that a particular program is loaded and executed. The operating system will search for the required executable file and copy it into the main memory, as suggested by the diagram above. Control is then transferred to the program that has been loaded, which may run until it finishes, or until it is interrupted.

The different steps in traditional compiling

Program text (source code) is created with the help of a text editor.

The compiler translates this program text to an object file.

The linker connects several object files to an executable file.

The operating system places the executable file in the main memory, and the program runs.

1.4 Compiling and executing Java programs

Imagine what it would be like if all the different types of computer understood the same machine code! Life would be much simpler. The same compiler could be used for all platforms, and the object code produced by this compiler would also be portable, so that it could be run on any computer, without the program needing to be compiled again. Now, as we know, reality is not like this. But we could pretend that a computer existed for all kinds of object code and this is precisely how Java works. Someone has come up with a *Java virtual machine*, an imaginary computer that understands the object code produced by a Java compiler. When Java programs are compiled, however, the code generated is not called object code but *Java bytecode*.[1]

---

[1] The word *byte* is a generally accepted designation of a group consisting of eight binary digits (zeros or ones).

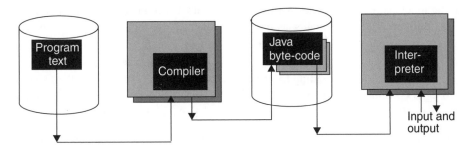

Figure 1.5

Since this virtual Java machine does not really exist, it must be simulated. This is done by a special program, an *interpreter*, which reads Java bytecode and ensures that the instructions in it are carried out; see Figure 1.5. On the face of it, it looks as though the Java program is "executed" in the virtual Java machine. The Java program reads input and produces output, just as in any "ordinary" program. Note, however, that it is really the interpreter that is being executed and that the Java bytecode is input to the interpreter. The Java program is never actually compiled into machine code. It is in the form of Java bytecode. We also see from Figure 1.5 that input to the interpreter can consist of several independent files, all of which contain Java bytecode. It can be said then that the interpreter also carries out dynamic linking and links all files with Java byte code which are necessary for the program to run.

Have we actually gained very much by using this technique? Since the Java compiler and the Java interpreter are ordinary programs compiled into machine code they have to be in different versions for different platforms. Different platforms, of course, have different machine code, but the work of adapting the Java compiler and the Java interpreter for different platforms needs to be done *only once* per platform. It is not the Java programmer who needs to do this; it has already been done by the development teams that produce Java. Programs written by the Java programmer are always immediately moveable between different platforms, without the programs having to be changed. This is not the case when we are programming in traditional programming languages and want to move programs from one platform to another. Then, every program being moved has to be adapted to the new platform; this is work that can be very taxing for the ordinary programmer.

The technique of interpreting is not something new that only applies to Java. Programming languages which make use of interpreting have been around for a long time. The most well-known languages previously using this technique are LISP and

Smalltalk. The disadvantage with interpreting is that it takes a lot longer to interpret a program than it does to execute a program that is already in the form of machine code. This difference does not matter as much as it might have done in the past, however, given the speeds of modern computers. It should also be remembered that Java programs often are interactive and have a graphical user interface. Most of the time, a program will be paused, waiting for the user to generate input data. Where the speed of a program is of paramount importance, it will be better for the programmer to use C++, for example, or Ada, where compiling takes place in the traditional way.

In order to increase the execution speed of Java programs, a technique called *just-in-time-compiling* is often used. This means that the interpreter really compiles the instructions in the Java bytecode into proper machine code during execution. Where these instructions are repeated later in the program, execution will proceed more quickly, since they can be executed "properly", without being interpreted.

If speed is important, another technique that is possible is that of writing central, complex parts of the program in a traditional language, most often C or C++, and letting the Java program call up these parts of the program. However, if this technique is used the program will no longer be platform-independent.

1.5 The first program

By using a simple example, we shall now demonstrate how compiling and execution in Java is carried out in practice. In order to do this, we need to have a Java compiler and a Java interpreter. Both of these programs are included in Sun's J2SDK, and we will assume that the latest version has been installed. This is not particularly difficult to do. (For an appropriate web address, see Section 1.2.)

A modern integrated program development system, an IDE (Integrated Development Environment), normally offers the programmer an environment with all the resources necessary to develop programs. Such systems also exist for Java. Some examples are Sun's Java Workshop, Borland's JBuilder, Symantec's VisualCafé and Microsoft's Visual J++. There are also a number of shareware systems on the Internet. Not only are the obvious resources of text editor, compiler and interpreter available in an IDE but there is support to keep account of the different parts of a programming project. There is also a *debugger* (a program that makes it possible to test-run programs step by step and search for errors), and there are help texts, documentation and examples. The professional programmer will certainly make use of an IDE but here we are dealing with student programmers. We merely assume that J2SDK has been installed.

Our first Java program is comprised of only a few lines:

```
class Message1 {
  public static void main (String[] arg) {
    System.out.println("Welcome to Java");
  }
}
```

When this program is run, it will print out the text `Welcome to Java`. Before we discuss how compiling and execution are handled, we should note the appearance of the program. (More detailed descriptions of the different program constructs will naturally come later in the book.)

A Java program normally consists of several *objects* which work in conjunction with one another. The different objects are created dynamically during execution. In order to describe how these objects look and behave, we use a construct called *class*. Our simple program consists of a definition of a single class with the name `Message1`. This class definition is introduced with the word `class`, followed by the name of the class. Any name will do. On the first line, there is a left-hand curly bracket and on the last line, a right-hand curly bracket. These brackets indicate where the class description begins and ends. (The characters { and } correspond to the words "begin" and "end", used in many other programming languages.)

When the program starts, there are no objects, so there must be a starting point in the program where we have the opportunity of creating the first object (or objects). When the Java interpreter begins to execute the program, therefore, it requires the presence of a so-called *method* with the special name of `main`. In this simple example the definition of `main` begins on the second line. Let us see what there is on this line.

The word `public` indicates that the method `main` should be accessible from outside. It must be if the interpreter is to be able to call it. (If the word `public` had not been included, the method would only have been recognized inside class `Message1`.)

The word `static` means that the method `main` is a *class method* (or *static method*, as we also say in Java). A class method is one which is not particular to one object but relates to the class itself. (A better description of this will be given later in the book.) Since there are no objects when the program starts, `main` must be a class method.

The word `void` means that the method `main` will not leave a result value.

The word `main` on the second line is, of course, the name of the method. We can normally give our methods any name we wish but in this case this method must have precisely the name of `main`. Note that Java differentiates between upper and lower case letters: we are not allowed to write `MAIN` or `Main`.

After the method's name, its *parameters* are found in brackets. In the case of main, we are able to pass arguments from the command line. We will not go further into this now but will merely state that this is the form it must have.

In a method the different steps to be performed are expressed by *statements*. A semicolon is written after each statement. In this example, there is only one statement, indicating that the text Welcome to Java is to be printed. This statement is found on the third line. The statement begins with the word System. System is a standard class found in the package java.lang in the Java API. System contains resources of a general nature. One of the items defined here is an *output stream* with the name System.out. This output stream is normally called *standard output*. Whatever is output in standard output will be automatically written in a text window on the screen. Output is generated by calling the method println for the output stream System.out. In the parentheses, we indicate the text to be written out: Welcome to Java. Note that this text must be included in double quotes.

Certain words in the program have been written in bold. These are *reserved words*, words with a special meaning in the language of Java. When we write our own programs, we do not have to mark these words in this way but we do it here simply to make the programs clearer. Note, however, that all reserved words must be written in lower case. All reserved words are listed in Appendix A.

We now type in the above program text with the help of a text editor and store it in a text file with the name Message1.java. As we can see, the file name has the *suffix* .java. All text files containing Java programs must have this suffix. In addition, the first part of the file's name must be identical to the name of the class. It is also important here to have the same upper- and lower-case letters in the file name as in the class name.

This is what we do if we are running Windows 95/98, Windows NT or Unix: Open a command window (called MS-DOS Prompt in Windows). Move with the help of the command cd to the folder with the file Message1.java. Then write the command:[1]

```
javac Message1.java
```

This command will start the program javac (Java Compiler) which compiles the Java program and generates a file containing the Java bytecode for the class Message1. This

---

[1] If we are running Windows and we give the command DIR, the name of the program file will be written out as Messag~1.jav. However, this is merely the MS-DOS way of truncating the file name to a maximum of eight characters, plus three characters for the suffix. The file is still called Message1.java, so it is important to indicate this name in the javac command.

file will be automatically given the name `Message1.class`. The suffix `.class` is used to mark that a file contains Java bytecode.[1]

Then run the program by giving the following command:

```
java Message1
```

Note that we must *not* write the suffix `.class`. This command starts the Java interpreter, which reads the file `Message1.class` as input and executes the program given there. The result is that the text

```
Welcome to Java
```

is written out in the command window.

When a Java program is executed the just-in-time-compilation technique will normally be used to increase execution speed. This might cause problems when you debug a program. You will not be told exactly where in the program (in which lines) the errors occur. Therefore, when you debug a program it is a good thing to disable the just-in-time-compilation so that a pure interpretation is performed. To accomplish this, run the program by giving the following command:

```
java -Djava.compiler=NONE classname
```

Compiling and executing independent Java programs

Using a text editor, a file is created with the program text.
This file should be called `classname.java`.

The compiler translates the program text to Java bytecode.
This is done with the command

```
javac classname.java
```

The interpreter executes the program by reading the Java bytecode and ensuring that the instructions in it are carried out.

The interpreter is started by the command

```
java classname
```

When you debug a program it is better to use the command

```
java -Djava.compiler=NONE classname
```

---

[1] In an MS-DOS Prompt, it looks as though the file should be called `Messag~1.cla` but this is only the truncated form. The proper file name is `Message1.class`, which is what we see when we open the folder in a Windows window.

1.6 A simple GUI program

The program in the preceding section was a simple one that wrote in a text window. Most Java programs are rather more interesting than this, and they usually use graphics. Of course, this complicates matters. We shall now show a simple program with a graphical user interface. Our program will write out the same greeting as the text-based program in the preceding section but this time, the program will create a new window, and the text will be written there. When the program is run, we will get the text illustrated in Figure 1.6. (The text should really be blue on a yellow background but, of course, this is not possible with printout in black and white.)

Figure 1.6

We shall call our program `Message2`, placing it therefore in a file with the name `Message2.java`. The program is compiled with the command:

```
javac Message2.java
```

We then run the program in the normal way by writing:

```
java Message2
```

The program `Message2` looks like this:

```java
import java.awt.*;

class Message2 extends Frame {

  Font f;

  Message2() {                 // Constructor for the class Message2
    f = new Font("SansSerif", Font.BOLD, 24);
    setBackground(Color.yellow);
    setSize(400,150);
  }
```

```
public void paint(Graphics g) {                      // The method paint
  g.setFont(f);
  g.setColor(Color.blue);
  g.drawString("Welcome to Java", 100, 100);
}
public static void main (String[] arg) {
  Message2 m2 = new Message2();
  m2.setVisible(true);
}
}
```

We begin by discussing the first line of the program. There is a package in the Java API called `java.awt` (AWT is an acronym for Abstract Window Toolkit). This package contains a number of classes that can be used when writing GUI programs. There are graphics resources (fonts, colours, drawing tools, etc.), resources to create different components (menus, buttons, lists, etc.) and resources to conveniently organize and display components in windows. A package must be *imported* at the beginning of a program if its content is to be used. This is done using a special **import** command. In order to indicate that the package `java.awt` is to be imported, we write:

```
import java.awt.*;
```

The asterisk at the end can be read as "everything in the package". (Compare this with the technique which can be used in MS-DOS and Unix to indicate file names.) Single classes can also be imported individually. In the program we will be using the three classes `Graphics`, `Font` and `Color` from the package `java.awt`. We could then write the following three lines instead

```
import java.awt.Graphics;
import java.awt.Font;
import java.awt.Color;
```

But since it is much simpler to write `java.awt.*`, we will be using this technique from now on. Note that this makes the program neither slower nor longer. The Java interpreter is clever enough to include only the classes we need.

All the packages needed by a program must be imported. This applies both to packages included in Java and others, the only exception being the package `java.lang`, which is imported automatically into all Java programs, without anything having to be written.

There is a class called `Frame` in the package `java.awt`. When an object of class `Frame` is created, a window is generated automatically that can be displayed on the screen. We can then draw or write in the window, or place different components (such as buttons and menus) in it. Now, we want our program to have the same characteristics as the class `Frame`. When an object of class `Message2` is created, a window should also be created, and to make this happen, we make use of *inheritance*, a technique that is central to object-oriented programming. We allow the class `Message2` to inherit characteristics from class `Frame`. This can be done by allowing the second line in the program to have the following appearance:

```
class Message2 extends Frame {
```

(Here it should be mentioned that there is a slight problem with the standard class `Frame`. When a window belonging to class `Frame` has been displayed on screen, it is difficult to close it. It is no good clicking in the closure box, or choosing the option `Close`, or some equivalent, in the window's menu. Instead, we type Ctrl-C in the command window, or MS-DOS window, from which the program was started. Later in the book, we shall see how a subclass of `Frame` is used to avoid this problem.)

There are a couple of *comments* in the program. A comment is introduced by the characters `//` and applies to the rest of the line. In Java, there are also two other ways of writing comments. We will come back to this later.

Execution of the program begins as usual in the method `main`. The first thing that happens in `main` is that a new object of class `Message2` is created. This is done in the expression **new** `Message2()`. The result of this expression is a *reference* (a kind of pointer) to the new object. This reference is kept in a variable we call `m2`. The line

```
Message2 m2 = new Message2();
```

is, in fact, a *declaration* of a new variable with the name `m2`. The word `Message2`, which comes first, indicates that the new variable should be a reference and be able to refer to objects belonging to the class `Message2`. The word `m2` is the name we assign to this variable. The equality sign means that the variable should be *initialized*. The value to which the variable should be initialized, is written to the right of the equality sign.

When the new object is created, an accompanying window is generated. However, this window is not yet shown on the screen. For this to be done, it must be expressly requested, and this is done with the statement

```
m2.setVisible(true);
```

When a new object is created, a *constructor* for the object is called automatically. A constructor is a kind of method in which the initializations required for the new object can be carried out. A constructor always has the same name as the class it is in. In our program, the constructor begins on the fourth line. We first initialize the variable `f` in the constructor, so that it refers to a new font object which will then be used to determine the font in the printout.

```
f = new Font("SansSerif", Font.BOLD, 24);
```

The name of the font, `SansSerif`, is given here. We then indicate whether we would like normal, bold or italic style, by writing, `Font.PLAIN`, `Font.BOLD` or

`Font.ITALIC`. The number 24 indicates the font size. Fonts directly supported are `Serif`, `SansSerif`, `Monospaced`, `Dialog` and `DialogInput`. The first three correspond to the fonts `TimesRoman`, `Helvetica` and `Courier`.

We now indicate in the constructor the background colour we wish to have in the window. The method `setBackground` should have a reference to an object of the class `Color` as parameter. In the class `Color` there are a number of pre-defined colour objects for the most common colours, `Color.yellow` for instance.

The statement

```
setSize(400,150);
```

indicates that the window should be 400 pixels wide and 150 pixels high.

Every time the window has to be drawn on the screen, a method with the name `paint` is called automatically. This does not only happen the first time the window is drawn but also when it has been moved or has to be redrawn because it has been partly covered by another component on the screen. We therefore have to write our own method called `paint`, and in it we indicate what should be drawn in the window. We see that the method `paint` has a parameter called `g`. This parameter is a reference to an object of the class `Graphics`. An object of this type is a kind of toolbox containing many different kinds of drawing aids. For example, we can write text and draw different kinds of figures. In this program we use the method `drawString` to write text in the window. The statement

```
g.drawString("Welcome to Java", 100, 100);
```

indicates that the text should be written beginning 100 pixels from the left and 100 pixels from the top of the window. (Coordinates are always indicated beginning from the window's upper left-hand corner.) The graphics toolbox keeps a check on the font and printout colour in use. The font and colour to be used can be indicated with the help of the methods `setFont` and `setColor`, respectively. The method `setFont` should have as parameter a reference to an object of class `Font`, and the variable `f`, declared in the third line of the program and initialized in the constructor, will serve this purpose. The methods `setColor` and `setBackground` should have a reference to an object of the class `Color` as parameter.

1.7 Applets

The two programs `Message1` and `Message2` are both examples of independent programs, or *standalone applications* as they are called. In this section, we shall give an introduction to *applets*. The word "applet" is an invented word designating a "small application", or a mini-program. An applet cannot be run independently. It is a part of a program and is called from another program. Applets are primarily intended to be called from a browser. To demonstrate how this works, we will begin by writing a third version of our program. We will call the class Message3 and place the program text in a file with the name Message3.java.

```
import java.awt.*;
import java.applet.*;

public class Message3 extends Applet {
  Font f;

  public void init() {
    f = new Font("SansSerif", Font.BOLD, 24);
    setBackground(Color.yellow);
  }

  public void paint(Graphics g) {
    g.setFont(f);
    g.setColor(Color.blue);
    g.drawString("Welcome to Java", 100, 100);
  }
}
```

As we can see, the class Message3 has very great similarities with the class Message2 on page 14. There are really only three differences.

We can see the first difference in the third line. The class Message3 *inherits its characteristics from the standard class* Applet and not from the class Frame. The class Applet is defined in the package java.applet, which we import in the second line. An object of the class Applet has in many ways the same characteristics as a Frame; there is a window associated with the object; we can write and draw in this window and display different components in it. (But the window does not have its own frame and it cannot be displayed by itself on the screen. It must be shown as a component in another window.) In addition, an object of class Applet has certain unique characteristics, enabling it to be called from a browser.

The other difference between the classes Message2 and Message3 is that in Message3 *a method with the name* main *is not needed*. We do not need to define any such method because an applet is not called directly from the Java interpreter. The browser takes care of creating a first object of class Message3. We could imagine the following line being executed by the browser:

```
Applet m3 = new Message3();  // performed in the browser
```

The third and final difference is that we have not defined a constructor in class Message3. Instead, *a method with the name* init *is defined*. Note that we do exactly the same thing in this method as in the constructor in class Message2, the only difference being that we have left out the call of the method `setSize`, for the window's size will be determined by the browser, which we will demonstrate shortly. The method `init` is called automatically by the browser as soon as an applet has been created. We could then imagine that the browser would here execute the statement

```
m3.init();  // is performed in the browser
```

The method `init` is therefore called once, when the applet object is created. The method `paint`, on the other hand, can be called several times. Just as in the case of class `Message2`, this occurs automatically each time the window needs to be redrawn. We therefore have to define our own `paint` method for our `Applet` classes.

Class `Message3` is compiled in the same way as other classes. We give the command

```
javac Message3.java
```

Then a file with Java bytecode is created, precisely as we saw earlier. This file will have the name `Message3.class`.

Note that we now *cannot* execute the file `Message3.class` through giving the command `java`. In order to do this, a method with the name `main` must exist, and, of course, we do not have one. The file `Message3.class` should instead be read and executed by the browser. A web browser normally reads text files containing instructions that describe how text and pictures should be shown on screen. These instructions are written in a special language called HTML (HyperText Markup Language). In order to tell a browser that it should start a particular applet, we have to create a text file with appropriate HTML instructions. Due to reasons of space, we cannot in this book describe the entire HTML language. We shall only show what is absolutely necessary to be able to execute applets. (The specification of HTML is on the website `www.w3.org`. A "Beginner's Guide" can be found at the site `www.ncsa.uiuc.edu/General/Internet/WWW`.)

With the help of the text editor, we will create the following file and give it the name `Message3.html`.

```
<html>
  <head>
    <title>Message3</title>
  </head>
  <body>
    My first applet
    <br>
    <applet code=Message3.class width=400 height=150></applet>
  </body>
</html>
```

19

An HTML file consists of different parts. Each part is introduced with a *tag* in the form `<name>` and is terminated by `</name>`. In an HTML document there must, first of all, be a head containing a title. Then follows a body containing the text and other items to be shown on the web page. Any kind of flowing text can be inserted here. For example, we have written the text `My first applet`. Headlines, lists and various kinds of editing commands can also be inserted. (The command `<br>` means that we should begin on a new line.)

What is especially interesting here is the line containing the `applet` tag:

```
<applet code=Message3.class width=400 height=150></applet>
```

This indicates that the browser should start the applet in the file `Message3.class`. The parameters `width` and `height` indicate the size of the window associated with the applets. For the call of the applets to work, files `Message3.html` and `Message3.class` must be in the same folder in the file system. If this is not the case, a `codebase` parameter must be given. Using this parameter, we can indicate the folder where the `class` file can be found. If, for example, the file `Message3.class` is in the folder `c:\own\jan\java\example\Chap1`, we can write

```
<applet code=Message3.class width=400 height=150
  codebase="c:\own\jan\java\example\Chap1"></applet>
```

Normally, the `class` file is in the same computer from which the browser has downloaded the HTML file. But the `class` file does not have to be in the same computer as the HTML file, for the parameter `codebase` can contain a complete web address.

```
<applet code=Message3.class width=400 height=150
  codebase="http://www.cs.chalmers.se/~skanshol/Java_dir/">
  </applet>
```

In order to execute `Message3`, we can now start the browser and indicate the address to the file `Message3.html`. Alternatively, we can double-click on the file `Message3.html`. If we use Internet Explorer, we will get a window as shown in Figure 1.7.

We may sometimes wish to test applets on our own computer without using a browser. We can then make use of the program `appletviewer`, which is included in J2SDK. The program `appletviewer` should, like a browser, have an HTML file as input. In order to test-run our applet `Message3`, we can give the command

```
appletviewer Message3.html
```

Then the window shown in Figure 1.8 will appear. The program `appletviewer` reads the entire HTML file but concentrates only on the contents of the applet tag.

To execute an applet, we always need to write an HTML file in addition to the file with the program text. From now on in this book, we will be working both with standalone

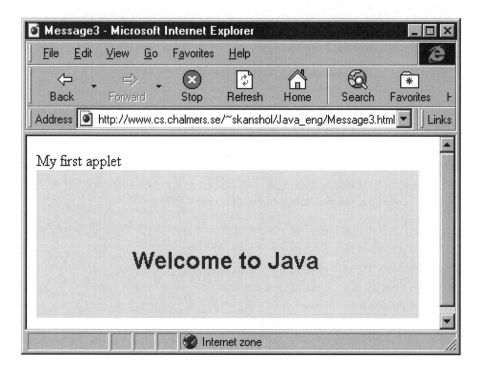

Figure 1.7

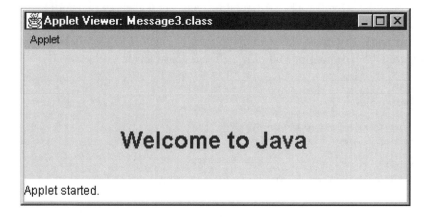

Figure 1.8

Compiling and executing applets

A file with program text is created by using a text editor.
This file is to be called `classname.java`.

The compiler translates program text to Java bytecode.
This is done by the command

```
javac classname.java
```

Create a corresponding HTML file using the text editor
(preferably with the name `classname.html`).
This file must contain an applet tag:

```
<applet code=classname.class width=n height=n> </applet>
```

Add `codebase` if the class file is not in the current folder.

The program can be executed by a browser. To do this, double-click on the HTML file, or give it as an address to the browser.

Alternatively, the program can be executed using `appletviewer`.
This is done by the command

```
appletviewer classname.html
```

GUI programs and with applets. Whenever we design applets, it will be assumed, unless something is said to the contrary, that there is an HTML file.

1.8 Graphics

In the class `java.awt.Graphics`, several methods are defined to draw different kinds of figures and texts. To acquaint ourselves with some of these drawing aids, we shall study an applet that draws the charming picture in Figure 1.9. We will be making use of Figure 1.10 to demonstrate how the picture is constructed.

```
import java.awt.*;
import java.applet.*;

public class Cat extends Applet {
  Font f = new Font("Serif", Font.ITALIC, 18);

  public void init() {
    setBackground(Color.white);
  }

  public void paint(Graphics g) {
    g.setColor(Color.black);
    g.drawRect(50, 50, 60, 60);      // head
    g.drawRect(80, 225, 140, 5);     // tail
```

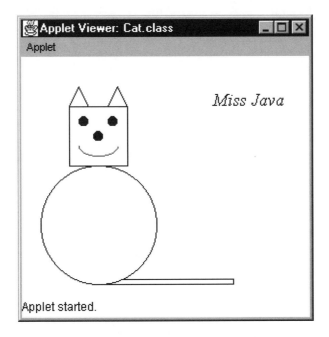

Figure 1.9

```
    g.setColor(Color.white);
    g.fillOval(20, 110, 120, 120);   // white body
    g.setColor(Color.black);
    g.drawOval(20, 110, 120, 120);   // paint body
    g.fillOval(75, 75, 10, 10);      // nose
    g.setColor(Color.blue);
    g.fillOval(60, 60, 10, 10);      // eyes
    g.fillOval(90, 60, 10, 10);
    g.setColor(Color.black);
    g.drawLine(50, 50, 60, 30);      // ears
    g.drawLine(60, 30, 70, 50);
    g.drawLine(110, 50, 100, 30);
    g.drawLine(100, 30, 90, 50);
    g.setColor(Color.red);
    g.drawArc(60, 80, 40, 20, 180, 180);  // mouth

    // draw name
    g.setColor(Color.black);
    g.setFont(f);
    g.drawString("Miss Java", 200, 50);
  }
}
```

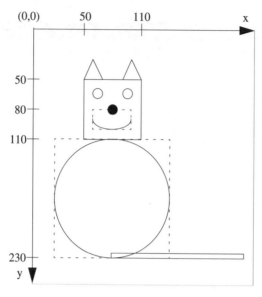

Figure 1.10

The method `init` is called when a new object of class `Cat` is created. Let us set the background colour to white. The interesting method is `paint`, which is called automatically every time the applets have to be redrawn. As we mentioned earlier, the parameter `g` refers to an object of the class `java.awt.Graphics`. All the methods in class `Graphics` have in common a coordinate system that begins from the upper left-hand corner of the drawing area. (See Figure 1.10.) The unit is one pixel.

1.8.1 Colours

All drawing takes place in the foreground colour, which is specified by calling the method `setColor`. The argument for this will be an object of class `Color`. Colours are described in Java by RGB numbers. These are three integers in the interval 0–255, which indicate how much red, green and blue are to be included in the colour. For example, yellow is described by the numbers (255,255,0), white by (255,255,255) and black by (0,0,0). There are a number of pre-defined colour objects in class `Color`, among them `Color.black`, `Color.white` and `Color.red`, which describe the most common colours. We can also define our own colours by combining the three RGB numbers in whatever way we wish. A light blue colour object, for example, can be created by the declaration

```
Color lightBlue = new Color(175,175,255);
```

Pre-defined colours in the class java.awt.Color			
`Color.black`	0, 0, 0	`Color.magenta`	255, 0, 255
`Color.blue`	0, 0, 255	`Color.orange`	255, 200, 0
`Color.cyan`	0, 255, 255	`Color.pink`	255, 175, 175
`Color.gray`	128, 128, 128	`Color.red`	255, 0, 0
`Color.darkGray`	64, 64, 64	`Color.white`	255, 255, 255
`Color.lightGray`	192, 192, 192	`Color.yellow`	255, 255, 0
`Color.green`	0, 255, 0		

1.8.2 Rectangles

When we draw rectangles, we can choose between ordinary rectangles, rectangles with rounded corners and ones in three dimensions. To draw the cat's head in the program, we choose the method `drawRect`, which draws an ordinary rectangle. The first two arguments for `drawRect` indicate the x- and y-coordinates, respectively, for the rectangle's upper left-hand corner. The last two arguments are the rectangle's width and height, respectively. The cat's tail is also drawn as an ordinary rectangle.

There is also a corresponding method called `fillRect`, which draws solid rectangles. `fillRect` has the same arguments as `drawRect`. To draw rectangles with rounded corners, we use the methods `drawRoundRect` and `fillRoundRect`. If we had wanted to give the cat's head rounded corners, we could have written

```
g.drawRoundRect(50, 50, 60, 60, 10, 10);
```

The two extra arguments indicate the distance of the point from the corner, at which rounding is to begin, the last but one argument indicating the distance along the x-coordinate, while the last argument indicates the distance along the y-coordinate. The arguments indicate the diameter of the rounding. This means that if a value of *n* has been given as the argument, rounding will begin *n*/2 pixels from the corner.

The methods `draw3DRect` and `fill3DRect` draw rectangles in three dimensions.[1] They have one more argument than `drawRect`. This final argument indicates whether we want the rectangle to have a raised or lowered profile in relation to the screen. For example, we can make the call

```
g.draw3DRect(100, 200, 75, 60, true);
```

---

[1] Unfortunately, the three-dimensional effect is barely visible.

Here, `true` means that the rectangle will have a raised profile. If instead we had written `false`, the rectangle would have had a lowered profile.

1.8.3   Circles and ellipses

In order to draw circles and ellipses, we use the methods `drawOval` and `fillOval`. When we draw an ellipse, we imagine it is inscribed in a rectangle; this is suggested in Figure 1.10. The arguments for the methods `drawOval` and `fillOval` define this rectangle's position and dimensions. These arguments are therefore the same as those of the method `drawRect`, that is, they are the x- and y-coordinates indicating width and height, respectively.

We draw the tail before the body because the tail's upper left-hand corner should be hidden by the body. To achieve this result, the colour is first changed from black to white, and then the body is drawn as a solid circle. The tail's upper left-hand corner will then be drawn over in white. Once this has been done, we return to the use of black and draw the body's contours. The cat's nose and eyes are also drawn as circles. Again, note that it is the coordinates and dimensions of the outer rectangles that are given.

1.8.4   Lines

The cat's ears are drawn as lines, each ear as two lines. In order to draw lines, the simple method `drawLine` is used. This method has four arguments. The first two indicate the x- and y-coordinates for the line's starting point and the last two indicate the x- and y-coordinates of the line's end point. Unfortunately, there is no way of indicating line thickness, or of producing broken lines. Only lines of standard thickness are drawn.

1.8.5   Arcs and segments

The cat's mouth is drawn as an arc, with the method `drawArc`. An arc is a section of an ellipse. The first four arguments for `drawArc` define, exactly as for the method `drawOval`, the position and size of the rectangle in which the ellipse is inscribed. In our program, the call for `drawArc` looks like this:

```
g.drawArc(60, 80, 40, 20, 180, 180);  // mouth
```

The surrounding rectangle then has its upper left-hand corner at the point (60,80) and is 40 pixels wide and 20 pixels high. An enlargement of this is shown in Figure 1.11.

The last two parameters indicate the part of the ellipse to be drawn. To describe this, we make use of angle measurements. We imagine that there is a clock at the centre of the ellipse, as indicated in the figure. We go anti-clockwise, beginning at three o'clock,

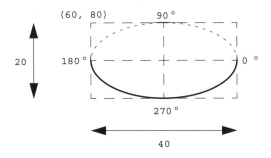

Figure 1.11

corresponding to 0°. A whole circle comprises 360°. This means that twelve o'clock corresponds to 90°, nine o'clock to 180°, and six o'clock to 270°. The fifth argument for drawArc indicates the beginning of the section of the arc that has to be drawn. In our example, we should therefore begin at 180° (nine o'clock). The final argument for drawArc does *not* indicate, as we might expect, the end point of the arc to be drawn. It indicates the length of the arc, that is, the angle corresponding to this length. In our example, the last argument has a value of 180°, which corresponds to half a circle.

In order to draw segments of circles and ellipses, we make use of the method fillArc, which has exactly the same arguments as drawArc. The difference is that fillArc draws all of the "pie" indicated and not only the contours.

1.8.6 Texts

To write out the name in Figure 1.9 is easy. This is done with the program lines

```
g.setColor(Color.black);
g.setFont(f);
g.drawString("Miss Java", 200, 50);
```

The text itself is printed on the last line, which says that the text will be placed at the point (200, 50). The vertical distance is to the text's *base line*, not the upper left-hand corner, as for rectangles. The text should be written out in black, with the font and size indicated in the Font object f.

If we wish to position the text more exactly and to know its exact width and height, we can make use of the standard class FontMetrics, but we won't now go into the details we would have to know.

When texts are written out in GUI programs, the method drawString is not usually used. Instead, the standard GUI component Label is used. This will be described in Section 5.2.

Some graphical methods	
`drawLine(x1,y1,x2,y2)`	Draw a line from point (x1,y1) to (x2,y2)
`drawRect(x,y,w,h)` `fillRect(x,y,w,h)`	Draw a rectangle and a solid rectangle, respectively, of width w and height h, with upper left-hand corner at (x,y)
`drawRoundRect(x,y,w,h,m,n)` `fillRoundRect(x,y,w,h,m,n)`	Draw a rounded rectangle and a solid, rounded rectangle, respectively, of width w and height h, with upper left-hand corner at (x,y). Rounding is m/2 wide and n/2 high.
`draw3DRect(x,y,w,h,up)` `fill3DRect(x,y,w,h,up)`	Draw a rectangle and a solid, 3-dim. rectangle, respectively, of width w and height h, with upper left-hand corner at (x,y). up=true ⇒ raised, up=false ⇒ lowered
`drawOval(x,y,w,h)` `fillOval(x,y,w,h)`	Draw an ellipse and a solid ellipse, respectively, which is inscribed in a rectangle of width w and height h, with upper left-hand corner at (x,y)
`drawArc(x,y,w,h,s,l)` `fillArc(x,y,w,h,s,l)`	Draw an arc, a segment, respectively, of an ellipse inscribed in a rectangle of width w and height h, with upper left-hand corner at (x,y). s is the starting point (in degrees) of the arc and l, the arc's length (in degrees)

`drawPolygon(xp, yp, n)`
`drawPolygon(p)`
`fillPolygon(xp, yp, n)`
`fillPolygon(p)`
`drawPolyline(xp, yp, n)`
	Draw a polygonal, or solid polygonal and a number of connected lines, respectively. `xp` and `yp` are arrays (see Section 6.4) with the points' x- and y-coordinates. n is the number of points. In the alternative forms, p is a `Polygon` (see Section 6.10)

drawString(txt,x,y)	Draw the text txt with its beginning at point (x,y). The y-coordinate indicates the text's base line.

1.9 Packages

A package is a collection of classes that can be useful in different programs. For example, the programs `Message2` and `Message3` made use of Java's standard packages to produce graphics. In this section, we shall show how we can design our own packages for use in our own programs.

The first thing that should be done when designing a package is to find a name for it. In order to differentiate between package names and names of classes, we usually let the names of packages begin with a lower-case letter. Suppose, for example, that we want to design a package with the name myPackage. The next step is to create a folder in the file system where the package is to go. The name of the folder must be the same as that of the package. In our example then, the package should be called myPackage. This folder can be put anywhere in the file system. Suppose that we put it in c:\own\java\classes.

The third step is to design the classes that are to go into the package. In Java, we do not collect all the classes of a particular package into a single file. Instead, the different classes are usually defined separately, each one in its own file. On the first line in each such file, we should give a special **package** command, in front of any **import** command, indicating into which package the class is to go. If no **package** command is first included in a program file, the package defined in the file will land in an *anonymous* package in the folder in question.

As an example, we define a class C1 which will go into the package myPackage. As usual, we give the file the same name as the class and add the suffix .java. The file including class C1 will, therefore, be called C1.java. We put the file C1.java into the new folder c:\own\java\classes\myPackage. Class C1 has the following form. (What it looks like inside class C1 does not interest us at the moment.)

```
// the file C1.java
package myPackage;        // C1 will be included in myPackage

public class C1 {         // a visible class
  ...
}
```

Each file is then compiled as usual. Class C1 is compiled with the command

```
javac C1.java
```

A file with the name C1.class is then generated in the folder c:\own\java\classes\myPackage. (It is really the class files which must be placed into a folder with the same name as the package; the java files may be placed anywhere but it is simplest to have them in the same place.)

We now define yet another class which is placed in the package myPackage in the same way.

```
// the file C2.java
package myPackage;        // C2 will be included in myPackage

class C2 {                // a local class
  ...
}
```

Class C2 looks almost the same as class C1 but there is an important difference. On the third line is written **class** C2, while **public class** C1 is on the third line in the file C1.java. If the word **public** is given first in a class definition, the class will generally be visible everywhere in a program, even in other packages, but if the word **public** is missing, the class will be a local class and visible *only* in the package it is in. For every class included in a package, we can therefore indicate whether the class should be local (only visible inside the package), or visible everywhere.

Up to now, we have assumed that each class definition has been placed in its own file. This is the normal thing to do but in fact it is permissible to place several class definitions in the same file, in which case at most one of the classes may be **public**, and the name of this class will determine the name of the file. The other classes in the file must be local and they will not be accessible to classes lying outside the file in question. This is useful if a class needs to make use of one or more help classes not visible from outside. The help classes are then defined as local in the same file as the public class.

As was mentioned above, a package can contain other packages, that is, it can be said to contain *subpackages*. We call such a package a *superpackage*. A subpackage must have a name consisting of the superpackage's name followed by a dot and then the subpackage's name. For example, we can create a new package myPackage.special, which will be placed in myPackage. (Compare with the way a file name is given in a file system.) The folder in the file system where a subpackage is placed must have the same name as the subpackage, and the folder must be placed in the folder where the superpackage is. If, for example, the package myPackage is in the folder c:\own\java\classes\myPackage, the subpackage myPackage.special should be placed in the folder c:\own\java\classes\myPackage\special. The hierarchical construction of the packages should be directly mirrored in the folders created in the file system.

We can now define a class C3 and place it in the new package myPackage.special.

```
// the file C3.java
package myPackage.special;

public class C3 {
  ...
}
```

We place the `C3.java` file in the folder `c:\own\java\classes\myPackage\special`.

Of course, a subpackage may in turn be a superpackage and contain other packages. For example, we can create a package with the name `myPackage.special.more`. If, as before, we assume that the classes in the package `myPackage` are in the folder `c:\own\java\classes\myPackage`, the classes in `myPackage.special.more` must be in the folder `c:\own\java\classes\myPackage\special\more`.

With the help of subpackages, we can design a hierarchical package structure, where the position of the packages corresponds to their logical role in the program. Class libraries, that is, collections of generally useful packages, can be designed in this way. Java's standard packages also follow this model. We start with a superpackage called `java`, then the different subpackages, for example, `java.awt`, `java.io` and `java.util` will be included in this folder.

When a program wants to use one of the classes in a package, it must, as we saw earlier, import the class. The simplest thing here is to import the entire package. For example, if we wish to use classes `C1` and `C2` in a program, we can write

```
import myPackage.*;
```

since both classes lie in the package `myPackage`. If we wish to use class `C3` from package `myPackage.special`, we can write

```
import myPackage.special.*;
```

A package can be placed anywhere in a file system. So that the Java interpreter can find the packages we wish to import, we have to tell it where to look. This we do by setting the environment variable `CLASSPATH`. This should contain a list of the names of folders (or *zip files*) that will be searched. In MS-DOS, for example, we can give the command

```
set CLASSPATH=.;c:\own\java\classes;d:\project\div
```

We write a semicolon between the different names in the list. In this way, we have indicated three folders here – first, `.`, which means the folder we are in now, then `c:\own\java\classes` and finally `d:\project\div`. It is convenient to place this command in the initiating file `AUTOEXEC.BAT`. It will then be performed automatically every time the computer is started.

If Unix is run, the command may instead have the following appearance. A colon is used between the different names in the list.

```
setenv CLASSPATH .:/own/java/classes:/project/div
```

This command is conveniently placed in an initializing file (`.cshrc`, `.profile`, or the equivalent, depending on the version of Unix). Then we won't have to rewrite the command each time we log on.

31

If we use an integrated program development system and do our compiling and programs from this, there may be a menu with setting options where we are able to indicate the CLASSPATH we would like to have.

In our CLASSPATH we do not have to indicate the location of the standard classes in the Java API, because the Java compiler and Java interpreter will still know where they are to be found. If we do not use our own packages, therefore, we will not need to set the environment variable CLASSPATH.

Packages

By using a **package** command, which must first be placed in a program file, we indicate that a class should go into a particular package.

package *packagename*;

The classes in a package must be placed in a folder with the name *packagename*. The folder *packagename* must be found in a folder indicated in CLASSPATH.

A package can, in turn, contain other packages. The dot notation is then used.

package *packagename.subpackagename*;

The classes in a subpackage must be in a folder with the name *packagename\subpackagename*.

It is a good idea to have a folder where we can put all our own private "standard packages", since they will then be directly accessible in all the programs we write. In addition, we will not need to copy any of the classes in this package and we will avoid having to maintain several different versions. In this book, we will use our own standard package in this way. It will contain classes, making it easier for the reader to write his own programs. We will give our standard package the name extra. It can be placed anywhere in our file system but we will put it in the folder c:\own\java\classes. When we discussed the program Message2 we saw that we had a problem with exiting programs that used the standard class Frame. It was not possible to click "close" in the window's box, or choose the Close option (or equivalent). To overcome this, we define our own class with the name ExtendedFrame and put the class in the package extra. The definition of this class will look like this:

```
package extra;
import java.awt.*;
import java.awt.event.*;
```

```
public class ExtendedFrame extends Frame {
  private static boolean first = true;
  private boolean isFirst = first;

  public ExtendedFrame() {
    addWindowListener(theListener);
    first=false;
  }

  WindowAdapter theListener = new WindowAdapter() {
    public void windowClosing(WindowEvent e) {
      dispose();
      if (isFirst)
        System.exit(0);
    }
  };
}
```

It is not necessary now to understand how the class `ExtendedFrame` is constructed.[1] The interesting thing is that when we write a standalone program with a graphic user interface, we can use the class `ExtendedFrame` instead of class `Frame`. Then the window generated by the program will close normally. For example, taking the program `Message2` from page 14, we can write:

```
import java.awt.*;
import extra.*;
class Message2 extends ExtendedFrame {
  // as previously
}
```

In this way, we have allowed the class `Message2` to inherit characteristics from class `ExtendedFrame` and not from class `Frame`. Note too, that we have imported our own standard package `extra`.

If we wish, from now on we can use class `ExtendedFrame` instead of class `Frame` in all the examples in the book.

1.10 Exercises

1. Check to see whether Sun's Java 2 Platform SDK is installed on your computer. Open a text window and write the command:

---

[1] It will inherit all the characteristics of class `Frame` but we have also added the characteristic that it will "listen" and discover whether the person running the program is trying to close the window. If this is the case, it removes the window from the screen and, if it is the first window opened by the program, the method `System.exit` is also called, closing the program. This is discussed in more detail in Chapter 10.

```
java -version
```

If Java is installed, the version number will be written out. This should be 1.2 or later for you to be able to run all the examples in this book. If Java is not installed, install it (or ask the person in charge of the system to do so). You will find the web address in Section 1.2 on page 3.

2. Write and test-run a Java program that writes out your name in a text window.

3. Write and test-run a standalone GUI Java program that prints out your name. Try different fonts, background colours and text colours. In addition, compose your own colour by indicating RGB numbers.

4. Follow the instructions of the preceding exercise but, instead, design your program as an applet. Also write an accompanying HTML file. Test-run the program, both with the help of a browser and the program `appletviewer`.

5. Write and test-run an applet which draws a picture of your own.

6. Create a "standard package" with the name `extra` on your own computer. You can put the folder with the package anywhere in the file system. Then place the class `ExtendedFrame` (see page 33) in the new package. Define the environment variable `CLASSPATH` so that the Java interpreter finds your package. Finally, make the changes in the program shown on page 33 and compile and test-run the program.

Classes and objects

In object-oriented programming, programs are constructed from a number of well-defined units called *objects*. In this chapter we shall discuss basic concepts and the associated terminology, with particular attention to *classes* and *objects*, and shall demonstrate how these are constructed in Java. In order to do this, we shall also describe how *variables* and *methods* can be declared.

2.1 Object-orientation

The classical picture of a computer program is of a "box" into which we put input data and from which we take output data. The task the program has is to transform a flow of data. This traditional way of looking at computer programs is usually called the *function-oriented* view. The *object-oriented* view is quite different. There, a computer program is conceived as a kind of *model* of the reality the program has to work with. The separate units in a program, the *objects*, are then models of real, or devised, things in the program's environment. It is then the task of the computer program to manipulate these objects. To represent and describe characteristics of objects, we use classes, as illustrated in Figure 2.1.

Let us begin by discussing the concept of an object in detail. Each object has a unique identity. We deal with objects by their names or by references (as used in Java). For instance, we could construct the object `theFlower`, representing a real flower, or the object `theWindow`, which describes a window on the screen. Every object has certain properties, which can be described by *attributes* and *operations*. Attributes are used to keep track of the object's status, since each object has a definite status which can be changed during execution. Each object has its own unique set of attributes. Normally, they are hidden within the object so that they are not accessible from outside and can only be changed by the object itself. This is called *information hiding*. As an example, we can study an object `theLift`, whose status can be described using two attributes, `direction` and `floor`. The attribute `direction` can have one of the values `stationary`, `up`, or `down`, while the attribute `floor` can contain an integer stating which floor the lift

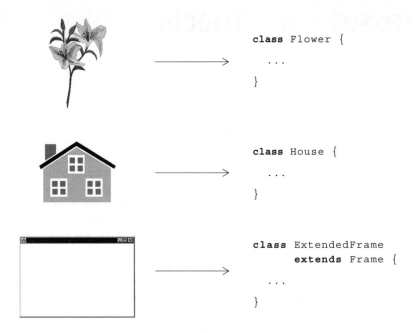

```
class Flower {

    ...

}
```

```
class House {

    ...

}
```

```
class ExtendedFrame
      extends Frame {

    ...

}
```

Figure 2.1 Models

is currently at. Different object-oriented languages use different terms for "attribute". In Java, the term "instance variable" is used, in C++ it is called a "data member", and in Ada, a "component". From now on we will be using the term *instance variable*. We may sometimes use the simpler term *variable* when it is clear that an instance variable is intended and not some other kind of variable.

The second category of properties for an object is the *operations* that can be performed on it. For the object `theLift`, for instance, there might be the operations `goTo`, `stop` and `whichFloor`. The method `goTo` is used to get the lift to a particular floor, `stop` is used to stop the lift, and `whichFloor` is used to find out which floor the lift is currently at. In Java, an operation like this is called a "method", in C++ it is a "member function", while in Ada the term "primitive operation" is used. From now on, we will be using the term *instance method* to emphasize that a particular method is employed for a particular instance of a class.

As stated, an object is a model of a real or devised thing. How then is an object described in a program? This is where the concept of *class* comes in. A class is a kind of template or pattern which describes the appearance of a collection of objects with a common construction and set of properties. A class is therefore a *description*, and different classes can describe different sets of objects. A diagram of class `Lift` is given

Object
Model of a real or devised thing. The properties can be described by *attributes* and *operations*. In Java these are called *instance variables* and *methods*, respectively.

Class
A description of a group of objects with the same properties

in Figure 2.2. In our diagrams we will use UML[1] (Unified Modeling Language). UML contains rules for visual presentation of classes, objects, and other concepts related to object-orientation. UML has been adopted as standard by the OMG (Object Management Group) and has been generally accepted.

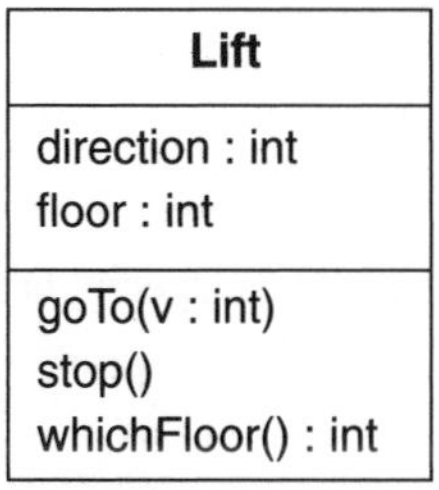

Lift
direction : int
floor : int
goTo(v : int)
stop()
whichFloor() : int

Figure 2.2 A class diagram

In UML a class is drawn as a rectangle with three compartments. The class name is placed in the top compartment, the attributes are placed in the middle compartment and the operations in the bottom compartment. In Figure 2.2 the types of the attributes and the types of the operations' parameters and return values are given. This is not necessary. It is permitted just to state the names of attributes and operations. (In the figure the direction of an elevator is described by an integer number. We can let –1 mean down, 0 stationary, and 1 up.)

An object which belongs to a particular class is said to be an *instance* of the class. Several objects may belong to any one class. Figure 2.3 contains a UML diagram showing two instances of the class Lift. An object diagram contains two

---

[1] *UML Notation Guide* (available from the website www.omg.org). Good text books:
Oestereich, B. (1999) *Developing Software with UML*, Addison-Wesley Longman
Pooley, R. and Stevens, P. (1999) *Using UML*, Addison-Wesley Longman

compartments. In the top compartment the name of the object and the class to which the object belongs are shown underlined. The second compartment shows the attributes and their current values.

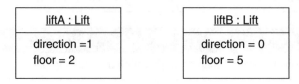

Figure 2.3 Object diagrams

In the figure there is one lift on the way up and currently at floor no. 2 and another one has stopped at floor no. 5. In UML, if the name of an object is of no interest it may be omitted. In that case the colon should still be kept. If we omit the name of a `Lift` object, for instance, the top compartment should show the text : Lift.

2.2 Class definitions

As we have already seen, there is in Java a special language construct to define classes. The definition of class `Lift` will have the following form, for example:

```java
class Lift {
    // instance variables
    private int direction;   // -1 down, 0 stationary, 1 up
    private int floor;

    // methods
    public void goTo(int v) {
        ...
    }

    public void stop() {
        ...
    }

    public int whichFloor() {
        ...
    }
}
```

A class definition is always introduced by the reserved word **class**. The name of the class is indicated after the word **class**, and in this case it is `Lift`. Inside the class definition, we have placed the instance variables first and the methods last. (We are not obliged to have this order. We may place the different declarations in a class in any order we choose, but we will be following this model in the book.) The definitions of methods have only been shown schematically so far but in the following sections we will be describing in detail how instance variables and methods can be declared.

Class Definition

```
class name {
    declarations of instance variables
    definitions of methods
}
```

When we declare a class, we ourselves may decide what it is to be called. The name of something in a program usually goes under the name of *identifier*. An identifier can have an arbitrary length and consist of letters, digits, dollar signs or underline marks but it must not begin with a digit. By "letter", we do not merely mean the letters "a" to "z", as in the English alphabet but also foreign characters. It is therefore eminently possible to use letters such as ê, ã and ö in identifiers. Note that lower-case and upper-case letters are treated as being different. The names n1 and N1 would indicate two different things. We are not allowed to use reserved words as names. For example, we may not declare variables called while and if, since these are reserved words.

We previously wrote the class name Lift, starting with a capital L. From now on, we will let all class names begin with a capital. We will be giving instance variables and methods names beginning with small letters, such as sec, for instance, or width. (This is a convention that is generally accepted in Java.) We do this to make it easy to differentiate class names from the names of variables and methods. If a name includes several words, such as ExtendedFrame, numberOfCars, highestValue and timeForLunch, we normally let each word begin with a capital (excepting the first word, in the case of variables and methods).

2.3 Variables

Variables can be used in different places in a Java program. They may be used as instance variables, for example. In Java there are two categories of variable, *reference variables* and *simple variables*. Reference variables are used to refer to objects, while simple variables act as a kind of container to hold data. A certain type of simple variable can only contain data of a certain kind and of a certain *type*. Similarly, a certain kind of reference variable can only refer to objects belonging to a certain class (or subclass of this).

2.3.1 Variable declarations

Before we can begin to use a variable in a program, we have to determine the name of the variable and the type it is to have. When we do these things, we *declare* the variable. A variable declaration has the following form:

```
modifier type variablename = initializationvalue;
```

Modifiers are reserved words, such as **final** and **private**, which indicate that the variable is to have certain specific properties. We use the initialization value if we wish to indicate that the variable is to contain a particular value from the beginning. The initialization value can be a simple, constant value, or an expression that has to be calculated. Modifier and initialization values may be left out, in which case the simplest form of the variable declaration is:

```
type variablename;
```

If an initialization value is left out for an *instance* variable, it will automatically be initialized to a *default* (standard) *value*, and what this might be would depend on the type. The default value for simple numerical variables is, for example, 0, while the default value for reference variables is null, an empty reference. This means that a reference variable that lacks an initialization value will not refer to an object.

Note that this does not apply to local variables declared inside methods. They must always be initialized before their value is used for the first time.

If several variables are to have the same type, they can be declared on the same line.

```
modifier type name1, name2, name3;
```

We can indicate initialization values here as well. For instance, we could have the form:

```
modifier type name1 = init1, name2, name3 = init3;
```

An initialization value only applies to the variable it stands next to, which in this example means that the variable *name1* will get the initialization value *init1* and *name3* the initialization value *init3*. The variable *name2* is automatically initialized to the default value for the actual type.

The word **final** is a special modifier. We use this word when we wish to declare *constant* variables. We can write:

```
final type v = init;
```

This means that the variable v will get the value *init* from the beginning and then it cannot be changed. In fact, we are also allowed to leave out initialization when we declare a variable marked **final**. In this case, the variable should be given a value before it is used for the first time. This value may not then be changed.

2.3.2 Simple variables and built-in types

Simple variables are ones whose type is one of the built-in types in Java. There are eight such types. These are `boolean` and `char`, together with six types used to describe *numerical* data, that is, ordinary numbers. The type `boolean` is used to describe logic values. Type `char` is used to describe individual characters such as letters. A variable of type `char` always consists of 16 bits indicating a character code. Type `char` will be discussed in Chapter 6.

Numerical types

The types `byte`, `short`, `int` and `long` are used to describe whole numbers or integers (numbers without decimals), while types `float` and `double` are used for real numbers (numbers with decimal parts). What distinguishes the different numerical types, apart from their ability to store decimals, is the number of bits in the computer's memory that variables of these types will take up. A variable of type `byte` is always 8 bits long, for example, while a variable of type `int` is always 32 bits long; see details in the table below. The type we choose will depend on the size of the numbers we wish to store in a program. We will generally be making use of type `int` for integers and type `double` for real numbers ("double" stands for "double precision", a relic from the programming language C).

Built-in numerical types			
type	size	least value	greatest value
`byte`	8 bits	−128	127
`short`	16 bits	−32 768	32 767
`int`	32 bits	−2 147 483 648	2 147 483 647
`long`	64 bits	−9 223 372 036 854 775 808	9 223 372 036 854 775 807
`float`	32 bits	Roughly -3.4×10^{38} to an accuracy of 7 digits	Roughly 3.4×10^{38} to an accuracy of 7 digits
`double`	64 bits	Roughly -1.7×10^{308} to an accuracy of 15 digits	Roughly 1.7×10^{308} to an accuracy of 15 digits

An instance variable, which is one of the numerical, built-in types, is automatically initialized to the value 0 unless a special initialization value is indicated in the declaration. Here are some examples of declarations of simple numerical variables.

```
int i, j, lowestPoint=10, highestPoint=50;;
final int maxSize=500;
double x, y;
```

Expressions for the calculation of numerical numbers often occur in programs. Such expressions are called *numerical expressions*. With these we can use the ordinary mathematical operations of addition, subtraction, multiplication and division, indicated by the signs `+`, `-`, `*` and `/`, respectively. The most common form of numerical expression has two operands which can be variables or constant values. Some examples are:

```
i + j        x + 12.6        1 - i           x - y
x * y        i * maxSize     i / 10          x / y
```

The two operands may be of different numerical type. The type which the result of a numerical expression gets is determined by the type of the operands. If one of the operands has type `double`, the result will be of this type. Otherwise, a search is made to see whether one of the operands has type `float` and if so, the result will be of type `float`. If not, a search is made to see whether one of the operands has type `long`, and if so, the result will be of type `long`. Otherwise, the result will be of type `int`, independent of the type the operands have.

Division requires further explanation. If one of the operands is a real number, nothing unusual will happen. Ordinary division takes place and the result will be a real number, the quotient of the two operands. If, on the other hand, both the operands have an integer type, for example, `int`, then *integer division* is performed. This means that we will see how many times the right-hand operand "goes into" the left-hand one. If, for example, the variables `i` and `j` are of type `int` and have the values `14` and `5`, respectively, the result of the expression `i/j` will be `2`, since `5` goes `2` times into `14`. The result will *not* be `2.8`. To obtain the remainder in a division operation, we can use the operator `%`. If, as previously, the variables have values of `14` and `5`, respectively, the expression `i%j` will produce a result of `4`.

More complicated expressions can be created by combining several operators. We then obtain an expression that contains several part-expressions. An example is `i+j*maxSize`. In a complicated expression, the priorities of the different operators determine the order in which the expression is calculated. Operators with higher priority are calculated before those with lower priority. If two operators have the same priority, calculation will be performed from left to right. In the case of numerical operators, `*`, `/` and `%` have the highest priority, while the operators `+` and `-` have the lowest priority. An example is the expression `-2+4/2*3`, which will have the value `4`. Parentheses can also be used to control the order of calculation. For instance, the expression `(-2+4)/2*3` will have a value of `3`. A list of all the operators in Java is given in Appendix A.

We often need to indicate constant values in an expression. We have already seen several examples of this. In the following example, `12.6` and `10` are constant values.

```
x + 12.6     i / 10
```

Such constant values are normally called *literals* in a programming language. In Java, we differentiate between integer literals and real literals. In the above expression, `10` is an integer literal and `12.6` is a real literal. It is normal to indicate integer literals in ordinary *decimal* form. They will then consist of the digits 0–9. If we let an integer literal begin with the digit 0, the compiler will interpret this as an *octal* number and the literal may then only contain the digits 0 to 7. The literal `025`, for example, is interpreted as 21 in the decimal system (2 * 8 + 5). Integer literals can also be given in *hexadecimal* form. The literal is then introduced by the signs `0x`, or `0X`, and then a number of hexadecimal digits are given. These hexadecimal digits are the normal digits 0 to 9, together with the letters A, B, C, D, E and F. (We can also use lower-case letters.) The integer literal `0x2c`, for example, is interpreted as 44 (2 * 16 + 12). Integer literals normally have type `int`. If we had to represent so large a number that it could not be contained in a variable of type `int`, we would write the letter L last in the literal. The literal would then have type `long` instead. For example, we can write the literal `150000000000L`.

Real literals can be written either in the ordinary way or in exponential form. In the ordinary form, there are a number of integer digits, a decimal point and a number of decimals. Note that it should be a decimal *point* and not the Continental decimal *comma*. We are allowed to leave out integer digits or decimals but never the decimal point. Some examples of this are

```
12.3     0.057     789.     .5     0.
```

The exponential form is handy when indicating very small or very large numbers. Some examples of numbers in exponential form are

```
1.234E2     23.456e-32     1.E16     .56e-55     832E12
```

The exponential part introduced by the letter E, or e, indicates how the number is to be raised. For example, `1.234E2` means "`1.234` times 10 raised to the power of `2`" and `23.456e-32` means "`23.456` times 10 raised to the power of `-32`". A real literal will have type `double`. (We can write the letter F right at the end, for example `7.8e17F`, if we want a real literal to have type `float`.)

There is a corresponding class in the package `java.lang` for each of the eight built-in types. This class will have the same name as the type but with a capital letter to begin it. There is, for instance, a class called `Byte` and another called `Double`. The exceptions to this rule are types `int` and `char`. The corresponding classes here are called `Integer` and `Character`, respectively. All of these classes are called "*wrapper classes*". They contain diverse constants and methods associated with the actual built-in type. All wrapper classes (except the class `Boolean`) contain the two constants `MIN_VALUE` and `MAX_VALUE`, which indicate the lowest and highest value, respectively, which an actual type can have. (In relation to the types `float` and `double`, `MIN_VALUE` will indicate the lowest positive number that is greater than zero.) For instance, we can make the following initializations:

```
int k = Integer.MIN_VALUE;
double z = Double.MAX_VALUE;
```

Then k is initialized to the least possible value of type `int` and z to the greatest possible value of type `double`. The classes `Float` and `Double` also contain the constants `NEGATIVE_INFINITY` and `POSITIVE_INFINITY` which describe an infinitesimally large negative number and infinitesimally large positive number, respectively. We can use the method `isInfinite` to test whether a value is infinitesimally large. For example, the expression `Double.isInfinite(z)` gives the value `true` if z contains an infinitesimally large number. Certain numerical operations, division by 0, for instance, give an undefined result. There is a method called `isNaN` in the classes `Float` and `Double`, which can be called to check whether a real variable contains such an undefined value. (NaN stands for "not a number".)

The type boolean

Type `boolean` is used to describe logical values and for this type only two values are allowed, `false` and `true`. An instance variable of type `boolean` that has not been explicitly initialized will automatically get the value `false`. It is perhaps a little unusual to find variables of type `boolean`. Type `boolean` is mostly used in connection with comparisons which, as we shall see, may be found in `if` statements and `while` statements. A *comparison expression* has type `boolean` and is constructed using a *comparison operator*. The different comparison operators are:

```
<     >     <=     >=     ==     !=
```

They mean "less than", "greater than", "less than or equal to", "greater than or equal to", "equal to" and "not equal to", respectively. Note especially that the operator "equal to" is written with two equal signs. Here are some examples:

```
i > j        lowestPoint == 10        x <= 5.75        i != 0
```

Comparison Operators					
==	equal to	<	less than	>	greater than
!=	not equal to	<=	less than or equal to	>=	greater than or equal to

We can construct more complicated *logic expressions* with the help of the operators &&, || and !, which carry out the operations *and*, *or* and *not*. These operators also yield a result of type **boolean**. The expression A&&B is true if *both* A and B are true and false otherwise. The expression A||B is true if *at least one* of A or B is true and false otherwise. The expression !A is true if A is false and false if A is true. Some examples:

```
temp>20 && temp<30
i==1 || i==3 || i==5 || i==7 || i==9
!(temp>20 && temp<30))
```

The operators && and || have lower priority than the arithmetical operators +, -, * and / and the comparison operators <, >, etc. This means that expressions such as

```
i + j > k * l && m == n
```

are interpreted as

```
(i + j) > (k * l) && (m == n)
```

The operators && and || are calculated from left to right, and the calculation is terminated as soon as possible. This means that if the left-hand operand of the operator && is false, the right-hand operand will never be calculated. Conversely, if the left-hand operand of the operator || is true, the right-hand operand will never be calculated. This can be very important, as, for example, in the following expression, where we want to avoid carrying out division if the variable k is equal to zero.

```
k != 0 && n/k > 10
```

Logic Operators		
A && B true if *both* A and B are true	A || B true if *at least one* of A or B is true	! A true if A is false
&& and || have *lower* priority than comparison operators ! has *higher* priority than arithmetical operators and comparison operators		

2.3.3 Reference variables

In Java, we cannot access objects directly. We always have to access them through a reference. Suppose, for example, that we have defined a class called Lift which describes how lifts work. We can then declare a new variable, which we will call a.

```
Lift a;
```

This does not mean, as we might perhaps be inclined to believe, that the variable a has type Lift. It means that a is a *reference variable* which has the ability to *refer to* lifts;

a has the type "reference to Lift". Since no initialization value has been indicated in the declaration, a will automatically get the default value null. This means that the variable a will not, for the present, be referring to an object. We can look upon a as being a container which contains an empty reference. This is illustrated in Figure 2.4.

Figure 2.4 An uninitialized reference variable

To make a refer to an object, we first have to *create* an object, that is, create a new instance of the class Lift. This is done with the operator **new**. We can write, for example:

```
a = new Lift();
```

Then we will have the situation in Figure 2.5. Note that the object itself lacks a name.

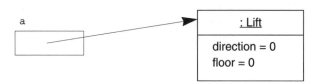

Figure 2.5 A reference variable and an object

It is the reference that is called a. We can now reach the object through the reference. We can, for instance, write:

```
a.goTo(5);
```

Naturally, it is possible to initialize reference variables directly in the declaration.

```
Lift b = new Lift();
```

We now have two reference variables and two lifts. See Figure 2.6.

When we use the operator **new**, the Java system reserves memory space for the new object. The space for objects no longer in use must be returned so that accessible memory space will not be exhausted. In some programming languages, such as C++, a programmer had to take great care that this was done correctly but in Java this is extremely simple: we do nothing! There is no operator to return memory space. The system automatically carries out *garbage collection* and if it discovers objects without

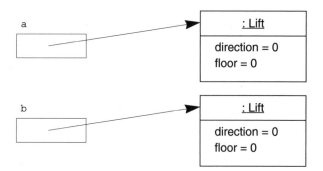

Figure 2.6 Two reference variables and two objects

references to them, it will return their memory space. If we know that we no longer have need of an object, we can make it possible for the system to return memory space by ensuring that there is no longer a reference to the object. For example, we can assign the value `null` to a reference variable. If we have reference variables declared inside methods, we do not even need to do this, since these reference variables will cease to exist once execution of the method is complete. We should also point out that in Java, it is not possible to have *lingering* references to objects that no longer exist. This is because we cannot declare objects directly but always have to use `new`. The system will not release memory space as long as there is a reference to it.

Automatic garbage collection is naturally very convenient for the programmer. There is only one disadvantage: it can take time. This means that Java is not always a convenient programming language to use for the construction of real-time programs.

It is often asserted that there are no pointers in Java but this is not true. In fact, it could be said that the opposite is nearer the truth; as soon as we start working with objects, we will be using pointers, for reference variables are nothing other than pointers. When people say that there are no pointers in Java, what they really mean is that there are few opportunities for the programmer to manipulate pointers. The programmer can only declare reference variables and assign values to them.

From now on, we will be mentioning references less, out of practical considerations. If we make the call `a.goTo(5)`, for example, it would be correct to say that we are calling the method `goTo` for the object variable `a` it is referring to but this is clumsy. So we simply say that we are calling the method `goTo` for object `a`. Everything takes place through references, however, and it is important to remember that `a` in this case is not an object but a reference to an object. When it is important to emphasize the difference between references and objects, for example when making assignments, we will naturally keep the two concepts separate.

2.3.4   Assignments

Variables, as we have seen, may be initialized directly upon declaration but we can also make use of an *assignment statement*. One of these might have the form:

```
variablename = expression;
```

What is happening here is that the expression to the right of the equal sign is being calculated first. This value is then placed in the variable. For a value to be assigned to a variable, the value must have the same type as the variable. Therefore, the expression to the right of the equal sign in an assignment statement must either have the same type as the variable to the left, or its value must be able to be converted automatically into the type of this variable. Where *numerical types* are concerned, that is, types containing mathematical numbers, it is important that "safe" type conversions can take place automatically. (A type conversion is safe when the value cannot be corrupted, that is, when the value can always be held in the new type.) Conversions from an integer type to a longer one are safe, as is the conversion from an integer type to a real type. Here are some examples of assignments:

```
int i;
double d;
d = i;      // OK! Safe type conversion
i = d;      // INCORRECT!! Attempt at a dangerous type conversion
```

If we wish to make "dangerous" type conversions, we must use an explicit type conversion, a *cast*. We will then write the type we wish the value of the expression to be converted to in parentheses, in front of the expression in the right-hand section. We can then write, for example:

```
i = (int)d;      // OK. Explicit type conversion
```

We can also make assignments to reference variables. If we suppose, as previously, that the variables a and b are references to the class Lift, we can write:

```
a = new Lift(); // OK! new gives a reference as result
a = b;          // Permissible but probably not what we intended
```

In the last assignment statement, we assigned b to a. This will mean that the reference in variable b will be assigned to variable a. After the assignment both references will then be pointing at the *same* object. See Figure 2.7. The object that b points to will *not* be copied to the object that a points to.

Certain classes, but not all, have a method called clone which can be called if we wish to make a copy of the whole object. For example, the standard class Calendar, which we will be using later, has such a method. Now suppose that we have two reference variables c1 and c2, which can refer to objects of class Calendar. In order to make a copy of the object c2 refers to and to let c1 refer to the copy, we can write:

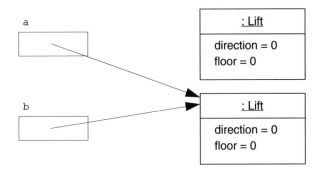

Figure 2.7 Assignment to reference variables

```
c1 = (Calendar) c2.clone();
```

(Here we need an explicit type conversion, since the method `clone` gives a reference to an object of the base class `Object` as result.) Not only standard classes can have a method called `clone`. We could also define one for our own classes but this is more complicated so we will not go into it now.

Assignment

variablename = expression;

The value of the expression to the right of the equal sign is calculated first. This value is then placed in the variable on the left.
The variable's earlier value is destroyed.
The expression on the right must have the same type as the variable, or be able to be converted automatically to this type.
"Safe" type conversions are made automatically for numerical types.

Where assignments to reference variables are concerned, the reference itself is changed, not the object the variable refers to.

Explicit type conversions are sometimes necessary:
variablename = (desired type) expression;

2.3.5   Text variables

There is a standard class `String` which is used to describe texts. An expression of the form `"a text"` is understood as a constant object of class `String`. In the declaration

```
String s1 = "Welcome";
```

the initialization expression is an object of class `String` and `s1` is a reference variable which is initialized to refer to this object. A `String` object can be displayed in a text window using the method `System.out.println`. The following statement will produce the printout `Welcome`.

```
System.out.println(s1);
```

Objects of class `String` are always constant; we cannot change anything inside the text. On the other hand, we can use the operator + to produce new objects.

```
String s2 ="to Java";
s1 = s1 + " " + s2;
```

The variable `s1` will now refer to a *new* `String` object containing the text `"Welcome to Java"`. The object `s1` referred to earlier (the one containing the text `"Welcome"`) will no longer be used and its space will be returned automatically when the system performs garbage collection. Operands for the operator + should be of type `String`. Automatic type conversion to `String` is performed for the built-in types. The following lines demonstrate how a value of type **int** is automatically converted to type `String`.

```
int i = 5;
s2 = "Number " + i;
System.out.println(s2);
```

The printout will then be:

```
Number 5
```

Values of types other than the simple built-in types can be automatically converted to type `String` but for this to be possible, the class in question must have a method called `toString`. This should return a value of type `String`.

Automatic conversions to `String` do not only occur in connection with the operator +. They can also take place when the method `System.out.println` is called. For example, we can write:

```
System.out.println(i);
```

2.4 Methods

Methods describe what we can do with objects, or how objects can be manipulated. In order to generate discussion on the subject, let us begin with the following class which describes the time of day. The class `Time` has three instance variables, `h`, `m` and `s`, which are used to hold hours, minutes and seconds. In addition, there is an instance variable `showSec`, which indicates whether the seconds should be shown in the printout. There are seven methods. We call method `set` when we wish to set an object to describe a particular time. We call method `setShowSec` to indicate whether the seconds should be shown. The methods `getHour`, `getMin` and `getSec` return the values of h, m and s, respectively. The method `tick` moves the time forward one second. Method `toString` returns as result a text with the form `hh:mm:ss`, or `hh:mm`, depending on whether the seconds are to be shown. We have defined this method so that automatic type conversions from class `Time` to class `String` can take place. If the variable t is a point in time, we will be allowed to write expressions such as `"The time is" + t`. The method `toString` will then be automatically called to make the conversion.

```java
class Time {
  // instance variables
  private int h, m, s;
  private boolean showSec = true;

  // methods
  public void set (int hour, int min, int sec) {
    // check that the time is OK
    if (hour>=0 && hour<24 &&
        min>=0 && min<60 && sec>=0 && sec<60) {
      h=hour; m=min; s=sec;
    }
    else
      System.out.println("Illegal time");
  }

  public void setShowSec(boolean show) {
    showSec = show;
  }

  public int getHour () {
    return h;
  }

  public int getMin () {
    return m;
  }

  public int getSec () {
    return s;
  }

  public void tick()     // moves the time forward by one second
    s = s+1;
    if (s==60) {
      s = 0;
      m = m+1;
    }
    if (m==60) {
      m = 0;
      h = h+1;
    }
```

```
    if (h==24)
      h=0;
  }

  public String toString () { // gives a text with the form
    String t = h + ":" + m;   // hh:mm:ss or hh:mm
    if (showSec)
      t = t + ":" +  s;
    return t;
  }
}
```

2.4.1 Method definitions

There are two parts to a method definition, a *head* and a *body*. In the method's head, we show how the function is to be used. By way of an example, let us study the method set. The head will look like this:

```
public void set (int hour, int min, int sec)
```

We first indicate the method's visibility (more of this later). We then indicate the type of the result that is returned from the function. In this example, we have the reserved word **void**, which means that the method will not be returning a value. The method's name is now shown and after this we indicate what is to be put into the method by listing the method's *parameters*. We will give the type and name for every parameter. Our program indicates that the method has three parameters hour, min and sec, which all are of the built-in type **int**. This is very much like a declaration of three variables, and these parameters will act as variables within the method set. They only exist while the method is being executed. When the method is called, hour, min and sec will contain the values given as arguments for the method. Note that when we declare parameters, we have to repeat the type name in front of *every* parameter name, so that we are not allowed to write (**int** hour, min, sec), which is possible when we are declaring variables. Neither is it allowed to initialize parameters. A number of methods lack parameters. The method getHour, for example, has the head

```
public int getHour ()
```

We then write empty parentheses after the method's name. We can also see that the method getHour should return a value of type **int** as result. A method can give a result of any type, including built-in types and references.

Inside a method's body, indicated by curly brackets, is described what will happen when the method is called. We usually write the declarations first (if there are any), followed by the statements that can be performed. There are no declarations in getHour and there is only one statement:

```
return h;
```

+---+
| **Method Definition** |
+---+
| *modifier resulttype name (type1 param1, type2 param2,* etc.) { |
| *local declarations* |
| *and statements* |
| } |
+---+

A `return` statement does two things. It indicates the value to be returned as a result from the method and it terminates the method. (If there were another statement immediately after the `return` statement, it would not be performed.) There should be an expression after the word `return`. The type for this expression should be the same as the type indicated first in the method's head. If this is not the case, an automatic type conversion to this type will occur (if this is possible). If a method returns a reference, the object the reference refers to will not be copied and returned. Instead, it will be the reference itself that will be given as the result. For instance, if we wrote in a method

```
MyClass r = new MyClass();
...
return r;
```

the return value will be a reference to an object created on the first line. There will not be a copy of this object.

It is possible to have several `return` statements in a method but it is very common to have only one, last in the method's body. All methods which have a return type that is not `void` must have a `return` statement. Methods with the return type `void`, that is, methods which do not leave a value, do not need to have a `return` statement and in this case execution in the method will be terminated when the final right-hand bracket has been reached. Methods with the return type `void` can have one or several `return` statements but then there must not be an expression after the word `return`.

+---+
| **return Statement** |
+---+
| `return` *expression*; |
| |
| Terminates a method and returns the value *expression* as result.|
| The expression's type should be the same as the method's result type.|
| Must be in methods with result types other than `void`. |
| |
| Methods with the result type `void` may have `return` statements; these will|
| then have the form |
| `return`; |
+---+

2. Classes and objects

The instance variables declared in a class are directly accessible inside the methods of the class (but not in methods defined with the modifier **static**). Let us look a little more closely at the methods in class Time. The three methods getHour, getMin and getSec are easy. They simply return the value of the corresponding instance variable. The method setShowSec is also quite simple. It has a parameter of type **boolean**, and the only thing it does is to assign the parameter's value to the instance variable showSec.

The method set is a little more complicated. It will have as parameters the three integers hour, min and sec, which will give the relevant time. The method's job is to set the instance variables h, m and s to hour, min and sec, respectively, but before it does this, it has to check that it has the permissible values in the parameters. Negative values are not allowed. In addition, the parameters min and sec may be 59 at most and the parameter hour at most 23. An **if** statement is used to carry out the checking.

```
if (hour>=0 && hour<24 && min>=0 && min<60 &&sec>=0 &&sec<60) {
    h=hour; m=min; s=sec;
}
else
    System.out.println("Illegal time");
}
```

The conditional expression inside the parentheses is calculated first in an **if** statement. This expression should be an expression of the built-in type **boolean**. If the expression is true, the statement(s) after the right-hand parenthesis is/are carried out. If there are several statements after the right-hand parenthesis, as in the **if** statement above, these statements must be put between curly brackets. If the conditional expression is false, these statements will not be performed but the statement(s) coming immediately after **else** will be. Here too, we will need curly brackets, if there is more than one statement. An **if** statement does not need an **else** part and if indeed there is none, nothing will be done when the conditional expression is false. The different forms an **if** statement can have are summarized in the Revision Table. When there are curly brackets around the statements after **if**, there should not be a semicolon in front of **else** but when there are no curly brackets, there *must* be a semicolon. To make it easier to see which statements are to be carried out conditionally, when dealing with **if** statements, we usually *indent* the text in the line.

The method tick also uses **if** statements but they do not have an **else** part.

```
if (s==60) {
    s = 0;
    m = m+1;
}
```

if statement, different forms	

if (*expression*)
    statement;
 	
if (*expression*)
    statement;
else
    statement;
 	
if (*expression*)
{
    one or more statements
}
else
{
    one or more statements
}
	if (*expression*)
	{
	    one or more statements
	}
	
	if (*expression*)
	    statement;
	else
	{
	    one or more statements
	}
	
	if (*expression*)
	{
	    one or more statements
	}
	else
	    statement;

The method `tick` should move the time forward by one second and this is done in the following way. We first increase the seconds by 1. If the number of seconds then comes to 60, a whole minute will have gone. We therefore increase the minutes by 1 and set the seconds at zero. If the minutes are then equal 60, exactly an hour will have gone. We now increase the hours by 1 and set the minutes at zero. If, in the end, exactly 24 hours have gone, then a whole day will have passed and we can set the hours at zero.

The method `toString` looks like this:

```
public String toString () {  // gives a text with the form
   String t = h + ":" + m;    // hh:mm:ss or hh:mm
   if (showSec)
     t = t + ":" +  s;
   return t;
}
```

On the second line, a *local variable* with the name `t` is declared. Local variables are variables which are needed temporarily in a method, for example, to contain certain partial results in a calculation. Declarations of local variables may be placed anywhere among the statements in a method but we usually put them first, as we have done here. The variable `t` is a reference variable which refers to an object of the standard class `String`. It is initialized to a text in the form `hh:mm`, where `hh` and `mm` are values of the instance variables `h` and `m` in text form. (As we saw in Section 2.3.5, integer variables are automatically converted to type `String` when we use the operator `+` for texts.) If the seconds are also to be shown, we create a new text in which the seconds are placed last. The text which has been constructed is given as a result from the method.

Local variables, like parameters, have a limited life and only exist while the method is being executed. We may compare this with the life of an instance variable which exists as long as the actual object exists, that is, as long as there is a reference to the object.

2.4.2   Method calls

A method definition is merely a description of how a particular event is to be performed. In order to really do anything, we have to *call* the method. To demonstrate this, let us look at a program that uses the class Time.

```
class TimeDemo {
  public static void main(String[] arg) {
    Time t1 = new Time();
    Time t2 = new Time();
    int a=17, b=8, c=20;
    t1.set(a, b, c);
    t2.set(23, 59, 59);
    t1.tick();
    t2.tick();
    t2.tick();
    System.out.println(t1);
    System.out.println(t2);
  }
}
```

(Please note that the calls of println cause the method toString in class Time to be called automatically.) A test-run of the program gives the output:

```
17:8:21
0:0:1
```

First, the two reference variables t1 and t2 are declared. Each of these refers to its own instance of class Time. Thus, there are two separate instances. Note that every object of a class has its *own* instance variables that are *independent* of other objects. There is, therefore, one collection of the variables h, m and s in t1 and another one in t2.

A method is called with the help of the *dot operator.* We write the name of the object[1] on which we wish to perform our method, followed by a dot and then the name of the method. The line

---

[1] Actually, as was mentioned earlier, we write the name of the variable which refers to the object on which we wish to perform the method but from now on, we will be expressing ourselves rather more succinctly.

```
t1.set(a, b, c);
```

is, for instance, a call of the method set for the object t1.

We are allowed, in a method, to call other methods for the same class. Then we will not need to write an object name and a dot before the method's name, for it is understood that the call applies to the same object as the one being dealt with.

When we call a method, we write a list of *arguments* after the method's name. (Sometimes the term *actual parameters* is also used.) When the call is executed, the values of the arguments are calculated first. (In the call of the method set, no calculations are necessary, since values are already available in the variables a, b and c.) The values of the arguments are then put into the method. These are *copied* to corresponding parameters. When set is called, the first argument's value is put into the parameter hour, the second argument's value is put into the parameter min and the third argument's value is put into the parameter sec. Note that none of the variables a, b and c have been in any way affected by this, or by what will later occur in method set. The technique of transferring the values of arguments to a method is normally called *call by value*. The arguments' values are thus *copied*, becoming local copies inside the method. Another way of expressing this is to say that hour, min and sec are *value parameters*. Call by value is *always* used in Java. All parameters are thus value parameters. However, *when there are parameters of reference type, the reference itself is copied and not the object that is being referred to*. Let us suppose, for example, that the class TimeDemo, in addition to main, also contains method tickBoth, with the following appearance (for the moment, do not worry why the word **static** is included):

```
static void tickBoth(Time x, Time y) {
    x.tick();
    y.tick();
}
```

Further suppose that we add the following lines last in main:

```
tickBoth(t1, t2);
System.out.println(t1);
System.out.println(t2);
```

We will then get two more lines of output as follows:

```
17:8:22
0:0:2
```

This demonstrates that there really are references which are copied when tickBoth is called. If the objects themselves had been copied, the objects t1 and t2 refer to would not have been changed by the call. Thus, x will refer to the same objects as t1 in this case and y will refer to the same objects as t2.

---

method Calls

---

referencename.methodname (a1, a2, ... an)

A reference name and dot can be left out if another method in the same class is called. The call then applies to the same objects.

a1, a2, ... an are *arguments*. They are allowed to be expressions.

Their types should agree with corresponding parameters.

The following takes place:

1. The values of *a1, a2, ... an* are calculated.
2. Arguments *a1, a2, ... an* are copied to their corresponding parameters.
   This is termed *call by value*.
   If the arguments are references, they are copied, and not the objects.
3. The statements inside the method are carried out.
4. The method is terminated in a `return` statement, or when the last statement has been executed.
5. Methods with a return type other than `void` must have a `return` statement.
   For such methods, the method's call value will equal the value in the `return` statement.
6. Execution continues after the method has been called.

A call of a method that does not leave a result (as does the result type `void`, here) is regarded as a *statement* in the program. Calls of the methods `set` and `tick` are therefore statements in the program. A call of a method that does not have the result type `void` is regarded as an *expression* and may therefore be put anywhere in a program where we are allowed to put expressions. This might be as a part of a long expression. In the following declaration, for instance, the text to the right of the equal sign is an expression:

```
int totalHour = t1.getHour()+t2.getHour();
```

Arguments of a method may be expressions. They do not have to be simple variables either. We can write, for instance:

```
t1.set(totalHour+2, t1.getMin(), 0);
```

2.5 Encapsulation and visibility

The instance variables `h`, `m` and `s` in class `Time` in the preceding section were automatically initialized to 0 in each new instance of class `Time`. Because the methods `set` and `tick` are the only methods which change instance variables and since both of these methods check that these instance variables have correct values, we would like to be certain that an object of type `Time` will always describe a correct time of day. But suppose that someone succeeded in directly changing one of the instance variables without making use of either of the methods `set` and `tick`. Then we could not be sure that the time was correct. In order to prevent such a possibility, the instance variables have been encapsulated in the class so that they cannot be accessed directly from without. We achieve this by writing `private` in the declaration of the instance variables. On the other hand, we want all methods to be visible and able to be called from without. For this reason, they have first been declared with the word `public`. These words are modifiers and indicate the nature of the *visibility* to be applied.

When instance variables and methods are declared, we can indicate the nature of their visibility for each of them and write one of the reserved words `public`, `private`, or `protected`. The word `public` means that what is being declared is accessible from anywhere in the program, even from other classes. The word `private` means that what is being declared is only accessible inside the actual class. The word `protected` means that what is being declared is only accessible within the actual class, in other classes within the actual package and in any subclasses of other packages.

Visibility				
visible in	`private`	*package*	`protected`	`public`
another class in the same package	no	yes	yes	yes
a subclass in another package	no	no	yes	yes
a class in another package	no	no	no	yes

If we do not write one of the words `public`, `private`, or `protected` when we declare an instance variable or a method, whatever we declare will have *package visibility*. This means that the instance variable or method will be visible in all other classes in the package in which the actual class is included but never from classes which are part of other packages. The idea here is that all the classes included in a particular package should be able to "rely on" each other, so that it would be safe to allow them free access to instance variables. However, the problem is that if we do not indicate that the class we are defining is to go into a special package, it will go into a default package that includes all of the classes in the actual folder of the file system and we cannot be sure that these classes will belong together to the degree that they can have access to each other's instance variables.

Visibility can be marked in UML diagrams. An example of this will be shown in Figure 2.8 on page 70.

2.6 Object initializations

When we declare a variable, the variable will automatically get a default value, as mentioned earlier. We can also give the variable an explicit initialization value. This applies to instance variables as well. We defined the class `Lift` on page 38. This had two instance variables, `direction` and `floor`. Both were uninitialized and therefore automatically got the default value 0 but we could very well initialize the variables explicitly, if we wanted to. If we want the instance variable `floor` to be initialized to 1, we could write the following text, in which case *every* new `Lift` that is created will be at floor 1 from the beginning.

```
class Lift {
  // instance variables
  private int direction;
  private int floor = 1;

    as previously
}
```

It is useful to be able to initialize instance variables directly but if we have to do more complicated initializations, or if we wish to allow the creator of a new object to affect initialization values, this mechanism will not suffice. We will then have to make use of something called a *constructor*. A constructor is a special initialization method that is called *automatically* every time an object of the actual class is created.

As an example, we will write a new variant of class `Time` on page 51.

```
class Time {
  // instance variables
  private int h, m, s;
  private boolean showSec=true;
 // constructors
  public Time() {}
  public Time(int hour, int min, int sec) {
    set(hour, min, sec);
  }
  // methods
  as earlier
}
```

Lines 6–9 are interesting here. A constructor may be a kind of method but it is special in that it will have the *same name* as the class in which it is included. In addition, it *cannot have a return type*. We have in fact defined *two* constructors here, both with the name `Time`. In Java, we may have several constructors for the same class, provided they have a different number of parameters, or different types in these parameters. The first constructor in class `Time` lacks parameters and the second has three parameters of type **int**. The first constructor does not do anything at all, since it does not contain statements. This means that all the instance variables will get the default value 0. The second constructor will use the parameters' values to initialize the instance variables but it will not do so directly. It will call the method `set` to do the job. The initializations are not made directly in the constructor because the contents of the parameters have to be checked for the correct values. The method `set` does this, and it is easier to call it than to repeat the checks in the constructor. Note that an object name and dot in front of the method name are not written when `set` is called. This is because we have called a method in the *same class* and the call applies to the *same object* that we are in the process of initializing.

Constructors are not called in the same way as ordinary methods. Instead, they are called automatically every time a new object is created. The constructor to be called is determined by the argument given in the expression after **new**. Suppose, for instance, that we have the following program lines:

```
Time t1 = new Time();
Time t2 = new Time(10, 20, 30);
System.out.println(t1);
System.out.println(t2);
```

The constructor lacking parameters will be called on the first line, since no arguments have been indicated. On the second line, the constructor with three parameters is called. The three instance variables in `t1` all get the value 0 and in `t2`, they get the values 10, 20 and 30. The printout from the program lines will therefore be:

```
0:0:0
10:20:30
```

Perhaps it may seem unnecessary to define the constructor without parameters. It is not doing anything and the instance variables are, of course, initialized automatically, since there is no explicit initialization. We still have to define a constructor lacking parameters; this is because we need one if we write expressions of the form **new** `classname()`, that is, if we do not indicate arguments. If we are dealing with a class where no constructors at all have been defined, the Java compiler will *itself* define a constructor without parameters (one that does nothing). This is why we were able to create objects of class `Time` previously, despite our not having defined constructors. However, if we have declared one or more of our own constructors for a class, the Java compiler will *not* define a constructor without parameters. We must do so ourselves, if we wish to have one. Of course, we can give the instance variables in a constructor without parameters whatever values we wish, and not merely the default values.

Thanks to the two constructors for class `Time`, there are two ways of creating new objects with **new**. Either we indicate hours, minutes and seconds as arguments, or we

> ### Constructors
>
> Constructors have the same name as the class.
>
> They are not allowed to have a return type.
>
> There may be several of them but then they must have a different number of parameters, or parameters with different types.
>
> Unless we define our own constructors, a constructor without parameters is defined automatically (and this does nothing).
>
> If we define our own constructors, we have to define a constructor without parameters ourselves, if we want one.
>
> A constructor can call another constructor:
>
> ```
> this (argument);
> ```

do not give any arguments at all. However, we may wish to have times shown without the seconds attached, in which case we should leave out the seconds, only indicating the hours and minutes, or only the hours. We would like to be able to write, for example:

```
Time t3 = new Time(15, 45);
Time t4 = new Time(18);
```

To achieve this, we add two constructors.

```
class Time {
  // instance variables
  private int h, m, s;
  private boolean showSec=true;

  // constructors
  public Time() {}

  public Time(int hour, int min, int sec) {
    set(hour, min, sec);
  }

  public Time(int hour, int min) {
    this(hour, min, 0);
    showSec = false;
  }

  public Time(int hour) {
    this(hour, 0);
  }

  // methods
  as previously
}
```

Now there are four constructors. The first two are those we discussed earlier. The third has hours and minutes as parameters and the last one has only hours as parameter. What is interesting here are the two lines containing the word **this**. We used the reserved word **this** inside a method to get a reference to the object we are currently dealing with. Constructors are not called as ordinary methods but one constructor can, in fact, call another constructor. To do so, we use **this**. For example, the statement

```
this(hour, min, 0);
```

means that the constructor with three parameters will be called. Similarly, the constructor with one parameter will call the constructor with two parameters. It is often useful to allow one constructor to call another, since whatever has to be done in the different constructors is often largely the same thing. Then we do not have to repeat the statements they have in common.

2.7 Overloaded methods

In the previous section we saw that, although all constructors in a class had the same name (the name of the class), we were allowed to have as many constructors as we wanted, as long as they had different parameters. This also applies to ordinary methods. We can have as many methods of the same name as we like, provided that these methods either have a different number of parameters, or parameters with different types. Methods with the same name are called *overloaded* methods. When we call an overloaded method, the compiler will decide which of the methods is intended by looking at the argument indicated. The method is chosen in which the number of arguments and types agree with the parameters. If none of the methods are suitable, or if more than one can be chosen, an error will arise in the compilation of the program.

As an example, let us extend the class Time with one more method called tick. It would be a little unusual if we wanted time to go forward by only one second, so the new method will have an integer parameter indicating the number of seconds by which the time is to advance.

```
class Time {
  as previously

  public void tick(int n) {
    while (n>0) {
      tick();
      n = n - 1;
    }
  }
}
```

The two methods `tick` will be overloaded, and we can now make calls with both of the following forms. In the second case, the method `tick` is called.

```
t1.tick();
t1.tick(35);
```

Inside the definition of the new method, we see for the first time a statement that produces repetition. This is a **while** statement. The execution of the **while** statement proceeds in the following way. First, the conditional expression between parentheses, after **while**, is computed. Exactly as for **if** statements, this expression will be of type **boolean**. So it can be either true or false. If the expression is false, nothing further is done – execution of the **while** statement is finished. On the other hand, if the expression is true, the statements in the curly brackets are performed once. When this has been done, the expression in parentheses is computed once more. If the result is false, the **while** statement is terminated, and if it is true, the statements in parentheses are performed yet another time, and so on.

In method `tick`, we will make as many rounds with our **while** statement as the parameter n indicates. The earlier version of method `tick` is called once during every round, which means that the time advances by one second per round. The variable n is decreased by 1 at every round. After each round, n will therefore contain the number of remaining seconds to be ticked forward. When n becomes zero, the test expression will be false and the **while** statement will be terminated. If we were to attempt to make the time go back, by calling `tick` with a negative argument, nothing would happen, since the test expression would be false from the outset.

In a **while** statement we can, exactly as in an **if** statement, omit the curly brackets if there is only one statement to be performed at every round.

while Statement, different forms	

while (*expression*)
    statement;
	while (*expression*)
	{
	    one or more statements
	}

Sometimes we may need to abort a **while** statement right in the middle of a repetition. We can then use a **break** statement.

2.8 The standard class `Point`

To further our knowledge of classes, let us look at the standard class `Point` in the package `java.awt`. The class `Point` describes a point in a window. This class contains

```
                          break Statement
```

May be placed among the statements performed at every round of a
repetition statement. Immediately aborts the repetition statement.
There is a jump to the first statement after the repetition statement.
Is often placed in an `if` statement:

```
if (conditions_to_end)
    break;
```

the two instance variables `x` and `y`, indicating the point's x- and y-coordinates,
respectively. The class `Point` has the following appearance:

```java
public class Point {
  // instance variables
  public int x;
  public int y;

  // constructors
  public Point() {
    this(0, 0);
  }

  public Point(Point p) {
    this(p.x, p.y);
  }

  public Point(int x, int y) {
    this.x = x;
    this.y = y;
  }

  // methods
  public void setLocation(Point p) {
    setLocation(p.x, p.y);
  }

  public void setLocation(int x, int y) {
    move(x, y);
  }

  public void move(int x, int y) {
    this.x = x;
    this.y = y;
  }

  public void translate(int dx, int dy) {
    x = x + dx;
    y = y + dy;
  }
```

```
public boolean equals(Object obj) {
    // checks whether obj is a point and whether it has the same
    // x- and y-coordinates as this point
    ... // the details are left out
}
}
```

There are three constructors: one without parameters, one which gets the new point's x- and y-coordinates and one which makes the new point a copy of another point p. There are methods for moving a point to a particular place, for shifting it in both its x and y elements and for comparing two points with each other.

One point worth noting is that in a couple of places in the class, for example in the method move, we have written **this**.x and **this**.y. This has been done because there are parameters called x and y, exactly like the instance variables. If we simply write x and y, we mean the parameters, while by **this**.x and **this**.y we mean the instance variables.

java.awt.Point	
new Point()	creates a new point with value (0,0)
new Point(x,y)	creates a new point with value (x,y)
new Point(q)	creates a new point which is a copy of the point q
p.x	gives the x-coordinate for point p
p.y	gives the y-coordinate for point p
p.equals(q)	checks whether points p and q are the same
p.setLocation(q)	sets p to a copy of q
p.setLocation(x,y)	sets p to the value (x,y)
p.move(x,y)	the same as p.setLocation(x,y)
p.translate(dx,dy)	translates p dx in the x direction and dy in the y direction

2.9 Class variables and class methods

Sometimes we deal with attributes common to all the objects belonging to a certain class. Such components are usually called *class variables* in the context of object-orientation. In Java they are also called *static variables*. This name is an unfortunate relic of C and C++ resulting from the fact that we make use of the reserved word **static** when we declare class variables. The word "static", which indicates that something does not change, is misleading. Class variables are not necessarily static in this sense. They can be changed. In order to avoid misunderstandings, therefore, we will be using the term "class variables" from now on but the word **static** must of course be used in the program code itself. What is special about a class variable is that it only exists in a single instance, and this instance is shared by all the objects belonging to the actual class. A good example of a class variable is a variable that keeps a check on how many instances of a particular class there are at any one time. Another, rather different example is a bank account. For every bank account, there is a particular balance and a particular account-holder. These data must, of course, be available in one instance for each account, and so they are ordinary instance variables. The interest rate, on the other hand, is a class variable. Since all accounts (at least accounts of the same kind) will have the same interest rate, it will be wholly unnecessary to store the interest rate in every single account. It suffices that it can be found in one place, being common for all accounts. We shall then use a bank account as an example and write its definition:

```
class Account {
  // class variables
  private static double interestRate;

  // class methods
  public static double getInterest() {
    return interestRate;
  }

  public static void setInterest(double newInterest) {
    interestRate = newInterest;
  }

  // instance variables
  private int customerNo;
  private double balance, interestEarned;

  // constructor
  public Account(int customer) {
    customerNo = customer;
  }

  // instance methods
  public double getBalance() {
    return balance;
  }

  public void transaction (double amount) {
    //negative amount => withdrawal
    if (amount<0 && balance+amount<0)
      System.out.println("Withdrawal cannot be done!");
    else
      balance = balance+amount;
  }

  public void getDailyInterest() {
    interestEarned=interestEarned+balance*interestRate/100/365;
  }
```

```
   public void addInterest() {
     balance = balance+interestEarned;
     interestEarned = 0;
   }
 }
```

For every account there are three class variables which keep a check on customer numbers, the current balance and the interest earned during the year. Interest earned is calculated on a daily basis but is not added to the balance until the end of the year.

First, we shall briefly describe the operations that have nothing to do with class variables. The constructor initializes a new account. A unique customer number is provided as argument to the constructor. The instance variables `balance` and `interestEarned` will automatically get a value of 0. We call the method `getBalance` if we wish to check the balance in a particular account. The method `transaction` is called each time a deposit or withdrawal is made on the account. A deposit is indicated as a positive amount and a withdrawal as a negative amount. If we try to take out more money than is available in an account, we get an error text. The method `getDailyInterest` is called once a day and it calculates the interest earned during that day. The interest earned is added to the instance variable `interestEarned`. The interest rate is expressed as a percentage and must therefore be divided by 100. Division by 365 is carried out because we want to calculate the interest earned for one day and not a whole year. The method `addInterest` is called at the end of every year (or when the account is closed). This method adds the total interest earned during the year to the balance, and the class variable `interestEarned` is then set at zero.

There is a class variable, `interestRate`. This is declared by the reserved word **static**. There are also two methods, `getInterest` and `setInterest`, which are used to read and change the interest rate. These functions are special in that they do not deal with individual accounts and do not use instance variables. A method with this property is called a *class method*, and methods of this kind are marked with the word **static**. In Java, class methods are also called *static methods* but this term, like the term "static variable", is a relic from C and C++ and is misleading. From now on we shall use the term "class method".

A class variable is only found in one place. A class variable is initialized when the class is loaded into the Java interpreter, that is, when the class is used for the first time in a program. As with other variables, we can indicate a special initialization value if we wish. If we had wanted the interest rate automatically to be 5% every time we started the program, we would have been able to write

```
   static double interestRate = 5;
```

If no initialization value has been indicated, then the class variables, like other variables, will get a default value. In class `Account`, the class variable `interestRate` will get a value of 0. Constructors are *not* used to initialize class variables. The job of constructors is, of course, to initialize the variables dealing with a particular *instance* of the class. If we want to create more complicated initializations of class variables, we can use special *class initializers* (also called *static initializers* in Java). They might look like this:

```
static {
    declarations and statements
}
```

and could be placed anywhere inside the class definition. What is happening is that the declarations and statements inside the class initializer are executed just once, when the class is loaded in the Java interpreter. The class variables can then be initialized.

Ordinary instance methods have access to the class variables and can read and change them. For example, the interest rate is necessary in the method `getDailyInterest` in order to calculate the daily interest. If a class variable is changed in an instance method, the change will affect all the objects of the actual class, since they all share this class variable.

Class Variables

are declared with the word **static**.
exist only in one edition, common to all objects belonging to the class.
are initialized when the class is loaded into the interpreter.
exist for the remainder of the program.
can be initialized if necessary in a special class initializer.

A class method is not called for one special object, and so it can be called even if there are no objects of the actual class. The calls

```
Account.setInterest(4.5);
double ir = Account.getInterest();
```

change and read interest. When a class method is called, the class name is written in front of the dot. It is also possible to call class methods in the same way as instance methods, by writing the name of an object instead of the class name. We can write:

```
Account acc = new Account(12345);
acc.setInterest(5.1);
```

However, this is pointless and even misleading, since the function `setInterest` does not in any way read or change the object `acc`. What it does do is change something that affects all the objects of the class.

Class Methods
are declared with the word `static`. may only use class variables and not instance variables. calls have the form 　*classname . methodname* (*argument*)

We finish this section by showing, in Figure 2.8, a UML diagram for the class `Account`.

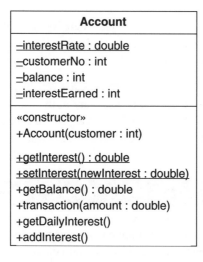

Account
−interestRate : double −customerNo : int −balance : int −interestEarned : int
«constructor» +Account(customer : int) +getInterest() : double +setInterest(newInterest : double) +getBalance() : double +transaction(amount : double) +getDailyInterest() +addInterest()

Figure 2.8 A class diagram with class variables and methods

In UML class variables and class methods are underlined, as shown in the figure. The visibility of the variables and methods of a class can be shown in a UML diagram. In that case the name is preceded by a visibility marker which is one of the characters "+", "−" or "#", denoting public, private and protected visibility, respectively. If the visibility marker is omitted, the visibility is not defined. Also note that a UML diagram can contain keywords enclosed in « ». This is called a *stereotype*. In the figure the constructor is marked in this way.

2.10 The standard class Math

Let us now discuss the class `Math` in the package `java.lang`, which is an example of a serviceable class containing class methods. There are a number of methods in this class used to calculate ordinary mathematical functions, for example trigonometric functions, square roots, exponents and logarithms. There are also methods, min and max, which can be used to calculate the least or greatest of two numbers. We can also find the mathematical constants π and e in class Math. A synopsis is given in the Revision Table. Note that angles are measured in *radians*. A complete revolution (360 degrees) corresponds to 2π radians.

java.lang.Math	
PI	the number π
E	the number e
abs(a)	gives the absolute value of a
max(a,b)	gives the greatest of a and b
min(a,b)	gives the smallest of a and b

The following methods return a value of type **double**.
The arguments x and y should also be real numbers.

exp(x)	gives e^x
log(x)	gives the natural logarithm (ln) of x
sqrt(x)	gives $\sqrt{x}$
ceil(x)	gives the least integer that is >= x
floor(x)	gives the greatest integer that is <= x
pow(x, y)	gives x^y (If x<=0, y must be an integer)
round(x)	rounds off x to an integer of type **long**
random()	gives an random number in the interval 0 to 1
sin(x), cos(x), tan(x)	x is indicated in radians
asin(x), acos(x), atan(x)	gives arcsin etc.
sinh(x), cosh(x), tanh(x)	hyperbolic functions

Calls of the methods in Math can be a part of numerical expressions such as:

```
3.6*Math.sqrt(z)    Math.log(z)/Math.PI    Math.abs(Math.sin(y))
```

Note that the class name must be written first, since the methods in class Math are all class methods.

2.11 Exercises

1. Construct a class Counter, which calculates integers that may only take on values within a certain interval. When a counter is initialized, the counter's start value should be indicated, and we should also be able to indicate the least and greatest values the counter can assume. (If no limit values are indicated, the counter will be allowed to assume all values of type **int**.) Methods should be found to increase

and decrease a counter by 1. If a counter then gets a value that is not allowed, error text should be printed out. We should also be able to read the counter's value.

2. Construct a class `Person`. A person should have a name, an address and an age. Make use of the class `String`. Form a constructor and some appropriate methods for class `Person`.

3. Construct a class `Card` which describes a card in an ordinary pack of cards. The value and colour of a card should be indicated when the card is created. Methods should be found to read the value and colour of a card. In addition, define a method `toString` that makes it possible, in a simple way, to write out the card in the form `Queen of Hearts`, `8 of Clubs`, `Ace of Spades`, etc.

4. A company has a storeroom which contains several different types of article and there may be several different examples of each article in stock. The following information will be interesting to know for each article: the *article identification* (a code of 4 characters), the article description (a text with at most 30 characters), the *number of articles* of a particular kind in stock and the *sales price*. Write a class `Article`, which defines an article. Methods should be found so that articles of the actual kind can be bought and sold. We should also be able to get information about an article.

5. In the package `java.awt`, there is a standard class called `Dimension`. Check the documentation on this class and try to define your own variant of it. (For simplicity's sake, you may assume that the method `equals` has a parameter of type `Dimension` instead of type `Object`.)

6. In the package `java.awt`, there is a standard class called `Rectangle`, which makes use of class `Point` from Section 2.8 and class `Dimension` from Exercise 5. Check the documentation on class `Rectangle` to see if you can understand how it is used and what the different methods do.

7. Write a class `C` which contains a class variable `totNumber`, which automatically holds the total number of objects of class `C` that have been created. The class `C` should also contain a class method which returns the value of the class variable.

8. Develop the previous exercise so that every object of class `C` has an instance variable that is automatically assigned a unique identification number. (*Hint*: Devise a constructor without parameters and read off the class variable `totNumber` in it.) There should be a method that makes it possible to read the identification number but it should not be possible to change it.

Reading and writing

Up to now we have only dealt with programs that wrote output and drew visuals. In this chapter we will be looking at how we can read input from the keyboard and format output in a text window. We shall also learn how to read and write data in text files. Different countries may have different conventions for presenting data. We will begin by describing how programs can be adapted to follow the conventions of the country in which the program is to be run.

3.1 Language conventions and number formatting

Let us for a moment return to the class `Time` on page 51. The printout of the times of the day is not really satisfactory. For example, we might get the printout

```
17:8:22
```

whereas we would always like the hours, minutes and seconds to be printed out as two digits, irrespective of their value. The conversion from integers to text is done by the method `toString` in class `Time`. If we write an expression of the form

```
h + ":" + m
```

the values of the integer variables `h` and `m` will be converted into text, and in this text there will be exactly as many characters as are needed to indicate the value of the variables. If `h` has a value of 17 and `m` a value of 8, there will be two characters for `h`'s value and one character for `m`'s value, and this cannot be changed by the programmer.

To format the text into the form we want, we must make use of an object of class `NumberFormat`. This class is defined in the package `java.text` and contains what we need. There are various aids for formatting numbers in different ways. The conventions for writing numbers varies from country to country. For example, the English-speaking countries use a dot between the integers and the decimals, while in most of the European countries, for example, a decimal comma is used. Conventions are normally determined by the operating systems in use. If we have a English system, for example, we will use English conventions. We can also explicitly indicate the conventions we want by calling the method `setDefault` in the standard class `Locale` of the package `java.util`. We must then give as arguments the codes for the language and country.[1] For example, English has the code `en`, Chinese `cn`, Russian `ru`, Spanish `es`, French `fr`, German `de`, Italian `it` and Portuguese `pt`. Some examples of country codes are: Great Britain `GB`, USA `US`, Canada `CA`, Australia `AU`, Argentina `AR` and Brazil `BR`. For example, to indicate that we want to have Spanish conventions, we can write:

```
Locale.setDefault(new Locale("es","ES"));
```

The class `Locale` also contains some pre-existing `Locale` objects for a number of "common" countries and languages. Some examples are shown in the Revision Table.

---

java.util.Locale

Conventions for different languages are handled with the help of the class `java.util.Locale`. An object of this class describes a local convention. Local conventions determine such things as the format for dates, times and numerals. There is always a default `Locale` object set by the system from the beginning.

In the following list, `l` indicates a variable of type `Locale`.

new `Locale("`*language*`","`*country*`")`	Creates a new `Locale` object. *language* and *country* are ISO codes
`Locale.getDefault()`	Gives a reference to the default `Locale` object.
`Locale.setDefault(l);`	Gives `l` to the default `Locale` object.
`Locale.UK`	A British `Locale` object.
`Locale.US`	An American `Locale` object.
`Locale.JAPAN`	A Japanese `Locale` object.
`Locale.CHINESE`	A `Locale` object for Chinese.
`Locale.FRENCH`	A `Locale` object for French.
`l.getLanguage()`	Returns the language code for `l` (a `String`)
`l.getCountry()`	Returns the country code for `l` (a `String`)

If we now make the declaration

```
NumberFormat sp = NumberFormat.getInstance();
```

we will get a `NumberFormat` object which makes use of the conventions currently set as default. In this example, the conventions are Spanish. A `NumberFormat` object can be obtained for any convention, without changing the default conventions. We would get a `NumberFormat` object following the American conventions if we wrote, for example:

---

[1] We can use a method `getAvailableLocales` in the class `NumberFormat` to check the languages and countries that are installed on the computer used.

```
NumberFormat us = NumberFormat.getInstance(Locale.US);
```

In class `NumberFormat` there is a method called `format`. It is called to format a number, and the result of a call is a text. Suppose, for example, that `x` is a number with the value `2318604.123` and that we write the statement

```
System.out.println(sp.format(x));
```

The object `sp` will direct the formatting here. We will get Spanish conventions, and the printout will be

```
2.318.604,123
```

If we had instead given the statement

```
System.out.println(us.format(x));
```

the printout would have been

```
2,318,604.123
```

There are methods in class `NumberFormat` for controlling the number of integer characters and the number of decimals. (See the Revision Table.) We can also indicate

---

Number formatting

Use class `java.text.NumberFormat`

Get an object of class `NumberFormat`:

```
NumberFormat f = NumberFormat.getInstance(); // local conventions
```
or
```
NumberFormat f = NumberFormat.getInstance("language","country");
```

Call the method `format` to convert a number `x` into text
```
f.format(x)
```

Formatting characteristics are given by the method calls:
```
f.setMaximumFractionDigits(n);  // maximum of n decimals, default 3
f.setMaximumIntegerDigits(n);   // maximum of n integer digits
f.setMinimumFractionDigits(n);  // minimum of n decimals
f.setMinimumIntegerDigits(n);   // minimum of n integer digits
f.setGroupingUsed(true);        // the digits should be grouped
f.setGroupingUsed(false);       // the digits should not be grouped
```

---

whether the digits in a number are to be grouped, that is, put together in groups of three, to make them more readable. These possibilities suffice for most formatting work. The characteristics of a `NumberFormat` object may be changed through calling

75

different methods. We could also use several different `NumberFormat` objects with different characteristics. As an example, we will show how to get 6 decimals in the printout.

```
NumberFormat nf = NumberFormat.getInstance();
nf.setMaximumFractionDigits(6);
nf.setMinimumFractionDigits(6);
System.out.println(nf.format(x));
```

Rounding-off will then take place to 6 decimal places. If we do not indicate the number of decimal places, rounding-off will, as in the examples above, take place to a maximum of 3 decimal places.

We should point out here that the method `format` cannot, at the moment, manage to format very small or very large numbers; such numbers as need to be written in exponential form to be shown correctly. There is a method `useExponent` in class `extra.ExtendedWriter`, discussed in Section 3.2.2, that we can use to test whether a number cannot be formatted by the method `format`.

Let us now return to the method `toString` in class `Time`. We will write a new version in which we use a `NumberFormat` object. In order to get access to class `NumberFormat`, we begin by inserting the line

```
import java.text.*;
```

in the file where class `Time` is defined. The method `toString` now has the appearance:

```
public String toString () {
  NumberFormat nf = NumberFormat.getInstance();
  nf.setMinimumIntegerDigits(2);
  String t = nf.format(h) + ":" + nf.format(m);
  if (showSec)
    t = t + ":" + nf.format(s);
  return t;
}
```

As a result of this amendment to the method `toString`, printout from the demonstration program on page 56 will now have the appearance:

```
17:08:21
00:00:01
```

Using `NumberFormat` objects can become a little complicated. In Section 3.2.2 we shall see how we can use our own help class `Std` to print out text. We will then avoid using a `NumberFormat` object, which will simplify matters. However, when we want to show numerical results in programs with a graphical user interface, we may be obliged to use a `NumberFormat` object to get the printout into the desired format.

3.2 Input and output

A program can communicate with the real world in many different ways. So far, we have merely seen how data is written. We have used the method System.out.println to write text in a text window. In this section we will be looking at how we key in data from the keyboard. Unfortunately, it is not necessarily easy to carry out input and output in Java, especially if we have to enter numerical data or want to format output. There are several reasons for this. One is that Java was primarily intended for the construction of GUI programs. Another reason is that Java is so general. When we input or output data, we use *streams*. Much can be done with streams but big demands are made of the programmer if he or she is to use them correctly. A third reason is that, because Java offers so much, we tend to raise our expectations of our programs, as compared to other programming languages. We do not have to produce input and output in a standard form dictated by the programming language. We can opt for the format used by the country in which we happen to be. The text input and output can also be coded in different forms in the various countries, and completely different alphabets can be used. We no longer have to put up with a situation where incomprehensible gobbledegook appears on the screen as soon as we use letters other than the "basic" a to z, that is, accented letters of the type ñ, ë and à.

If we try to write data making use of the standard classes in Java, we soon find out that it is a difficult business. When we program, however, it is essential to be able to input and output text easily. Even if the programs we write are GUI programs we may have to produce test output while developing the program. We may also need to read or write data from files. Unfortunately, there are no standard classes in Java for input and output that are easy to use. To make it easier for the programmer, therefore, we have constructed our own help classes, and these are described in Section 3.2.2. However, we shall begin by describing how we can read and write text with the help of Java's standard classes. (Those who prefer to use our own simpler help classes can skip the first section and go directly to Section 3.2.2.)

3.2.1 Reading and writing by using standard classes

The language of Java does not itself contain constructs for data input and output. To read and write data, therefore, we have to make use of streams. The stream classes are defined in the standard package java.io. A *stream* is a flow of data streaming in or out of a program; we differentiate between *input streams* and *output streams*. A stream may be originally from a file, from the keyboard, from a communication line such as a modem, or from some other input unit in the computer. Similarly, an output stream may be stored in a file, shown on the screen, or be sent out on a communication line. The class System (in the package java.lang) contains three different streams we can use in our Java programs. They are defined as class variables, with the names `System.in`, `System.out` and `System.err` and correspond to *standard input, standard output* and *standard error.* Normally, *standard input* is connected to the keyboard, which means that everything we write there lands in the stream `System.in`. Both *standard output* and *standard error* are usually connected to a text window.

Printout

The stream `System.out`, which we have used in the book until now, is an object of class `PrintStream`. Two of the methods for this class are `print` and `println`. The difference between these two is that `println` places the printout cursor in a new line after printout has taken place. When there are repeated printouts, `println` sees to it that every printout lands in a new line. When we use `print`, on the other hand, printouts will follow each other on the same line. If, for example, we want to print out

```
What is your name?
```

we will use `print`:

```
System.out.print("What is your name? ");
```

We should not need to use `println` here, since it is natural for the user to print out the answer on the same line as the question.

We should know in connection with the stream `System.out` that it uses a *buffer*. This means that the printout will not necessarily be directly visible in the text window when it has been printed out by the program. This is particularly misleading in *interactive programs*, which write out questions for the user to answer. The program can wait for an answer to its question, although the question has not yet been presented to the user of the program. To be sure text shows up immediately, we sometimes have to empty the buffer, which is done by calling the method `flush`.

```
System.out.flush();
```

This should be done after method `print` has been called. If, on the other hand, we call `println`, this will not be necessary, as the buffer will be emptied automatically.

One problem with the stream `System.out` is that we do not always get correct printout, that is, when `LATIN_1` code (see Section 6.1) is not used in the text window. This is especially common when we use MS-DOS Prompt in Windows 95/98 or Windows NT. It can also happen when the user is working in a language not based on the Latin alphabet. For instance, we may give the statement:

```
System.out.println("Would you like some pâté?");
```

This printout looks fine if we are running a Unix system, for instance, which uses `LATIN_1` to code characters. But if we are running a PC (even if we are using Windows

95/98 or Windows NT), then LATIN_1 is not used in MS-DOS windows,[1] for historical reasons. Printout can then assume the sinister appearance

```
Would you like some pótú?
```

The coding used in MS-DOS works well with LATIN_1 when we only need the first 128 characters, but for the remaining 128 (amongst them, all the accented letters) another coding system is used. This is not a problem that only involves MS-DOS. In all the countries that do not use the Latin alphabet, text is coded in some way other than with LATIN_1.

Let us now look at how we can print out numerical data for the stream System.out. The easiest way is simply to call the method print or println directly, with a numerical variable as argument, or to use the operator + together with a text. The numeral will then be converted automatically to text. We can write, for example:

```
int n = 8150;
double d = 0.058;
System.out.println(d);
System.out.println("n = " + n);
```

The printout will then be:

```
0.058
n = 8150
```

We will always get a standard format, where the number of decimals is determined automatically. Note, too, that we will always get a decimal point in the printout, even if we have a non-English installation. The standard format generally works well with integers, but in the case of real numbers it can look awful. Let us insert the statement:

```
System.out.println("Result: " + (n*d));
```

We will then get the printout:

```
Result: 472.70000000000005
```

For technical reasons, the last decimal place of the result may not always be exact when using real numbers.

If we want to be able to format printout, or use local conventions, we have to use a NumberFormat object, as described in Section 3.1. For example, if we run a Spanish system and give the statements:

```
NumberFormat nf = NumberFormat.getInstance();
nf.setMaximumFractionDigits(1);
System.out.println("Result: " + nf.format(n*d));
```

---

[1] In Windows windows, on the other hand, LATIN_1 is used. This is why this problem does not arise in GUI programs.

the printout will be:

```
Result: 472,7
```

Note that we now get the decimal comma automatically, instead of a decimal point.

Input

Data written at the keyboard will land in the stream System.in, which is an object of the class java.io.InputStream. We cannot read directly from this stream, however. Instead, we have to connect another stream to it. We do this using the model in Figure 3.1. In the program it is convenient to use a stream of class BufferedReader. This

Figure 3.1

cannot be connected immediately to the stream System.in. We have to use an intermediary stream of class InputStreamReader, as shown in the figure. When we create a new stream in a program, we indicate, as parameter to the constructor, the other stream the new stream should read from. In order to create a new stream myIn, in accordance with the figure, we write the declaration:

```
BufferedReader myIn = new BufferedReader
                     (new InputStreamReader(System.in));
```

In class BufferedReader, there is a serviceable method called readLine, which reads in a whole line at a time. In order to use readLine, we must declare a variable of type String which will refer to the input line.

```
String s;
```

We then write out a question to the user:

```
System.out.print("What is your name? "); System.out.flush();
```

Note that we have to call flush, since we are using print and not println. The input itself is now done with the method readLine. It returns a reference to a String object containing the input line.

```
s = myIn.readLine();
```

We finish by writing out the greeting:

```
System.out.println("Hello " + s + "!");
```

Note that the method `readLine` waits until the user has entered a whole line and finished it by pressing the Enter key. The end-of-line character (or end-of-line characters, if the Enter key produces more than one) is read by `readLine` but will *not* be included in the text that is returned.

Input errors may sometimes arise when entering data. The input methods, for example `readLine`, will then generate a kind of error signal of class `IOException`. We call such error signals *exceptions*. The method in which such an exception arises must either itself deal with it, or send it on. How we deal with exceptions is described later in the book. We choose the simpler alternative here, sending the exception further on. This will happen automatically but at the beginning of the method, where the reading is done, we must indicate that an exception might arise. We do this by writing **throws** *event name* after the parameter list at the beginning of the method. If, for example, the call of `readLine` lies in the method `main`, the introduction to `main` must have the following appearance:

```
public static void main (String arg[]) throws IOException {
```

When entering data, the user often has to indicate that he or she does not intend to write any more. A technique using *end of file* is used where, at the keyboard, the user writes a special combination of characters indicating an end to the input. In MS-DOS this combination of characters is usually Ctrl-Z and in Unix Ctrl-D. If *end of file* is indicated when the program has called the method `readLine`, `readLine` will return the value **null**, that is, an empty reference. Note that this is not the same thing as a blank line. If we simply press Enter when the program has called `readLine`, it will return not **null** but a reference to a `String` object containing a text of length 0.

There is also a method in class `BufferedReader` called `read`, which reads a single character at a time. For example, we can give the following statements:

```
System.out.print("Type a character "); System.out.flush();
char c = (char) myIn.read();  // type conversion needed
System.out.println("You typed " + c);
```

The method `read` will give, not as we might think, a **char** as result but a value of type **int**. This is why an explicit type conversion to type **char** must be made before the result can be assigned to the variable `c`. The method `read` does not return a **char** because `read` gives the value −1 when the user has indicated *end of file*. A value of type **char** cannot be negative, so type **int** is used instead.

The method `read` waits, just like method `readLine`, until the user has pressed the Enter key. The difference is that `read` only reads *a single character*. Suppose, for example, that the execution of the program lines given above produce the following output:

3. Reading and writing

```
Type a character Z  (the user presses the Enter key having typed Z)
You typed Z
```

When the user presses the Enter key, one or two characters are put in the input stream. If we are running a Unix system, the character '\n' will be produced, and in MS-DOS the two characters '\r' and '\n' are produced. (These characters are described in Section 6.1.) This, or these, character(s) remain in the input buffer after the character 'Z' has been read into the program and will be the first character, or characters, to be read the *next* time read or readLine is called. The method readLine is recommended rather than read, since readLine functions in the same way in both Unix and MS-DOS.

Unfortunately, the standard class BufferedReader contains no methods for the input of numerical data. Therefore, if we want to read an integer or a real number, we first have to read the input line in the form of text and then make a type conversion to the numerical type we want. The following lines demonstrate how we can read an integer for the variable i and a real number for the variable x:

```
System.out.print("Enter an integer number: ");
System.out.flush();
String s = myIn.readLine();
int i = Integer.parseInt(s);
System.out.print("Enter a real number: "); System.out.flush();
s = myIn.readLine();
double x = Double.parseDouble();
```

To make the type conversion from text to the numerical types, we use the methods parseInt and parseDouble included in the wrapper classes Integer and Double. Errors might arise in a type conversion of this kind if the user entered incorrect input data. In this case, the type conversion methods will generate an error signal of class NumberFormatException.

The type conversion method parseDouble, above, assumes that the program's user has entered the numerical values in "English" format, with a decimal point. If we want to use a format following local conventions, for example use of the decimal comma instead of the decimal point, the method parseDouble should not be used. Instead, we would use the method parse in class java.text.NumberFormat; see Section 3.1. This method functions like the method format in the same class but "the other way around". A NumberFormat object has to be declared first. For example, we can say:

```
NumberFormat nf = NumberFormat.getInstance();
```

The same NumberFormat object can be used for both the method format and the method parse. To read an integer to the variable i and a real number to x, we can then write the statements:

```
System.out.print("Enter an integer number: ");
System.out.flush();
String s = myIn.readLine();
int i = nf.parse(s).intValue();
System.out.print("Enter a real number: "); System.out.flush();
s = myIn.readLine();
double x = nf.parse(s).doubleValue();
```

Input data can now be entered, in accordance with the conventions determined by the NumberFormat object nf. The method parse will also generate an error signal if the user has entered incorrect input data. This signal is of the kind ParseException. The same rules apply to this kind of error as for IOException; either we have to deal with the error, or we can send it on. It is easiest to send it on, in which case we write ParseException after the word **throws** at the beginning of the method. If all the statements lie in the method main, in the introduction we will have to write:

```
public static void main (String arg[]) throws IOException,
                                          ParseException {
```

3.2.2   Reading and writing with the use of help classes

As we can see from the last section, it could be complicated to read and write using Java's standard classes. In this section we shall be describing the three classes ExtendedReader, ExtendedWriter and Std, which will make things much easier for the programmer. We will put these three classes into our own "standard package" extra. For this package, see page 32. These program texts are available from the book's website. In order to take advantage of help classes, users will have to take home the program texts and compile them. Users must then make sure that the compiled files are in the package extra. They must also set the environment variable CLASSPATH so that the Java interpreter can find the package extra. How this is done is dealt with on page 31.

The class ExtendedReader is a subclass of the standard class BufferedReader, and it contains several methods for various kinds of data input. We can input text, either in the form of entire lines, or in words and numerals.

The class ExtendedWriter is a subclass of the standard class PrintWriter. With the help of class ExtendedWriter we can print out and format various kinds of data. Real numbers can be written either in standard form or exponentially. If a real number is so small or so large that it cannot be written in the normal way, printout in the exponential form will take place automatically.

The class Std contains declarations of three ready-made streams, in, out and err. The stream in is an object of the class ExtendedReader, and the streams out and err are objects of class ExtendedWriter. These three streams correspond to *standard input,*

Methods in the class extra.ExtendedReader	
readLine()	reads a line, returns a String, always begins reading on a new line, gives null upon *end of file*
readWord()	reads a word (a sequence of non-blank characters), returns a String, gives null upon *end of file*
readInt()	reads and returns an int, makes error checks
readLong()	reads and returns a long, makes error checks
readDouble()	reads and returns a double, makes error checks
readChar()	reads a character, returns an int with the character code, gives –1 upon *end of file*
lookAhead()	looks ahead at the next character in the input stream without taking it up yet, gives the same return value as readChar
skip(n)	skips n characters, returns a number of skipped characters
skipLine()	skips the rest of the line read in
more()	gives true if there are more non-blank characters to be read
setFormat(r)	indicates that the NumberFormat object r will be used
getFormat()	returns the NumberFormat object that is used
getFileReader(*name*)	a class method that returns a new ExtendedReader object which reads from the file *name* (*name* is a String)
close()	closes the file connected to the stream

standard output and *standard error*, respectively. *Standard input* is normally related to the keyboard, and the two others to a text window on the screen. From now on, we shall be using the streams Std.in and Std.out to read and write.

To demonstrate how reading and writing proceeds using the new help classes, let us look at a program that calculates the cost of hiring a car. We will assume that we know the number of days for which we wish to hire the car, together with the hire charges per day. It would then be easy to calculate the total cost. However, we shall make the program a little more realistic by supposing that we are in Spain on holiday and that the hire cost is given in euro. Shunning mental arithmetic, we want the program to write out the total cost in both euro and US dollars. To this end, we will have to give the current exchange rate as input data. We also would like to be able to make several calculations, consecutively, to compare the costs for different numbers of days and different cars with varying daily hire charges. The exchange rate does not change between calculations, so we shall enter this only once at the beginning. We now show what such a program looks like. Whatever is written in italics has been written by the user. Everything else will have been written by the program.

Instance methods in the class extra.ExtendedWriter	
`println()`	begins a new line in the printout
`print(x)`	writes out x with exactly the number of positions needed. x can be a value of one of the simple built-in types, a `String`, a **char** array, or of a class having the method `toString`
`println(x)`	the same as `print(x)` followed by `println()`
`print(x,n)`	the same as `print(x)` but using *at least* n positions in the printout; filling-up takes place to the left of x for numerical types and for the types **bool** and **char**, filling-up takes place to the right of x for other types, and blank characters are used if `setFillChar` has not been called
`println(x,n)`	the same as `print(x,n)` followed by `println()`
`print(x,n,d)`	writes out a real number x, with a total of at least n positions, of which d are used for decimals
`println(x,n,d)`	the same as `print(x,n,d)` followed by `println()`
`printExp` and `printlnExp`	write out a real number exponentially; they exist in the same variants as `print` and `println`, respectively
`setFillChar(c)`	indicates that c will be a fill-in character
`setFormat(r)`	indicates that the `NumberFormat` object r will be used
`getFormat()`	returns the `NumberFormat` object used by the stream
`close()`	closes the stream
`flush()`	empties the stream's buffer

```
Exchange rate? 1.068
Type of car? Renault Twingo
Number of days? 3
Cost per day? 31
Total cost for Renault Twingo: 93.00 euro ($99.32)
Type of car? Volvo S70
Number of days? 3
Cost per day? 38.50
Total cost for Volvo S70: 115.50 euro ($123.35)
Type of car? (here the user indicates end of file)
```

The program is terminated when the user indicates that he or she does not intend to enter more input data, by writing a special combination of characters at the keyboard. In an MS-DOS window this is usually Ctrl-Z and in Unix Ctrl-D.

The program will look like this:

```
import extra.*;
class CarRent {
  public static void main (String[] arg) {
    String car;
    int dayNo;
    double dailyRate, totalCost;
    final double exchangeRate;
    Std.out.print("Exchange rate? ");
    exchangeRate = Std.in.readDouble();
    while (true) {
      Std.in.skipLine();
      Std.out.print("Type of car? ");
      car = Std.in.readLine();
      if (car == null)  // end of file ?
        break; // the while statement
      Std.out.print("Number of days? ");
      dayNo = Std.in.readInt();
      Std.out.print("Cost per day? ");
      dailyRate = Std.in.readDouble();
      totalCost = dayNo * dailyRate;
      Std.out.print("Total cost for " + car + ": ");
      Std.out.print(totalCost, 1, 2);
      Std.out.print(" euro ($");
      Std.out.print(totalCost*exchangeRate, 1, 2);
      Std.out.println(")");
    }
  }
}
```

First, we declare the variables that will be used. The variable exchangeRate has been declared as **final** because it will not be changed once it has got its value.

The class std is constructed so that printout will take place in accordance with local conventions. If we use println for some output, the output marker will automatically be moved forward to a new line *after* the data is printed out, while the output marker remains at the end of the same line if we use print. When real numbers are written out, for example in the statement Std.out.print(totalCost,1,2);, format arguments can be given. The second argument means that output should take place with *at least* 1 output position. The last argument means that we want 2 decimals in the output.

When we used the stream system.out, we had problems with output in windows not using LATIN_1 code. This applied, for example, to MS-DOS windows in Windows 95/98 or Windows NT. We do not have this problem with standard.out. If, for example, we give the statement:

```
Std.out.println("Would you like some pâté?");
```

the printout will be correct:

```
Would you like some pâté?
```

The class `Std` is constructed such that at the start of the program it checks to see whether Windows 95/98 or Windows NT is running. This done, it will check the language that is used in the installation, and the streams will be initialized so that translation takes place automatically to and from the MS-DOS coding used in the actual country. (If an English system is being run, MS-DOS code 437 will be used.)

When the stream `System.out` was used in interactive programs, the method `flush` had to be called following output to ensure that text would show up immediately. If instead we were to use `Std.out`, we would not have to worry about this, as the output buffer will be emptied automatically before the input operation. Interactive questions and answers will then always take place in the correct order.

Let us now read from the stream `Std.in`. We use either method `readInt` or method `readDouble` to read in numerals. These methods give as result an **int** and a **double**, respectively, and if we do not indicate anything else, they will assume that input data follows local convention. Both these methods will check to see that input data has been indicated correctly. Were we to make a mistake, for example by writing a letter instead of a digit, we would get an error message asking us to enter the number again.

```
Exchange rate? 1.0t8
Illegal number. Try again
1.068
Type of car? Renault Twingo
```

The car model is a text, and to read texts, we use the method `readLine`. This method reads in a whole line and gives as result a reference to a `String` object containing the text read in. If the user writes Ctrl-Z (or Ctrl-D) to indicate *end of file*, `readLine` will return an empty reference, that is, the value **null**.

When we want to write out numerical values together with texts, we can also use the operator + for texts. The printout of the result for our car hiring program could then take place with the statement:

```
Std.out.println("Total cost for " + car + ": " + totalCost +
                " euro ($" + totalCost*exchangeRate + ")");
```

But then the conversion from numerals to text will not be carried out by class `Std`, but in standard fashion. We will neither get local conventions in the printout nor be able to format the number of positions and the number of decimals in the printout. If we had used this statement in the car hire program, the final output in our example on page 85 would have had the appearance:

```
Total cost for Volvo S70: 115.5 euro ($123.34500000000001)
```

The stream `Std.out` uses a `NumberFormat` object internally to format output; in the same way, `Std.in` uses a `NumberFormat` object to interpret input numbers. If we do not want local conventions for reading and writing, we can tell these streams to use another `NumberFormat` object. We do this with the help of the method `setFormat`. If we want French conventions in our program, we can write, for instance:

```
NumberFormat r = NumberFormat.getInstance(Locale.FRENCH);
Std.in.setFormat(r);
Std.out.setFormat(r);
```

A decimal point is then used instead of the decimal comma for input and output. We can also change the characteristics of a `NumberFormat` object. For example, if we want the digits to be grouped in threes when numerals are printed out, we can enter:

```
Std.out.getFormat().setGroupingUsed(true);
```

There are also some serviceable class methods in class `extra.ExtendedWriter`, the method `formatNum`, for example, which formats a numeral in the same way as with output, but instead of writing out the number, the formatted number is returned as a `String`.

3.3 Text files

The variables used in a program exist in a computer's primary memory but only exist as long as the program is running. However, many programs need to store data permanently. To do this, we have to use a secondary memory (often a disk memory). Data in the secondary memory is stored in the form of *files*. A file is an arbitrarily long sequence of bytes (8 bits). These bytes most often contain characters coded in accordance with the LATIN_1 code (see Section 6.1) or some other code. A file containing such characters is called a *text file*. But there are many files which do not contain text. Such files are usually called *binary files*. In this section we shall only be discussing text files. To read or write a file in Java, we have to connect a stream to the file. The simplest way of doing this is to use our own help classes `ExtendedReader` and `ExtendedWriter`. After describing how this is done, we describe the procedure, in Section 3.3.2, should we only want to use Java's standard classes.

3.3.1 Using help classes

To connect a new stream to an existing text file, we can use the class method `getFileReader` in the class `ExtendedReader`. This method should have an argument of type `String` which contains the file's name (the name the file has in the file system). We can give either a simple name, or a search path. For example, we can write:

Class methods in the class extra.ExtendedWriter	
`formatNum(x)`	formats x with exactly as many positions as are required; x can be a value of a simple numerical type, gives as result a value of type `String`
`formatNum(x,n)`	the same as `formatNum(x)` but uses *at least* n positions, filling-up takes place with blank spaces to the left of x
`formatNum(x,n,t)`	the same as `formatNum(x,n)` but filling-up takes place with the character t to the left of x
`formatNum(x,n,d)`	the same as `formatNum(x,n)` but with d decimals
`formatNum(x,n,d,t)`	the same as `formatNum(x,n,d)` but filling-up takes place with the character t to the left of x
`formatExp`	formats a real number in exponential form; exists in the same variants as `formatNum`
`useExponent(x)`	gives **true** if the number x is so small or large that it must be written out or formatted in exponential form
`adjustLeft(s,n,t)`	returns a copy of the text s adjusted to the left in at least n positions; filling-up takes place with the character t
`adjustRight(s,n,t)`	returns a copy of the text s adjusted to the right in at least n positions; filling-up takes place with the character t
`toFixedLength(s,n)`	returns a copy of the text s adjusted to the left in precisely n positions; truncation or filling-up takes place with spaces
`setStaticFormat(r)`	sets the `NumberFormat` object r to be used by the class methods
`getStaticFormat()`	returns the `NumberFormat` object used by the class methods
`getFileWriter(`*name*`)`	gives a new `ExtendedWriter` object, which writes to a new file *name* (*name* is a `String`)
`getFileWriter(`*name*`, `**true**`)`	gives a new `ExtendedWriter` object, which adds text to the end of the file *name*

```
ExtendedReader f1=ExtendedReader.getFileReader("report.txt");
ExtendedReader f2=ExtendedReader.getFileReader(" c:\\x\\y.dat");
```

Note that we must write a double \\ character. This is because the character \ has special significance. Two streams are created here, f1 and f2. (If the file indicated as argument does not exist, the method getFileReader will return the value **null**.) We can then use the methods in class ExtendedReader and read from the files exactly as we do from std.in. For example, if we wish to read in the first line in file f1, we write:

```
String line = f1.readLine();
```

We shall now write a program that illustrates how input is read from text files. Suppose we have a situation involving an automatic pump at a self-service petrol station. Every time a customer buys petrol, the pump will register the number of litres bought, the date, the time of day and the number of the customer's account card, on magnetic tape. From time to time, the service staff come to retrieve the magnetic tape. Information on it is read into a computer and stored in the form of a text file, in which there is a line for every purchase. Each line has the form:

```
nnn.nn dd/mm/yy hh:mm:ss xxxxxxxxxxxx
```

As can be seen, the number of litres of petrol sold comes first in the line. Let us suppose that the file has the name log.txt. Our program will then read in all the data recorded and write out the total amount of petrol sold within a certain period. Output can look like this:

```
First time: 14/10/00 09:14:25
Last time:  17/10/00 11:02:37
Total number of litres: 5679.18
```

The program will have the following appearance:

```java
import extra.*;
class Petrol {
  public static void main (String[] arg) {
    ExtendedReader f = ExtendedReader.getFileReader("log.txt");
    // read the first line
    double litre  = f.readDouble();
    String date   = f.readWord();
    String time   = f.readWord();
    String cardNo = f.readWord()
    double tot    = litre;
    Std.out.println("First time: " + date + " " + time);
    // read other lines
    while (f.more()) {
      litre = f.readDouble();
      tot += litre;
      date = f.readWord();
      time = f.readWord();
      cardNo = f.readWord();
    }
    Std.out.println("Last time:  " + date + " " + time);
    Std.out.print  ("Total number of litres: ");
    Std.out.println(tot, 1, 2); // left-adjusted, 2 decimals
  }
}
```

Note that we have to use the method more to see when the file will end. This is because numerals come first in every line. If we try to call the method readDouble or readInt when the file has ended, we will get an error message.

It is just as easy to store output in a text file. We then use the method `getFileWriter` in class `ExtendedWriter` to connect a stream to a file. For example, we can write:

```
ExtendedWriter w = ExtendedWriter.getFileWriter("newfile.txt");
```

If the file `newfile.txt` does not already exist, it will be created. But if there is a file with this name already, it will be overwritten with new information. To avoid this, we can use an alternative form:

```
ExtendedWriter w = ExtendedWriter.getFileWriter
                   ("newfile.txt", true);
```

The existing file will not be overwritten. Instead, the new information will be added at the end of the file. If, for some reason, a new file cannot be created, the method `getFileWriter` will return the value **null**.

We can now use all of the methods in class `ExtendedWriter` to write to the file, in exactly the same way as we write to `Std.out`. For example, we can write:

```
w.print("Result: ");
w.println(x, 1, 3);
```

The next program we will look at copies one text file to another. When the program starts, it asks for the names of the two files. When copying is finished, the program tells us the number of lines copied. This could look like this:

```
Input file? myfile.txt
Output file? copy.txt
518 lines copied
```

If the input file does not exist, or if an output file cannot be created, the program produces an error message and will be interrupted. The program reads one line at a time from the input file. It is an easy matter to see when the file has ended, since the method `readLine` returns the value **null** when it can read no further.

```
import extra.*;

class FileCopy {
  public static void main (String[] arg) {
    // open the input file
    Std.out.print("Input file? ");
    String name = Std.in.readWord();
    ExtendedReader inFile = ExtendedReader.getFileReader(name);
    if (inFile == null) {
     Std.out.println("Cannot find " + name);
     System.exit(1);
    }
```

```
// open the output file
Std.out.print("Output file? ");
name = Std.in.readWord();
ExtendedWriter outFile =ExtendedWriter.getFileWriter(name);

if (outFile == null) {
 Std.out.println("Cannot create" + name);
 System.exit(2);
}

// copy
int n=0;
while (true) {
  String line = inFile.readLine();
  if (line == null)
    break;
  outFile.println(line);
  n = n + 1;
}
outFile.close();  // NB Important!
Std.out.println(n + " lines copied");
    }
}
```

Note that we should always close an output file when we have finished writing. If this is not done, characters remaining in the buffer will never be printed out.

3.3.2   Using standard classes

If we want to make use of standard classes only, it is simplest to use the classes `FileReader` and `FileWriter`. Using these classes, we can connect a stream to the file we want to read from or write to. When creating the stream, we simply give the file's name as parameter to the constructor. Let us begin by discussing how files are read. In a program, we should not read directly from a stream of class `FileReader`. Instead, we should use a stream of class `BufferedReader` and connect it to the `FileReader` stream. (Compare this with our procedure for reading from standard input, in Section 3.2.1.) For example, we can create a stream `inFile` and connect it to the file `indata.txt`.

```
BufferedReader inFile = new BufferedReader
                        (new FileReader("indata.txt "));
```

If there is no file with this name, the constructor would give an error signal of type `FileNotFoundException`; if we did not trap this error, we would have to write the words **throws** `FileNotFoundException` at the beginning of the actual method. The method `readLine` can now be used to read one line at a time from the file. If we want to read in numerical data, then we ourselves must make the conversion from text to the numerical type we want, exactly as we did when reading from the keyboard.

When writing output in a program, we may want to make use of a stream of class PrintWriter. The methods print and println are in this class, and they can be used in exactly the same way as when we write to the stream System.out. A PrintWriter stream should be connected to a file using a FileWriter stream but we do not do this directly. Instead, we make use of an intermediary stream of class BufferedWriter. For example, we can make the following declaration to create outFile, a PrintWriter stream which can be used for output to a file called outdata.txt.

```
PrintWriter outFile = new PrintWriter(new BufferedWriter(
                          new FileWriter("outdata.txt")));
```

There will be an error signal here too, of type FileNotFoundException if the file cannot be opened.

We conclude by giving an alternative version of the program FileCopy, on page 91.

```
import java.io.*;
class FileCopy2 {
  public static void main (String[] arg)
                      throws IOException, FileNotFoundException {
    // create a stream from standard input
    BufferedReader myIn = new BufferedReader
                            (new InputStreamReader(System.in));
    // open the input file
    System.out.print("Input file? "); System.out.flush();
    String name = myIn.readLine();
    BufferedReader inFile = new BufferedReader
                              (new FileReader(name));
    // open the output file
    System.out.print("Output file? ");
    name = myIn.readLine();
    PrintWriter outFile = new PrintWriter(new BufferedWriter
                                  (new FileWriter(name)));
    // copy
    int n=0;
    while (true) {
      String line = inFile.readLine();
      if (line == null)
        break;
      outFile.println(line);
      n++;
    }
    outFile.close();
    System.out.println(n + " lines copied");
  }
}
```

3.4 Exercises

1. Write a program that calculates and prints out the number of kilometres a car has travelled during the last year and, in addition, calculates the car's average petrol consumption per kilometre. Input data for your program should be the daily meter reading and the meter reading for a year, together with the number of litres of petrol consumed during the year (indicated as a real number). The output should look like this:

   ```
   Number of kilometres travelled:    1487
   Number of litres of petrol:        1235.4
   Consumption per kilometre:         0.83
   ```

2. When a car is to be insured, it is customary to choose a comprehensive insurance for the car if it is relatively new (for example, less than 5 years old). If the car is older, a third-party insurance might be sufficient.

   a) Write a program that indicates which type of insurance should be chosen. The program should get as input data the actual year (current year) and the year of manufacture of the car. One of the texts: *Choose a comprehensive insurance* or *Choose a third-party insurance* should be written out, depending on whether the age of the car is less or more than 5 years.

   b) A number of insurance companies arrange special insurance for antique cars which are at least 25 years old. Complement your program so that it gives the printout: *Choose an antique car insurance* if the car is at least 25 years old.

3. Write a program that calculates the amount of change you should receive when you have gone shopping, together with the type of bills. Input data for the program should be the price to be paid for goods and the amount actually tendered. For the sake of simplicity, let us suppose that all amounts are a whole number of US dollars. For example, if your shopping cost $51 and you paid with a $100 bill, your program should write out that you get change consisting of two $20 bills, one $5 bill, and four $1 bills (or coins).

4. Suppose that a bank gives $p\%$ interest on deposited capital. Suppose further that you can deposit d dollars. Write a program that shows how the capital accrues interest, calculated as compound interest, during the first 10 years. The output of your program should indicate the size of your capital, including interest, after each of the 10 years. The interest rate and the capital deposited should be the input data for your program.

5. A text file called `temp.txt` contains temperatures that are recorded at one o'clock in the afternoon at a certain place, for one month. Write a program that reads the file, and calculates and prints out the highest recorded temperature, together with the average of all temperatures.

6. A text file contains information about a number of persons, and there are two lines in the file for every person. The person's name and address are on the first line, while on the second line are the person's age, height and weight. The height is given in centimetres (cm). In order to carry out a medical enquiry on very tall persons, you want to try to find all persons at least 200 cm tall. Your task is to write a program that reads files containing personal data. Your program should create a new text file that only contains data on very tall persons. The name of this file should be read in by the program.

Object-oriented program development

When we develop big programs with object-oriented design we say that we carry out *object-oriented program development*. Object-oriented program development is normally divided into the different phases of object-oriented analysis, object-oriented design and object-oriented programming, and we will be discussing these phases.

A feature of object-oriented program development is the relationship between different objects. We will demonstrate how UML (Unified Modeling Language) can be used to give a visual presentation of such relationships, and we will also discuss how relations between objects are described in Java.

4.1 Object-oriented analysis

In Chapter 2, we stated that object-oriented program development was a kind of model building. The first question we might now ask ourselves is "What shall I build a model of?" To be able to answer this question, we have to try to understand and establish what the program is supposed to do. In object-oriented program development, this phase is termed *object-oriented analysis*. In this phase, we try to get the feel of the problem, to understand the conditions involved and make a first, fairly rough model of our program. To put this in more concrete terms, we must

- find the objects that will be part of the model
- describe the different attributes of objects
- establish the relations between the different objects
- put the objects into groups.

It may be necessary to go through these steps repeatedly, since we have to make sure that all the required operations are carried out by an object. The result of an object-oriented analysis is documented in various forms by diagrams that illustrate the model, while these diagrams can be complemented with tables and other written information. In the following discussion we talk about objects, but we must keep in mind that the discussion is also about classes, since we use classes to describe objects.

The first step, to find the objects, may seem complicated. How do we find the "right" objects? If the program is considered as a model of reality, there is a natural way to let every real "thing" in the environment be represented as an object. At this stage, we should also be doing our utmost to reuse previously constructed classes. Examples of these are different types of container classes, such as tables or queues, or classes which describe visuals on the screen.

Another strategy that has been suggested is to write down, in words, an informal description of what the system should do. In this description, we underline all the nouns and let them be candidates for an object. All the verbs would be candidates for the operations on the objects. This may seem straightforward but the problem with this strategy is that there probably will be too many objects. Nouns need not only designate prospective objects. A noun could also indicate a property, or a condition of an object.

We could also study how the system works as a whole and select a number of *use cases*, or scenarios. If we think of an object as something that provides services, we could check that all these services in our use cases are available. If, for example, a program is to be constructed to check a bank's cashpoint, we could look at the use case, "a customer wants to withdraw money", "a customer wants to check the balance of an account" and so on.

Of course, no one collection of objects will be the only right one. Different collections can produce results that are equally good. Clearly, the quality of a program will finally depend on the experience, knowledge and intuition of its creator.

In order to see more clearly when constructing big programs, we group objects, that is, we divide a program into its *subsystems* and select the objects to be included in the different subsystems. One way of doing this is to collect all the objects that work closely together and communicate often with one another, and establish a subsystem for them. We may allow objects that interface with their surroundings to form their own subsystems. For instance, there might be a subsystem that handles communication with a database. If we can isolate a group of objects with a small and well-defined interface in respect of the rest of the system and this group can offer well-defined services to the other subsystems, then we will have found a "client–server" model.

In Java, packages can be used to create subsystems. We have seen how it was possible, for every class that was a part of a package, to indicate whether the class should be local (only visible inside the package) or visible everywhere. When packages are used to form subsystems in an object-oriented program, classes used internally in the subsystem may be allowed to be local. Visible classes are used to give the subsystem a well-defined interface for other subsystems in a program. Then these other subsystems will only see the visible classes and need not "know" how the package is constructed internally.

To be able to carry out an object-oriented analysis in a big program development project, we must have the support of a *system development method*. This is a sort of work schedule which indicates how we will accomplish the process of constructing models, that is, of finding objects, attributes and relations. This method also stipulates the different forms of the diagrams to be produced, and it usually provides software support, that is, programs which help with the selection of diagrams and other information that might be required. Examples of some common object-oriented system development methods are OMT,[1] Objectory[2] and Coad/Yourdon's OOA-OOD.[3]

In this section we will use UML notation in our diagrams, just as we did in Chapter 2. UML is not a system development method, but different methods can prescribe that UML should be used.

An object-oriented analysis should establish the relations between the various objects. We will discuss three different kinds of relation:

- *knows*
- *has*
- *is*

In UML, a relationship between classes is called an *association*. An association exists between the classes c_1 and c_2 if, for instance, c_1 has attributes of type c_2, if c_1 calls methods in c_2 or if some of the methods in c_1 have parameters of type c_2. Figure 4.1

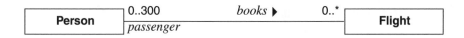

Figure 4.1 Association

shows an association between the classes Person and Flight. The relation is illustrated as a *path* (a line) between the class diagrams. An association can be given a *name*, which is written near the path. In Figure 4.1 the name is *books*. The name may have an optional small black triangle which indicates the direction in which the association name should be read. (It is not always necessary to read from left to right.) At the end of an association path it is possible to write a *rolename* which indicates the role played by the class in the association. In our example a person is a *passenger*. At

---

[1] Rumbaugh, J. et al. (1991) *Object-Oriented Modeling and Design*, Prentice Hall

[2] Jacobsson, I. et al. (1992) *Object-Oriented Software Engineering*, Addison-Wesley

[3] Coad, P. and Yourdon, E. (1991) *Object-Oriented Analysis*, 2nd Edition, Prentice Hall
   Coad, P. and Yourdon, E. (1991) *Object-Oriented Design*, Prentice Hall

the end of an association we may also attach a *multiplicity*. A multiplicity could be either a simple number or an interval. a..b means that the number of objects of the current class should be in the interval a to b. The character * means un limited number. (The interval 0..* may be written as a single star *.) In Figure 4.1 a person can book a seat on 0 or more flights and a flight can have at most 300 passengers.

Figure 4.1 describes a *knows* relation. A passenger must know which flights he or she has booked a seat on and a particular flight must have a passenger list, that is, know its passengers. In other words, Figure 4.1 describes a relation in both directions. But relations need not always be bi-directional. This is demonstrated in Figure 4.2.

Figure 4.2 One-way association

A customer list must contain information about all the customers, but it is not necessary for the customers to know that they are on a list. Arrows may be attached to the ends of an association path to indicate the direction of the association, its *navigability*. In Figure 4.2 the arrow at the class Person shows that the association is from right to left. UML does not state how an association without arrows should be interpreted. It could mean that the association is bi-directional, but it could also mean that no information about navigability is given.

The "diamond" on the path near the class CustomerList in Figure 4.2 indicates that the class CustomerList is an *aggregate*. This means that it is composed of a number of persons. When the diamond is hollow, as in Figure 4.2, it means that the aggregate "knows of" its parts.

Associations may also exist between objects of the same class. A person may be married, for example, and therefore have an association with his wife or her husband. This is demonstrated in Figure 4.3.

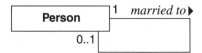

Figure 4.3 Association to the same class

Figures 4.1, 4.2 and 4.3 all describe the *knows* relation. The next relation we will describe is the *has* relation, which states that an object is constructed with the help of another object, that it has this object as one of its parts. This is also sometimes called *composition*. For example, a car has a motor, and a book has a number of different chapters. Figure 4.4 illustrates how we can graphically describe that a motor has a

Figure 4.4 Composition

number of cylinders. Note that the "diamond" should be filled. In UML composition is considered to be a stronger form of aggregation, a form where the parts are *encapsulated* in the aggregate. If, for instance, the aggregate is copied then all its parts would also be copied.

Of course, an object can consist of several different sub-objects. In Figure 4.5 we illustrate that a car is composed of a motor, wheels, body and interior.

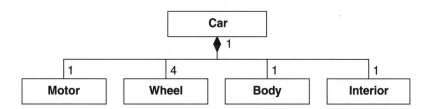

Figure 4.5 Composition with different classes

It is easy to confuse the *knows* relation with the *has* relation. We should not be fooled by the word "has". That a car has an owner does not mean that an owner is a component in the construction of the car. The *knows* relation is represented in programs with the help of references. To describe, for example, that a car has an owner, we let the class Car contain an instance variable which is a reference to an object belonging to the class Person.

The third important relation in object-oriented program development is the *is* relation. This is used to state that a class has certain general properties that can be common to other classes: "a squirrel is a mammal", "a dog is a mammal". The common properties are then described in a separate superclass (in our example, in the class Mammal). We can have *is* relations in several stages: "a mammal is an animal", "an animal is a living

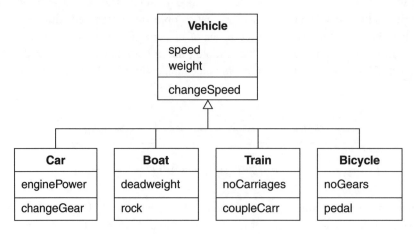

Figure 4.6 Generalization

thing". Figure 4.6 illustrates *is* relations for different kinds of vehicle. In UML the word *generalization* is used to denote this kind of relation. In Figure 4.6 the class Vehicle is a generalization of the more specific classes Car, Boat, Train, and Bicycle. In a UML diagram there should be a hollow arrow from the specific class to the general class.

In object-orientation, we make use of the concept of *inheritance* to describe *is* relations. When we have to describe a class, we can begin with a class that already exists and add or subtract attributes. The new class is said to *inherit* the properties of the old class, which is said to be a *superclass* of the new class. The new class is then a *subclass* of the old class. Suppose, for example, that we have a class Person. Some of the instance variables in this class will be name and address. Suppose further that we wish to describe students at a university. We can then create a new class Student, a subclass of the class Person. This means that the new class will automatically get all the attributes in the class Person. Therefore, we do not have to redefine the instance variables name and address. The only thing that we need to do is to declare the new attributes and relations we want to have in the subclass Student. We could conceive of relations that indicated the courses a student had taken, as well as an operation that could give a printout of the grades the student had achieved. Figure 4.7 uses both *inheritance* and *knows* relations to illustrate the classes Person, Student, Teacher and Course. Both students and teachers are persons. A student takes a number of courses. A teacher teaches a certain number of courses. A course has one teacher. A course has several students.

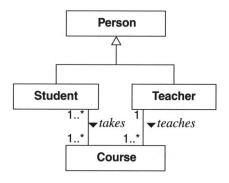

Figure 4.7

A class that is a subclass of another class can in turn be a superclass with its own subclasses. This means that a class hierarchy, with a tree-like structure, can be built. One of the ideas behind inheritance is that the programmer can make use of "ready-made" classes kept in a *class library*. In Java, there is, of course, the API. In this way, we will not have to keep writing new program code. Moreover, ready-made classes have been tested and are more likely to be free of errors than those we have constructed ourselves.

4.2 Object-oriented design

So far, we have mainly discussed object-oriented analysis – the first phase in object-oriented program development. After the analysis phase comes the design phase. *Object-oriented design* may be said to be the activity where plans are drawn up and "drawings" made for object-oriented programs.

The boundary between the analysis and design phases is rather vague. Generally, it can be said that in the analysis phase an idealized model is made, while in the design phase this model is given substance. Another way to express this is to say that during the analysis phase we think about *what* is to be done, while in the design phase we consider *how* it is to be done.

The design phase can be divided into two parts: *system design* and *object design*. System design has to do with making global decisions for the system. At this point we ask questions such as how the new system is to be split into subsystems and how it will communicate with its environment. The operating system to be used for the new system is also something that has to be decided. Part of the environment for the new system might well be a GUI (as Windows or X), database handlers and communication programs. This is easier when we program in Java, since most things are platform-independent.

During the object design phase, we start with the objects that have been selected in the analysis phase, then add all the details, object by object. For example, we determine how an object's various methods are to be performed through the application of appropriate algorithms (see Section 4.4) and describe the parameters the different methods will have. In the object design phase, we also determine how objects are to be constructed internally and whether previously constructed objects can be used again.

A decision as to which programming language will be used to write the program must be made before the design phase is over, since the program language will affect aspects of different objects as well as the system's method of communicating with its environment.

It should be pointed out again here that object-oriented analysis and design often merge, that it is not unusual for the analysis phase to encroach on the design phase. It is also an *iterative* process, where a return to the analysis phase is sometimes necessary if something in the design phase has to be changed or if new functionality is to be added. The programmer must be flexible in developing object-oriented programs.

4.3   Object-oriented programming

The object of the programming phase is to implement the system, that is, to realize it in the form of a computer program that can be run. Naturally, we try to write as "good" a program as possible. A program is "good" if it satisfies the following requirements:

- it is correct
- it is effective
- it is reusable
- it is adaptable

The first requirement is that the program should be *correct*. It should be able to perform the operations defined in earlier phases of the program development without error. Of course, this is a very important requirement. If a program is littered with errors, it will not matter that it has good properties.

The next requirement is that a program should be *effective*, that is, it should use the resources of the computer system well. Under certain conditions, for example, in connection with real-time systems, this may be a deciding factor in whether the program can be used but this requirement may not always be of great importance.

Is a correct and effective program always a good program? Naturally, it depends on what we mean by "good". To shed some light on this issue, we can look at the cost of producing software. This can be divided into two parts: development costs and maintenance costs. Program development would be simplified if we had greater freedom in using pre-existing program components in the same way as occurs with mechanical and electronic systems. In other words, we can require software to be reusable. It is advantageous if we can construct software with the help of ready-made, reusable and well-tested components, instead of writing everything ourselves. Then we can achieve

- lower program development costs
- faster program development
- improved software quality.

It is a known fact that many programmers spend much of their time programming variants of satisfactorily developed programs. Why must this be so? One of the reasons may be that programmers are not used to reusing programs. They may think that it must take at least as long to find a program component and find out how it works, as to write it themselves. Another reason may be that it is not as easy for a programmer to find a suitable program component as it is, say, for an electronics design engineer to find a VLSI circuit. If software components are to be reusable, they must conform to certain conditions, whether it is a question of the operating system or the ability to handle certain kinds of data. The number of variants can be endless. What is required of a reusable program component is that it should be applicable under different conditions. In other words, it should be "general". In this context, Java can provide the programmer with many advantages, since its various components are platform-independent.

Before proceeding further with our discussion on reusable programs, a few words should be mentioned concerning the other side of program development costs: *maintenance costs*. A program does not deteriorate, so software maintenance costs cannot be compared with, for example, the maintenance costs for a car. The two main aspects of maintenance costs are: correcting errors in the software that should already have been discovered during its construction, and adapting software to changed circumstances and requirements. That the latter should be necessary is probably because the program specifications were incorrect from the beginning, because there was a lack of foresight, or because it was simply not possible to forecast how certain conditions would develop with the passing of time.

Maintenance costs can be low, therefore, if it has been possible to keep a program free of errors from the beginning (by the use of well-tested components, for example), and if the program is intrinsically adaptable.

The program will tend to be more adaptable if it is constructed from several independent modules, each one being employed for a special, well-defined task. Then changes in the program will simply entail a procedure where a component is exchanged or removed as with the repair of a TV set. Therefore, we will want to avoid interfering with the structure of programs, as far as possible. If changes have to be made, they should be well thought out.

Our ability to take in a complex situation is limited. So it is extremely important that the number of contact paths between modules in a system, together with each module's interface with anything outside it, be kept to a minimum. All the information in a module that is local, that is only necessary to be known for the module itself, should be hidden. When the module is used, the user should not need to think about its internal construction. This is where the concept of *information hiding*, which was touched on earlier, comes in. Again, it is a question of packaging, and the packaging can have a favourable effect on both development and maintenance costs.

In object-oriented programming, we try to write programs that are correct, effective, reusable and adaptable, by allowing individual modules in a program to be constructed of objects – objects which facilitate information hiding. Objects are, of course, described with the help of classes, and to know which objects are required, we have to refer back to the design phase.

For the result to be satisfactory, an *object-oriented programming language*, a language with the relevant constructs, should be used. There are, above all, two constructs which are usually required of an object-oriented programming language:

- *Information hiding*. It should be possible to put everything that describes an object's properties into one place in a program. This includes both data and operations. The details belonging to a particular object should be capable of being hidden so that other objects do not need to see these details or have access to them. In Java we use classes to accomplish this.

- *Inheritance*. When describing a class, we should begin with the properties of other classes, adding the new properties as required. In other words, we should try to use previously constructed classes and, making use of the inheritance mechanism, modify and adapt them to our own actual requirements.

These constructs can be found in Java but also in other object-oriented languages such as C++ or Ada.

4.4 Algorithms

When constructing methods for various objects, we are confronted with the difficulty of finding appropriate ways of solving subproblems. A description of how certain (parts of) problems are solved, a calculation method, is called an *algorithm*. An algorithm consists of a number of elementary operations and directions concerning the order in which operations should be performed. We can make demands of an algorithm:

- It should solve the given problem.
- It should be unambiguous (not "fuzzy" in its formulation).
- If the problem has an ultimate objective (for example, that it should calculate a certain value), the algorithm should terminate after a finite number of steps.
- Note that not all algorithms should terminate. If you have, for example, an algorithm which describes how a control program in a nuclear power station should function, you will not want this algorithm to come to an end.

As a matter of fact, we come across different kinds of algorithms every day. One example is a cookery recipe. Here the problem is to prepare a certain dish, and the algorithm gives us the solution. Another example is provided by assembly instructions (who has not attempted to assemble a bookshelf from IKEA?) and other kinds of operational instructions. Anyone who knits will realize that a knitting instruction is an algorithm.

Algorithms can be expressed in many different ways. A common way is to indicate the algorithm in normal language. Pictures and symbols can also be used (IKEA again) or formalized language (e.g. mathematical notation). Flow charts are another well-known example. We will be dealing with programming here, so what is naturally most interesting for us is that algorithms can be expressed in a programming language.

Algorithm
Description of how a particular problem is to be solved (a calculation method).

Let us look at an example. We shall describe an algorithm that shows how the sum `1+2+3....+n` can be evaluated, where `n` is a given integer > 0. One way of describing the algorithm in natural language is:

1. Set 'sum' to 0 and the counter `k` equal to 1.
2. Repeat the following steps until `k` is greater than `n`:
   2.1 Add 'sum' and `k` and save the result in 'sum'.
   2.2 Increase the value of `k` by one
3. The result required is now the number in 'sum'.

Expressed as part of a Java program, the algorithm looks like this:

```
int sum=0, k=1;
while (k<=n) {
   sum = sum + k;
   k = k + 1;
}
// the result is now in the variable sum
```

To enable it to construct general algorithms, the description method we use must be able to express the following three constructs:

- A *sequence* is a series of steps that are carried out sequentially in the order they have been written. Each step is performed exactly once.

  An example is the assembly instructions for bookshelves:
     1. Put the side pieces in position
     2. Screw the back piece on to the sides
     3. Put the shelves into the frame

- *Selection*. Selection means that one of two or more alternatives should be chosen.

  Example. Calculate the absolute value of a number t.
     If t > 0, the result is the same as t
     otherwise the result is –t.

- *Iteration*. Part of the algorithm should be capable of repetition either a defined number of times, or until a certain condition has been met.

  We saw an example of repetition a defined number of times in the algorithm above, when the sum 1+2+3+....+n was calculated.

  An example of the other type of repetition could be:
     Whisk the eggs vigorously
     until they become fluffy

The most important algorithmic constructs
Sequence — series of steps Selection — choice between alternative paths Iteration — repetition

Another kind of construct that is commonly used in algorithms and which can sometimes replace iteration, is *recursion*. This construct seldom appears in "everyday" algorithms and may, therefore, seem a little strange. The principle is to break down the original problem into smaller but structurally similar problems. The smaller problems can then be solved by reapplying the same algorithm. The previous example, calculating `1+2+3+...+n`, can be solved using recursion in the following way:

1. If `n`= 0, set the result to 0,
2. otherwise do this:
   2.1 Compute the sum 1+2+3+...(`n`-1) using the algorithm.
   2.2 The required result is obtained by adding `n` to the result from step 2.1

When a complicated problem has to be solved, it is helpful to split it into smaller subproblems and solve them separately. These subproblems can then be split into further subproblems and so on. This is a very important technique in algorithm and program design and is known as *top-down design*. Let us look at a real-world algorithm that describes how to wash a car. A first, rough algorithm may be simply:

1. Wash car

This can quickly be expanded to:

1.1 If you are feeling lazy:
   1.1.1 Wash it at a car wash
1.2 otherwise
   1.2.1 Wash it by hand

Step 1.1.1 can be refined to:

1.1.1.1 Drive to the nearest car wash
1.1.1.2 Buy a token
1.1.1.3 Wait in line
1.1.1.4 Have the car washed

Step 1.1.1.4 can be refined further:

1.1.1.4.1 Drive into the car wash
1.1.1.4.2 Check that all the doors and windows are closed
1.1.1.4.3 Get out of the car
1.1.1.4.4 Put the token into the machine
1.1.1.4.5 Wait until the car wash is finished
1.1.1.4.6 Get into the car
1.1.1.4.7 Drive away

In this way, different parts of an algorithm can be refined until a level is reached where the solution becomes trivially simple.

There are usually several alternative algorithms for solving a particular problem. In general, it is sensible to design an algorithm that is as simple and easily understood as possible, because there is a better chance that it will work as it was intended.

Top-down design
Divide a problem into subproblems. Solve the subproblems individually. Divide the subproblems into further subproblems. Continue in this way until all the subproblems are easily solvable.

4.5 Relations in Java

In this section we shall illustrate the various kinds of relation, discussed in Section 4.1, in greater detail.

4.5.1 The *knows* relation

Because we always make use of references in Java, it will be a simple matter to describe the *knows* relations. We will use class `Person` as an example. A person has a name and address and, in addition, we have added another relation that says that a person can be married. Compare with Figure 4.3 on page 100. We let class `Person` have an instance variable `husbOrWife` that is a reference variable.

```java
class Person {
  private String name, address;
  private Person husbOrWife;  // reference to another Person

  // constructor
  public Person(String n) {
    name = n;
  }

  public String getName() {
    return name;
  }

  public void setAddress(String adr) {
    address = adr;
  }

  public String getAddress() {
    return address;
  }

  public void marry(Person p) {
    husbOrWife = p;      //provide a reference to husband or wife
    p.husbOrWife = this; //let husb. or wife refer to this person
  }
```

```
  public void divorce() {
    husbOrWife.husbOrWife = null;
    husbOrWife = null;
  }
  public Person marriedTo() {
    return husbOrWife;
  }
}
```

Because the instance variable husbOrWife is not initialized in the constructor, husbOrWife will from the beginning contain the value null for every new person. To establish a relation between two persons, the method marry is called. We can write:

```
Person p1 = new Person("Robert");
Person p2 = new Person("Carol");
p1.marry(p2);
```

In the call of the method marry, we allow the object p1 refers to, that is, the object Robert, to be the actual object. As argument, we give a copy of p2, in other words, a reference to the object Carol. The method marry does two things: on the one hand, it permits the instance variable husbOrWife in the actual object to refer to the same object as the parameter p, and on the other, it changes the instance variable husbOrWife in the object p refers to, so that it refers to the actual object. As a result, a bi-directional relation arises. (We do not always need bi-directional *knows* relations but in this example, it is necessary.) After the call of the method marry, the two reference variables p1 and p2.husbOrWife will refer to the same object (to Robert). Similarly, p2 and p1.husbOrWife will refer to the same object (to Carol).

Each Person object has its own name and its own address. For example, we can make the call:

```
p1.setAddress("2 Old Mill Road");
p2.setAddress("36 Prince Street");
Std.out.println(p1.getAddress());
```

The output will be:

```
2 Old Mill Road
```

which shows that Robert's address remains unaffected by the second call. As a result of the *knows* relation, any changes that might be made in one of the two objects will indirectly affect the other. For example, we can reach Carol's new address via Robert:

```
Std.out.println(p1.marriedTo().getAddress());
```

The method marriedTo returns a copy of the instance variable husbOrWife, in this example a reference to Carol. The output will be:

```
36 Prince Street
```

If we are dealing with a *knows* relation but, for the time being, an object does not know some other object, we indicate this by giving the reference variable the value `null`. If we call the method `divorce`:

```
p1.divorce();
```

the reference variable `husbOrWife` in the method `divorce` is set to `null` for both objects involved. Note that the two statements:

```
husbOrWife.husbOrWife = null;
husbOrWife = null;
```

inside the method `divorce` must be performed in the right order. Once the reference variable `husbOrWife` in the actual object has been set to `null`, the connection will be broken and we will not be able to reach the other object to alter it.

4.5.2   The *has* relation

When we use classes to construct models of reality, we often find that certain objects are constructed with the help of others, which are encapsulated in the bigger object. In other words, there is a *has* relation. As an example of how we describe this in Java, let us look at the class `Flight`, which describes regular flights. Every flight is described by five instance variables: the flight number, destination, commentary, departure time and time of arrival. The first three are text strings but it is the departure and arrival times that are the interesting things here, and there is a *has* relation involved. A flight *has* a departure time and arrival time. These times are described with the help of two objects of class `Time` from Chapter 2. However, since we cannot declare objects directly in Java, we will have to use two reference variables. The class `Flight` then has this appearance:

```
class Flight {
  private String no, destination, comment = "";
  private Time dep, arr;  // departure and arrival times
  // constructor
  public Flight (String flightNo, String dest,
                 int depHour, int depMin,
                 int arrHour, int arrMin) {
    no  = flightNo;
    destination = dest;
    dep = new Time(depHour, depMin);
    arr = new Time(arrHour, arrMin);
  }
  // methods
  public void setComment(String com) {
    comment = com;
  }
```

```
public void delay (int min) {
  dep.tick(min*60);
  arr.tick(min*60);
  setComment("Delayed");
}

public Time getDep() {
  return new Time(dep.getHour(), dep.getMin());
}

public Time getArr() {
  return new Time(arr.getHour(), arr.getMin());
}

public String getDestination() {
  return destination;
}

public String toString() {
  return no + " " + destination + " " + dep + " " + comment;
}
}
```

The constructor has six parameters. When we create a flight, we indicate the flight number, destination and departure and arrival times, expressed in hours and minutes. For example, we can write:

```
Flight f = new Flight("BA1853", "London", 8, 10, 10, 55);
```

The constructor creates two new objects of class `Time` and allows the instance variables `arr` and `dep` to refer to these. We can set the instance variable `comment` separately by calling the method `setComment`.

We use the class `Time` in class `Flight` in the normal way. The method `delay`, which we call to indicate that a flight has been delayed, will in turn call the method `tick` for class `Time` (the second version, the one with a parameter) both for the time of departure and the arrival time. Note that class `Flight` has no more knowledge of class `Time` than any other outsider. It cannot reach the enclosed instance variables in any of the time objects directly but instead must use the methods defined for this purpose.

We find in the method `toString` the expression

```
no + " " + destination + " " + dep + " " + comment
```

Since `dep` is an object of class `Time`, the method `dep.toString` for class `Time` will be automatically called to make the conversion to type `String`.

The method `toString` for class `Flight` will be called automatically if we try to write out a flight object with the help of the method `println`. The three statements:

```
Std.out.println(f);   // f.toString is called automatically
f.delay(15);
Std.out.println(f);   // f.toString is called automatically
```

for example, give the output:

```
BA1853 London 08:10
BA1853 London 08:25 Delayed
```

In order to read from outside the departure and arrival times and the destination of a flight, we call the methods getDep, getArr and getDestination, respectively. These are very interesting. Note that in getDep and getArr we do not directly return the instance variables dep and arr. Instead, we create *copies* of the objects that dep and arr point to and return references to these copies. We do this so that an outsider will not have direct access to the private instance variables. For example, we may make these statements from outside:

```
Time t = f.getDep();
t.tick(60);
```

If t had been a reference to the same time object as the one f.dep refers to, we would naturally have changed the departure time "behind the back" of the flight object, which would not have been a good thing, but because this change is made in a copy, it is quite safe to do so.

Because we also have to use reference variables for *has* relations in Java, we must be careful to hand back references. If we allow an outsider class to have access to a reference to an enclosed object, one that we "have", then it will no longer be a question of a *has* relation but a *knows* relation, in which case, various objects will be able to know an enclosed object and affect it. The difference between *has* relations and *knows* relations is sometimes very subtle, indeed.

Let us look at the method getDestination. We do not make a copy in this. It merely says **return** destination. What happens then if we make the following statements?

```
String s = f.getDestination();
s = "Paris";
Std.out.println(f);
```

Won't the destination for flight f be changed? When the first line is executed, s of course refers to the same text as f.destination. Then should not the text also be changed for f? No, because there is never any danger where references to objects of the standard class string are concerned. As we saw in Section 2.3.5, we can never *change* anything in an object of this kind. The second line, above, therefore means that a *new* string object is created containing the text Paris and that s is set to refer to the new object. The instance variable f.destination will not be affected. It will still refer to the old string object, the one with the text London.

4.5.3   The *is* relation

The third relation we now look at is that of inheritance, or the *is* relation. Inheritance is dealt with thoroughly in Chapter 7, which is devoted entirely to this concept. We merely give a brief introduction here. When we define a new class, we can start with an already existing class and add or change characteristics. We then say that the new class is a *subclass* of the old one and that the old class is a *superclass* of the new one. We have already seen examples of this. The class ExtendedFrame was a subclass of the standard class Frame. As a demonstration of this relationship, we will define a new class TimeWithAlarm.

```java
import java.awt.*;
import extra.*;

class TimeWithAlarm extends Time {
  private int ah, am, as = -1;

  public void setAlarm (int hour, int min, int sec) {
    if ( hour>=0 && hour<24 &&
         min>=0 && min<60 && sec>=0 && sec<60) {
      ah=hour; am=min; as=sec;
    }
    else
      Std.out.println("Incorrect time");
  }

  public void stopAlarm() {
    as = -1; // the instance variable s can never get this value
  }

  public void tick() {
    super.tick();
    if (getHour()==ah && getMin()==am && getSec()==as) {
      Toolkit.getDefaultToolkit().beep();
    }
  }
}
```

This class is used to trigger the functioning of an alarm clock. The instance variables ah, am and as indicate when it is time for the alarm to ring. On the third line, we see that the reserved word **extends** has been used to indicate that a class will be a subclass of another class. The new class inherits both instance variables and methods from the superclass. This means, for example, that an object of class TimeWithAlarm, in addition to the instance variables ah, am and as, also has the instance variables h, m and s, inherited from class Time. An object of class TimeWithAlarm also has all the methods in class Time, for example set and getHour, in addition to the new methods setAlarm and stopAlarm. The method tick requires a comment. It exists in class Time but has been redefined in class TimeWithAlarm. If we call the method tick for an object of class TimeWithAlarm, the new version will then be called.

The new version of tick begins by calling the version of **tick** in the superclass. This is done by the statement **super**.tick(). A check is then made to see whether the time is equal to the alarm time. If so, the method beep (in the standard class Toolkit) is called to get the computer to emit a "beep". For example, we may have the following program lines:

```
TimeWithAlarm ta = new TimeWithAlarm();
ta.set(11, 59, 58);
ta.setAlarm(12,0,0);
ta.tick();
ta.tick();
```

The computer will then "beep" when the last statement has been executed. To shut off the alarm function, we use a little trick. We set as to –1. Since the instance variable s can never take on negative values, the condition in the **if** statement in tick can never be true, and the alarm clock will not ring.

Inheritance is a crucial, central mechanism in object-oriented programming. It is the best way of making use of such ready-made program parts as the standard GUI classes.

4.6 Exercises

1. Construct a class Car that describes a car. A car should have a registration number and a text containing the make and model of the car. A car should also know its owner, a member of the class CarOwner, which will be a subclass of the class Person (cf. ex. 2, page 72). In addition, define the class CarOwner. For simplicity's sake, you should specify that a car owner may only own one car. Write methods that can be called when a car is bought or sold.

2. Construct the classes Vehicle and Train in Figure 4.6.

3. Construct the classes Person and Teacher in Figure 4.7.

4. A table contains n different numbers. Describe, in natural language, an algorithm which searches a table and finds the least number. The algorithm should give as result the position number in the table (an index between 1 and n) of this least number.

5. A table contains n different numbers. Describe an algorithm which changes the contents of the table so that the numbers appear in order of size (the smallest number first and the largest last). Use a method that first places the least number in the table's first position, then the next least number in the table's second position, and so on. (*Hint*: Make use of the algorithm in the previous exercise.)

GUI components

5

In Chapter 1, we saw that with the help of class `java.awt.Graphics`, we were able to draw figures and write texts in programs with graphical user interfaces (GUI). This can be rather complicated, as there are so many details that have to be specified. However, GUI programs have similar interfaces. They use buttons and menus, for instance. In order to make it easy to make up GUI programs, there are a number of standard classes in the package `java.awt`. These classes define GUI components which we can use in our programs. In this chapter, we will demonstrate how we construct an interface using standard GUI components. Those components that might constitute the parts of a window will be dealt with here, while dialogues and menus will be discussed in Chapter 11.

This chapter is also intended to demonstrate the power and usefulness of the concept of a class and how we can make use of ready-made classes to produce advanced programs with relative ease.

5.1 An overview

In Figure 5.1, we show the standard classes that describe GUI components. These different subclasses are:

- `Button` describes buttons which can contain text, for example `OK` and `Interrupt`, which the user can click on.

- `Checkbox` describes a box with an accompanying text which the user can indicate or not, depending on whether he wishes a particular option to apply. An example is a box with the accompanying text `Show visuals`. Several `Checkbox` components may be connected to give a group in which only one option can be chosen. These are called "radio buttons".

- `Choice` describes a pop-up menu with different options, where the programmer can choose one. When the user does not use the menu, a box is displayed with the chosen alternative.

117

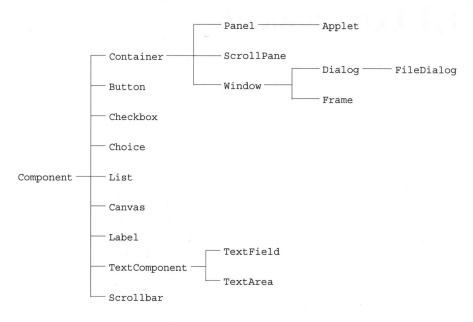

Figure 5.1 GUI components

- `List` describes a menu displayed in a box. If there are more options than can fit into the box, there is a scrollbar, enabling the user to scroll down the list of options and make a choice of one or more of these.

- `Canvas` describes a canvas on which arbitrary figures can be drawn. To do this, we use the class `Graphics`, in the same way as in Chapter 1.

- `Label` describes a simple text that can be displayed in a window. The text can be changed by the program but not by the user.

- `TextComponent` is a superclass of the two classes `TextField` and `TextArea`. We use class `TextField` when we want a single line in which the user can enter input data for the program. If more than one line must be displayed and edited by the user, the class `TextArea` is used.

- `Scrollbar` describes a scrollbar, where the user can manipulate a value lying between two given values. For instance, we could create a scrollbar which allows the user to choose values between 1 and 10.

- `Container` is a superclass of several other classes. GUI components cannot be displayed separately on the screen but instead must be placed in a container. Such containers are described in class `Container`. In class `Container`, a method `add` is defined which is used to put components in a window.

- `Window` describes a standalone window on the screen. A `Window` component does not have borders and a title bar.

- `Frame` describes a standalone window with borders and title line.

- `Dialog` describes a dialog window which can be displayed and removed during execution of the program. Messages are one of the things that can be displayed in the window.

- `FileDialog` describes a window in which the user can choose a file name.

- `Panel` describes a part of a window, a sub-window. A `Panel` cannot be displayed alone on the screen. It must be enclosed in a `Container`, for example in a `Frame`. We use the class `Panel` to design complicated GUIs hierarchically. We can let a window contain several panels. The various panels can be constructed independently of each other and they can in turn be divided into panels, and so on.

- `Applet` is a `Panel` and can therefore contain components. An `Applet` does not have a window of its own and cannot be displayed alone on the screen. An applet is normally called from a web browser, or from the program `appletViewer`, which creates a window for the applet.

- `ScrollPane` is a `Container` which can contain one component only. A `ScrollPane` can be smaller than the component it contains, in which case we can make use of scrollbars at the borders to see part of a component at a time.

As can be seen from Figure 5.1, all GUI components are subclasses of the standard class `Component`. All GUI components therefore inherit certain common, standard characteristics from this class (see Revision Table). For instance, we can indicate the component's background and foreground colours, together with the font to be used in texts. Suppose, for example, that `b` is a button, an object of class `Button`, and we want its foreground colour to be blue. We then write:

```
b.setForeground(Color.blue);
```

GUI components (excepting objects of class `Window`, or one of its superclasses) cannot be displayed separately on the screen. They must be put into a window, and this window must be an object of a subclass of the standard class `Container`. In Figure 5.1 we can see that the two standard classes `Applet` and `Frame`, which we have used up to now, are subclasses of class `Container`. Since our own class `ExtendedFrame` from Section 1.9 is a subclass of class `Frame`, it will also be a subclass of class `Container`. This means that we can set out GUI components in windows of classes `Applet`, `Frame`

GUI components	

Are subclasses of the standard class `java.awt.Component`.
Some common methods:

`setBackground(c)`	sets the background colour to `c` (of class `Color`)
`setForeground(c)`	sets the foreground colour to `c` (of class `Color`)
`setFont(f)`	indicates which font is to be used
`setVisible(b)`	displays/hides the component (b is a **boolean**)
`paint(g)`	is called automatically when the component must be redrawn (g is of class `Graphics`).
`repaint()`	draws the component again (calls `paint`)
`getParent()`	gives the `Container` the component is placed in
`setSize(x,y)`	sets the component's size
`getSize().width,` `getWidth()`	gives the component's width
`getSize().height,` `getHeight()`	gives the component's height

and `ExtendedFrame`. In this chapter, we shall also discuss the classes `Panel` and `ScrollPane`, which are also subclasses of `Container`.

There is a method `add`, for objects belonging to a subclass of `Container`, which we can use to place components in a window. If, for example, we have an object w of the class `Applet`, `Frame` or `ExtendedFrame` and an object b of class `Button`, we can put b in the window w:

```
w.add(b);
```

Note that this does not mean that the `Button` object b is directly displayed on the screen. Every `Container` has a list that contains references to the GUI components that are to be put into the window. The method `add` puts only the object b in this list. The actual drawing by the components in the window is carried out whenever the window w is drawn. This can be either the first time the window is drawn, or whenever it is redrawn because it has been partly or wholly hidden by other windows.

Java aims to make programs portable between different platforms. A programmer should no longer have to indicate details of size and position for the different GUI components in a window. Instead, he or she will indicate a *strategy* for how these things will be done. There are five different strategies that can be used and there is a standard class for each of these strategies in the package `java.awt`. The classes are `FlowLayout`, `BorderLayout`, `GridLayout`, `GridBagLayout` and `CardLayout`. These classes are all subclasses of class `LayoutManager`. Each time a window is redrawn, the window calls a `LayoutManager`, which handles the layout of components in the window. We let the window know which `LayoutManager` is to be used, by calling the method `setLayout`.

This has a `LayoutManager` as parameter. For instance, if we want the strategy `FlowLayout` to be used to place components in the window `w`, we write:

```
w.setLayout(new FlowLayout());
```

Briefly, this strategy means that the components are arranged neatly on a line from left to right. If there is no room for a component on the actual row, a new row is begun under the previous one.

In our first few examples, we shall use the strategy `GridLayout` to arrange components. With this strategy, the window is divided into a number of equally large boxes, and we indicate the number of rows and columns we want in the window. If we want `r` rows and `c` columns in a window `w`, we write:

```
w.setLayout(new GridLayout(r,c));
```

The components are then arranged in rows, from left to right. Each component will automatically be large enough to fill up its own box.

java.awt.Container

An object `w` that is a subclass of the class `Container` can contain GUI components. Some methods:

`w.add(x)`	places the GUI component `x` in `w`
`w.remove(x)`	removes the GUI component `x` from `w`
`w.removeAll()`	removes all the GUI components from `w`
`w.setLayout(l)`	indicates that `l` will be used as `LayoutManager`
`w.getLayout()`	gives the `LayoutManager` used by `w`
`w.pack()`	arranges `w`'s components and calculates `w`'s size (Note: Exists only for subclasses of `Window`.)
`w.paint(g)`	is automatically called when `w` must be reshaped (`g` is of class `Graphics`) Automatically redraws all components in `w`
`w.setVisible(true)`	displays `w` and its components
`w.getComponents()`	gives a list (an array) with the components in `w`

The size of a `Container` is determined by the kind of `Container` in question and the `LayoutManager` being used. It is true that the method `setSize` exists for all `Container` objects, but it cannot be guaranteed to be always effective. An applet's size is indicated in the HTML file from which the applet is started, and certain `LayoutManagers`, for example `GridLayout`, will themselves determine the size of the various components, also for `Container` objects arranged as components. For standalone windows, such as classes that are subclasses of `Window`, the method `pack` can be used to calculate the window's size automatically. The window will then be big enough for its components to fit.

Apart from the classes in Figure 5.1, there are some classes which we use to create menus. Menus differ from the classes in Figure 5.1 in that they cannot be put anywhere in a window. They must be put under the window border, or they must be pop-up menus. The menu classes are not, therefore, subclasses of class Component.

5.2 Label

We will begin by discussing the simplest of the GUI standard classes, the class Label. An object of class Label displays a simple row, with text in a window. When we create a new Label object, we can indicate the text we want to display:

```
Label l = new Label("Welcome to Java");
```

As an extra argument, we can add Label.LEFT, Label.CENTER or Label.RIGHT to indicate that the text should be left-justified, centred, or right-justified in the printout box. If nothing is indicated, the text will be placed to the left. If we want the text to be centred, we write:

```
Label l = new Label("Welcome to Java", Label.CENTER);
```

There is also a constructor without parameters, so we do not need to indicate a text when we create a Label object. The method setText can be used to change the text for an already existing object. For example, we can write:

```
l.setText("Good bye");
```

There is also a method setAlignment that makes it possible to change the text justification. For example, if we want the text to be aligned to the right, we write:

```
l.setAlignment(Label.RIGHT);
```

The two methods getText and getAlignment can be used to check the text and alignment that applies to a particular object. Note that only the program can change the text in a Label object. The text displayed on the screen cannot be changed by the person running the program. If we want this to be possible, we should use class TextField. This class will be discussed later.

In order to demonstrate all of this, we now give a new version of the program that displays the text Welcome to Java in a window on the screen. The window will look as in Figure 1.6 on page 14.

```
import java.awt.*;

class Message4 extends Frame {
  public static void main (String[] arg) {
```

```
    Message4 w = new Message4();
    Label l = new Label("Welcome to Java", Label.CENTER);
    l.setFont(new Font("SansSerif", Font.BOLD, 24));
    l.setBackground(Color.yellow);
    l.setForeground(Color.blue);
    w.setLayout(new GridLayout(1,1));
    w.add(l);
    w.setSize(400,150);
    w.setVisible(true);
  }
}
```

In this program, we have used the strategy `GridLayout` for arranging components in a window. In our program, there is only one component, so we have indicated that there should be 1 row and 1 column.

java.awt.Label	
Displays a text on the screen	
new `Label("text")`	creates a `Label` justified to the left, with the text `"text"`
new `Label("text",adj)`	creates a `Label` with the text `"text"`. *adj* can be `Label.LEFT`, `Label.CENTER` or `Label.RIGHT`
`l.setText("text")`	sets the text in `l` to `"text"`
`l.getText()`	returns the text in `l`
`l.setAlignment(adj)`	justifies the text in `l`. *adj* can be `Label.LEFT`, `Label.CENTER` or `Label.RIGHT`
`l.getAlignment()`	gives `Label.LEFT`, `Label.CENTER` or `Label.RIGHT`

Using standard GUI components and `LayoutManager` is not only simpler for programmers than shaping in detail all the components in a window, but it also gives them more flexibility, since a `LayoutManager` will always automatically adapt the size of components to the window size. If readers test-run both the program `Message2`, on page 14, and `Message4`, constructed here, they will find that if they drag on the windows to change their sizes, the text in the window produced by `Message4` will always be centred, while the text from the `Message2` program will always have a fixed placement.

We have allowed class `Message4` to be a subclass of the standard class `Frame` but, as we mentioned in Section 1.6, this will mean that it could be difficult to close the window. We would have to press Ctrl-C in the command window from which the program was started. In order to close the window in the normal way, we can instead allow class `Message4` to be a subclass of our own class `ExtendedFrame` (see Section 1.9). From now on, this will generally apply to all classes which are subclasses of class `Frame`.

5.3 Designing our own GUI components

We can make use of graphics standard components in other ways than simply by using them directly, as we did in the Message4 program. We can also use them to create our own GUI components by letting one of our own classes inherit properties from one of them. To demonstrate this, we will show how class Label can be used to allow our class Time, from Chapter 2, to be displayed on the screen. We shall let class Time be a subclass of the standard class Label. This then means that an object of class Time can be handled in the same way as a Label object. We will therefore give a new definition of class Time.

```java
import java.text.*;
import java.awt.*;

class Time extends Label {
  // instance variables
  private int h, m, s;
  private boolean showSec=true;

  private NumberFormat nf = NumberFormat.getInstance();

  // constructors
  public Time() {
    this(0,0,0);
  }

  public Time(int hour, int min, int sec) {
    set(hour, min, sec);
    nf.setMinimumIntegerDigits(2);
    setFont(new Font("Monospaced", Font.BOLD, 18));
    setBackground(Color.lightGray);
    setAlignment(CENTER);
  }

  public Time(int hour, int min) {
    this(hour, min, 0);
    showSec = false;
  }

  public Time(int hour) {
    this(hour, 0);
  }

  // methods
  public String toString () {
    String t = nf.format(h) + ":" + nf.format(m);
    if (showSec)
      t = t + ":" +  nf.format(s);
    return t;
  }
```

```
    public void paint(Graphics g) {
      setText(toString());
    }
```
    other methods are defined as previously
}

Comparing this with our earlier version, we can discern the following changes:

- Appearing on the third line is **extends** `Label`. This means that `Time` will be a subclass of class `Label` and inherit all its properties.

- In the other constructor (the one with three parameters), we have added statements indicating the font, background colour and placement of the text we want when an object of class `Time` is displayed on the screen. Because all of the other constructors call this one, these statements will be carried out for every new object of class `Time`.

- A new method `paint` has been added to indicate how an object of class `Time` is to be displayed on the screen. This is quite straightforward. Since a `Time` is a `Label`, the method `setText` simply has to be called to select the text to be displayed. The method `paint` will be called automatically every time the window, in which the time object is displayed, needs to be redrawn.

We can now write a demonstration program that displays two times. When the program is run, we will get a window looking like the one in Figure 5.2. This picture has been constructed by four GUI components, arranged in two rows and two columns. In the first row are placed two `Label` objects and in its second row, two `Time` objects.

```
import java.awt.*;
class TimeDemo2 extends Frame {
  Time t1;
  Time t2;

  TimeDemo2() {
    t1 = new Time();
    t2 = new Time(10,20,30);
    setSize(250,100);  // the window's size
    setLayout(new GridLayout(2,2,5,5)); // 2 rows, 2 columns
    add(new Label("Time 1", Label.CENTER));
    add(new Label("Time 2", Label.CENTER));
    add(t1);
    add(t2);
    setVisible(true);  // display the window
  }

  public static void main (String[] arg) {
    TimeDemo2 demo = new TimeDemo2();
  }
}
```

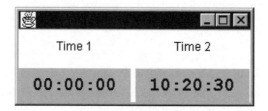

Figure 5.2 Label

In the statement

```
setLayout(new GridLayout(2,2,5,5));
```

the first two parameters indicate that there should be 2 columns and 2 rows. The last two parameters indicate the distance (given in pixels) between the different components. The last but one parameter gives the horizontal distance, while the last one gives the vertical distance.

When these components are arranged in the window using the method add, the order in which this is done will determine the way the components land in the window. When the window is visible, the components in it will automatically be drawn.

5.4 Panel

The next standard class we shall discuss is the class Panel. The class Panel, like class Label, is a subclass of class Component. An object of class Panel can, therefore, be a component in a window. The interesting thing about class Panel is that it is also a subclass of class Container. As a result, an object of class Panel has the property that GUI components can be arranged in it, with the help of method add. We use panels as aids when we have to construct GUIs on a more complicated level. The window can then be built hierarchically, since every panel has its own coordinate system and its own LayoutManager. Each panel can be described separately, then all the panels can be put together into a larger window.

To demonstrate how this is done, we shall write a program that displays flight information. Our aim then is to write a program that displays the picture in Figure 5.3.

As we can see, the picture is made up of four rows, with each row containing information about a flight. We could say that the picture is made up of four sub-windows, one placed under the other. Sub-windows can be described with the help of the standard class Panel. We shall let Flight be a Panel and redefine class Flight on page 112.

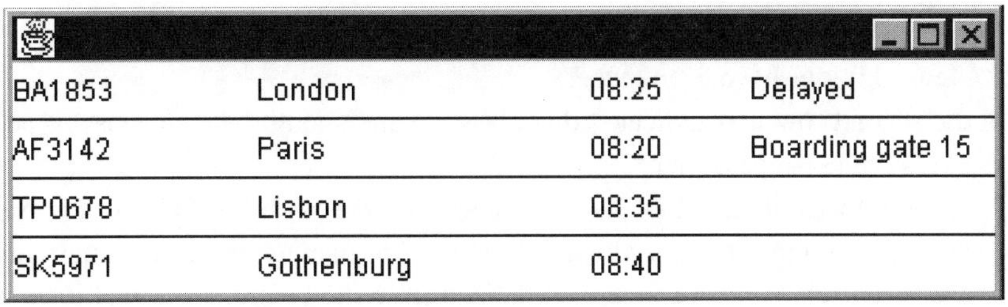

Figure 5.3 Panel

```java
import java.awt.*;
class Flight extends Panel {
  String no, destination,
         comment="                                 ";
  Time dep, arr;

  Label comLabel = new Label(comment);

  public Flight (String flightNo, String dest,
                 int depHour, int depMin,
                 int arrHour, int arrMin) {
    no  = flightNo;
    destination = dest;
    dep = new Time(depHour, depMin);
    arr = new Time(arrHour, arrMin);
    setLayout(new GridLayout(1,4));
    setBackground(Color.white);
    dep.setFont(getFont());
    dep.setBackground(getBackground());
    add(new Label(no));
    add(new Label(destination));
    add(dep);
    add(comLabel);
    setVisible(true);
  }

  public void delay (int min) {
    dep.tick(min*60);
    arr.tick(min*60);
    setComment("Delayed");
  }

  public void setComment(String com) {
    comment = com;
    comLabel.setText(comment);
    repaint();
  }
```

Only a few additions have been made:

- In the second row it is indicated that class `Flight` should be a subclass of `Panel`. **extends** `Panel` appears here.
- A new instance variable `comLabel` is declared on the sixth line. This is a reference to an object of class `Label`, which will be used to display any commentary on the actual flight. This object `Label` is initialized from the beginning so that it contains blank text. The text contains a lot of blank characters so that the system will have room in the window for a commentary.
- The constructor has been enlarged with statements indicating the GUI components to be included in the actual flight. Each flight will be displayed with the four components, namely flight number, destination, departure time and commentary, and these will be arranged in a row, one after the other. Therefore, `GridLayout` is used, with 1 row and 4 columns. The flight number and destination are components of class `Label`. We never have to change them, so no reference to them is required. On the other hand, the commentary might change. This is why we use the instance variable `comLabel`. The departure time is of class `Time` but since this is a subclass of the class `Label` (see page 122), the time can be put directly into the flight panel. The only thing we need to do, to make it look good, is to indicate that the departure time should be displayed in the same font and background colour as the other components. (The methods `getFont` and `getBackground` give as result the font and actual background colour for the actual component, that is, for the flight panel.)
- The text in `comLabel` is updated in the method `setComment`. We have also added a call of `repaint`, so that the actual flight will be updated on the screen.

Now we only need a class that creates the flights we want to have, arranging them one under the other in a window. We create a window with 4 components placed in 4 rows. Because flights are a subclass of `Panel`, they can be put directly into the window. We make the background colour black and leave 1 pixel between the components, arranged vertically. We will then get horizontal lines between the components.

---

java.awt.Panel

`Panel` is a subclass of class `Container`.
A `Panel` object can therefore contain GUI components.

`Panel` is also a subclass of `Component`.
A `Panel` object can therefore be a component in a `Container`.

Used to describe sub-windows.
Has its own `LayoutManager`.

```
import java.awt.*;

class FlightDemo2 extends Frame {
  Flight f1, f2, f3, f4;

  FlightDemo2() {
    f1 =  new Flight("BA1853", "London",      8, 10, 10, 55);
    f2 =  new Flight("AF3142", "Paris",       8, 20, 10, 50);
    f3 =  new Flight("TP0678", "Lisbon",      8, 35, 12, 40);
    f4 =  new Flight("SK5971", "Gothenburg", 8, 40,  9, 30);
    add(f1);
    add(f2);
    add(f3);
    add(f4);
    setLayout(new GridLayout(4, 1, 0, 1)); // 4 rows, 1 column
    setBackground(Color.black); // gives black lines

    pack();                     // calculates the window's size
    setVisible(true);
    f1.delay(15);
    f2.setComment("Boarding gate 15");
  }

  public static void main(String[] arg) {
    FlightDemo2 demo = new FlightDemo2();
  }
}
```

The call of method `pack` is important. This method sets the window's size so that its components will have exactly the space they require.

5.5 `TextField` – text input

Up to this point, we have only discussed how we could input data from a text window. We shall now see how data can be input in a GUI program. Inputting of text can be done with the help of the standard class `TextField`. The standard class `Label` was discussed in connection with this, in Section 5.2 on page 122. The class `TextField` is also used for texts but the main difference is that the user can *change* the text that is displayed. This cannot be done in the case of `Label` objects. We can create a new object of class `TextField` in one of the following four ways:

```
TextField t = new TextField();
TextField t = new TextField(n);
TextField t = new TextField("a text");
TextField t = new TextField("a text", n);
```

The first declaration gives an empty `TextField` object of indeterminate (short) length. The second declaration gives an empty `TextField` object with space for n characters.

The third declaration gives a `TextField` object, which from the beginning contains the text `"a text"`. The last declaration gives a `TextField` object that can hold n characters and from the beginning contains the text `"a text"`.

An object of class `TextField` can be put, exactly like other GUI components, into a window (a `Container`) with the help of the method `add`. If, for example, we have a window w, we can put the `TextField` object t into the window w with the statement:

```
w.add(t);   // put t into the window w
```

The exact placement of t in the window w is, as usual, determined by the `LayoutManager` used for the window w.

A `TextField` object is displayed as a box on the screen. The size of a `TextField` object can be changed at any time by calling the method `setColumns`.

```
t.setColumns(n);   // change the size to n characters
```

From the program we can indicate the text to be displayed in the box, using the method `setText`:

```
t.setText("a text");   // display the text "a text"
```

The interesting thing about a `TextField` object is that the user can enter text in its box. In the program, we can see what the user has written by calling the method `getText`, which gives as result the text in the box.

```
String txt = t.getText(); // read text written in
```

If we do not want whatever the user has written in the box to be visible – the user should perhaps write a secret password, we could indicate that the inserted characters should be replaced by a special character in the box. For example, if we wanted the inserted characters to be displayed by * in the box, we would give the statement:

```
t.setEchoChar('*');   // inserted characters displayed as *
```

If we want, we can select text in a window. Text is then displayed in an unusual way, for example in white on a blue base. This is done with the method `selectAll`.

```
t.selectAll();     // select the entire text
```

We can also select a part of the text

```
t.select(i, j); // select characters i to j
```

and the selected part of the text can be read with the method `getSelectedText`:

```
String txt = t.getSelectedText(); // read selected text
```

As can be seen, it is quite easy to enter text with the help of a `TextField` object but we are still faced with a problem that has to be solved: How does the program know when the user has changed text in a `TextField` object? To answer this question, we shall look at an example of a GUI program. When we run the program, a window is displayed on the screen containing a box in which the user can write his or her name. When this has been done, a greeting will be displayed in the window. Figure 5.4 illustrates this.

Figure 5.4 TextField

The program begins by drawing the window on the screen. After this, it cannot do anything until the user has written his or her name in the box, so it will wait until this is done. The user will write his or her name, then press the Enter key. An *event* is then generated which tells the program that something has happened. The program then reads the text in the box and writes out the greeting. Next, it will wait until someone writes another name in the box, and so on. The program is not terminated until the closure box in the window border is clicked.

This is an example of an *event-driven program*. In this type of program, the program waits for the different kinds of events that might occur – for example, that the user writes something, or clicks with a mouse button. The program will perform different things for the different events. In this example, the program cares only about one kind of event, namely that the user presses the Enter key.

In an event-driven program, we specify what is to take place when different events occur. In Java, this is done by defining special *event listeners*. There are a number of different event listeners for different types of event. When the Enter key is pressed in a TextField box, an event of the ActionEvent type is generated; this kind of event will then be trapped by an event listener of the ActionListener type. In general, a listener will be an object of a special listener class but we can often simplify things. We can indicate that the GUI component we construct should also function as a listener. We will make use of this technique in this chapter. A more general account of listeners and listener classes is given in Chapter 10. Let us see what the program looks like:

```
import java.awt.*;
import java.awt.event.*;
```

```
class Hello extends Frame implements ActionListener {
  TextField answer      = new TextField(25);
  Label     greeting = new Label();

  // Constructor
  Hello() {
    // define the appearance of the window
    setFont(new Font("Dialog", Font.PLAIN, 14));
    setLayout(new GridLayout(2,2)); // 2 rows, 2 columns
    add(new Label("What is your name? ", Label.RIGHT));
    add(answer);
    add(greeting);
    greeting.setAlignment(Label.RIGHT);
    pack();                // calculate the window's size
    answer.addActionListener(this); // connects a listener
    setVisible(true); // display the window
  }

  public static void main (String[] arg) {
    Hello h = new Hello();
  }

  // listeners
  public void actionPerformed(ActionEvent e) {
    // this method is called when an event occurs
    if (e.getSource()==answer) { // an event in the answer box?
      String name = answer.getText();
      greeting.setText("Welcome " + name + "!");
    }
  }
}
```

The classes dealing with event listeners are defined in the standard package `java.awt.event`. This package is therefore imported in the second line. Note that **implements** `ActionListener` appears at the beginning of the definition of class `Hello`. This says that objects of class `Hello` (among other things) are to be listeners for events of the kind `ActionEvent`. The word **implements** has to do with *interfaces*, and it signals a special kind of inheritance. A better account of this is given in Section 7.9.

An object of class `Hello` is created in the method `main`. A constructor is called automatically for this class. The constructor begins by defining the different GUI components which are to be found in the window. We will have two rows of components. There will be a `Label` object in the first row to the left, with the text `"What is your name? "` and to the right, an object of class `TextField`. We will call this object `answer`. There is only one GUI component in the second row, a `Label` object with the name `greeting`. There is no component in column 2, in row 2. The components `answer` and `greeting` have been declared as instance variables at the beginning of the program. They must be declared outside the constructor in order to be accessible in the listener later.

The last but one row in the constructor is important. It looks like this:

```
answer.addActionListener(this);
```

The method `addActionListener` is called here for the `TextField` object `answer`. Its argument is the object that is to be the listener for events occurring in this component. Here, it is a question of events of the `ActionEvent` kind, that is, events that occur when the user presses the Enter key. We have given the argument **this** here. This means that the actual object (the actual `Hello` object) will itself be a listener. A listener must always be registered in this way in order for it to know which component it is to be connected to and listen in.

A listener of type `ActionListener` must have a method called `actionPerformed`. This method will be called automatically when the actual event occurs. In our program, this method will be called whenever the user presses the Enter key in the answer box. We ourselves must define the method `actionPerformed` in the listener. This method has a parameter `e` which is of class `ActionEvent` (defined in the package `java.awt.event`). The parameter `e` contains diverse information on the kind of event that has occurred, and there is a method `getSource`, which gives a reference to the object in which the event has occurred. In the **if** statement:

```
if (e.getSource()==answer) { // an event in the answer box?
  String name = answer.getText();
  greeting.setText("Welcome " + name + "!");
}
```

only the two enclosed statements are performed if the event has occurred in the object `answer`. Then the text the user has written in the answer box will be read and the `Label` object `greeting` is changed so that the new name can be displayed.

5.6 `ExtendedTextField` – inputting numerical data

When we want to input numerical data into a GUI program, we can also make use of the standard class `TextField`. The text that the user has written, a `String` object, is input. The text is then analyzed and converted into a number. (Compare this with how we were obliged to proceed on page 82, when we could only read from the keyboard with the help of the standard classes.) This should be done in such a way as to enable us to deal with errors that arise due to incorrect writing by the user, for example where letters are written instead of digits. To simplify the input and conversion of data, we shall now use the class `ExtendedTextField`, a subclass of the class `TextField`. The class `ExtendedTextField` is a class that we ourselves have set up. It is therefore *not a standard class.* But we can easily make it accessible in all our programs by putting it into our "standard package" extra, together with the classes ExtendedFrame, Std, ExtendedReader and ExtendedWriter; see Section 1.9. The class ExtendedTextField is accessible on the book's website.

Two new methods have been added in class ExtendedTextField: getInt and getDouble. Exactly as with the method getText, these methods read the text the user has written in the box but they do not return a value of type String. They return an **int** and a **double**, respectively. Otherwise, class ExtendedTextField functions exactly like class TextField.

We shall demonstrate how class ExtendedTextField is used by writing a new version of the program that calculates the cost of hiring a car. The version of the program shown in Section 3.3.2 used a text window to communicate with the user. The new version will use a graphical user interface. The program can look like Figure 5.5 when

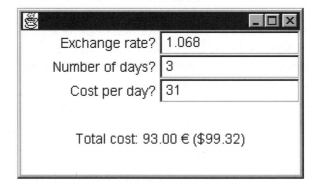

Figure 5.5 ExtendedTextField

we run it. The window is divided into an upper and a lower section; so the window has two rows and one column. In the lower section of the window a Label component is placed that displays the result of the calculation, and in the upper section a Panel component, which in turn contains three rows and two columns. Three Label components have been arranged in the left-hand column and three components of the new class ExtendedTextField in the right-hand column.

The program has the following appearance: an object of class CarRent2 is created in the method main. The constructor for the class is then called, and this draws the different components in the window. We let the actual object be listener to events in all three of the ExtendedTextField components, so we must call the method addActionListener for each one of these components. The program looks as follows:

```java
import java.awt.*;
import java.awt.event.*;
import java.text.*;
import extra.*;

class CarRent2 extends Frame implements ActionListener {
  ExtendedTextField exchAnswer = new ExtendedTextField(15);
  ExtendedTextField dayAnswer  = new ExtendedTextField(15);
  ExtendedTextField costAnswer = new ExtendedTextField(15);
  Panel p = new Panel();              // upper half
  Label result = new Label();  // lower half

  // Constructor
  CarRent2() {
    setFont(new Font("Dialog", Font.PLAIN, 14));

    // arranges the components in the window's upper half
    p.setLayout(new GridLayout(3,2));   // 3 rows 2 columns
    p.add(new Label("Exchange rate? ", Label.RIGHT));
    p.add(exchAnswer);
    p.add(new Label("Number of days? ", Label.RIGHT));
    p.add(dayAnswer);
    p.add(new Label("Cost per day? ", Label.RIGHT));
    p.add(costAnswer);

    // arranges the components of the entire window
    setLayout(new GridLayout(2,1)); // 2 rows 1 column
    add(p);            // the uppermost panel
    add(result);   // the result text at the bottom
    result.setAlignment(Label.CENTER);
    pack(); // calculates the window's size

    // indicates the listener to be used
    dayAnswer.addActionListener(this);
    costAnswer.addActionListener(this);
    exchAnswer.addActionListener(this);
    setVisible(true);   // displays the window
  }

  public static void main (String[] arg) {
    CarRent2 car = new CarRent2();
  }
```

```
// a listener
public void actionPerformed(ActionEvent e) {
  if (e.getSource()==exchAnswer|| e.getSource()==dayAnswer ||
     e.getSource()==costAnswer) {
  // read the three answer boxes
  int dayNo = dayAnswer.getInt();
  double dailyRate = costAnswer.getDouble();
  double exchangeRate = exchAnswer.getDouble();
  double totalCost = dayNo * dailyRate;
  // edit the result text
  NumberFormat r = NumberFormat.getInstance();
  r.setMinimumFractionDigits(2);  // 2 decimals
  r.setMaximumFractionDigits(2);
  String s = "Total cost: " + r.format(totalCost)+" \u20AC";
  s = s + " ($" + r.format(totalCost*exchangeRate) + ")";
  result.setText(s);  // display new result
  }
 }
}
```

The listener method `actionPerformed` is defined according to the same model as in the program `Hello`, on page 132. This method is called automatically when the user presses the Enter key. First we check whether the event applied to one of the three answer boxes, by calling the method `getSource` for the actual event. If it did, we try to read the values in the answer boxes in order to calculate and display the result.

The methods `getInt` and `getDouble` are called. These methods read the text in the answer box and attempt to interpret it as a number. If the user has written correct input data, the methods will return an `int` and a `double`, respectively. The program will continue normally, calculating and displaying the new result. In the listener a `NumberFormat` object named `r` is used to format the text to be displayed. The strange character sequence `\u20AC` is a Unicode sequence. Such sequences could be used to represent characters that cannot be typed on the keyboard. The sequence `\u20AC` denotes the euro symbol. (Characters and Unicode will be discussed in Section 6.1.)

If the user makes a mistake, so that the input text cannot be interpreted as a correct numerical number, the methods `getInt` and `getDouble` will emit a "beep", and the incorrect text will be selected in the answer box, enabling the user to see where the fault lies. If the user has written something incorrect, these two methods will not be able to return a value. Instead, they will give an error signal, an *exception* of type `NumberFormatException`. This signal is forwarded to a place in the program where the method was called and where, if we wish, it can be trapped. The procedure for this is described in Chapter 8. If we do not trap the error signal, we will get an error text in the text window where the program started. In this example the method `actionPerformed` will be terminated without the contents of the window being changed.

---

java.awt.TextField and extra.ExtendedTextField

Are used for inputting text and numerical numbers, respectively.

NB `ExtendedTextField` is *not* a standard class.

Create an object x in one of the following ways (the same for `ExtendedTextField`):

```
new TextField()
new TextField(n)                    space for n characters
new TextField("text")               contains the text text from the beginning
new TextField("text",n)
```

Connect a listener l of class `ActionListener` to x:

```
  x.addActionListener(l)
```

Define the method `actionPerformed` in the listener:
```
 public void actionPerformed(ActionEvent e) {
    // we get here when the user presses the Enter key
    ...
 }
```

The following methods can be called in the listener:

`e.getSource()`	returns the object where the event occurred
`x.getText()`	returns the text in the answer box

In class `ExtendedTextField` there are, in addition:

`x.getInt()` and	returns the integer and real number, respectively,
`x.getLong()` and	that is typed in the answer box, gives
`x.getDouble()`	`NumberFormatException` if illegal data is typed

Unless otherwise stated, class `ExtendedTextField` will assume that local conventions be used when numerical values are entered. Should we want another convention, we can call the class method `setFormat` for class `ExtendedTextField`. All the objects of this class will then in future use the other convention. For example, if we want to have Spanish conventions, we can write:

```
NumberFormat r = NumberFormat.getInstance
                             (new Locale("es","ES"));
ExtendedTextField.setFormat(r);
```

We can mention here that there are easier ways in this program of editing output in method `actionPerformed`. If we use the class method `formatNum` in the help class `ExtendedWriter` (see page 89), editing can be carried out with the following statement:

```
result.setText("Total cost: " +
   ExtendedWriter.formatNum(totalCost,1,2) + " \u20AC ($" +
   ExtendedWriter.formatNum(totalCost*exchangeRate,1,2) + ")");
```

The first argument of the method `formatNum` is the number to be edited, the second argument indicates the minimum number of positions that will be found in the result and the last argument indicates the number of decimals. Note that the class `ExtendedWriter`, like class `ExtendedTextField`, is not a standard class.

5.7 TextArea

We use the class `TextField` to make it possible for the user to give input data in one row. If we wish to display a longer text, or make it possible for the user to edit more than one row, we can use the class `TextArea`. This class shares many similarities with class `TextField` (both have a common superclass, `TextComponent`). In both classes from the program, for instance, we can read the text the user has written, or the part of the text the user has selected.

When we create an object of class `TextArea`, there are many possibilities open to us. If we wish to create a `TextArea` with r rows and c columns, we write:

```
TextArea a = new TextArea(r, c);
```

Then we will get a box with both a vertical and a horizontal scrollbar, so that the user can scroll the text. We also have the option of indicating that we do not want a scrollbar.

The user can write text in the area and cut and paste in the normal way. We can also insert and remove text from the program. In addition, we can indicate that only the program is allowed to change text inside the text area. This can be useful if we wish to display text, for example a help text, for the user. There is a synopsis of the most important methods in the Revision Table. Note that when the user changes the text in a `TextArea`, an event of class `TextEvent` is generated and not one of class `ActionEvent`. To trap an event of this class, we need a listener of class `TextListener`. We will be showing an example in which class `TextArea` is used in Section 5.15.

5.8 Canvas

In Chapter 1, we drew directly in a window. We created subclasses of classes `Applet` and `Frame`, and then we made our own version of the method `paint`. The method `paint` is defined in the standard class `Component`, which is superclass of all the other GUI standard classes. This means that we can draw in subclasses of all the GUI standard classes, for example in subclasses of `Applet` and `Frame`. But if we only want to draw, it is convenient to create our own subclass of the standard class `Canvas`. A `Canvas` is, as the name suggests, simply a blank surface on which we can draw. A `Canvas` is a `Component` and can therefore be arranged in a `Container`. In this way, a `Canvas` is like

---

java.awt.TextArea

new TextArea()	with scrollbar
new TextArea("*text*")	with the text *text* , with scrollbar
new TextArea(r,c)	r rows and c columns
new TextArea("*text*",r,c)	with the text *text* , with scrollbar
new TextArea("*text*",r,c,*sb*)	*sb* can be TextArea.SCROLLBARS_NONE,
	TextArea.SCROLLBARS_HORIZONTAL_ONLY or
	TextArea.SCROLLBARS_VERTICAL_ONLY
a.setEditable(*bool*)	indicates whether the user is allowed to edit in a
a.append("*text*")	appends the text "*text*" last in text area a
a.insert("*text*",i)	inserts the text "*text*" with the beginning in position i
a.replaceRange("*text*",i,j)	replaces the text between positions i and j with "*text*"
a.setText("*text*")	changes the text in a to "*text*"
a.getText()	returns the text in the area
a.getSelectedText()	returns the selected parts of the text
a.select(i,j)	selects the text between positions i and j
a.selectAll()	selects the entire text
a.getSelectionStart()	gives the position where selection has begun
a.getSelectionEnd()	gives the position where selection ends
a.setRows(r), a.setColumns(c)	sets the number of rows and columns
a.getRows(), a.getColumns()	returns the number of rows and columns

Connect a listener l of class TextListener to a:

```
a.addTextListener(l)
```

Define the method textValueChanged in the listener:

```
public void textValueChanged(TextEvent e) {
  // we get here when the user makes changes inside the text
}
```

e.getSource()   returns the object where the event occurred

---

a Panel but an important difference is that a Canvas is not a Container. We can only draw in a Canvas and not arrange any other components in it. As an example, we will write an applet that displays the window in Figure 5.6. There are two GUI components in the window, a Canvas uppermost and a Label object at the very bottom that contains the text "A circle". We begin by defining a subclass of the class Canvas.

Figure 5.6 Canvas

```
import java.awt.*;
public class CircleCanvas extends Canvas {
  public boolean filled = true;
  public boolean inTheCentre = true;
  public boolean blackBackground = false;

  public void paint(Graphics g) {
    int diam = Math.min(getSize().width, getSize().height);
    int x0 = 0;

    if (inTheCentre)
      x0 = (getSize().width-diam)/2;
    if (blackBackground)
      setBackground(Color.black);
    else
      setBackground(Color.white);
    if (filled)
      g.fillOval(x0, 0, diam, diam);
    else
      g.drawOval(x0, 0, diam, diam);
  }
}
```

The only method this class contains is our own version of paint. A circle is drawn in paint. The three instance variables filled, inTheCentre and blackBackground are declared as **public** so that they can be changed from without. If the instance variable filled is true, the circle will be drawn filled in. The instance variable inTheCentre decides whether the circle will be drawn centred, or furthest to the left. Note that a Canvas has its own coordinate system, with the point (0,0) furthest up towards the left

140

in the drawing area. The circle will be of a size to fit in the drawing area, and its diameter will therefore be equal to this area's length or width, whichever is the shortest. When we are going to draw a circle, we should indicate the coordinates of the rectangle containing the circle, in the upper left-hand corner. The circle will be placed at the top of the drawing area, so its y-coordinate will be equal to zero. If the circle is centred at the side, its x-coordinate will be calculated to allow equal space to the right and left of the circle. Otherwise, the x-coordinate will be equal to zero. We can now define the applet that generates the picture in Figure 5.6.

```java
import java.awt.*;
import java.applet.*;

public class CircleDemo extends Applet {
  CircleCanvas c = new CircleCanvas();
  Label  l = new Label("A circle", Label.CENTER);

  public void init() {
    c.setForeground(Color.blue);
    l.setFont(new Font("Serif", Font.BOLD, 18));
    setLayout(new GridLayout(2,1));  // 2 rows and 1 column
    add(c);
    add(l);
    setVisible(true);
  }
}
```

Two components are declared, a `CircleCanvas` c and a `Label` l. The window is divided into two rows and one column. The object c is placed at the top and l at the bottom. The size of the window will be determined by whatever is in the HTML file where the applet started. As we are using `GridLayout`, the size of the drawing area c will automatically be adapted to the size of the window. If we had used another `LayoutManager`, `FlowLayout`, for example, it might have been necessary to indicate the drawing area's size explicitly with the help of the method `setSize`.

5.9 Button

The next graphics standard class we now look at is the class `Button`. We use this class when we wish to arrange buttons in a window, buttons that the user can click on. Buttons can be created with and without a text:

```java
Button okButton = new Button("OK");
Button aButton = new Button();
```

In order to demonstrate how buttons can be used, we shall make a new version of the applet `CircleDemo` from the previous section. This time, we will generate a window that looks like the contents of Figure 5.7. The window is divided into two parts. In the

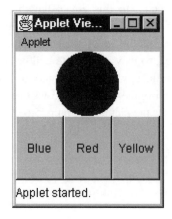

Figure 5.7 `Button`

top part, there is, as there was previously, a `Canvas`. The lower part consists of a `Panel` in which we have placed three buttons. When the user clicks on one of the buttons, the circle is changed so that it is drawn in the corresponding colour. The new version of the applet has the following appearance: the class `CircleCanvas` is unchanged and looks as it did in the previous section.

```
import java.awt.*;
import java.awt.event.*;
import java.applet.*;
public class CircleDemo2 extends Applet implements ActionListener
{
   CircleCanvas c  = new CircleCanvas();
   Panel   p  = new Panel();
   Button b1 = new Button("Blue");
   Button b2 = new Button("Red");
   Button b3 = new Button("Yellow");

   public void init() {
     c.setForeground(Color.blue);
     setLayout(new GridLayout(2,1)); // 2 rows, 1 column
     add(c);    // a Canvas at the top
     add(p);    // a Panel at the bottom
     p.setLayout(new GridLayout(1,3));   // 1 row, 3 columns
     p.add(b1); p.add(b2); p.add(b3);    // arrange the buttons
     // connect listeners
     b1.addActionListener(this);
     b2.addActionListener(this);
     b3.addActionListener(this);
```

```
    setVisible(true);
  }

  // define listeners
  public void actionPerformed(ActionEvent e) {
    // check which button the user has clicked on

    if (e.getSource()==b1)
      c.setForeground(Color.blue);
    else if (e.getSource()==b2)
      c.setForeground(Color.red);
    else if (e.getSource()==b3)
      c.setForeground(Color.yellow);
    c.repaint();
  }
}
```

Here we see a new example of an event-driven program. When the user clicks on a button, an event of type `ActionEvent` is generated. The method `actionPerformed` is then called automatically in the listener connected to the button. A listener must, therefore, be connected to a button. This is done for each button by calling the method `addActionListener`. In this example, we use the `Applet` object itself as listener for all three buttons. We therefore write **implements** `ActionListener` at the beginning of the class definition. In method `actionPerformed`, we have to check which of the buttons the user clicked on. As we saw earlier, the method `getSource` in class `ActionEvent` can be used to see in which component the event was generated.

java.awt.Button	
new `Button()`	creates a new button
new `Button("`*text*`")`	creates a new button containing the text *text*
`b.setLabel("`*text*`")`	puts the text *text* in button b
`b.getLabel()`	returns the text in button b
`b.setActionCommand("`*text*`")`	connects the text *text* to button b

Connect a listener 1 of class `ActionListener` to button b:

```
  b.addActionListener(1)
```

Define the method `actionPerformed` in the listener:

```
 public void actionPerformed(ActionEvent e) {
   // we get here when the user presses the button
 }
```

The following methods can be called in the listener

`e.getSource()`	returns the object where the event occurred
`b.getLabel()`	returns the text in the button

5.10 Checkbox

The next GUI component we demonstrate is Checkbox. We shall write yet another variant of the program that draws a circle. This time, the program will generate a window, as in Figure 5.8. At the top, there is, as there was previously, a Canvas with

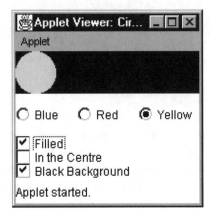

Figure 5.8 Check boxes and radio buttons

the circle. In the middle, there is a group consisting of three *radio buttons*. With these buttons, we can choose which colour the circle is to be drawn with. Radio buttons have the property that only one can be selected at a time. If the user selects a button, the button previously selected is de-selected automatically. There are three *check boxes* at the bottom. These are not connected to each other but several boxes can be selected at the same time here.

Both radio buttons and check boxes are set up with the help of the standard class Checkbox. We begin by describing how check boxes are constructed. To create a check box, we can enter one of the following:

```
Checkbox x1 = new Checkbox();        // not selected, without text
Checkbox x2 = new Checkbox("text"); // not selected, with text
Checkbox x3 = new Checkbox("text", false); // not selected,
Checkbox x4 = new Checkbox("text", true);   // selected
```

Check boxes are their own GUI components and are arranged individually. In Figure 5.8, we have chosen to put them one under the other but they could be put anywhere.

Radio buttons are created in almost the same way as check boxes. We begin by declaring a group, which will be of the standard class CheckboxGroup.

```
CheckboxGroup gr = new CheckboxGroup();
```

We then create the radio buttons that are to belong to the group.

```
Checkbox r1 = new Checkbox("text1", bool, gr);
Checkbox r2 = new Checkbox("text2", bool, gr);
Checkbox r3 = new Checkbox("text3", bool, gr);
```

The last parameter gives the group they belong to. The parameter *bool* can be `true` or `false`. Because only one radio button in a group can be selected, only one can have the value `true`. In spite of the fact that radio buttons belong to a group, they are, like check boxes, their own GUI components and are arranged individually.

---

java.awt.Checkbox

`new Checkbox()`	unselected without text
`new Checkbox("text")`	unselected with text
`new Checkbox("text", bool)`	with text (*bool* means `true` or `false`)
`new Checkbox("text", bool, g)`	radio button with text, belongs to group g
`new CheckboxGroup()`	creates radio button group
`x.setLabel("text")`	puts the text *text* into the `Checkbox` object x
`x.getLabel()`	gives the text for x
`x.setState(bool)`	selects or de-selects x
`x.getState()`	gives `true` if x is selected
`x.setCheckboxGroup(g)`	indicates that x will belong to group g
`x.getCheckboxGroup()`	gives the group x belongs to
`g.setSelectedCheckbox(x)`	indicates that x in the group g will be selected
`g.getSelectedCheckbox()`	gives the `Checkbox` in group g that is selected

Connect a listener l of class `ItemListener` to x:

```
x.addItemListener(l)
```

Define the method `itemStateChanged` in the listener:

```
public void itemStateChanged(ItemEvent e) {
   // we get here when the user clicks on a checkbox
   ...
}
```

The following method can be called in the listener:

    `e.getSource()`   returns the object where the event occurred.

There are methods in class `Checkbox` which are common to check boxes and radio buttons. The most important of these is the method `getState`, which can be called to check whether a particular check box or radio button has been selected or not. There are also a couple of methods for class `CheckboxGroup` that can be used to see which radio button in a particular group is selected, or to select from the program a particular button in a group; see the Revision Table.

The applet that generates the window in Figure 5.8 has the following appearance. The window is divided into three parts, one placed under another. At the top, there is an object of class CircleCanvas. This class is defined exactly as before, so we will not repeat it here. In the middle of the window, there is a Panel p1, which contains three radio buttons placed in a row. At the bottom, there is a Panel p2 which contains three check boxes, arranged one under the other.

```java
import java.awt.*;
import java.awt.event.*;
import java.applet.*;

public class CircleDemo3 extends Applet implements ItemListener {
  CircleCanvas c  = new CircleCanvas();
  Panel p1  = new Panel();

  CheckboxGroup group = new CheckboxGroup();
  Checkbox f1 = new Checkbox("Blue",    true,  group);
  Checkbox f2 = new Checkbox("Red",     false, group);
  Checkbox f3 = new Checkbox("Yellow", false, group);
  Panel p2 = new Panel();
  Checkbox x1 = new Checkbox("Filled", true);
  Checkbox x2 = new Checkbox("In the Centre", true);
  Checkbox x3 = new Checkbox("Black Background", false);

  public void init() {
    c.setForeground(Color.blue);
    setLayout(new GridLayout(3,1));   // 3 rows (c, p1 and p2)
    add(c);
    add(p1);
    // arrange the radio buttons
    p1.setLayout(new GridLayout(1,3));   // 3 columns
    p1.add(f1); p1.add(f2); p1.add(f3);
    f1.addItemListener(this);
    f2.addItemListener(this);
    f3.addItemListener(this);
    add(p2);
    // arrange the check boxes
    p2.setLayout(new GridLayout(3,1));   // 3 rows
    p2.add(x1); p2.add(x2); p2.add(x3);
    x1.addItemListener(this);
    x2.addItemListener(this);
    x3.addItemListener(this);
    setVisible(true);
  }
```

```
// Listeners
public void itemStateChanged(ItemEvent e) {
  // checks which Checkbox the user clicked on
  if (e.getSource()==f1)
    c.setForeground(Color.blue);
  else if (e.getSource()==f2)
    c.setForeground(Color.red);
  else if (e.getSource()==f3)
    c.setForeground(Color.yellow);
  else if (e.getSource() == x1 || e.getSource() == x2 ||
           e.getSource() == x3) {
    c.filled = x1.getState();
    c.inTheCentre = x2.getState();
    c.blackBackground = x3.getState();
  }
  c.repaint();
}
}
```

When the user clicks on a check box or a radio button, an event of class ItemEvent is generated (and not ActionEvent, as for class Button). In order to trap an event of this kind, we have to connect a listener of class ItemListener to the check box or the radio button. This is why **implements** ItemListener appears at the beginning of the definition of the applet. A method called itemStateChanged must be defined in the listener, and this method will be called automatically when the event occurs. The method itemStateChanged has a parameter of class ItemEvent that describes the actual event. We can call the method getSource for class ItemEvent to find out in which component the event arose.

5.11 Choice **and** List

In this section, we describe the two classes Choice and List. With the help of these two, we can produce such things as are shown in Figure 5.9. As before, there is a CircleCanvas at the top, and under this we have placed a Panel which in turn contains a Choice object and a List object next to each other. A Choice object is a menu in which we can choose an alternative. Normally only the chosen alternative is displayed (as on the left, in Figure 5.9). When we press on the arrow with the mouse button, the whole menu is displayed, and a choice can be selected; see the window on the right in Figure 5.9. We create a menu offering a choice by first creating a Choice object and then adding the various options.

```
Choice colours = new Choice();
colours.add("Blue"); colours.add("Red"); colours.add("Yellow");
```

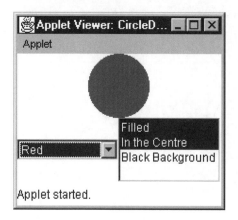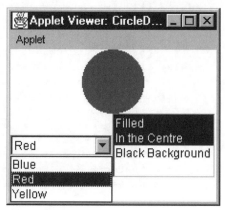

Figure 5.9 Choice *and* List

There is a List object on the right in the windows in Figure 5.9. This is a list from which an arbitrary number of choices can be made. If the list is not long and the window is sufficiently large, the whole list is displayed (as in Figure 5.9) but if the whole list does not have enough room, there is a scrollbar to the right of the list enabling it to be scrolled. List objects are created according to the same model as Choice objects. The list is first created, then alternatives are added.

```
List l = new List(3, true);
l.add("Filled"); l.add("In the Centre");
l.add("Black Background");
```

The parameter **true** indicates that more than one alternative can be chosen from the list. The first parameter indicates the number of alternatives that can be displayed at one time. However, it should be pointed out that if we have a LayoutManager that itself determines the size of the components, for example GridLayout, this parameter will have no effect. The number of alternatives displayed will depend on the size the List object will get.

The applet that generates the window in Figure 5.9 will have the following appearance. When the user selects an alternative in a Choice object, or a List object, then an event of class ItemEvent is generated. In this way, we will connect a listener of class ItemListener to the Choice object and the List object. We therefore write **implements** ItemListener at the beginning of the applet definition. For a Choice object, we can use the method getSelectedIndex to find out which alternative has been chosen, while for a List object, we can call the method isIndexSelected to check whether a particular alternative has been chosen. The alternative's number is then given as parameter. (Alternatives are numbered starting with 0.)

---

	java.awt.Choice and java.awt.List
new Choice()	creates a choice menu
new List(n, *bool*)	creates a list of alternatives, n visible alternatives
	if *bool* == **true**, several alternatives may be chosen
x.add("*text*")	adds the alternative *text* to x
x.select(n)	selects alternative no. n
x.getSelectedIndex()	gives the number of selected alternatives, or −1 if
	no alternative is selected, or several are selected.
x.isIndexSelected(n)	gives **true** if alternative no. n is selected
	(only for List objects)
x.getItemCount()	gives the number of alternatives

Connect a listener l of class ItemListener to x:

```
x.addItemListener(l)
```

Define the method itemStateChanged in the listener:

```
public void itemStateChanged(ItemEvent e) {
  // we get here when the user selects or
  // de-selects an alternative
}
```

The following method can be called in the listener:

   e.getSource()   returns the object where the event occurred

If the user *double*-clicks on an alternative in a List object,
an event of class ActionEvent is generated.

```
import java.awt.*;
import java.awt.event.*;
import java.applet.*;

public class CircleDemo4 extends Applet implements ItemListener {
  CircleCanvas c  = new CircleCanvas();
  Panel p = new Panel();
  Choice colours = new Choice();
  List l = new List(3, true);

  public void init() {
    c.setForeground(Color.blue);
    setLayout(new GridLayout(2,1));
    add(c); add(p);
    p.setLayout(new GridLayout(1,2));
    p.add(colours);
    colours.add("Blue"); colours.add("Red");
    colours.add("Yellow");
```

```
      colours.select(0);   // blue from the beginning
      colours.addItemListener(this);
      p.add(l);
      l.add("Filled"); l.add("In the Centre");
      l.add("Black Background");
      l.select(0); l.select(1); // filled and centred
      l.addItemListener(this);
      setVisible(true);
   }

   // Listeners
   public void itemStateChanged(ItemEvent e) {
      if (e.getSource()==colours) {
         if (colours.getSelectedIndex() == 0)
            c.setForeground(Color.blue);
         else if (colours.getSelectedIndex() == 1)
            c.setForeground(Color.red);
         else
            c.setForeground(Color.yellow);
      }

      else if (e.getSource()==l) {
         c.filled          = l.isIndexSelected(0);
         c.inTheCentre     = l.isIndexSelected(1);
         c.blackBackground = l.isIndexSelected(2);
      }
      c.repaint();
   }
}
```

We should mention that if the user double-clicks on an alternative in a List object, an ActionEvent will be generated and not an ItemEvent. If we wish to trap an event of this kind, we also have to connect an ActionListener to the List object.

5.12 Scrollbar

As we have seen, the inputting of numerical data into a GUI program may take place with the help of the class ExtendedtextField but in some cases, the class Scrollbar offers a more elegant alternative. A Scrollbar object is a scrollbar into which the user can insert values. To demonstrate how class Scrollbar functions, we will write another applet that draws a circle. This time, the user will be able to get any colour in the circle. There will be three scrollbars, one for each base colour. The user can insert an arbitrary value between 0 and 255 for each base colour, and the colour of the circle will be displayed with the adjusted colour combination. This is shown in Figure 5.10.

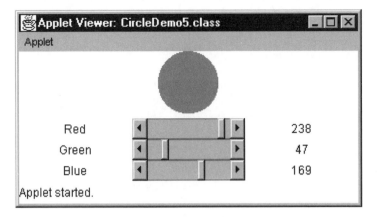

Figure 5.10 scrollbar

When we create a scrollbar object, we can indicate different properties for it. To create the scrollbar lying uppermost in Figure 5.10, for example, we write:

```
Scrollbar sR=new Scrollbar(Scrollbar.HORIZONTAL, 0, 1, 0, 256);
```

The first argument indicates orientation. We can choose Scrollbar.HORIZONTAL and Scrollbar.VERTICAL. The second argument indicates the initialization value for the scrollbar. The third argument indicates the width of the scroll box, the part of the scrollbar that can be moved back and forth (or up and down). The last two arguments indicate the minimum and maximum values of the scrollbar, respectively.

A scrollbar's value can be read from the program. We then use the method getValue. Note that when we read the scrollbar's value, we read the value of the scroll box's lower left edge. Since the scroll box in this example has a width of 1 and we wish the highest readable value to be 255, we must give the last argument in the constructor the value of 255+1, or 256.

Users can manipulate the scrollbar in three ways: they can drag on the scroll box, click on the scrollbar's arrows and click on the scrollbar between an arrow and the scroll box. We can indicate by how much the scrollbar increases, up or down, in the last two cases. (The default value is 1 if the arrows are clicked on, and 10 if we click between an arrow and a scroll box.) The methods setUnitIncrement and setBlockIncrement, respectively, are used for this.

The applet that generates the picture in Figure 5.10 will have the following appearance. The window is divided into two parts. At the top we have a CircleCanvas and at the bottom, a Panel p containing three rows. In each row, there is a Label object with the name of a colour, a `Scrollbar` object, and a `Label` object that displays the scrollbar's current value.

```java
import java.awt.*;
import java.awt.event.*;
import java.applet.*;
public class CircleDemo5 extends Applet
                         implements AdjustmentListener {
  CircleCanvas c  = new CircleCanvas();
  Panel  p = new Panel();
  Scrollbar sR=new Scrollbar(Scrollbar.HORIZONTAL,  0,1,0,256);
  Scrollbar sG=new Scrollbar(Scrollbar.HORIZONTAL,  0,1,0,256);
  Scrollbar sB=new Scrollbar(Scrollbar.HORIZONTAL,255,1,0,256);
  Label lR = new Label("0",   Label.CENTER);
  Label lG = new Label("0",   Label.CENTER);
  Label lB = new Label("255", Label.CENTER);

  public void init() {
    c.setForeground(Color.blue);
    setLayout(new GridLayout(2, 1, 0, 5)); // 2 rows, 1 column
    add(c);
    add(p);
    p.setLayout(new GridLayout(3,3));

    // arrange the texts and the scrollbars in panel p
    p.add(new Label("Red",  Label.CENTER)); p.add(sR);p.add(lR);
    p.add(new Label("Green",Label.CENTER)); p.add(sG);p.add(lG);
    p.add(new Label("Blue", Label.CENTER)); p.add(sB);p.add(lB);
    sR.addAdjustmentListener(this);
    sG.addAdjustmentListener(this);
    sB.addAdjustmentListener(this);
    setVisible(true);
  }

  // Listeners
  public void adjustmentValueChanged(AdjustmentEvent e) {
    if (e.getSource()==sR || e.getSource()==sG ||
        e.getSource()==sB) {
      int r=sR.getValue(), g=sG.getValue(), b=sB.getValue();
      // display the values read
      lR.setText(String.valueOf(r));
      lG.setText(String.valueOf(g));
      lB.setText(String.valueOf(b));
      c.setForeground(new Color(r, g, b));
      c.repaint();  // redraw the circle with the new colour
    }
  }
}
```

When the user adjusts a scrollbar, an event of type `AdjustmentEvent` is generated. In order to deal with such events, we have to connect a listener of class `AdjustmentListener` to the three scrollbars. Note that **implements** `AdjustmentListener` appears at the beginning of the applet's definition. The method called in the listener when an event occurs is called `AdjustmentValueChanged`, and we have to write our own version of this. We will read the three scrollbars there, display their value in the `Label` objects and redraw the circle with the new colour.

---

java.awt.Scrollbar

new `Scrollbar`(*position, init.value, scrollbox, min.value, max.value*)
      position is `Scrollbar.HORIZONTAL` or `Scrollbar.VERTICAL`,
      scrollbox=width of scroll box

`x.setUnitIncrement(n)`	changes the value by ±n when an arrow is clicked on
`x.setPageIncrement(n)`	changes the value by ±n when inside x is clicked
`x.setValue(n)`	sets the value at the scroll box's left/lower edge
`x.getValue()`	reads the value at the scroll box's left/lower edge

Connect a listener `l` of class `AdjustmentListener` to x:
  `x.AdjustmentListener(l)`

Define the method `adjustmentValueChanged` in the listener:
```
public void adjustmentValueChanged(AdjustmentEvent e) {
   // we get here when the user changes a scrollbar
   ...
}
```

The following method can be called in the listener:
    `e.getSource()`   returns the object where the event occurred

5.13 `ScrollPane`

Sometimes we may wish to study a picture that cannot be accommodated by the window on the screen. Then we can make use of the class `ScrollPane`. A `ScrollPane` object is a `Container` that can only contain a single component. This component may often be a `Canvas` but it could be any component at all, a `Panel`, for example. If the component the `ScrollPane` object contains is bigger than the `ScrollPane` object, the scrollbars can be produced at the sides, enabling the user to determine the part of the component he or she would like to see. As an example, let us look at a program that displays the window in Figure 5.11. The window contains two `ScrollPane` objects placed next to each other. The picture of the cat from Chapter 1 is displayed on the left and on the right, a

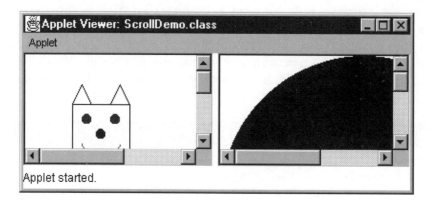

Figure 5.11 `ScrollPane`

`CircleCanvas` from this chapter. Both `ScrollPane` objects are smaller than the components they contain, so the scrollbars have been put in.

We begin by adjusting the class `Cat` from Chapter 1 (see page 22). Because we have decided that this class is not to be an applet but instead a component that can be arranged in a window, we remake class `Cat` to be a subclass of `Canvas`. The only difference is that the method `init` will be eliminated and replaced by a constructor. Note that we explicitly give the size of a `Cat` object in the constructor. This was not necessary when class `Cat` was an applet, because the size was given in the HTML file.

```
public class Cat extends Canvas {
  as previously

  public Cat() {  // replaces the method init
    setBackground(Color.white);
    setSize(300,260);
  }

  as previously
}
```

We now create a `ScrollPane` object and place a `Cat` in it with the statements

```
ScrollPane sp1 = new ScrollPane();
Cat miaow = new Cat();
sp1.add(miaow);
```

There can be an extra parameter in the constructor in class `ScrollPane`, `ScrollPane.SCROLLBARS_ALWAYS` or `ScrollPane.SCROLLBARS_NEVER`, which will indicate whether we always, or never, want to have scrollbars. If, as is the case here, nothing in particular is indicated, scrollbars will be automatically set there if the `ScrollPane` object is smaller than the component it contains. The entire applet generating the window in Figure 5.11 looks like this:

```java
import java.awt.*;
import java.applet.*;
public class ScrollDemo extends Applet {
  ScrollPane sp1 = new ScrollPane();
  ScrollPane sp2 = new ScrollPane();
  Cat miaow = new Cat();
  CircleCanvas cc = new CircleCanvas();

  public void init() {
    cc.setSize(300,300);
    sp1.add(miaow);
    sp2.add(cc);
    setLayout(new GridLayout(1, 2, 5, 0));
    add(sp1); add(sp2);
    setVisible(true);
  }
}
```

The sizes of the `Cat` object and the `CircleCanvas` object are both fixed but we have not indicated anywhere how large the two `ScrollPane` objects are to be. Since we are using `GridLayout`, their sizes as usual will be determined by the size of the surrounding window, and they will automatically be changed if we drag on the window to make it bigger or smaller. If we make the window so large that the whole of the `Cat` object and the `CircleCanvas` object can be seen, the scrollbars will automatically disappear.

java.awt.ScrollPane	
`new ScrollPane()`	automatically gives a scrollbar when needed
`new ScrollPane(s)`	s is `ScrollPane.SCROLLBARS_ALWAYS` or `ScrollPane.SCROLLBARS_NEVER`
`x.add(c)`	the component c will be displayed in x
`x.getHScrollbarHeight()`	gives the horizontal scrollbar's height
`x.getVScrollbarWidth()`	gives the vertical scrollbar's width
`x.setScrollPosition(x,y)`	changes the scrollbars so that the point (x,y) can be seen

If we use a `LayoutManager`, where the size of the components does not change automatically, we will have to indicate the size of the `ScrollPane` object explicitly with the help of the method `setSize`. In order to work out the total size, including the scrollbars, we can use the two methods `getHScrollbarHeight` and `getVScrollbarWidth`, which give the height of the vertical scrollbar and the width of the horizontal one, respectively.

5.14 Layout Managers

As we have seen, the arrangement of the components in a `Container` object is controlled by a `LayoutManager`. There are five subclasses of class `LayoutManager`: `FlowLayout`, `GridLayout`, `BorderLayout`, `CardLayout` and `GridBagLayout`. Up to now, we have only made use of class `GridLayout`. It is now time to introduce the others.

5.14.1 `FlowLayout`

Perhaps the simplest of the `LayoutManager` class is `FlowLayout`. When `FlowLayout` is used, the components are arranged in rows from left to right. If there is no room for a component in a row, a new row is automatically begun, and the component is put to the left extremity of this row. The size of the individual components is not changed by the `LayoutManager`. For example, a `Button` or a `Label` object will be just large enough for text to be given room. We now give an example. We arrange five components in a window in the following applet: two buttons, a `Label` object, a `TextField` object and a `Canvas`. The size of the first four components is determined by their texts but it is worth noting that we have to indicate the size for the `Canvas` object explicitly, or it will have a length and width of zero and will not be seen.

```
import java.awt.*;
import java.applet.*;

public class LayoutDemo extends Applet {
   Button b1 = new Button("1");
   Button b2 = new Button("Button 2");
   Label   l3 = new Label("Label 3");
   TextField t4 = new TextField("Text 4");
   Canvas c5 = new Canvas();

   public void init() {
      c5.setBackground(Color.lightGray);
      c5.setSize(75,75);
      setLayout(new FlowLayout());
      add(b1); add(b2); add(l3); add(t4); add(c5);
      setVisible(true);
   }
}
```

When this applet is run, it can look as in the window on the left in Figure 5.12. What is particular to `FlowLayout` is that the arrangement of components will automatically be changed if the height or width of the window is changed. In the part on the right in Figure 5.12, for instance, we have made the window narrower and longer. As a result, two new rows have been created automatically in the window.

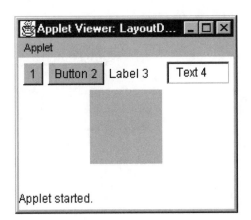 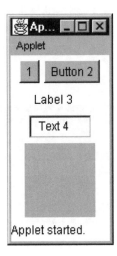

Figure 5.12 `FlowLayout`

When components are arranged in a row, they will normally be centred but when we create a new `FlowLayout` manager, we can indicate that the components should be arranged from the left or the right. We can also indicate that there should be a distance between components. Unless otherwise indicated, they will be put next to each other.

java.awt.FlowLayout
Is used as a default for the classes `Applet` and `Panel`

new `FlowLayout()`	the components are centred
new `FlowLayout(a)`	*a* is `FlowLayout.LEFT` or `FlowLayout.RIGHT`
new `FlowLayout(a, dx, dy)`	*dx* and *dy* indicate the distance between the components

5.14.2 `GridLayout`

We have seen many examples of the use of `GridLayout`. The window is divided into a number of rows and columns, and components are arranged in a row from left to right. All the components will be equally large, regardless of anything else having been indicated. If, for example, we make the following changes in the method `init` in class `LayoutDemo` from Section 5.14.1:

```
setLayout(new GridLayout(3,2));   // 3 rows, 2 columns
add(b1); add(b2); add(13); add(t4); add(c5);
```

the window will look as in Figure 5.13. We can see that the size of the components is

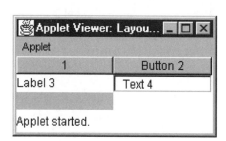
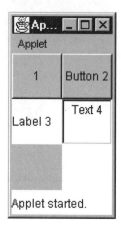

Figure 5.13 `GridLayout`

entirely determined by the window size and that it will be changed automatically when we drag on the window.

java.awt.GridLayout
new `GridLayout(r,c)`   puts the components into *r* rows and *c* columns 0 indicates an arbitrary number of rows and columns
new `GridLayout(r,c, dx, dy)` *dx* and *dy* indicate the distance between components

5.14.3 `BorderLayout`

When we use `BorderLayout`, the window is divided into five sections. The components are arranged along the window's four sides and in the middle of the window. When we add components to the window, we set an extra argument that will indicate which of the five sections the components are to be put into. A point of the compass is used to identify sections. In order to demonstrate this, we once more make changes inside method `init` in class `LayoutDemo`, on page 156.

158

```
setLayout(new BorderLayout());
add("West", b1); add("North", b2);
add("East", l3); add("South", t4);
add("Center",c5);
```

The window will look as in Figure 5.14. If a window's size is changed, for example by

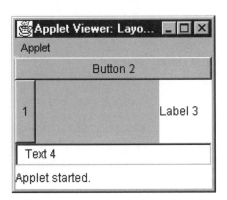
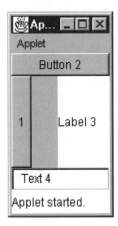

Figure 5.14 `BorderLayout`

dragging on it, the size of its components will automatically be changed, as demonstrated by the figure. However, the components' inner placement will remain unchanged. The size of the different components is determined automatically in the following way: the components `"North"` and `"South"` will have exactly the height they need but will be stretched out horizontally to fill out the whole window. The components `"East"` and `"West"` will have exactly the width they need. They will be stretched out vertically to fill out the space between the components `"North"` and `"South"`. Finally, the component `"Center"` will be large enough to fill out the space left over when the other components have been arranged in the window.

java.awt.BorderLayout

Is used as default by classes `Frame` and `Dialog`	
`new BorderLayout()`	
`new BorderLayout(`*dx,dy*`)`	*dx* and *dy* indicate the distance between components
`add("`*place*`", c)`	arranges the component c. *place* can be
	`North, South, East, West` or `Center`

5.14.4 `CardLayout`

`CardLayout` differs from other `LayoutManagers` in that its components are not all seen at the same time. Instead, we define a kind of card system that the user can scroll through, looking at one card at a time. (This is the same idea that has been used in many places in Windows 95. If, for instance, we select the icon, "My computer" and press the right-hand mouse button to choose the alternative, "Properties", a window will come up containing several cards and we can choose which of the cards we wish to see by clicking on one of the "tabs" at the top.)

We can declare a panel p, in which we wish to place three cards which are, in their turn, panels. We also declare a `LayoutManager` of class `CardLayout`:

```
Panel p = new Panel();
Panel one = new Panel();
Panel two = new Panel();
Panel three = new Panel();
CardLayout m = new CardLayout();
```

We can then indicate that m will be the `LayoutManager` for panel p and put the three panels one, two and three as cards in p:

```
p.setLayout(m);
p.add("no 1", one);
p.add("no 2", two);
p.add("no 3", three);
```

When we use `CardLayout`, we can assign a name to each card, as we have done here. A text is given as an extra parameter to the method `add`. We can then use this name when we want to indicate the card to be displayed. There is a method `show` in class `CardLayout`, which can be called in the following way:

```
m.show(p, "no 2");
```

There are also methods in class `CardLayout` to display the first or last card, or to scroll through the cards. For instance, we can write:

```
m.first(p);
```

To demonstrate all this, we will remake the applet `LayoutDemo` so that it produces windows as in Figure 5.15. We shall define three different cards. The first card contains two buttons, the second card a `Label` object and a `TextField` object, and the third card a `Canvas` object. The first and the third cards are shown in Figure 5.15. The components to be arranged in the three cards are declared as previously:

java.awt.CardLayout	
m = **new** CardLayout()	one component (a card) is displayed at a time
m = **new** CardLayout(*dx,dy*)	*dx* and *dy* indicate the distance around the card displayed
w.add(c)	w is a Container object
w.add("*name*", c)	adds to the component c the name *name*
m.show(w, "*name*")	displays the component (the card) *name*
m.first(w)	displays the first component (the first card)
m.last(w)	displays the last component (the last card)
m.next(w)	displays the next component (card)
m.previous(w)	displays the previous component (card)

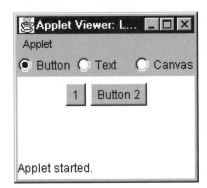 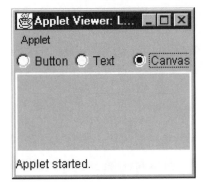

Figure 5.15 CardLayout

```
Button b1 = new Button("1");
Button b2 = new Button("Button 2");
Label  13 = new Label("Label 3");
TextField t4 = new TextField("Text 4");
Canvas c5 = new Canvas();
```

To enable the user to choose the card that will be visible, we have divided the window into two sections. We have put a row with radio buttons in the top part, and we display the different cards in the lower part. When the user clicks on a radio button, the corresponding card is shown in the lower section of the window. The three radio buttons are Checkbox objects, and we put them into a Panel with the name index. We arrange for the three Checkbox objects to be included in a group, so that only one button at a time can be chosen.

```
Panel index  = new Panel();
CheckboxGroup indexGroup = new CheckboxGroup();
Checkbox i1 = new Checkbox("Button", true, indexGroup);
Checkbox i2 = new Checkbox("Text",   false, indexGroup);
Checkbox i3 = new Checkbox("Canvas", false, indexGroup);
```

We put a `Panel` with the name `cards` in the lower part of the window. This `Panel` will contain the three cards. We provide for each card in turn to be a `Panel`. We can then arrange any components we want in the different cards.

```
Panel cards = new Panel();
Panel card1 = new Panel();
Panel card2 = new Panel();
Panel card3 = new Panel();
```

The method `init`, where all the arranging takes place, looks as follows. `BorderLayout` is used to arrange the two main components `index` and `cards`. The panel `index` is put into the `"North"` space. The panel cards is put into the `"Center"` space and so will fill out the remainder of the window.

```
public void init() {
    setLayout(new BorderLayout());

    // arrange index
    add("North", index);
    index.setBackground(Color.lightGray);
    index.setLayout(new GridLayout(1,3));
    index.add(i1); index.add(i2); index.add(i3);
    i1.addItemListener(this);
    i2.addItemListener(this);
    i3.addItemListener(this);

    // arrange the pile of cards
    add("Center", cards);
    cards.setBackground(Color.white);
    cards.setLayout(new CardLayout(2,2));
    cards.add(i1.getLabel(), card1);
    cards.add(i2.getLabel(), card2);
    cards.add(i3.getLabel(), card3);

    // arrange the components in the cards
    card1.add(b1); card1.add(b2);
    card2.add(l3); card2.add(t4);
    card3.setLayout(new BorderLayout());
    card3.add("Center", c5);
    c5.setBackground(Color.lightGray);
    setVisible(true);
}
```

The interesting component here is the panel `cards`. `CardLayout` is used for this to arrange the three components `card1`, `card2` and `card3`. We will use the texts of the corresponding radio buttons `i1`, `i2` and `i3` as names for the three cards.

We have connected the actual applet object as listener to the radio buttons, as we did before. Thus, **implements** `ItemListener` will be at the beginning of the applet's definition. When the user selects one of the radio buttons, we will get into the method `itemStateChanged`. We give the following definition:

```
public void itemStateChanged(ItemEvent e) {
  if (e.getSource()==i1 || e.getSource()==i2 ||
      e.getSource()==i3) {
    Checkbox c = (Checkbox) e.getSource();
    CardLayout manager = (CardLayout)cards.getLayout();
    manager.show(cards, c.getLabel());
  }
}
```

Here we have used the method `getSource` to get a reference to the radio button selected. Since this method gives a result of class `Component`, we must make an explicit type conversion to class `Checkbox`. To be able to call the method `show`, we have to have a reference to the `CardLayout` manager that deals with the panel `cards`. An explicit type conversion will be needed here, too. The method `getLayout` returns a reference to a `LayoutManager`, but we want a reference to the subclass `CardLayout`.

5.14.5 `GridBagLayout`

We have saved the most powerful, but also the most complicated `LayoutManager` until the end. When we use `GridBagLayout`, the window is separated into a number of boxes, exactly as with `GridLayout`, but all the windows are of unequal size. In addition, we can let certain components monopolize several boxes. To demonstrate how `GridBagLayout` works, we shall design the window in Figure 5.16. To the left in the figure is displayed the window when it is just big enough for all components to have the space they need, and to the right the window has been dragged out in respect of both its length and its width.

The window is divided into four rows and three columns. The rows are numbered from the top and the columns from the left. Note that we begin numbering with 0. The uppermost row is then row no. 0 and the column furthest to the left column no. 0. There are two `Checkbox` objects in the window; they are placed in boxes (0,0) and (1,0). The dark field is a `Canvas` object. It takes up four boxes, that is, the columns 1 and 2 and rows 0 and 1. In the third row (row no. 2), there is a `Label` object with the text `"File"` to the left (in column no. 0). In columns 1 and 2, there is a `TextField` object. The last row (no. 3) contains three buttons, each in its column.

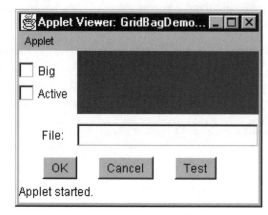

Figure 5.16 `GridBagLayout`

When we want to use `GridBagLayout`, we begin by declaring a `LayoutManager` of class `GridBagLayout`. This is easy, since there is only one constructor, which has no parameters. It would be a good idea to give the `LayoutManager` a name, since we will have to refer to it later. We shall call it `m` here. We also indicate that `m` will be the `LayoutManager` in the actual window.

```
GridBagLayout m = new GridBagLayout();
setLayout(m);
```

The different components will then be added, one by one. What is different with `GridBagLayout` is that when we add each component, we have to indicate explicitly the *properties* each one is to have. Such properties might indicate, for example, where the component is to be placed. In the Revision Table, there is a synopsis of the properties that can be indicated. A special class called `GridBagConstraints` is used to indicate a component's properties. We begin by declaring a reference variable for an object of this class. Note that we wait a while before creating the object itself.

```
GridBagConstraints con;
```

For every component (or group of similar components), a new object of class `GridBagConstraints` is created:

```
con = new GridBagConstraints();
```

We then fill this object with the components we want. If, for example, we want a component to begin in box (2,3), we write:

```
con.gridy = 2; con.gridx = 3;   // row and column
```

and if we want it to be two boxes high, we write:

Properties for java.awt.GridBagLayout	
`gridx` `gridy`	Indicate the column no. and row no., respectively, for the box in which the component is to begin. (Numbering starts with 0.) <u>Default value: `Relative`</u>, which means that the component is put to the right of (`gridx`) or under (`gridy`), the component last added.
`gridwidth` `gridheight`	Indicate the number of boxes which the component will include horizontally and vertically. <u>Default value: 1</u>. The value REMAINDER means the remainder of the row or column.
`fill`	Indicates how the component will fill out the whole box (or boxes). Permitted values: NONE, BOTH, HORIZONTAL and VERTICAL. <u>Default value: NONE</u>.
`anchor`	Indicates where in the box (or boxes) the component is to be put if it is smaller than the space available. Permitted values: CENTER, WEST, NORTH, EAST, SOUTH, NORTHWEST, NORTHEAST, SOUTHWEST and SOUTHEAST. <u>Default value: CENTER</u>.
`ipadx` `ipady`	Indicates the extra space (expressed in pixels) the component will be allotted in addition to its minimum size. <u>Default value: 0</u>.
`insets`	Indicates the amount of filling-out that will be put *around* the component. Is assigned a value of class `Insets`, which has the constructor `Insets`(*up, left, down, right*). <u>Default value: `Insets(0,0,0,0,)`</u>.
`weightx`	Is used to determine how the extra horizontal space will be allotted among the columns. For each column the value of `weightx` for all its rows is examined and the maximum of these `weightx` values will be the actual column's weight. The horizontal extra space is then allotted among the columns in proportion to their weights. If all the columns have a weight of 0, no column will get extra space. <u>Default value: 0</u>.
`weighty`	Is used to determine how the extra vertical space is to be allotted between the rows. Works in the same way as `weightx`. <u>Default value: 0</u>.

```
con.gridheight = 2;
```

When we have indicated all the properties we want, we connect them to the component in question. For example, if the component is called `comp`, we write:

```
m.setConstraints(comp, con);
```

We then add the component to the actual window in the usual way.

```
add(comp);
```

This procedure is repeated for all components. It is convenient to create a new GridBagConstraints object for every component because there are many different properties that may be specified. For each property, there is a default value (a value that applies in the absence of something else being indicated). Creating a new GridBagConstraints object means that we can be sure that all of its properties have this default value.

We will now show how the window in Figure 5.16 is built up. We begin as before by declaring a LayoutManager and a reference to a GridBagConstraints object.

```
GridBagLayout m = new GridBagLayout();
setLayout(m);
GridBagConstraints con;
```

We first arrange the two check boxes Big and Active. We set weighty to 1 for both row no. 0 and row no. 1. This will mean that any extra vertical space will be allotted to these two rows (each one gets the same amount).

```
// The check boxes
Checkbox bx1 = new Checkbox("Big");
Checkbox bx2 = new Checkbox("Active");
con = new GridBagConstraints();
con.weighty = 1;
con.anchor = GridBagConstraints.SOUTHWEST;
con.gridy = 0; con.gridx = 0;   // row and column
m.setConstraints(bx1, con);
add(bx1);
con.anchor = GridBagConstraints.NORTHWEST;
con.gridy = 1; con.gridx = 0;   // row and column
m.setConstraints(bx2, con);
add(bx2);
```

The next component to be arranged is the Canvas which takes up four boxes.

```
// the Canvas object
Canvas ca = new Canvas();
ca.setBackground(Color.darkGray);
con = new GridBagConstraints();
con.gridy = 0; con.gridx = 1;          // row and column
con.gridwidth = 2;                     // takes up two columns
con.gridheight = 2;                    // takes up two rows
con.fill = GridBagConstraints.BOTH;    // fills up all the space
m.setConstraints(ca, con);
add(ca);
```

We now put the two components in the third row. There will be a Label object with the text File: in the left-hand column, and in the other two columns a TextField object.

```
// the Label object
Label       dl = new Label("File: ", Label.RIGHT);
con = new GridBagConstraints();
con.gridy = 3; con.gridx = 0;          // row and column
con.insets = new Insets(10,0,10,0); // 10 pixels above and below
m.setConstraints(dl, con);
add(dl);
// the TextField object
TextField dt = new TextField();
con.gridwidth = 2;                              // takes up two columns
con.fill = GridBagConstraints.HORIZONTAL;// fill up both
con.gridy = 3; con.gridx = 1;                   // row and column
m.setConstraints(dt, con);
add(dt);
```

Finally, we put the three buttons OK, Cancel and Test in the lowest row.

```
// The last row
Button ok = new Button("OK");
Button cl = new Button("Cancel");
Button te = new Button("Test");
con = new GridBagConstraints();
con.gridy = 4; con.gridx = 0;   // row and column
con.ipadx = 5; // enlarge the buttons before and after the texts
con.anchor = GridBagConstraints.EAST; // adjust the first one to
                                      // the right
m.setConstraints(ok, con);
add(ok);
con.weightx = 1; // give columns no.1 and no.2 any extra space
con.gridy = 4; con.gridx = 1;   // row and column
con.anchor = GridBagConstraints.CENTER;
m.setConstraints(cl, con);
add(cl);
con.gridy = 4; con.gridx = 2;   // row and column

con.anchor = GridBagConstraints.WEST;
m.setConstraints(te, con);
add(te);
```

Here we have set weightx to 1 for columns nos 1 and 2, so that these will be allotted all the extra horizontal space. Because we had previously allotted all the extra vertical space to rows 0 and 1, the canvas object will be enlarged automatically if we make the window larger (see the right-hand window in Figure 5.16).

5.15 Example – a text editor

We shall round off this long chapter by demonstrating quite an advanced program, a text editor. With the help of the graphics standard classes and our own classes `ExtendedReader` and `ExtendedWriter` (see Section 3.3.1), it is surprisingly easy to design the program. When we run it, we get a window as in Figure 5.17.

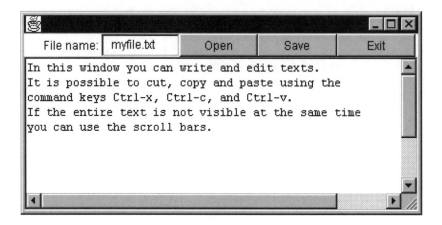

Figure 5.17 A text editor

The user can edit text in the text area in the usual way. If we want to open and read in an existing text file, we write the file's name in the text field at the top on the left, then click on the `Open` button. The text area's previous contents are then wiped away, and the new file is read in. If there is no file with the given name, the program will emit a hollow, metallic sound to signal to the user that an incorrect name has been entered. If we click on the `Save` button, the program will save whatever is displayed in the text area in the file indicated.

The window has been divided into two sections. At the top there is a panel with five components: a `Label`, a `TextField` object and three buttons. The components in the panel have been arranged with `GridLayout` (one row and five columns). Under the panel, there is a `TextArea` object. The panel and the texts are arranged in the window with `BorderLayout`. The text area is placed in the `Center` position, which means that it will get all the extra space if the window is enlarged. The program looks like this:

```
import java.awt.*;
import java.awt.event.*;
import extra.*;
```

```
class TextEdit extends Frame implements ActionListener {
  Panel p = new Panel();
  TextField name  = new TextField();
  Button     open = new Button("Open");
  Button     save = new Button("Save");
  Button     exit = new Button("Exit");
  TextArea   area = new TextArea(10,60);

  TextEdit() {
    p.setFont(new Font("SansSerif", Font.PLAIN, 12));
    area.setFont(new Font("Monospaced", Font.PLAIN, 12));

    // arrange the components in panel p
    p.setLayout(new GridLayout(1,5));
    p.add(new Label("File name: ", Label.RIGHT));
    p.add(name); p.add(open); p.add(save); p.add(exit);
    name.addActionListener(this);
    open.addActionListener(this);
    save.addActionListener(this);
    exit.addActionListener(this);

    // arrange the panel and the text area
    setLayout(new BorderLayout());
    add("North", p);
    add("Center", area);
    pack();
    setVisible(true);
  }

  public void actionPerformed(ActionEvent e) {
    // check which button the user has pressed
    if (e.getSource()==name || e.getSource()==open)
      readFile(name.getText());
    else if (e.getSource()==save)
      saveFile(name.getText());
    else if (e.getSource()==exit)
      System.exit(0);
  }

  void readFile(String name) {
    area.setText("");    // empty the text area
    ExtendedReader inFile = ExtendedReader.getFileReader(name);
    if (inFile == null) {              // the file does not exist
      Toolkit.getDefaultToolkit().beep(); // give a sound signal
      return;
    }
```

```
    // the file exists, read it in and display it in the text
       area
    String s;
    while ((s=inFile.readLine()) != null) // read line by line
      area.append(s + "\n"); // add the line + line feed
      inFile.close();
  }

  void saveFile(String name) {
    ExtendedWriter outFile =ExtendedWriter.getFileWriter(name);
    outFile.print(area.getText());   // write out the whole text
                                     area
    outFile.close();
  }

  public static void main (String[] arg) {
    TextEdit t = new TextEdit();
  }
}
```

As usual, we arrange for the actual object of the main class also to be a listener. The button the user has pressed is checked in the listener method `actionPerformed`.

We should comment on a small detail. The method `readFile`, called when the user presses the `Open` button, reads in the file row by row and adds the rows last in the text area so that they will be seen in the window. Every row in a text file is terminated by one or two characters that indicate the end of the row. The method `readLine` reads a whole row, including the characters indicating the end of a row, but this indication is not included in the text that `readLine` gives as a result. If we were to add the rows read one after the other in the text area, they would all end up in the same row there. We therefore have to insert an end-of-line marker after every row read in. This kind of end-of-line marker is indicated by the character \n. (We will deal with this at greater length in Chapter 6.) When we then write out the whole of the text area to a file, the end-of-line markers will be in the text.

5.16 Exercises

1. Give the class `Car`, in Exercise 1 on page 116, the property that it is a `Panel`, so that it can be used as a GUI component. The registration number and make of a car should be displayed. Then write a program that displays three cars side by side in a window.

2. What changes would have to be made in the program `FlightDemo2` on page 129, for the program to become an Applet instead?

3. Write a GUI program that allows a user to enter his name, his height and his weight in three black boxes. When the user has written the input data, the program should display a text having the form *Hello NN. Your weight is xx.x kg/cm.*

4. Solve Exercise 1 on page 94, letting the program have a graphical user interface.

5. Solve Exercise 2 on page 94, letting the program have a graphical user interface.

6. Solve Exercise 3 on page 94, letting the program have a graphical user interface.

7. Write a program that shows two thermometers next to each other. One thermometer should show the temperature expressed in degrees Celsius (°C) and the other, in degrees Fahrenheit (°F). The thermometers will be displayed with the help of two `Scrollbar` objects. When the user drags on the scroll box of the first thermometer, the other one should also change. The actual values of the thermometers should be written out at their sides, in digital form. 0°C corresponds to 32°F and 100°C corresponds to 212°F. The formula °C=(°F–32)×5/9 can be used to convert °F to °C.

8. With the help of `GridBagLayout`, design a window that can be used to enter various details about a programmer. In addition to the person's name, we should be able to indicate their age, civil status (single, married or someone's partner) and this programmer's favourite programming language (there should be a list to choose from). There should also be two buttons: one marked `Interrupt`, which interrupts the program, and another marked `Finished`. When this one is clicked on, the information about the programmer appears in a text window (use the stream `std.out`). All the selections in the window should then be removed so that new information about a new programmer can be entered.

9. Write a program that plays "Scissors, stone and paper". The program should arbitrarily "think of" a stone, a pair of scissors, or a piece of paper and display a window with three buttons for the user to play. The program should then decide who won and display a message. See if you can devise the program so that it can run several times in succession and display the number of times the user has won or lost.

Texts and arrays

6

The largest amount of data on a computer is probably text rather than numerical information. We begin this chapter by describing how the smallest constituents of a program – individual letters and other characters – can be represented in Java. Later we will be discussing the standard class `String`, together with the way in which characters and texts are compared.

6.1 Character codes and character literals

We normally use a group of 8 bits to store a character in the computer. A group of this kind is called a *byte*. In the past, only seven of these eight bits were used. The eighth bit, or *parity bit*, was reserved for checking purposes. The other seven bits could be combined in 128 different ways, which meant that there were 128 different character codes. There is a generally accepted standard, called the *ASCII standard*, which determines the characters that can be coded with the seven available bits, and for each pattern of seven bits, there is one character designated in the standard. For example, `'%'`, `'9'` and `'A'` are represented, respectively, by

```
00100101 00111001 01000001
```

These bit patterns can be interpreted as binary integers, called *character codes*. The codes start with 0, so the character codes lie between 0 and 127; the characters `'9'` and `'A'` will, for example, have the character codes 57 and 65, respectively. The ASCII standard contains the letters a–z (both upper- and lower-case), the digits 0–9, various special characters (for example, `'!'` and `'.'`) and a set of non-printing control characters.

ASCII is an American standard that was developed on the assumption that the language used would be English. The English alphabet has the 26 letters, a–z, derived from the Latin alphabet. Almost all the other living languages use either the Latin alphabet, with other characters, or other non-Latin alphabets or characters. The ASCII standard is, however, spread throughout the world. The fact that ASCII only contains the letters a–z has been a problem and a constant source of irritation to everyone working in programming in the non-English-speaking countries. An obvious solution to this problem would be to allow for more characters in the standard. If we dropped the use of the first bit in each byte as a parity bit, we could have eight bits instead of seven, and 256 different characters could be represented instead of 128. We could then use the characters from 128 to 255 to represent new letters and other characters. There is an international standard (ISO 8859) specifying the characters to be designated by the different codes. When we use Windows or a Unix system (but not MS-DOS or Macintosh) we follow this standard. ISO 8859 corresponds to the ASCII standard for the character codes 0 to 127. Character codes 128 to 255 are used partly for non-printing control characters and partly for a set of printable characters. The latter, contained in the ISO 8859 standard, is called *LATIN_1*. Among the characters in LATIN_1 there are the letters with diacritics that are used in the Romance and Germanic languages, for example á, å, è, æ, ö, ü, ñ and ç. All these characters exist both in lower and upper case. The only exceptions are the German character ß, indicating a double s, and the character ÿ. Apart from the letters with diacritical marks, LATIN_1 also contains various graphic characters such as §, £ and ¶.

Of course, using LATIN_1 instead of ASCII only solves the problem for countries where the Western European languages are used. Java, however, aims to ensure that it can be used anywhere in the world and so it has gone a step further. Letters and characters are coded in Java with 16 bits instead of 8. As a result, no fewer than 65,536 different characters can be encoded. Java uses the Unicode standard, in which 38,887 characters (in version 2.1) are currently defined. These characters come from 25 different alphabets from all over the world. In addition, there are a number of special characters for graphics. The Unicode codes 0–255 agree with the LATIN_1 standard. A complete listing of all the Unicode characters can be found on the Internet at `www.unicode.org`.

In Java, variables of the standard type **char** are 16 bits long and contain character codes in accordance with the Unicode standard.

Character literals, or constant character values, are written between apostrophe marks. For instance, if we want to declare a variable of type **char** and insert a plus character into it, we can write:

```
char ch = '+';
```

The following assignments are also permitted:

```
ch = 'ê'; ch = '¿';
```

Character literals for characters that can be written can be easily indicated, as demonstrated above. Exceptions are the characters ' (apostrophe), " (double quotes) and \ (backslash). When we wish to indicate these characters, we have to use *escape sequences.* An escape sequence is introduced by the character \ and is interpreted as a single character. For example, to assign an apostrophe to the variable ch1 and a backslash to the variable ch2, we can write:

```
ch1 = '\'';   ch2 = '\\';
```

Escape sequences are also used to indicate the control characters that cannot be written. Some of the most common control characters have been given special escape sequences. For example, \n is the character for a new line and \t means tabulator. If we want to indicate a character that we cannot write and that lacks a special escape sequence, we can use an escape sequence where the character's code is directly indicated. If we want to indicate a character included in LATIN_1, we can write an *octal number*[1] consisting of, at most, three digits after the character \. The highest octal number that can be indicated in this way is 377, which corresponds to decimal 255. Some examples are:

```
'\0'   '\33'   '\177'   '\266'   '\377'
```

It is impossible to type most of the characters in the complete Unicode standard on a normal keyboard. To indicate characters with character codes higher than 255 (decimal), we can use a Unicode sequence. This has the form '\uxxxx'. The number xxxx will consist of four digits and is written in *hexadecimal* form.[2] If we have two variables ch1 and ch2, both of type **char**, for instance, we can write:

```
ch1 = '\u2663';   ch2 = '\u03A8';
```

Then the variable ch1 will contain the character ♣, while the variable ch2 will contain the character ψ. (These codes are given on the Internet at the address www.unicode.org.)

We do not only use Unicode in the type **char**. Java also uses Unicode internally in the compiled classes. It is, therefore, permissible to use Unicode letters in class names, variables, and so on, while we can also use Unicode sequences in the program code itself. If, for example, we write the declaration:

```
double π = 3.1416;
```

---

[1] Only the digits 0–7 may be used in an octal number. For instance, the decimal number 8 is written as 10 in octal form. Octal 20 corresponds to decimal 16 and octal 100 corresponds to decimal 64.

[2] The digits 0–9 are used in a hexadecimal number and the letters A–F are used to indicate the decimal numbers from 10 to 15. Thus the hexadecimal number F corresponds to decimal 15 and the hexadecimal number 10 corresponds to decimal 16. Hexadecimal 20 corresponds to decimal 32 and hexadecimal 100 corresponds to decimal 256.

Escape sequences		
\n	*new line*	moves the printout position to the beginning of the next line
\b	*backspace*	moves the printout position one step to the left
\r	*return*	moves the printout position to the beginning of the next line
\f	*form feed*	moves the printout position to the beginning of the next page
\t	*tab*	moves the printout position to the next tab stop
\'	*single quote*	apostrophe mark
\"	*double quote*	quotation marks
\\	*backslash*	gives the character \
nnn		the character with the octal character code *nnn*
\u*xxxx*		the character with the hexadecimal unicode *xxxx*

but do not have a text editor that allows us to enter the Unicode characters, we can instead write:

```
double \u03C0 = 3.1416;
```

As an example of how we deal with individual characters, we will demonstrate a small program that reads a text file and writes it out at the terminal. To read one character at a time the program will call the method readChar in our class ExtendedReader. This method works in the same way as the method read, discussed on page 81. In the printout, all the tab characters will be replaced by 3 blank characters; in addition, all upper-case letters will be converted to lower-case letters. The program begins by asking for the file's name, after which printout will take place.

In the program, the class methods isUpperCase and toLowerCase in the wrapper class Character (see page 43) are called. The method isUpperCase checks to see whether a character is a capital, and the method toLowerCase converts capitals to the corresponding lower-case letters. The standard class Character contains several other methods that are useful when dealing with individual characters; please see online documentation for the details.

```
import extra.*;
 class CharDemo {
   public static void main (String[] arg) {
     // open the input file
     Std.out.print("Input file? ");
     String name = Std.in.readWord();
     ExtendedReader inFile = ExtendedReader.getFileReader(name);
     if (inFile == null) {
       Std.out.println("Cannot find " + name);
       System.exit(1);
     }
```

```
// read and write out the file
int i;
while ((i = inFile.readChar()) != -1) {
    char c = (char) i;
    if (c == '\t')
        Std.out.print("    ");

    else if (Character.isUpperCase(c))
        Std.out.print(Character.toLowerCase(c));
    else
        Std.out.print(c);
}
Std.out.flush(); // NB! Important!
}
}
```

The expression after **while** might look somewhat strange, so we should say something about assignments in Java. An expression of the form a=b is called an *assignment expression*. In an expression of this kind, a's value is, of course, assigned to b but, in fact, the *whole* expression has a value in the same way that an expression of the form a+b has a value. The value of an assignment expression is the value that is assigned. The value of the expression:

```
i = inFile.readChar()
```

is, therefore, the value that is assigned to the variable i. In the **while** statement:

```
while ((i = inFile.readChar()) != -1)
```

the value of i is compared with –1. Note the importance of the parentheses around the assignment expression. The operator != has a higher priority than = and would have been carried out first had the parentheses not been included, producing a compilation error. Note, too, that we have to read in the characters to a variable of type **int** and not a variable of type **char**, since a variable of type **char** cannot, of course, contain the value –1.

We call the method flush last of all in the program to empty the printout buffer. If this were not done, a number of characters (perhaps all of them) that were to be written out could remain in the buffer and, therefore, not be seen on the screen. The printout buffer is cleared automatically every time println is called, or something is entered from the keyboard; since we have not done anything like this in the program, we have to empty the buffer expressly by calling flush.

6.2 The standard class `String`

In Section 2.3.5 on page 49, we began by describing the standard class `String`. An object of class `String` contains a text consisting of a series of elements of type **char**, that is, of elements coded with 16-bit Unicode. If a text contained a character that could not be written at the keyboard, we would be able to use Unicode sequences:

```
String s = "\u03B1\u03B2"; // s contains the text "αβ"
```

Ordinary escape sequences may also be used in texts. For example, we could make the statement:

```
Std.out.println("\"method\" is called \"function\" in C++");
```

The printout will then be:

```
"method" is called "function" in C++
```

We have seen two different ways of displaying texts in GUI programs. One way, which we used in the programs `Message2`, `Message3` and `Cat` in Chapter 1, is to define a method `paint` that gets a parameter `g` of class `Graphics`. The method `g.drawString` can then be called in the method `paint`. The other, rather simpler, way is to create an object `l` of class `Label` and call the method `l.setText`. In both cases we can use Unicode sequences in the text to be displayed. For example, we can write:

```
g.drawString("\u03B1\u03B2");
```

or

```
l.setText("\u03B1\u03B2");
```

The text αβ will then be displayed in the window. There are not many Unicode characters that can be displayed correctly in a normal installation. (An empty square is displayed instead.) For it to be possible to display a particular Unicode character, we must have installed a special font for the group of characters in question.

In Section 2.3.5, we stated that objects of class `String` were constant – they could not be changed. But *new* `String` objects can easily be created by using the + operator, for instance, in the following program lines:

```
String s1 = "class";
int i = 19;
String s2 = "super" + s1; // s2 contains "superclass"
s2 = s2 + i; // s2 contains "superclass19"
```

Class `String` contains many methods, a number of which can be used for text analysis. A synopsis appears in the Revision Table. The most important of these are `length`, `charAt`, `equals` and `compareTo`. The method `length` returns an **int** that gives the

java.lang.String

In the following list, `s1` and `s2` denote objects of class `String`, `c` a value of type **char** and `n` and `m` integer indices greater than, or equal to, 0.

`s1.length()`	gives the number of characters in `s1`
`s1.charAt(n)`	gives the character at position `n` in `s1`
`s1.substring(n)`	gives the subtext of `s1` that begins in position `n`
`s1.substring(n, m)`	gives the subtext of `s1` that begins in `n` and ends in `m-1`

`s1.compareTo(s2)` gives a value that is 0 if `s1` and `s2` are equal, <0 if `s1` comes before `s2` alphabetically and >0 if `s2` comes before `s1`. NB: Only works for the "pure" letters a–z.

`s1.equals(s2)`	gives `true` if `s1` and `s2` are equal, `false` otherwise
`s1.equalsIgnoreCase(s2)`	gives `true` if `s1` and `s2` are equal, `false` otherwise lower- and upper-case letters are regarded as being the same
`s1.startsWith(s2)`	gives `true` if `s1` begins with the subtext `s2`, `false` otherwise
`s1.startsWith(s2,n)`	gives `true` if `s1`, with its beginning in position `n`, contains the subtext `s2`, `false` otherwise
`s1.endsWith(s2)`	gives `true` if `s1` ends with the subtext `s2`, `false` otherwise
`s1.indexOf(c)`	gives the position for the first occurrence of the character `c` in `s1`, gives −1 if the character `c` is not in `s1`
`s1.indexOf(c,n)`	gives the position for the first occurrence, from position `n` and onwards, of the character `c` in `s1`
`s1.lastIndexOf(c)`	gives the position for the last occurrence of the character `c` in `s1`
`s1.lastIndexOf(c,n)`	gives the position for the last occurrence, from position `n` and backwards, of the character `c` in `s1`
`s1.indexOf(s2)`	gives the position for the first occurrence of the text `s2` in `s1`
`s1.indexOf(s2,n)`	gives the position for the first occurrence, from position `n` and onwards, of the text `s2` in `s1`
`s1.lastIndexOf(s2)`	gives the position for the last occurrence of the text `s2` in `s1`
`s1.lastIndexOf(s2,n)`	gives the position for the last occurrence, from position `n` and backwards, of the text `s2` in `s1`
`s1.trim()`	gives a copy of `s1`, where the beginning and ending blank characters and tab characters have been removed
`s1.replace(c1,c2)`	gives a copy of `s1` where the character `c1` has been exchanged for the character `c2` everywhere
`s1.toUpperCase()`	gives a copy of `s1` where all lower-case letters have been exchanged for capitals
`s1.toLowerCase()`	gives a copy of `s1` where all the capitals have been exchanged for lower-case letters
`String.valueOf(x)`	gives a text where the value of `x` has been converted into text form. `x` must be either of a simple, built-in type, or of a class where the method `toString` is defined.

length of the actual text. If, as before, the variable s2 referred to the text "superclass19", the statement:

```
Std.out.println(s2.length());
```

would give 12 as output.

The method charAt is used for checking individual characters in a text. This method returns a value of type **char**. As argument, we will give the number of the character to be checked. Numbering always begins at 0, so that the first character has the number 0. For example, the statements:

```
Std.out.println(s2.charAt(2));
Std.out.println(s2.charAt(s2.length()-1));
```

will give the output:

```
p
9
```

We use the method equals when we want to check whether two texts are equal:

```
if (s1.equals(s2))
  Std.out.println("The texts are equal");
```

The method equals gives as a result a value of type **boolean**, which will indicate whether the texts were equal or not. Note that we must not write s1=s2 or s1==s2 inside the parentheses in the **if** statement. The first expression is an assignment of s2 to s1. The second expression is, of course, a comparison but it compares the values of the reference variables and not what they refer to. Therefore, the second expression will only be true if both s2 and s1 refer to the *same* String object.

The method compareTo is used to check whether a certain text comes before or after another text in alphabetical order. The method returns a whole number. This number will be less than zero if the first text comes first, greater than zero if the second text comes first and equal to zero if the two texts are equal. For example, we write:

```
if (s1.compareTo(s2) < 0)
  Std.out.println(s1 + " is before " + s2);
else if (s1.compareTo(s2) > 0)
  Std.out.println(s2 + " is before " + s1);
else  // == 0
  Std.out.println(s2 + " and " + s1 + " are equal");
```

We must issue a warning for the method compareTo. It compares the two texts character by character and upper- and lower-case letters are regarded as being different. Furthermore, alphabetization is only carried out for the "pure" letters, a–z. Other letters, such as those with accents, will not be alphabetized. The method compareTo will, therefore, not be suitable for comparing texts containing natural language. In

Section 6.3 we shall describe how we compare texts in correct alphabetical order, in different languages.

6.3 Comparisons of characters and texts

An internal order is defined between the different values of type **char**, which is determined, quite simply, by the code representing the characters. A character with a small character code will come before a character with a larger code. Note especially that upper- and lower-case letters are not regarded as being the same and that the normal alphabetical order will not apply to letters with accents or other diacritics. The program lines below compare two characters and write them out in order of size. (We suppose that the variables ch1 and ch2 both have type **char**.)

```
ch1 = 'A'; ch2 = 'a';
if (ch1 < ch2)
   Std.out.println(ch1 + " is smallest");
else
   Std.out.println(ch2 + " is smallest");
```

The output will be:

```
A is smallest
```

Capitals are treated as being smaller than lower-case letters.

In Section 6.2 we saw that we were able to use the method compareTo in the standard class String to compare two texts. This method will compare the incoming characters one by one in the same method as above, that is, the character code determines their internal order. The method compareTo will, therefore, not function as we would like it to when we compare natural text, especially if the text is written in a language other than English. Let us take an example: let us suppose that the variables s1 and s2 have type String:

```
s1 = "pâté"; s2="prince";
if (s1.compareTo(s2) < 0)
   Std.out.println(s1 + " is before " + s2);
else if (s1.compareTo(s2) > 0)
   Std.out.println(s2 + " is before " + s1);
else
   Std.out.println(s2 + " and " + s1 + " are equal");
```

The output will be:

```
prince is before pâté
```

6. Texts and arrays

The solution to our problem is to use a *collator* that knows the rules for sorting letters in the language in question. We can get a collator by declaring an object of the standard class `java.text.Collator`:

```
Collator co = Collator.getInstance();
```

The class method `getInstance` gives a collator that knows the rules for the language currently serving as a default `Locale` (see page 74). For example, if we use French conventions, the collator `co` will know the French rules.

To compare two texts, we can now use the method `compare` for the collator `co`. We can write:

```
s1 = "pâté"; s2="prince";
if (co.compare(s1, s2) < 0)
   Std.out.println(s1 + " is before " + s2);
else if (co.compare(s1, s2) > 0)
   Std.out.println(s2 + " is before " + s1);
else
   Std.out.println(s1 + " and " + s2 + " are equal");
```

The method `compare` has, as parameters, the two texts to be compared. The result it gives is the same value as the method `compareTo` in class `String`, that is, a value that is 0 if the two texts are equal, or less than 0 if the first text comes before the second, and a value greater than 0 if the second text comes before the first. The output from these program lines will now be (with English conventions):

```
pâté is before prince
```

The comparisons will not be entirely perfect yet. For example, if we let `s1` contain the text `"Prince"` and `s2`, the text `"prince"`, we will get the output:

```
prince is before Prince
```

If we let `s1` contain the text `"Irene"` and `s2`, the text `"Irène"`, we will get the output:

```
Irene is before Irène
```

This is because the collator `co` regards upper- and lower-case letters as being different. Moreover, it also sees letters with accents and the corresponding letters without accents as being different. Meanwhile, we can solve this problem by telling the collator `co` how exacting it is to be when comparing different letters; this is done with the method `setStrength`. This has a parameter that indicates the collator's strength. There are three levels: PRIMARY, SECONDARY and TERTIARY. If the level is set at PRIMARY, the collator will only differentiate between different letters, upper- and lower-case letters being regarded as equal. Letters with diacritics are seen as being the same as letters without them. If the collator is set to SECONDARY, upper- and lower-case letters are regarded as equal but letters with diacritics are not seen as being the same as letters without them. If the TERTIARY level is chosen, upper- and lower-case letters are treated as being unequal, as are letters with and without diacritics.

If no level has been indicated for a collator, the TERTIARY level will be chosen, which is why the collator co, in our example above, sorted things in such an odd way. The best thing is to set the level to PRIMARY, which will give normal alphabetical comparisons:

```
co.setStrength(Collator.PRIMARY);
```

Using the same example as before, we will now get the correct comparisons:

```
prince and Prince are equal
Irène and Irene are equal
```

When we create a collator, we can indicate the language conventions we want to have. The class getInstance, for example, can have as parameter a Locale object. If we want a collator to make a comparison in accordance with Portuguese language rules, for instance, we can write:

```
Collator co_pt = Collator.getInstance(new Locale("pt", "PT"));
```

Summing up, we can say that if ordinary alphabetical comparisons are called for, a collator should be obtained that has been adjusted to the language conventions desired. The collator's level should then be set to PRIMARY.

We can also use a method equals, in class Collator, to check whether, from an alphabetical point of view, two texts are the same. We can write:

```
s1 = "Irene"; s2="Irène";
if (co.equals(s1,s2))
  Std.out.println(s1 + " and " + s2 + " are equal");
```

Alphabetical comparison of texts

Obtain a collator of class java.text.Collator:
```
Collator c = Collator.getInstance();
```
or
```
Collator c = Collator.getInstance(new Locale("language","country"));
```

Set the collator's level to PRIMARY:
```
c.setStrength(Collator.PRIMARY);
```

The texts are then compared with method compare or equals:

c.compare(s1,s2)	gives a value that is 0 if s1 and s2 are alphabetically equal, < 0 if s1 comes before s2 and >0 if s2 comes before s1
c.equals(s1,s2)	gives true if s1 and s2 are alphabetically equal, false otherwise

A collator has to consider several different language-related factors when making its comparisons. The methods `compare` and `equals` can, therefore, be quite demanding sometimes. As a result, programs can be slow if many comparisons are made, for example, when sorting texts. In order to avoid this, we can use *collation keys*. A collation key is an object of class `java.text.CollationKey`. Collation keys can be compared with one another effectively. For each text, a collation key can be obtained with the help of the method `getCollationKey` in the class `Collator`. For instance, we can calculate the collation keys for the texts `"prince"` and `"pâté"`:

```
CollationKey k1 = co.getCollationKey("prince");
CollationKey k2 = co.getCollationKey("pâté");
```

We can use a method `getSourceString` in class `CollationKey` to find the text corresponding to a particular collation key. For example, the call:

```
k1.getSourceString()
```

gives the value `"prince"`.

Instead of comparing the texts directly, as before, we can now compare their collation keys. This is done with the method `compareTo`, in class `CollationKey`. This method compares a particular collation key with another and returns, just as the method `compare` in class `Collator`, a value that is equal to 0, less than 0, or greater than 0, depending on the order of the two texts. For example, we can write:

```
if (k1.compareTo(k2) < 0)
  Std.out.println(k1.getSourceString() + " is before " +
                  k2.getSourceString());
else if (k1.compareTo(k2) > 0)
  Std.out.println(k2.getSourceString() + " is before " +
                  k1.getSourceString());
else
  Std.out.println(k1.getSourceString() + " and " +
                  k2.getSourceString() + " are equal");
```

Comparisons can also be carried out with the method `equals` in class `CollationKey`. The method gives as result a value of type **boolean**. An example:

```
if (k1.equals(k2))
  Std.out.println(k1.getSourceString() + " and " +
                  k2.getSourceString() + " are equal");
```

It is only worthwhile using collation keys when a particular text is to be compared to other texts *several* times, as is the case when sorting, for example. If a text will only be compared once, it is easier and more effective to compare the text directly, as we did earlier in this section.

6.4 Arrays of simple variables

A simple variable, for example, a variable of type `int` or `double`, can only contain one value at a time. However, we often need to be able to deal with collections containing several different values of the same type. We then make use of *arrays*. An array is a table that contains several components of the same kind, where the various components are numbered. We can use a special kind of reference variable to handle arrays. We can call this an *array variable*. We begin by declaring an array variable which we will call `f`.

```
double[] f;
```

Here it is clear that `f` is an array variable, that is, a reference variable that can refer to an array, and not an ordinary variable, since `[]` appears after the type name. The word `double` indicates that the array's components will be of this type. As is the case with all reference variables, `f` will automatically get the initialization value `null` unless we initialize it. There are two ways of initializing an array variable. The first is by using `new`.

```
double[] f = new double[5];
```

Initialization means that `f` will refer to an array with five components. We show this in Figure 6.1. Each component in an array is automatically initialized to its default value,

Figure 6.1

the value an ordinary, uninitialized variable of the actual type would have obtained. Because the components in the array are of type `double`, they are initialized to the value 0.

Every component in an array has a unique number, or *index*, as it is usually called. Note especially that the numbering of components *always* takes place from 0, so that the first component will have the index 0. (It is not possible in Java, as it is in several other languages, to indicate how we want the components to be numbered. The first component will always have the index 0.) It follows then that the index for the last component in an array will always be a number that is one less than the number of components in the array. The instance variable `length` can be used to determine the number of components in an array. Here, for example, the expression `f.length` will have a value of 5. When we want to access a particular component in an array, we make use of the component's index for *indexing*. If, for example, we wanted to put the value 2.75 into the last component (the one with the number 4) in the array f, we would write the statement:

```
f[4] = 2.75;
```

We also make use of square brackets here. The index indicated in square brackets does not need to be a constant. It could be an arbitrary integer expression. If the variables i and j are of type **int**, we can write:

```
f[i+j] = 2.75;
```

The important thing here is that the index expression should have a value lying inside the array's boundaries. In this example, the value of i+j will lie in the interval 0 to 4. The Java interpreter will check that the correct index has been indicated. If the value of an index expression lies outside the array's boundaries, an error signal is generated – an exception of type ArrayIndexOutOfBounds. If this error signal is not dealt with, the program will be interrupted.

The components in an array can be of arbitrary type. For instance, we can declare another array variable with the name a and let it refer to an array with 6 components of type **int**:

```
int[] a = new int[6];
```

As we have seen when creating an array, all its components will be initialized to a default value unless otherwise specified. An array can also be initialized when it is being created. If we wanted, we could write:

```
int[] b = {13, 23, 55, 4};
```

This is the other way to initialize an array variable. Note that we do not need to use **new** when writing in this way. A new array will still be created. The number of components in the new array will be determined by the number of components that are enumerated in the curly brackets. Here we create a new array having four components and they will get the initialization values 13, 23, 55 and 4. The initialization expressions inside the curly brackets do not need to be constants. They can be arbitrary expressions. For example, if the variables i and j had type **int**, we would write:

```
int[] b = {i, i-1, i+j, 18};
```

Note that it is only during the initialization stage that it is permissible to give values to the components all at once. For example, the following statement would not be allowed:

```
b = {0, 0, 0, 0};  // not allowed!
```

If, for example, we wanted to assign the value 5 to all the components in b, we could do this for each component, one at a time, like this:

```
int i=0;
while (i<b.length) { // b.length here has the value 4
   b[i] = 5;
   i = i+1;
}
```

This is a little unwieldy. Better is the following construction:

```
b = new int[]{5, 5, 5, 5};
```

But note that now we create a *new* array, letting b refer to the new array. The array that b referred to earlier will be an item for automatic garbage collection.

Because array variables are reference variables, we must be careful when making assignments of arrays. In the following statement, for example, the variable a is set to refer to the *same* array as the variable b.

```
a = b;    // copies the reference
```

What this would look like is shown in Figure 6.2.

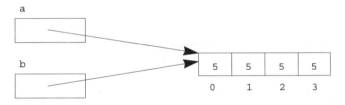

Figure 6.2

If we want to assign the whole array b to a, we must instead make a copy of the arrays b refers to. This we do by using the standard method clone.

```
a = (int[]) b.clone();   // copies the array
```

The method clone returns a value of class Object, and so an explicit type conversion to type int[] is required. Instead, we will now get the situation shown in Figure 6.3. Note that a is a reference and that it is the reference itself that is changed so that a will refer to a *new* array. This means that it does not matter what a referred to earlier. As can be seen, the length of the array that a referred to earlier does not need to agree with the length of array b.

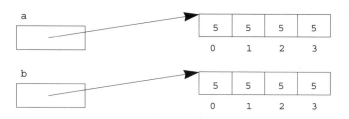

Figure 6.3

If we want to copy a number of components from one array to another, we can use the class method `arraycopy` in the standard class `System`. Suppose, for example, that we have declared yet another array:

```
int[] c = {10, 20, 30, 40, 50, 60};
```

Further suppose that array b looks as in Figure 6.3. We now make the call:

```
System.arraycopy(c,2,b,1,2);
```

The first argument is the array that we will copy from and the second indicates where in this array we will begin to copy. Copying will, therefore, begin with component number 2 in array c. The third argument is the array we will be copying to, and the fourth element will indicate the starting position in this array. Here copying will, therefore, take place to component number 1 and onwards, in array b. The last argument indicates the number of components to be copied, in this example, 2. The result of the above statement will thus be that components 1 and 2 in array b will be changed. Components 0 and 3 will remain unchanged. As a result, array b will contain the values {5, 30, 40, 5}. Note that `arraycopy` will change the contents of the array that b refers to. The reference b itself will not be changed. (Compare this with the use of the method `clone`, above.) Of course, it is possible to write a repetition statement instead of using `arraycopy`.

Care must be exercised when making comparisons of arrays. If we wrote, for example,

```
if (a == b)    // permitted but not what is intended
```

it would certainly be allowed, but the contents of the arrays would not be compared. Instead, a check is made to see whether a and b are referring to the *same* array.

The class `java.util.Arrays` contains some class methods (static methods) that are useful when dealing with arrays. A compilation of these is given in the Revision Table. For example, we can check whether two arrays f and g are equal by writing:

```
if (Arrays.equals(f,g))
```

Arrays, the basics

type[] f;	declares a reference to arrays
type[] f = **new** *type*[*number*];	declaration and initialization
type[] f = {*value*, *value* ... *value*};	declaration and initialization
f = **new** *type*[]{*value*, *value* ... *value*};	f is assigned a new array
f = g;	f refers to the same array as g
f = (*type*[]) g.clone();	f refers to a *copy* of g
f.length	gives the number of components in the array f
System.arraycopy(f1,*startpos1*,f2,*startpos2*,*number*);	
	copies *number* of components from f1[*startpos1*] to f2[*startpos2*]
f == g	checks whether f and g refer to the same array

java.util.Arrays

equals(a1,a2)	gives **true** if the arrays a1 and a2 are equal (contain the same number of components and the components are equal)
fill(a,v)	gives all the components in array a the value v
fill(a,i1,i2,v)	gives components no. i1 to i2-1 in array a the value v
sort(a)	sorts the components in array a in ascending order
sort(a,c)	as above but uses c to compare components (c will implement the interface Comparator, see Section 15.5)
sort(a,i1,i2)	sorts components no. i1 to i2-1 in array a
sort(a,i1,i2,c)	as above but uses c to compare components
binarySearch(a,k)	searches for component k in the array a, gives k's index in the array if k exists, otherwise −1
binarySearch(a,k,c)	as above but uses c to compare components (c will implement the interface Comparator)
asList(a)	converts an array a to a list (see Section 15.5)

Objects of standard type string contain an array in which the components are of type **char**. So it is easy to convert an array of **char** to a string object and vice versa. For example, we can write:

```
char[] v = {'J', 'a', 'v', 'a', ' ', 'c', 'l', 'a', 's', 's'};
String s = new String(v);    // s gets the value "Java class"
String t = new String(v,1,3); // t gets the value "ava"
char[] w = t.toCharArray();   // w gets the value {'a', 'v', 'a'}
```

On the third line we choose a subarray of v. The "one" means that the subarray will begin in position 1, and the "three" means that the subarray will be 3 characters long.

It is also easy to convert an array of **byte** to a string object and vice versa:

```
byte[] b = s.getBytes();  // b contains the text "Java class"
String p = new String(b);    // p gets the value "Java class"
String q = new String(b,1,3); // q gets the value "ava"
```

It should be mentioned here that (unfortunately) there is another way of declaring arrays in Java. The array variable f that we previously declared as

```
double[] f;
```

can also be declared in the following way:

```
double f[];
```

So we can set the square brackets after the variable name instead of after the type name. This way of writing is inherited from the programming language C, where arrays were declared in this way, but it is illogical and misleading, since the square brackets really are a part of the type indication. If we look at the following example:

```
int[] g1, h1;    // recommended way of writing
```

we see that this is written in the usual way. The result will be that the variables g1 and h1 both get type int[], which is quite natural. The indication of the type, that is, int[], comes first, and then the variables that will have this type are enumerated afterwards. However, if we write:

```
int g2[], h2[];
```

we see that the square brackets must be repeated for each variable. If these are omitted for a variable, the variable will not be an array but an ordinary variable. For instance, if we write the following, g3 will be an array variable, while h3 will be an ordinary int:

```
int g3[], h3;
```

We therefore recommend the normal way of writing, where square brackets are written together with the type name (even if old C programmers might be offended!).

6.5 The for statement

When we work with arrays, we often have to use repetition to run through the components in an array. So far we have only used **while** statements to produce repetition. In this section, we will introduce the **for** statement, an alternative to the **while** statement and often more convenient when dealing with arrays. We usually use a **for** statement when we have a repetition where there is a counter to count up or down in each round of the statement. A **for** statement differs slightly from the corresponding statement in most of the other programming languages (excepting C and C++). After the reserved word **for** come parentheses containing three separate sections, an initialization section, a condition section and a change section. A semicolon separates the three different sections. A **for** statement has the form:

```
for (init; condition; change)
   statement;
```

The statement on the second line can consist of several statements in curly brackets, just as for `if` statements and `while` statements. Execution proceeds in the following way: First *init* is computed and then *condition*. If *condition* is true, *statement* is performed. When this has been done, *change* is computed. Now *condition* is computed once again. If it is still true, another round is performed, which means that first *statement* and then *change* are computed again; *condition* is then computed and checked again, the whole process being reiterated until this expression is shown to be false. Note that *init* is only performed once, before the first round, while the other expressions are computed once per round, *condition* before each round and *change* after each round.

Here are a few examples of `for` statements. The following statement writes out the multiplication table for 12, that is, 1 times 12, 2 times 12 and so on, up to 12 times 12:

```
int i;
for (i=1; i<=12; i=i+1)
   Std.out.println(i*12);
```

If we have a counter, as we do here, computation need not take place with 1. The counter can be changed at will at the end of each round. For instance, we could just as well write:

```
int i;
for (i=12; i<=144; i=i+12)
   Std.out.println(i);
```

We could also declare the counter in the initialization expression. It will then only be known inside the `for` statement. (But the counter must not be given the same name as another variable declared outside the `for` statement in the actual method.)

```
for (int i=12; i<=144; i=i+12)
   Std.out.println(i);
```

We might as well take this opportunity to introduce the operators ++ and --, as well as the composite forms of the assignment operator. Statements such as:

```
i = i + 1;
k = k - 1;
```

are very common. In Java there are a couple of useful operators, ++ and -- to increase or decrease a variable's value by 1. These two may be used to simplify the way the two statements, above, are written:

```
i++;
k--;
```

The increment and decrement operators come in two variants. We can set ++ or -- either in front of the variable name (the *prefix* variant) or after it (the *postfix* variant):

```
++i;   // prefix
--k;   // prefix
```

In the above examples, it will not matter which of the two variants we choose but there is still an important difference. The expressions i++ and ++i both mean that the variable i is increased by 1 but the *values* of the expressions are different. The value of the expression i++ is the value i had *before* the increase, and the value of the expression ++i is the value i has *after* the increase. The same thing applies to the -- operator. This difference is best illustrated by an example:

```
int i, k, m, n;
i = 4; k = 7;
m = i++ * k--; // postfix.  m gets the value 4*7, or 28
i = 4; k = 7;
n = ++i * --k; // prefix.   n gets the value 5*6, or 30
```

Apart from increasing and decreasing it by 1, we may often wish to change a variable's value in other ways, for instance by adding a particular value to the variable, subtracting a particular value from the variable, or multiplying a variable by a certain number. Some examples are:

```
i = i + 2;
j = j - k;
k = k * i;
```

In such situations it can be useful to use the composite forms of the assignment operator. Then the above statements could be written as:

```
i += 2;    // same as i = i + 2;
j -= k;    // same as j = j - k;
k *= i;    // same as k = k * i;
```

There are several composite forms of the assignment operator (see Revision Table).

The operators ++, -- and composite assignments
++   increases the value of the operand by 1. The value of k++ is k's old value. The value of ++k is k's new value.
--   decreases the value of the operand by 1. The value of k-- is k's old value. The value of --k is k's new value.
+=   -=   *=   /=   %=   composite assignment operators.   The expression: x •= y;   is equivalent to: x = x • (y);

These operators work well together with the `for` statement. For example, we can write:

```
for (int i=1; i<=12; i++)
   Std.out.println(i*12);
```

or

```
for (int i=12; i<=144; i+=12)
   Std.out.println(i);
```

---

for statement

```
for (init; condition; change)
    statement;
```

The equivalent of the statements:

```
init;
while (condition) {
    statement;
    change;
}
```

Parts `init`, `condition` and `change` could be left out but the semicolon must remain.

Each part can consist of several expressions with the comma character in between.

Each of the three different parts `init`, `condition` and `change` in parentheses in the `for` statement could easily contain several expressions. For instance, we might sometimes want to initialize several variables at the beginning of a repetition. Here is an example where we want to compute the value of x^n. Let us suppose that x has type **double** and n type **int**. The result will be computed in a variable r of type **double**. Both the variable r and a counter i must be initialized before the first round. Note especially, that when one of the parts `init`, `condition` and `change` contains several expressions, the *comma character* must be inserted between them:

```
for (r=1.0, i=1; i <=n; i++)
   r *= x;
```

Sometimes the statement to be repeated in every round will be an *empty statement*, that is, nothing will be done, in which case we only write a semicolon on its own. The `for` statement, above, could then be written as follows:

```
for (r=1.0, i=1; i <=n; i++, r*=x)
   ;
```

But then, as in this example, the semicolon should be written in a separate line to show that there is an empty statement. Because a semicolon is interpreted as an empty statement and will be the statement repeated at every round, *a semicolon should never be written directly after a right-hand parenthesis character.* This applies to `while` statements as well.

One of the three parts of a `for` statement can be omitted. If, for example, there are no initializations to be done, the initialization part will not be necessary. If a part is omitted, it must be marked by a semicolon. There must always be two semicolons between parentheses in a `for` statement. We can even leave all the parts out. If the `condition` part is left out, it will be regarded as being "true":

```
for (;;)
   Std.out.println("Help, I can't stop");
```

As an example of the use of `for` statements, we will now look at a simple program which reads in, from the keyboard, several real numbers constituting a series of measurements. The program will then compute the mean value of the measurements and write it out. Finally, the program will write out all the measurements that are greater than the mean value:

```
import extra.*;

class ForDemo {
  public static void main (String[] arg) {
    Std.out.print("How many measurements? ");
    final int no = Std.in.readInt();
    double sum = 0;
    double[] m = new double[no];
    Std.out.println("Enter the measurements");
    for (int i = 0; i<no; i++)
    {
      m[i] = Std.in.readDouble();
      sum += m[i];
    }
    double mean = sum / no;
    Std.out.println("The mean is ");Std.out.println(mean);
    Std.out.println("Measurements greater than the mean:");
    for (int i = 0; i<no; i++)
      if (m[i] > mean) {
        Std.out.print("Measurement no. "); Std.out.print(i+1);
        Std.out.print(" is ");  Std.out.println(m[i]);
      }
  }
}
```

This could have the following appearance when the program is run:

```
How many measurements? 5
Enter the measurements
4.0   4.5   3.5   3.8   4.2
The mean is 4
Measurements greater than the mean:
Measurement no. 2 is 4.5
Measurement no. 5 is 4.2
```

6.6 Arrays of reference variables

The components of the arrays we have studied so far have been of simple, built-in types such as `int` and `double`, but we can also have arrays where the components are reference variables. By using arrays like these, we can build tables of objects. Suppose, for example, that we have defined a class `Point` that describes points on the screen:

```
class Point {
  int x, y;
  Point(int xx, int yy) {  // constructor
    x = xx; y = yy;
  }
}
```

There are two instance variables `x` and `y` and a constructor. We can now define an array variable that can be used to describe a pentagon:

```
Point[] f = new Point[5];
```

This will look as in Figure 6.4. Note that the individual components in the array are not

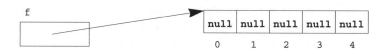

Figure 6.4

points but *references* to points. Initialization will take place automatically so that all the components will get the value `null`. If we want a component to refer to an object, we can make an assignment, exactly as for ordinary, simple variables. For example, we can write:

```
f[2] = new Point(4,3);
```

We will then get the situation in Figure 6.5.

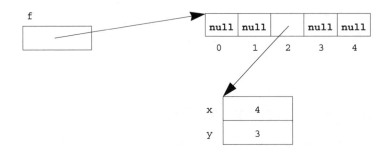

Figure 6.5

We can now access the object that component 2 in the array refers to, by using indexing. We could write the statement:

```
Std.out.println(f[2].x);
```

and this would give 4 as output.

It is also possible to initialize the components in an array when making a declaration. For example, we can write:

```
Point[] g = {new Point(1,1),  new Point(0,1),
             new Point(-1,1), new Point(0,0)};
```

Here we have an array with four components. Each component is a reference that refers to an object of class Point.

Of course, we can declare array variables where the components can be references to any kind of object. An especially interesting case is one where the components can be references to objects of class String. This makes it possible to create tables of texts, as in the following example. Note that the texts can be of different lengths.

```
String[] message = {"Turn off the tap",
                    "Open the window",
                    "Turn off the computer",
                    "Start the fan"};
```

As usual, we use indexing to get to the different texts. The statements:

```
i = 2;
Std.out.println(message[i]);
```

could give the printout:

```
Turn off the computer
```

We shall now demonstrate a slightly larger example of the use of arrays. Suppose that a company has a number of sales representatives working on commission. The total number of reps is at most 100. Every time a rep has sold something, a record of the sale is left with the company. A sales record consists of the rep's number and the amount the goods have been sold for. What we are now going to do is to construct a program which inputs a lot of sales records and outputs a compilation of how much the different reps have sold. In this compilation, we would also like to see how much commission the reps are to have. The commission on a sale is 10% of the total sales amount if this is less than, or equal to, $5,000. If the total sale exceeds $5,000, the commission is 15% of the amount exceeding $5,000. We show what the program could look like when it is run. Whatever is in italics has been written by the user. Everything else is written by the program. Sales figures can be entered in any order, and different sales figures can be entered for a particular agent (for instance, Linda Sands and Eric Anderson have each made two sales).

```
Agent? Linda Sands
Amount? 1000
Agent? Curt North
Amount? 50
Agent? Eric Anderson
Amount? 1200
Agent? Jenny Linden
Amount? 2500
Agent? Linda sands
Amount? 6000
Agent? Eric Anderson
Amount? 100
Agent? Katie Ward
Amount? 6000
Agent? The user enters Ctrl-Z here
```

	Amount	Commission
	======	==========
Linda Sands	7,000	800
Curt North	50	5
Eric Anderson	1,300	130
Jenny Linden	2,500	250
Katie Ward	6,000	650

The following class is used in the program to describe reps:

```
class Agent {
  static final double limit=5000;
  static final double proc1=0.1;
  static final double proc2=0.15;
  String name;
  double sum;

  Agent(String n) {      // constructor
    name=n;
  }

  double commission() {    // computes the commission
    if (sum <= limit)
      return sum * proc1;
    else
      return limit * proc1 + (sum-limit) * proc2;
  }
}
```

There are two instance variables called name and sum. The latter contains the total sum of a rep's sales. There are three constant class variables (limit, proc1 and proc2) used to keep account of the percentage rates and the limit applicable when sales commission is to be calculated. By defining these variables as constants, it is easy to make changes in the program if information has to be changed – for instance, if the limit for the higher percentage rate were to be raised. Note especially that the three constant variables are class variables (**static**). They will, therefore, only be found in a single edition that will be shared by all of the sales reps.

In class Agent, there is also a constructor and a method commission that calculates the commission for the agent concerned. The main program is in the following class:

```
import extra.*;
import java.text.*;

public class Report {
  static Collator co = Collator.getInstance();

  public static void main (String arg[]) {
    Agent[] a = new Agent[100];
    int noOfAgents = 0;
    co.setStrength(Collator.PRIMARY);
    // read in sales information
    while (true) {
      Std.out.print("Agent? ");
      String nn = Std.in.readLine();
      if (nn==null) // no more information
        break;
      Std.out.print("Amount? ");
      double amount = Std.in.readDouble(); Std.in.skipLine();
```

```
    // search for the name nn
    int i;
    for (i=0; i<noOfAgents && !co.equals(nn,a[i].name); i++)
        ;
    if (i == noOfAgents) {     // not found, create new rep
      a[i] = new Agent(nn);
      noOfAgents++;
    }
    a[i].sum += amount;
  }

  // write a compilation
  Std.out.getFormat().setGroupingUsed(true);
  Std.out.println();
  Std.out.println();
  Std.out.print(" ", 20);                        // 20 spaces
  Std.out.println("    Amount   Commission");
  Std.out.print(" ", 20);                        // 20 spaces
  Std.out.println("    ======   ==========");

  for (int j=0; j<noOfAgents; j++) {
    Std.out.print   (a[j].name, 20);
    Std.out.print   (a[j].sum,     10, 0);
    Std.out.println(a[j].commission(), 10, 0);
  }
 }
}
```

First, an array variable a is declared that is initialized so that it refers to an array with space for a maximum of 100 sales reps. The variable noOfAgents is used to keep an account of the number of reps that have handed in their sales information. This variable is equal to zero from the beginning.

The program begins by reading in the sales figures. This is done in a **while** statement. At each round, the program reads in the rep's name and the amount the rep has sold. The **while** statement is terminated if the user indicates *end of file* (presses Ctrl-Z or Ctrl-D) when the program asks for the rep's name. For every new sales figure read in, the program will check whether the rep concerned is already present in array a. This is done in the statements:

```
// search for the name nn
int i;
for (i=0; i<noOfAgents && !co.equals(nn,a[i].name); i++)
    ;
```

This is an example of a *linear search*. The array's components are checked from the beginning until either the desired component has been found, or all the components have been checked. Since the reps are put into the array beginning at 0, the rep put in last will be in position noOfAgents-1. The variable nn contains the name of the rep whose name has just been entered. In order to check that this name is the same as that of one of the reps already in array a, a collator co (see page 182) is used. It is worth noting that this collator treats upper- and lower-case letters as being the same. (We "happened" to write Linda Sands' last name with a small "s" when it came up for the second time in our example of the program running but everything still went well.)

If the variable i contains the value noOfAgents after the **for** statement has finished executing, this will mean that we have searched through all of the components without finding a rep with the name we have been looking for. A new rep is then created and placed last in the array a, while noOfAgents is increased by one. The total sales amount is then initialized automatically to 0 for the new rep.

The new amount is added to the previous amount for the actual rep in the **while** statement at the end of each round.

There will be three columns in the printout. The first will contain the names of the reps left-justified, while the two others will contain the sales amounts and the commissions right-justified. We would like the numbers to be written out in groups of three, so that it would be easier to read. To indicate this, we call the method setGroupingUsed for the editor used by class std. To get the printout adjusted, we make use of the fact that we can give an extra argument to the printout methods. This argument will indicate the total number of printout positions, so that when real numbers are printed out, the number of decimals desired can be indicated as well. Note that texts will be left-justified and numerical values right-justified, exactly as required in this program.

6.7 Arrays as parameters

We can, of course, have array variables as parameters for methods. An example of this can be shown by a method that can be called if we would like to give all the components in an array the same values:

```
static void initAll(int[] f, int value) {
   for (int i=0; i<f.length; i++)
     f[i] = value;
}
```

If, for example, we have made the declaration:

```
int[] a = new int[6];
```

we can make the call:

```
initAll(a,1);
```

Then all components in the array a will get the value 1. Note that the array itself is not copied during the call. The variable a is a *reference* to the array, and the parameter f will then be a copy of this reference. This means that f will refer to the same array as a.

Arrays of reference variables can also be parameters. To demonstrate this, we return to our program dealing with sales reps from the previous section. We note that the reps were not displayed in alphabetical order. If we would like this to be done, we will have to sort the array of reps before we write it out. *Sorting* is a standard exercise in data processing, and it can be carried out in many different ways. The standard class java.util.Arrays contains a class method that could be used to sort an array, but we shall not use it here. To demonstrate how sorting could be done we shall write our own sorting method by using a relatively simple technique usually called *insertion sort*. The idea here is to begin with an empty array, inserting the components one at time. The first component is placed in position number 0. The next one is put in front of, or after, the first component, depending on which is the greater. The third component is then put in the right order in relation to the two earlier ones, and so on. In this way, we ensure that the array we are building is correctly sorted after each component is inserted. Whenever we insert a new component in the array, we start at the back and work our way forwards in the array until we have found the correct position for the new component. At the same time as we carry out this process, we move the components we have searched one step to the right, in order to make space for the new component.

We can write the following method, which inserts a new rep into the array a. The last parameter indicates the number of components that were previously inserted into the array. These components lie in positions 0 to number-1.

```
static void insert(Agent newAgent, Agent[] a, int number) {
    int i=number-1;
    for (; i>=0 && co.compare(newAgent.name, a[i].name)<0; i--)
        a[i+1] = a[i];      // move one step to the right
    a[i+1] = newAgent;      // insert the new rep
}
```

We let the index i run through the array, from the back to the front. This process stops when i has become less than 0, or when the correct place has been found for the new element. The new rep's name is compared with the name of the reps in the array with the help of the collator co. A component that has been checked is moved one step to the right. When the run of the index through the array is interrupted, there will, therefore, be a free place for the new component.

This technique involves beginning with an empty array and putting the components in one by one. But how should we deal with a full array with its components unsorted? Let us look at the following method that sorts an already full array. The method has two parameters. The first is the array a that has to be sorted, and the other one indicates the number of elements in the full array. (If all the elements in the array were filled, this parameter would not be required, since we would then be able to find the number of components in the array by writing a.length.)

```
// insertion sort
static void sort(Agent[] a, int number) {
  for (int i=1; i<number; i++)
    insert(a[i], a, i);
}
```

The following idea has been used. There is a sorted part of the array on the left and an unsorted part on the right. From the beginning, the sorted part consists only of a single component (in the position 0). We then run through the unsorted part of the array, beginning at the index 1, inserting the components one by one into the sorted part. This is done with the method insert. The sorted part will then grow, until all of the components finally lie in this part and the array will be sorted.

To sort all the reps in our program from the previous section, we merely need to add the following call just before the table of reps is displayed:

```
sort(a, noOfAgents);
```

In our program of sales reps we read in information about the different reps one by one, inserting the new reps into array a. If we were able to use the method insert when inserting the reps, would the array not be sorted from the beginning, in which case we would not need to call the method sort? This is true. Let us look at how the sales rep program can be changed to accommodate this interesting idea.

When a new piece of sales information has been entered (a name and a sales figure) into the program, we have to check whether the actual agent is already in the array a. We used a linear search to do this before but, since array a is now sorted, we can use a more effective search method called a *binary search*. We carry out this search by a separate method we will call binarySearch and will begin by describing how a search in the method binarySearch is done.

We then need the array *sorted* in which we will search. To this end, we first look at the component in the middle of the array and suppose that this component contains the name *m*. If the name we are searching for comes alphabetically before *m*, we know that, if it exists, it must lie in the left-hand part of the array, since the array is sorted. If, on the other hand, the searched name comes alphabetically after *m*, then if it exists, it must lie in the right-hand side of the array. Otherwise it is possible that *m* is the name we are searching for. The solution is then simple, as we have found the name immediately. Having therefore looked at the component in the middle of the array, we will either have found the name we were looking for, or we will know which half of the array to continue searching in.

When we continue our search, we can deal with the half we are searching in as though it were a new array but smaller than the original one. We can then use the same idea from the beginning, that is, we look at the component in the middle of the new, smaller array. If the name we are searching for is not the same as the name in this component, we can decide whether to search in the array's left-hand or right-hand side. We can apply this technique yet again with the new, still smaller array. The procedure is repeated with ever-diminishing sub-arrays, until we have found the name we have been searching for, or the sub-array we are searching in has become so small that it does not contain any components. In this latter case, the searched name will not be in the array.

The method binarySearch has three parameters. The first is the name we are searching for. The second is the array and the third is an integer indicating the number of elements in the array. As result the method gives an index for the place in the array where the name that has been searched can be found. If the name is not to be found in the array, the value –1 is returned. We use the variables first and last to keep account of the first and last indices in the sub-array we are searching in.

```
// binary search
static int binarySearch(String searched, Agent[] a, int number)
{
    int first=0, last=number-1;
    while(first <= last) {
        int middle = (first + last)/2;

        if (co.compare(searched, a[middle].name) < 0)
            last = middle - 1;
        else if (co.compare(searched, a[middle].name) > 0)
            first = middle + 1;

        else // the same
            return middle;
    }
    return -1;   // not found
}
```

This search method is much more effective than a simple linear search. For example, if we have an array of 100 components, the binary search algorithm will have to check at most 7 components of the array to decide whether a particular name is in the array. If we had used a linear search, we might have had to check 100 components. Of course, the bigger the array, the more effective the binary search. In an array of 10,000 components, a binary search would require 13 components, at most, to be checked, while a linear search could require all 10,000 components to be checked.

We can now use the method `binarySearch` and assemble the part of the sales rep program where sales information is entered, as follows:

```
// read in sales information
while (true) {
  Std.out.print("Agent? ");
  String nn = Std.in.readLine();
  if (nn==null) // no further information
    break;
  Std.out.print("Amount? ");
  double amount = Std.in.readDouble();
  int i;
  // search for the name nn
  if ((i = binarySearch(nn, a, noOfAgents)) == -1) {
    Agent newAgent = new Agent(nn);
    newAgent.sum = amount;
    insert(newAgent, a, noOfAgents);
    noOfAgents++;
  }
  else
    a[i].sum += amount;
}
```

A check is made to see whether the actual sales rep is in array a, whenever a name and an amount is read in. In order to do this, the method `binarySearch` is called. The result of the search is assigned the variable i when the call is made, and then a check is carried out to see whether the value assigned to i was equal to −1. If it was, the rep was not found. We have to create a new rep and insert it into the array. The method `insert`, which we described earlier, is called to do this. If there already is a sales rep with the name nn in the array, a new rep will not be inserted into it. The variable i will then contain the index for this rep, and we instead increase the total sales amount for the sales rep concerned.

6.8 Parameters of `main`

In command operating systems such as Unix and MS-DOS, we start a program by writing a *command line*. In a command line, we first indicate the program's name, and after this we can also give arguments for the program. These arguments are normally names of files but there can be other kinds of arguments, too, such as flags of different kinds. The program name and its various arguments are usually bounded by blank characters. If, for example, we wrote the command line:

```
prog -x /r fill
```

this would mean that the program called prog should be run and that it should have the three arguments -x, /r and fill. This procedure can also be followed for Java programs. Let us suppose, for example, that we want to run the Java program MainDemo.class. Because Java programs cannot be executed directly but have to be executed by the Java interpreter, we write:

```
java MainDemo -x /r fill
```

As we have seen, a standalone Java program (but not an applet) must have a method main in which execution begins. Up to now, we have not worried very much about the appearance of the definition of main, so let us now look at the following simple class:

```
class MainDemo {
  public static void main (String[] arg) {
    for (int k=0; k<arg.length; k++)
      Std.out.println("Argument " + k + ": " + arg[k]);
  }
}
```

On the second line, we can see that the method main has one parameter. It is called arg and has type String[]. This parameter is, therefore, an array variable that refers to an array where the components are objects of class String, that is, texts. We do not call the method main as we do other methods, from inside the program. Instead, it is called from the Java interpreter when program execution begins. Let us suppose that we have written the command line as it stands above. The Java interpreter will then create an array with three components and give this array as argument to main. The text "-x" will be found in arg[0], the text "/r" in arg[1], and the text "fill" in arg[2]. We see that main in class MainDemo contains a for statement that runs for the same number of rounds as the length of the array arg. At every round, the text of the corresponding argument is displayed. The printout in this example will be:

```
Argument 0: -x
Argument 1: /r
Argument 2: fill
```

Let us take another example. The program MainDemo2 will display a message in a window. This might look as in Figure 6.6. The message for display is given as the first argument in the command line. A whole number, indicating the number of times the message is to be displayed, is given as the second argument. To get the printout in Figure 6.6, we start the program with the command:

```
java MainDemo2 "Time's up!" 3
```

Note that we have to put an argument in double quotes if it contains blank characters. The program will be shaped such that the second argument can be left out. The message will then be written out once. For example, we can write:

Figure 6.6

```
java MainDemo2 "Shut down the computer"
```

The program will have the following appearance:

```
import java.awt.*;
  class MainDemo2 extends Frame {

  public static void main (String[] arg) {
    MainDemo2 m = new MainDemo2();
    m.setFont(new Font("SansSerif", Font.BOLD, 18));
    int n;
    if (arg.length < 2)
      n = 1;   // argument no.2 is missing, write once
    else
      n = Integer.parseInt(arg[1]); // read argument no.2
    for (int i=1; i<=n; i++)
      m.add(new Label(arg[0], Label.CENTER));
    m.setLayout(new GridLayout(n,1));
    m.pack();
    m.setVisible(true);
  }
}
```

The variable n is used to keep an account of the number of times the message is to be displayed in the window. A check is made in the **if** statement to see whether the user has given both arguments or not. If the user has left out the second argument, n is set to 1. Otherwise, n should be set to the second argument. However, since n is an **int** and arg[1] is a text of type string, a conversion from text to type **int** must be made. This can be done with the help of the method parse, in a standard class called Integer.

```
n = Integer.parseInt(arg[1]);
```

(Or we could have used a NumberFormat object, as for reading input data.)

6.9 Parameters for applets

It is not only standalone programs that can have parameters. Applets, too, can have parameters. But since applets do not have a `main` method, a different way is used to send parameters to applets. Applets are started not from a command line but from an HTML file, and an applet's parameters are, therefore, given in the HTML file. As an example of this, we will look at an applet called `PolyDemo` that draws a polygon in a window. This applet will have two whole numbers as parameters. The first parameter indicates the number of corners the polygon is to have. If, for example, we give the parameter 7, a heptagon will be drawn. The second parameter indicates the heptagon's size. We have to imagine that the heptagon is inscribed in a circle, where the parameter indicates the circle's radius, expressed in pixels. Figure 6.7 shows the picture that the applet `PolyDemo` would generate if it were called with parameters of 7 and 100.

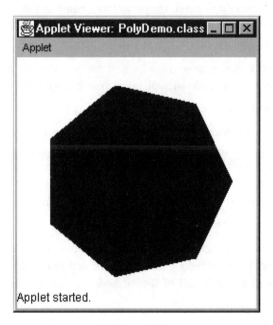

Figure 6.7

The HTML file that starts the applet `PolyDemo` will have the following appearance:

```
<html>
  <head>
    <title>PolyDemo</title>
  </head>
  <body>
    <applet code=PolyDemo.class width=250 height=250>
      <param name=number value=7>
      <param name=radius value=100>
    </applet>
  </body>
</html>
```

In an HTML file, the parameters are indicated inside an `applet` tag, between `<applet>` and `</applet>`. For every parameter, a `param` tag of the following form is added.

```
<param name=parameter name value=parameter value>
```

As can be seen, for every parameter, the parameter's name and value are indicated. We have given the parameter that indicates the number of corners, the name `number` and the parameter that indicates the circle's radius, the name `radius`.

There is a method called `getParameter` in class `Applet`. We use this method to access a parameter's value inside an applet. For example, we can write the statement:

```
String s = getParameter("number");
```

We give as argument the parameter's name. We get as result a `String` object containing the parameter's value in the form of a text. If the parameter, as is the case here, is a whole number, a conversion from text to type `int` must be made. As we saw in the previous section, this can be done with the help of the class method `parse` in the standard class `Integer`. If the variable n has type `int`, we can write:

```
n = Integer.parseInt(s);
```

In the usual way, there is a method `paint` in class `PolyDemo` that is automatically called each time the applet has to be redrawn. The polygon is drawn in the method `paint`, and this is done through a simple call of the method `fillPolygon` in the standard class `Graphics`.

```
g.fillPolygon(x, y, n);
```

The parameters x and y are two arrays of whole numbers. They will contain x- and y-coordinates for the polygon's corners. The third parameter is a whole number indicating the number of corners. The array variables x and y are initialized, and the values of the components are computed in the method `init` when the applet is initialized.

We put the polygon's centre in the middle of the window. This central point is described by the variables xo and yo. A little basic mathematics will now be necessary to understand how we calculate the coordinates to be placed in arrays x and y. (It is not necessary to understand this, so this part can be skipped.) To determine the points in the arrays x and y, we begin with a circle of radius 1, placed in the mid-point (x0,y0). The x-coordinate of a point (xi,yi) in a circle is given by the expression xi=x0+cos(v), where v is the angle between the x-axis and a line drawn from (x0,y0) to (xi,yi). The y-coordinate is similarly given by the expression yi=y0-sin(v). Mathematically speaking, there should normally be a + sign, but we have written a – sign instead because the y-axis goes downwards in a Java window and not upwards, as is usually the case. We get the angle v by dividing a complete revolution (360 degrees) into n equal angles, where n is the number of corners in the polygon.

We shall now use the standard class Math (see Section 2.10). We shall need the methods sin and cos in our program. These methods will have an angle as parameter, where it is expressed not in degrees but in radians. A complete revolution (360 degrees) corresponds to 2π radians. The coordinates in the arrays x and y can now be computed by the following statements:

```
angle = 2*Math.PI/n;
for (int i=0; i<n; i++) {
  double v = i*angle;
  x[i] = x0 + (int)Math.round(r * Math.cos(v));
  y[i] = y0 - (int)Math.round(r * Math.sin(v));
}
```

The method Math.round rounds off a real number to an integer of type **long**. We then have to make an explicit type conversion of this value to type **int** because the components in arrays x and y are of type **int**.

We are now ready to see the entire PolyDemo class:

```
import java.awt.*;
import java.applet.*;

public class PolyDemo extends Applet {
  int n, r, x0, y0;
  double angle;
  int[] x, y;

  public void init() {
    String s = getParameter("number");
    n = Integer.parseInt(s);
    s = getParameter("radius");
    r = Integer.parseInt(s);
    x0 = getSize().width/2;
    y0 = getSize().height/2;
```

```
    x = new int[n];
    y = new int[n];
    angle = 2*Math.PI/n;
    for (int i=0; i<n; i++) {
      double v = i*angle;
      x[i] = x0 + (int)Math.round(r * Math.cos(v));
      y[i] = y0 - (int)Math.round(r * Math.sin(v));
    }
  }

  public void paint(Graphics g) {
    g.fillPolygon(x, y, n);
  }
}
```

6.10 Multiple relations

In Section 4.5, we discussed how we could describe the different kinds of relations that exist between objects in Java. Arrays can be used to describe relations where an object has several sub-components of the same kind, or knows several other objects that are all of the same class. We then declare instance variables that are array variables. We will begin by describing a multiple *has* relation. As an example, we will look at the standard class Polygon in the package java.awt. This class is used to describe polygons that can be drawn into a window. The definition of the class has this structure:

```
public class Polygon {
   public int npoints = 0;   // number of corners
   public int xpoints[]; // x-coordinates for the corner points
   public int ypoints[]; // y-coordinates for the corner points

   public Polygon() {
     // creates a polygon without corners
   }

   public Polygon(int xpoints[], int ypoints[], int npoints) {
     // creates a polygon with the corner points xpoints, ypoints
   }

   public void addPoint(int x, int y) {
     // adds a new corner at the point (x,y)
   }

   more methods
}
```

The interesting things here are the two instance variables xpoints and ypoints, arrays containing the x- and y-coordinates of the corner points. This is a typical *has* relation:

a polygon *has* a number of corner points. These instance variables have been declared as **public** so that the corner points can be read from without.

There are two constructors. When we build up a polygon, we can either use the constructor that has corner points as parameter, or we can start with a polygon without corners and then call the method addPoint for each corner that is to be added. To demonstrate the latter technique we will show a new, somewhat simpler version of the applet PolyDemo on page 209. Instead of using two arrays to keep account of the corner points, we shall make use of an object of class Polygon:

```java
import java.awt.*;
 import java.applet.*;

 public class PolyDemo2 extends Applet {
    int n, r, x0, y0;
    double angle;
    Polygon p = new Polygon();

    public void init() {
       String s = getParameter("number");
       n = Integer.parseInt(s);
       s = getParameter("radius");
       r = Integer.parseInt(s);
       x0 = getSize().width/2;
       y0 = getSize().height/2;
       angle = 2*Math.PI/n;

       for (int i=0; i<n; i++)
          p.addPoint(x0 + (int)Math.round(r * Math.cos(i*angle)),
                     y0 - (int)Math.round(r * Math.sin(i*angle)));
    }

    public void paint(Graphics g) {
       g.fillPolygon(p);
    }
 }
```

Note that in method paint, we have called the method fillPolygon with an object of class Polygon as parameter. In the class Graphics, both of the methods drawPolygon and fillPolygon are overloaded. They exist in two versions, a version that has arrays with coordinates as parameters, and one that has an object of class Polygon as parameter.

The class Polygon has a number of useful methods. For example, we can check whether a particular point lies within a polygon or not; see the Revision Table.

We shall also see how the *knows* relation can be described with the help of arrays. A particular object can know several other objects that are all of the same kind. As an

java.awt.Polygon	
new Polygon()	creates a new polygon without corners
new Polygon(xp,yp,n)	creates a new polygon with n corners. The x- and y-coordinates are given by the arrays xp and yp
p.addPoint(x,y)	adds the corner (x,y) to the polygon p
p.npoints	the number of corners in the polygon p
p.xpoints	array with the x-coordinates of the corners in the polygon p
p.ypoints	array with the y-coordinates of the corners in the polygon p
p.translate(dx,dy)	moves the polygon p
p.contains(x,y)	gives **true** if the point (x,y) lies in the polygon
p.contains(q)	gives **true** if the point q (of standard class Point) lies in the polygon p
p.getBounds()	gives the smallest rectangle (of standard class Rectangle) that encompasses the polygon p

example, we will extend the class Person on page 110, so that it will be possible to describe that a person can have one child or several children.

```
class Person {
    private String name, address;
    private Person husbOrWife;
    private Person[] children = new Person[20];
    private int noOfChildren = 0;

    public void newChild(Person b) {
        children[noOfChildren++] = b;
    }

    public Person[] getChildren() {
        Person[] copy = new Person[noOfChildren];
        System.arraycopy(children,0,copy,0,noOfChildren);
        return copy;
    }

    other methods as on page 110
}
```

We have declared a private instance variable children that is an array variable, initialized so that it refers to an array with 20 components. This means that a person can have at most 20 children. The variable noOfChildren, which from the beginning has the value zero, is used to keep a check on the number of children the person has. The components in the array children are of type Person, that is, they are references to `Person` objects. As a result, persons have references to their children. They *know* their children. Each time a person gets a new child, the method `newChild` is called. We get a reference to the new child as parameter. This reference is put into the first available place in the array `children`, and at the same time `noOfChildren` is increased by one.

The method `getChildren` is called from without when we want to know which children a particular person has. This method could have been made very simple. It only needed to contain the statement:

```
return children;
```

But we have not chosen to do it like this – for two reasons. Firstly, the variable `children` is a reference to the array of children. If we had returned this reference, it would have been possible to change the children the person was a parent of, from without. This would have been contrary to the enclosure principle, which states that every object should determine its instance variables. Secondly, the length of the array the variable `children` refers to is always 20, irrespective of the number of children the person has. Had we chosen the easy way out, we would have had to add another method that returned the number of children.

We chose instead to let the method `getChildren` return a reference to a *copy* of the array the instance variable `children` refers to, and this copy has exactly as many components as the number of children. We then avoid both of the problems mentioned above at the same time.

Here are some program lines that demonstrate how the new methods in class `Person` can be called:

```
Person p = new Person("Carl Gustaf");
p.newChild(new Person("Victoria"));
p.newChild(new Person("Carl Philip"));
p.newChild(new Person("Madeleine"));
Person[] b = p.getChildren();
Std.out.println(p.getName() + " has "+ b.length + " children:");
for (int i=0; i<b.length; i++)
   Std.out.println("   " + b[i].getName());
```

The output will be:

```
Carl Gustaf has 3 children:
   Victoria
   Carl Philip
   Madeleine
```

Note that we can use `b.length` to find out the number of children there are, which would not have been possible if the method `getChildren` had returned the reference to the original array. Note, too, that making changes inside array b would have no effect on the instance variables inside the object p.

6.11 Multi-dimensional arrays

The arrays we have looked at up to now have provided us with an index to select individual components in the array. This kind of array is very useful for describing collections of several data objects, where these naturally lie in a long line. Sometimes, however, we are presented with tables that cannot be described in this way. An example of this is Table 6.1, which describes daily air and water temperatures in the Algarve, in Southern Portugal. In Java, we can make use of arrays with several indices,

	January	February	March	April	May	June	July	August	September	October	November	December
Minimum	11.5	12.0	12.9	13.5	17.0	20.5	22.2	22.5	21.5	16.0	13.5	9.9
Maximum	19.0	20.5	21.0	23.0	27.0	29.0	33.0	35.0	31.5	27.0	22.0	20.0
Medium	15.0	15.5	17.0	19.0	20.1	24.0	27.0	27.4	26.5	22.7	17.5	14.5
Water	17.0	17.5	20.5	21.0	21.5	23.0	25.0	26.0	26.0	22.7	21.0	17.5

Table 1: Daily air and water temperatures in the Algarve

or *multi-dimensional arrays*, to describe this kind of array. For example, we can declare an array variable m that can refer to tables where the individual components are of type int.

```
int[][] m;
```

The type for m is int[][]. The double square brackets indicate that m is an array variable with two indices. We can now let m refer to a table consisting of 3 rows and 4 columns.

```
m = new int[3][4];
```

We can, of course, initialize m directly with the declaration:

```
int[][] m = new int[3][4];
```

A two-dimensional arrangement of numbers is usually called a *matrix*. We could then say that m is a matrix of 3 rows and 4 columns. We are allowed to have as many indices as we like but, in practice, it is unusual to have more than two, so we will confine ourselves to just two.

The variable m is really a reference to a one-dimensional array of 3 elements, where each component is in turn a reference to an array consisting of 4 components of type int. We say that m is an *array of arrays*. Figure 6.8 shows what m will look like.

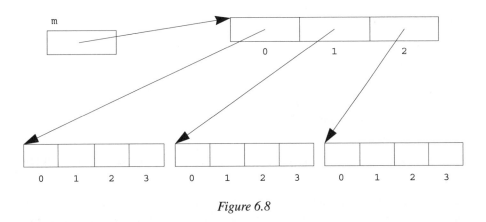

Figure 6.8

We do not have to create the dimensions of a multi-dimensional element all at once. For example, we can write:

```
int[][] f = new int[10][];
```

The array variable f is then initialized to refer to a one-dimensional array of 10 components. Each component is in turn a reference that is automatically initialized to the value null. We can then initialize the 10 components one at a time. For instance, we could write:

```
f[6] = new int[7];
```

The component number 6 in the array f would refer to an integer array of 7 components. Not all the components in a multi-dimensional array need refer to arrays that are of a similar length. If we made the statement:

```
for (int r=0; r<10; r++)
  f[r] = new int[r+1];
```

f would describe a triangular number formation, where the first row would have one component, the second row two components, the third three, and so on. We can use length to check the lengths of rows and columns. The expression:

```
f.length   // = number of rows
```

will get the value 10 and indicates the number of components in the array f refers to, or, in other words, the number of rows in the formation. The expression:

```
f[r].length   // the number of columns in row no. r
```

215

will give the number of columns in row no. r.

Multi-dimensional arrays can be initialized in connection with a declaration. For example, Table 6.1 could be described with the variable temp, declared in the following way:

```
double[][] temp =
  { {11.5,  12.0,  12.9,  13.5,  17.0,  20.5,
     22.2,  22.5,  21.5,  16.0,  13.5,   9.9},
    {19.0,  20.5,  21.0,  23.0,  27.0,  29.0,
     33.0,  35.0,  31.5,  27.0,  22.0,  20.0},
    {15.0,  15.5,  17.0,  19.0,  20.1,  24.0,
     27.0,  27.4,  26.5,  22.7,  17.5,  14.5},
    {17.0,  17.5,  20.5,  21.0,  21.5,  23.0,
     25.0,  26.0,  26.0,  22.7,  21.0,  17.5} };
```

We can see that every row of the table in the initialization expression comes between curly brackets.

Of course, we can have multi-dimensional arrays where individual components are references to objects. As an example, let us look at the following table that describes the team colours for different football teams. Each row in the table indicates the colours of a team's kit:

```
String [][]kit = { {"blue", "yellow"},
                   {"red", "white", "blue"},
                   {"red", "yellow"},
                   {"green", "black", "white"} };
```

Notice that it is permitted to have rows of different lengths even when a multi-dimensional array is declared in this way.

The easiest way of accessing an individual element in a multi-dimensional array is to use indexing. For example, we can write:

```
m[1][2] = 14;
```

We normally use repetition statements nested inside each other to run through multi-dimensional arrays. If, for instance, we want to set all the elements in the variable m to zero, we write:

```
for (int i=0; i < 3; i++)
  for (int j=0; j < 4; j++)
    m[i][j] = 0;
```

But it is pointless to insert constant values for the number of rows and columns. It would be better to use length, in accordance with the following model:

```
for (int i=0; i < m.length; i++)
  for (int j=0; j < m[i].length; j++)
    m[i][j] = 0;
```

Using this technique, we can also run through two-dimensional arrays where the rows are of different lengths:

```
for (int i=0; i<kit.length; i++) {
    Std.out.print("Team no. " + i + " :");
    for (int j=0; j<kit[i].length; j++)
      Std.out.print(" " + kit[i][j]);
    Std.out.println();
}
```

Multi-dimensional arrays are allowed to be parameters of methods. We now conclude by demonstrating a method that adds two matrices a and b, element by element, and puts the result into a third matrix c:

```
static void add (int a[][], int b[][], int c[][]) {
  for (int i=0; i < c.length; i++)
    for (int j=0; j < c[i].length; j++)
      c[i][j] = a[i][j]+b[i][j];
}
```

We have taken it for granted that the three matrices a, b and c have the same number of rows and columns.

6.12 Exercises

1. A text that can be read forwards or backwards, giving the same result, is an example of a palindrome (e.g. *madam*, *ada*). Write an applet that enters a word into a text box then writes out a message indicating whether the word is a palindrome or not. The test of the word entered should be done in a class method that will get a text as parameter, returning a value of type **boolean**.

2. Write a program that reads a text file and writes out the number of letters, digits and other characters the file contains. *Hint*: Make use of some of the class methods in the standard class Character.

3. In the Romany language, all the consonants are doubled and an "o" is placed between the doubled consonants. Vowels and other characters remain unchanged. A text file contains a secret message written in the Romany language. Write a program that reads in the file and writes out the secret message in plain English on the screen. If, for example, the file contains the text "hoheyoy alollol yoyou roromomanoniesos", the function should write out "hey all you romanies".

4. Reconstruct the program on page 176 so that it does not print out the file that has been read. The program should instead change the contents of the file so that all

tab characters are replaced by three spaces and all capitals are replaced by lower-case letters. *Hint*: Because only one file can be read or written, you must make use of another file, a temporary one. Write out the result in the temporary file, then copy the result to the original file.

5. A *prime number* is a positive integer greater than 1, which cannot be divided exactly by any other integer excepting itself and 1. A number will be a prime number if it cannot be divided exactly by a smaller prime number. Use this fact to construct a program that computes the first 50 prime numbers and puts them into a table. (If you want to decide whether a certain number k is a prime number or not, you can check to see whether k can be divided exactly by any of the numbers put into the table so far.) The program should terminate when the table with your 50 prime numbers has been printed out.

6. There is a very simple but not particularly effective sort algorithm called "bubble sort". With this method, we run through the array to be sorted, again and again. As soon as we find two elements in the array lying side by side that are not in the right order, we let them change places. Running through an array is terminated when none of the elements have changed places. The "lighter" elements, those having small values, will successively "bubble up" to the front of the array during execution – hence the name of this sort method. Write a class method that gets an integer array as parameter and sorts the array with the help of this algorithm.

7. In Exercise 3 on page 116, you had to construct the classes Person and Teacher in Figure 4.7. Your task is now to construct both of the other classes in Figure 4.7, that is, the classes Student and Course. A student can study several courses, and a course can have several students. Use multiple *know* relations.

8. The simplest form of noughts and crosses is played on a board of 3×3 squares. One player marks with crosses, and the other noughts, and they take it in turn to put their characters into a square. Thus, during a game, a given square can be empty, contain a cross, or contain a nought. The first player to get three characters in a row, column or diagonal has won.

   Construct a class Board that represents a board for the game of noughts and crosses. The class should be a subclass of the standard class Canvas, so that a board can be drawn in a window. The constructor should construct an empty board, and the following methods should exist:

   read returns a value of type **char**, which gives the marking of a particular square. Row and column numbers are given as parameters.

   place places a mark (a nought or a cross) into a particular square. Marking, rows and columns, are all given as parameters.

   move moves a mark from one square to another. Row and column numbers, for both the old and the new square, are given as parameters.

win indicates whether a player has won. Returns a `char` that contains the winner's mark. If nobody has won, a blank character is returned.

paint draws the board. It will, as usual, get a parameter of class `Graphics`.

9. In Exercise 4 on page 72 we defined a class `Article` that describes the kinds of article in stock. Your task now is to use this class to write a program that keeps track of all the articles in stock. You may assume that there is a text file containing information about the different kinds of articles. Each row in the file contains information about a kind of article, that is, the article designation, article description and the sales price. The program will first read the text file and place the information into an array with components of type `Article`. (Assume that there are no more than 1000 kinds of article in the warehouse.) Input can be terminated when, for example, the user of the program indicates the article designation "0000". The program will then repeatedly read commands from the keyboard and perform the tasks required. The different commands are (xxxx stands for the article designation):

info xxxx   Write out all the information about article xxxx
sell xxxx n Register that n items of article xxxx have been sold
buy xxxx n   Register that n items of article xxxx have been put into the warehouse

More about inheritance

What distinguishes an object-oriented language from a traditional programming language is the fact that it contains constructs enabling the use of *inheritance*. By making use of inheritance we can create new classes from already existing ones by extending them with new attributes and operations. We can, for instance, express relations such as "an athlete is a person", or "a book is a document". In Java inheritance is introduced by creating *subclasses* of already existing classes. In this chapter we shall be looking at how this is done.

By using inheritance we can create objects that are only partly equal to other objects. Such objects are defined by what are called *polymorphous classes*. In dealing with polymorphic classes, we make use of a mechanism called *dynamic binding*. Both of these important concepts are handled in this chapter.

7.1 Definitions of subclasses

By way of an introduction, we shall make use of the following class that describes houses in a very general way. The instance variables `length`, `width`, `noOfFloors` and `lastRenovation` (a year) are provided for a building, together with a method `area` that calculates the total surface area of the building. Apart from this method, there should be methods to change and read the instance variables but we shall leave this for the moment.

```java
public class Building {
    double length;
    double width;
    int noOfFloors;
    int lastRenovation; // year

    public double area() {
        return length * width * noOfFloors;
    }
}
```

7. More about inheritance

Now let us suppose that we want to describe a house, that is, a building made for people to live in. We can create a new class House that is a subclass of class Building. The new class will then automatically get the attributes that are to be found in class Building. Therefore, we shall not have to redefine the instance variables length, width, noOfFloors and lastRenovation. The only thing we need to do is to declare the new attributes we want in the subclass House. Now suppose that we want to add an instance variable indicating whether the house has been given additional insulation or not, together with a method that makes it possible to insulate a house after it has been built. The definition of class House will be:

```
public class House extends Building {
  boolean additionallyInsulated;

  public void insulate() {
     additionallyInsulated = true;
  }
}
```

Note that when we define a subclass, we use the reserved word **extends**, writing after this the name of the superclass. An object of class House will now get five instance variables, length, width, noOfFloors and lastRenovation, inherited from class Building, and additionallyInsulated, declared in class House. In addition, the inherited method area will be available for objects of class House. If we now make the declarations:

```
Building b = new Building();
House h = new House();
```

we will get the situation in Figure 7.1. Note that the object b refers to has only a Building part, while the object h refers to has both a Building part and a House part.

In class Building, we did not indicate visibility for the instance variables (**private**, **protected**, or **public** do not appear in our definition), which means that these instance variables will only be visible for other classes in the same package. If we suppose that class House lies in the same package as class Building, the instance variables in class Building will be directly visible in class House. If we want to be able to put subclasses into packages other than the package the superclass is in, we will have to indicate **protected** visibility for the instance variables we want to be visible in the subclasses.

A class that is a subclass of another class can in turn be a superclass of its own subclasses. For example, we can define a class that describes houses with several flats. We add to the new class an instance variable that indicates the number of flats in the building, together with an instance variable that indicates when the building's interior was last renovated. In addition, we have added a method that routinely computes the

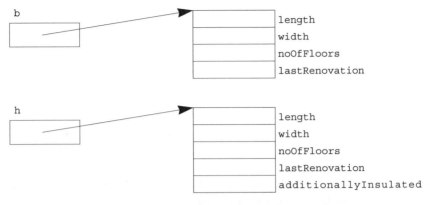

Figure 7.1

Definition of subclass

class *subclass name* **extends** *superclass name* {
    declarations of additional instance variables
    definitions of additional methods
}

rent that the building's owner can receive every year. The new class will have the following appearance:

```
public class BlockOfFlats extends House {
    int numberOfFlats;
    int lastRenovation; // refers to interior renovation
    static final double rentPerM2 = 100;

    public double calculatedRentalIncome() {
        return area() * rentPerM2;
    }
}
```

There are two things worth noting here. The first is that the variable rentPerM2 is a *class variable* and not an instance variable. This is because we gave the word **static**. The rent per square metre is, of course, not unique to each house. It applies to all the houses generally. This information does not therefore have to be included in all BlockOfFlats objects. As a result, an object of class BlockOfFlats will not have an instance variable called rentPerM2. Let us suppose that we now make the declaration:

```
BlockOfFlats f = new BlockOfFlats();
```

We will get the situation as shown in Figure 7.2.

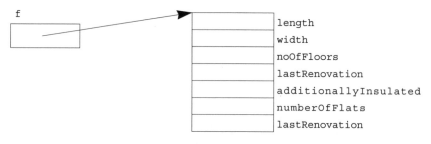

Figure 7.2

The second thing worth noting is that an instance variable was declared in class BlockOfFlats with the same name as an instance variable in a superclass. This was the instance variable lastRenovation. This is permitted and can sometimes be the intention of the programmer. In this example, we might let the instance variable declared in class Building refer to exterior renovation, while the one declared in class BlockOfFlats could refer to interior renovation. When we are dealing with two instance variables of the same name, what happens is that the instance variable in the superclass is *hidden* by the instance variable of the subclass. For example, if we write:

```
f.lastRenovation = 1998;
```

the instance variable declared in class BlockOfFlats will be changed. (We suppose that this statement lies in a class of the same package, so that the instance variables are directly visible.) How should we then proceed if we wanted to access a hidden variable? To demonstrate this, we must broach the subject of references to subclasses. We shall then return to the subject of hidden variables in Section 7.3.

A class may have several subclasses. The class Building, for example, can also have the subclasses FactoryPremises and Cinema and class House can have the subclass Bungalow. In this way, we can build a class hierarchy that will have a tree-like structure. The different classes we have discussed are illustrated in Figure 7.3.

One of the ideas behind inheritance is that, during the programming process, we should be able to make use of ready-made classes belonging to a *class library*. In Java, for example, there is the API. By so doing, we would not have to write so much program code. In addition, these ready-made classes would probably be better tested and contain fewer errors than classes we ourselves construct.

In Java, all the classes have a common, highest superclass called Object. If we wrote a class definition having the form:

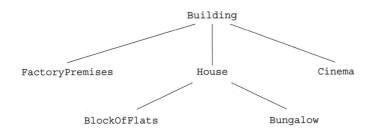

Figure 7.3

```
class C {
    ...
}
```

this would actually mean:

```
class C extends Object {
    ...
}
```

In Figure 7.3, therefore, we should really put class `Object` at the top. Class `Object` is defined in the package `java.lang` and has a number of methods common to all classes.

The word `final` can be written at the beginning of a class definition:

```
final class C {
    ...
}
```

This indicates that it is forbidden to define subclasses of this class.

7.2 References to subclasses

There are a couple of important rules governing the relations between references and subclasses. The most important of these is:

Wherever there is a value of the type "reference to C*", an expression of the type "reference to* Csub*" will suffice if* Csub *is a subclass of* C*. There is then an automatic type conversion to type "reference to* C*".*

This is because the instance variables of a superclass will always constitute a part of the object of the subclass. A `House`, for example, will always have a `Building` part – a `House` *is* a kind of `Building`. Suppose there is another method in class `Building` that compares whether the actual building is bigger than another building:

```
public boolean bigger(Building another) {
  return area() > another.area();
}
```

Let us further suppose that the variable b, as before, has type "reference to Building" and the variable h type "reference to House". Then we are allowed to write the expression:

```
b.bigger(h)
```

The next rule follows as a consequence of the first one:

A reference variable that has type "reference to c" may refer to objects that are of class c or a subclass of c.

It is, therefore, possible to do the following:

```
Building b = new Building();  // b now refers to a Building
House h = new House();
BlockOfFlats f = new BlockOfFlats();
b = h;   // b now refers to a House
b = f;   // b now refers to a BlockOfFlats
```

Note that a consequence of this rule is that a reference variable of type "reference to Object" is allowed to refer to any object at all, since class Object is a superclass common to all classes.

On the other hand, we cannot simply assign a reference of a superclass to a reference of a subclass. The assignment:

```
h = b;   // ERROR!!
```

is not allowed, for example. We cannot be sure that the object b refers to is a House. It might well be a FactoryPremises. If we are absolutely certain that the assignment is correct, we can use an explicit type conversion:

```
h = (House) b;  // Correct, but dangerous!
```

If b referred to something that was not a House there would be an interruption when the program was executed. A more reliable procedure would be first to test whether b referred to a House. To do this, we can use the **instanceof** operator:

```
if (b instanceof House)
  h = (House) b;      // Reliable
```

7.3   Hidden instance variables

We saw in Section 7.1 that there was an instance variable lastRenovation in class BlockOfFlats, with the same name as an instance variable in the superclass Building.

We wondered then how we might access the hidden variable of the superclass. Now, we must differentiate between two different instances of this: when we want to access the superclass's variable from a method in the subclass and when we want to access the superclass's variable from without. We will begin with the first case. As an example, we shall demonstrate how a method `renovate` in class `BlockOfFlats` can be added. This method has two parameters that indicate when an exterior or interior renovation was last carried out:

```
public void renovate(int exterior, int interior) {
    super.lastRenovation = exterior;
    lastRenovation = interior;
}
```

We can see here that, in a method of a subclass, we can use the reserved word **super** to gain access to things in a superclass.

If we want to access a hidden variable from without, the word **super** cannot be used. Instead, we have to use references. If we wrote:

```
Building b;
f = new BlockOfFlats();
b = f;
```

the reference variables b and f would refer to the same object, a `BlockOfFlats`, after the last statement. If we now write the statement:

```
b.lastRenovation = 1999; // exterior renovation
```

the instance variable declared in class `Building` will be affected. If, on the other hand, we write:

```
f.lastRenovation = 1999; // interior renovation
```

the instance variable declared in class `BlockOfFlats` will be affected. When we deal with hidden instance variables, it is thus the *reference variable's type* that will decide which variable is intended.

Hidden instance variables

An instance variable v in a subclass that has the same name as an instance variable in the superclass *hides* the instance variable in the superclass.

We can write **super**.v to access the instance variable in the superclass.

If a is a reference variable of type "reference to superclass" and b is a reference variable of type "reference to subclass", then b.v is the subclass's variable and a.v is always the superclass's variable, regardless of whether a happens to refer to a superclass or to a subclass.

A method is also allowed to have the same name in a subclass as in a superclass but then it will not function in the same way. We shall discuss this in the next section.

7.4 Polymorphism and dynamic binding

We saw in Section 7.1 that we were allowed to indicate the same name of an instance variable in a subclass as in a superclass. One or more of a superclass's methods can also be redefined in a subclass. It can then be said that the new subclass's method *overrides* the method in the superclass. To demonstrate this, we extend class BlockOfFlats with a new method that calculates the total surface area for a block of flats. When the surface area of the flats is calculated, the area covered by the stairs has to be deducted. (We shall suppose that the stairs take up 5% of the building's total area.) The method area in class Building will not therefore give the correct result. The new method has the following appearance:

```
public class BlockOfFlats extends House {

    as previously

    public double area() {
        return length * width * noOfFloors * 0.95;
    }
}
```

We now declare two objects, a House and a BlockOfFlats, and we give them the same length, width and number of floors.

```
House h = new House();
BlockOfFlats f = new BlockOfFlats();
h.width = 10; h.length=20; h.noOfFloors = 3;
f.width = 10; f.length=20; f.noOfFloors = 3;
```

We now calculate their area:

```
Std.out.println(h.area());
Std.out.println(f.area());
```

The result will be:

```
600.0
570.0
```

In the first case, the method area in class Building is called, and in the second the method area in class BlockOfFlats. We now declare a new reference h2 of type "reference to House" and let it refer to the same BlockOfFlats as the variable f:

```
House h2;
h2 = f;
```

We now calculate the area with the help of the new reference:

```
Std.out.println(h2.area());
```

The result will be:

```
570.0
```

It is very important in this connection to note that it is the method area in class BlockOfFlats that is called, in spite of the fact that the reference has type "reference to House", because where redefined (overridden) methods are concerned, it is the *object's class* that determines the method to be chosen. The type of the reference is of no importance. Note that this is the exact opposite of the situation in relation to hidden instance variables.

All this goes by the name of *polymorphism*. When dealing with objects belonging to polymorphous classes, we can find operations going by the same name that, logically speaking, should do the same thing on the different objects but because of the nature of the object concerned, will do something different. Let us suppose, for example, that we have two different kinds of bank account, one where interest is calculated on a daily basis and another where a minimum amount must have been deposited for a certain length of time for the account to earn interest. Logically speaking, the operation "calculate interest" does the same thing for the two different types of bank account but the computation will be done in a different way. There is a mechanism in the object-oriented languages called *dynamic binding* which provides a standard procedure for dealing with the kind of objects we have discussed here. We do not have to determine the nature of the object ourselves; instead, a language mechanism sees to it that the correct operation is performed when the program is executed.

In Java, *dynamic binding* can best be explained by the following illustration. When a method m is called through a reference r, that is, when a call of the form r.m(*arguments*) is made, the Java interpreter will examine the kind of object r refers to. Let us suppose that the object belongs to the class c. If for class c there is a method called m that has parameters that match the given arguments in number and type, then this method is called. If such a method cannot be found in class c, the Java interpreter will check to see whether there is one in c's nearest superclass s1. If such a method can be found here, it is called. If it cannot be found in s1 class s1's nearest superclass s2 will be examined, and so on. The Java interpreter begins at the bottom in the inheritance hierarchy, searching its way up until it finds the method it is looking for. If we tried to write a program where an appropriate method could not be found either in class c or in one of its superclasses, we would get an error message when trying to compile the program.

In fact, earlier in the book we saw a number of examples where dynamic binding was used, and this was in all of the programs using a graphical user interface. These programs had in common the fact that they contained classes that had a method called paint. This method is defined in class Component, a superclass for all classes that describe GUI components. Many of the different subclasses of Component overrode the method paint and defined their own version. (For example, we saw several examples where we wrote our own version of method paint.) As we saw, the method paint was called automatically every time a component had to be redrawn. The call was made with dynamic binding; as a result, different versions of method paint were called for different kinds of graphics components.

Note that dynamic binding is quite a different mechanism to overloading, which we looked at in Section 2.7. Overloaded methods might have the same name but *different* parameters and the methods could be defined in the same class. We saw how the compiler chose the method appropriate to the parameters and the arguments given when the call was made. In the case of dynamic binding the methods will have *both* the same name and the same parameters but they must lie in different classes.

In Section 7.3 we saw that the reserved word **super** could be used inside a method in a subclass to access hidden instance variables in a superclass. The word **super** can also be used if we want to call overridden methods. For example, we can give an alternative version of the method area in class BlockOfFlats:

```
public double area() {
   return super.area() * 0.95;  // call area in class Building
}
```

This can often be useful when we want to do roughly the same thing in a subclass as in a superclass.

Dynamic binding

A method m in a subclass that has the same name and parameters as a method in the superclass *overrides* the method in the superclass.

If r is a reference variable and the call r.m(*arguments*) is made,
the class of the object that r refers to determines the method to be called.
The type of the reference r is irrelevant. The search for the first appropriate method takes place from the bottom upwards in the class hierarchy.

We can write **super**.m in the subclass to access the method in the superclass.

Sometimes we may want to prevent a particular method from being overridden in subclasses. Then we can write the reserved word **final** in the definition of the method. If, for example, we had written in class Building:

```
public class Building {
   . . .
   public final double area() {  // must not be overridden
     return length * width * noOfFloors;
   }
   . . .
}
```

we would not have been allowed to redefine the method area in one of the subclasses of class Building, for example in class BlockOfFlats. We can use final as a safety measure to make sure that the actual method will not be changed in a subclass. In this connection, we should point out that methods defined with the word private cannot be overridden (they are, of course, not visible outside the class). Class methods, that is, methods defined with the word static, must not be overridden, either. Of course, it is not possible to override methods lying in classes that are defined with the word final (see page 225), as these classes cannot have subclasses.

7.5 Constructors and inheritance

Objects belonging to a subclass are initialized, as are other objects, by making use of constructors. When one of these is called, the data members inherited from the superclass must also be initialized. This will happen when a constructor for the superclass is called. The constructor will initialize the part of the object inherited from the superclass. The rest of the object will be initialized by the constructor defined especially for the subclass. In this section we shall see how this is done and consider the rules that apply. We continue to use class Building, with its subclasses, as an example.

In Section 2.6, we learned that if we failed to define a constructor for a class, the Java compiler would itself define a constructor without a parameter. This applies to all classes, both superclasses and subclasses. Up to now in this chapter, we have created new Building objects of different kinds by writing expressions having the form new Building(), new House() and new BlockOfFlats(). This worked well precisely because automatically generated constructors without parameters existed.

Meanwhile, we can define our own constructors, and this applies to subclasses as well. To demonstrate this, we begin by defining two constructors for the superclass Building:

```
public class Building {
   double length;
   double width;
   int numberOfFloors;
   int lastRenovation;

   Building() {}

   Building(double l, double w, int f) {
      length=l; width=w; noOfFloors=f;
   }
```

   as previously
```
}
```

The first constructor is one without parameters that does nothing. We only define it to be able to create new houses without indicating arguments. We should like to write:

```
Building b = new Building();
```

The second constructor is one that makes it possible to indicate the length, width and number of floors for a building when it is created. For instance, we can now write:

```
Building b = new Building(10,20,3);
```

Of course, we saw in Section 2.6 that if we defined our own constructor as we have done here, the compiler would no longer define a parameterless constructor itself.

The following four steps take place in succession when a constructor for a subclass is executed:

1. All the variables in the subclass are set to their default values (that is, the value 0, or equivalent).
2. A constructor for the superclass is called.
3. The instance variables in the subclass with explicit initialization expressions are initialized to these values.
4. The statements in the subclass's constructor are executed.

In order to demonstrate this, we shall define some constructors for the class House:

```
public class House extends Building {
   boolean additionallyInsulated;

   House(boolean insul) {
      additionallyInsulated=insul;
   }

   House() {
      additionallyInsulated=true;
   }
```

```
House(double l, double w, int f, boolean insul) {
  super(l, w, f);
  additionallyInsulated=insul;
}
House(double l, double w, int f) {
  this(l, w, f, true);
}
```
as previously
```
}
```

The first constructor makes it possible to write something like:

```
House h = new House(true);
```

In step 2, above, a constructor was called for the superclass. If nothing in particular has been indicated in the subclass's constructor, the superclass's *parameterless* constructor will always be called. In that case, if no parameterless constructor is available in the superclass, the program will be faulty. In this example, this means that the instance variables `length`, `width` and `noOfFloors` will all get the default value 0, as the parameterless constructor for class `Building` does nothing. The instance variable `additionallyInsulated` is then set to the given value.

The second constructor for the subclass `House` is a parameterless constructor. Because nothing in particular is said, this one will automatically call the parameterless constructor in superclass `Building`.

If, in step 2, we want a constructor other than the parameterless one to be called, we have to indicate this explicitly. In order to do this, we use the reserved word **super**. This is shown above in the third constructor for class `House`, where the constructor for the superclass with three parameters is called. Note that when we use the word **super** in this way to indicate the constructor to be used, the call of the superclass's constructor must be the *first statement* of the superclass's constructor. We can now create houses with expressions of the form:

```
House h = new House(10,20,3,false);
```

We can also use the word **this** in subclasses to let a particular constructor call another for the same class, exactly as in Section 2.6. This is shown, above, in the fourth constructor. Making use of this, we can give expressions of the form:

```
House h = new House(10,20,3);
```

Then the instance variable `additionallyInsulated` will get the value **true**. What happens is that the fourth constructor is called first. It calls the third constructor, which in turn calls the superclass's constructor with three parameters.

These rules apply to all inheritance levels. If, for instance, we defined the following parameterless constructor for class BlockOfFlats:

```
BlockOfFlats() {}
```

it would call the parameterless constructor for class House, which would then function as described above.

7.6   The method finalize

Constructors are called automatically to initialize new objects. Similarly, there is a method called finalize that is called automatically just before an object is to be subjected to garbage collection (see page 46). This method is defined in the following way in class Object and is inherited by all classes:

```
protected void finalize() throws Throwable { }
```

As we can see, the method does nothing but it can be redefined in classes that have a special need to "clean up after them". This may apply to classes that use files which should be closed afterwards. This may look like this:

```
public class C extends A {
   ExtendedReader in = ExtendedReader.getFileReader(filename);
   public void finalize() throws Throwable  {
     in.close();       // clean up in this class
     super.finalize(); // clean up in the superclass
   }
   other methods
}
```

Note that we should always call the method finalize for the superclass. Constructors always call a constructor for the superclass automatically but there is no such mechanism for the method finalize.

In addition to files, there are other system resources that sometimes have to be set free explicitly, but in the large majority of cases, it is not necessary to redefine the method finalize. Finally, we should point out that method finalize may not be called every time an object is no longer required. If no garbage collection has to be carried out, finalize will not be called. If a program ends without garbage collection, the system resources used are usually set free by the operating system.

7.7 Object collections and class `Vector`

Dynamic binding is a powerful mechanism that is central to object-oriented programming languages. It is often used in dealing with collections of several objects. The objects in a collection can be of different classes but these classes must have a common superclass. In Java this is not a problem, as all classes automatically have a common superclass, `Object`. Objects placed in a collection usually have a common property, for instance, that they can be drawn on the screen or written out in a file. We can find an example of object collections in the standard GUI class `Container`. A `Container` object has an internal list of all the components included in the container, and all the objects in the list have in common the fact that they are of classes that are subclasses of the class `Component`. All the objects in the list can, therefore, be drawn on the screen by a call of the method `paint`.

To study collections of components, we shall begin with the following classes that describe different kinds of vehicle. Class `Vehicle` is the superclass that all the classes will have in common. It has two subclasses, `MotorVehicle` and `Bike`. Class `MotorVehicle` has in turn the two subclasses `PrivateCar` and `Truck`. For each class, we have defined a simple constructor that initializes new objects of the class. Note that we have used the technique of calling the superclass's constructor in some of these constructors. We have also defined for class `Vehicle` a method called `print` that writes out information about the object concerned. This method has then been overridden in the different subclasses, as a result of which each class has its own version of it. Note, too, that in the subclasses `PrivateCar` and `Truck` in the methods `print`, we call the superclass's version of `print` to write out the part of the information that is found in the superclass. The different vehicle classes will look like this:

```
import extra.*;

public class Vehicle {
  public void print() {
    Std.out.println("A vehicle");
  }
}

public class MotorVehicle extends Vehicle {
  String regNum;

  public MotorVehicle(String no) {
    regNum = no;
  }

  public void print() {
    Std.out.println("A motor vehicle with reg no: " + regNum);
  }
}
```

```
public class PrivateCar extends MotorVehicle {
  int numSeats;

  public PrivateCar(String no, int n) {
    super(no);
    numSeats = n;
  }

  public void print() {
    super.print();
    Std.out.println("A private car with " + numSeats +" seats");
  }
}

public class Truck extends MotorVehicle {
  int maxL;

  public Truck(String no, int load) {
    super(no);
    maxL = load;
  }

  public void print() {
    super.print();
    Std.out.println("A truck with " + maxL + " kg maximum load");
  }
}

public class Bike extends Vehicle {
  int numGears;

  public Bike(int g) {
    numGears = g;
  }

  public void print() {
    Std.out.println("A bike with " + numGears + " gears");
  }
}
```

Let us now suppose that there is a company that hires out cars and bicycles. To keep track of all the company's vehicles, we use a computer program with the following array. We will assume that the company has a maximum of 100 different vehicles:

```
Vehicle[] veh = new Vehicle[100];
```

We can then let the different components in array veh describe different vehicles:

```
veh[0] = new PrivateCar("ABC123", 5);
veh[1] = new Truck("XYZ999", 10000);
veh[2] = new PrivateCar("PPP000", 6);
veh[3] = new Bike(10);
```

Note that in spite of the fact that the components in the array `veh` will be references to objects of class `Vehicle`, we are allowed to let the components refer to objects belonging to subclasses of this class. We say that we have a *heterogeneous object collection*, as the objects included in the collection are not of the same type.

Now let us suppose that we want to output information about all of the firm's vehicles. We can then construct a repetition statement that runs through all of the components in the array `veh` and gives information for all the components not equal to `null`.

```
for (int i=0; i<veh.length; i++)
   if (veh[i] != null) {
     veh[i].print();  // dynamic binding
     Std.out.println();
   }
```

To output the information, we call the method `print` for every object. Note that these calls all take place with dynamic binding. This means that different versions of `print` will be called for different types of object. In our example, we get the printout:

```
A motor vehicle with reg no: ABC123
A private car with 5 seats

A motor vehicle with reg no: XYZ999
A truck with 10000 kg maximum load

A motor vehicle with reg no: PPP000
A private car with 6 seats

A bike with 10 gears
```

We have used an array to build up an object collection. It is relatively easy to use arrays for this but there are a number of disadvantages. For instance, we have to determine the array's size when creating it, and elements cannot be inserted without moving the other elements in the array. However, there is a very useful standard class called `Vector` in the package `java.util` that more or less functions like an array but without its limitations. To demonstrate how we can use this class, we shall build a vector that contains texts. We begin by declaring a `Vector` object:

```
Vector v = new Vector();
```

We then get a vector of size 0, that is, one that does not contain any components. There are different methods we can use to add components to a vector. The simplest one is `addElement`, which adds a new element to the last position in the vector. We can write:

```
v.addElement("EEE");
v.addElement("VVV");
v.addElement("XXX");
```

where the vector `v` will contain the three components `"EEE"`, `"VVV"` and `"XXX"`, in positions 0, 1 and 2, respectively. A vector's size can be determined by calling the method `size`. The call `v.size()`, therefore, returns the value 3. It is also possible to indicate a vector's size explicitly by calling the method `setSize`. If the size is reduced, the components that cannot be accommodated are removed from the vector; if the size of the vector is increased, the new components will get the value `null`.

The method `insertElementAt` adds a new component to a certain position. The components that are already there are moved a place to the right to make way for the new component. Indexing takes place, as usual, from 0. For example, if we write:

```
v.insertElementAt("JJJ", 0);    // put in "JJJ" first
```

the component `"JJJ"` will be placed in position number 0, that is, first in the vector. The three components already in v will be moved a place to the right, landing in positions 1, 2 and 3, and the size of v will be increased from 3 to 4.

Individual components can also be changed; this is done with the method `setElementAt`. For instance, we can change component number 1 so that it will contain the text `"AAA"`:

```
v.setElementAt("AAA", 1);       // change "EEE" to "AAA"
```

The three methods `addElement`, `insertElementAt` and `setElementAt` all have in common the fact that their first parameter is of type `Object`. Because all Java classes have class `Object` as a superclass, it will be possible to insert any kind of object into a vector. (Remember the rule on page 225!) It is even possible to insert different kinds of objects into the same vector. We then get a heterogeneous data collection.

The method `removeElementAt` can be used to remove components. We indicate as argument the index for the component to be removed. For example, we can write:

```
v.removeElementAt(3);    // remove "XXX"
```

When a component is removed, all the components to the right of the component removed are moved a place to the left, and the size of the vector is reduced by one.

The method `firstElement` can be used to read the value of the first component in a vector without changing anything inside the vector, `lastElement` will return the vector's last element, and `elementAt` has an index as parameter that indicates the component to be read. These three methods all return a value of type `Object`, that is, a reference to any object whatsoever. This means that we often have to make an explicit type conversion to the type we want. Let us suppose, for example, that we want to write out component number 1 in the vector v. We can then make the statements:

```
String s = (String) v.elementAt(1);   // explicit type conversion
Std.out.println(s);
```

In the first line, there is an explicit type conversion from type `Object` to type `String`. (As it happens, we would not have needed to make an explicit type conversion in this case, because the method `println` can also be found in a version that has a parameter of type `Object`.) Another example of the use of the method `elementAt` is given in the following line where element number 1 is copied and the copy put last in the vector. (It is the reference to the text object that is copied and not the text itself.)

```
v.addElement(v.elementAt(1));   // copy "AAA"
```

We may often wish to run through all the elements of a data collection. If we want to do this for all the elements in a vector v, we can first make a **for** statement where we let an index run from 0 to `v.size()-1`, calling `v.elementAt` at every round. Meanwhile, there is a more general technique that we can use in all data collections. We can use an *iterator*. An iterator is an auxiliary object that can be connected to a particular data collection. This auxiliary object will have knowledge of how the data collection is constructed internally and will be able to run through it efficiently. To do this, we call methods in the iterator, instead of calling methods in the data collection itself. We will begin by describing how iterators of the standard class[1] `java.util.Enumeration` are used. In order to get an iterator of type `Enumeration` that is connected to a particular vector, we call the method `elements`. The expression `v.elements()` gives as result an iterator that is able to run through the vector v. The class `Enumeration` only has two methods: `hasMoreElements`, which returns the value **true** if there are components remaining in the data collection being scanned, and the method `nextElement` that returns the next component in the data collection. The method `nextElement` returns a value of type `Object`, as do the methods `firstElement`, `lastElement` and `elementAt`, so we usually have to make an explicit type conversion when we call `nextElement`. To show how all of this works, we construct a **for** statement to run through and write out all the components in vector v. The variable e is the iterator we use. It is an object of class `Enumeration` and is initialized to be connected to the vector v:

```
for (Enumeration e=v.elements(); e.hasMoreElements(); ) {
  s = (String) e.nextElement();
  Std.out.println(s);
}
```

The printout will be:

```
JJJ
AAA
VVV
AAA
```

In J2SDK version 1.2 many new standard classes for collections were introduced. (We will discuss them in Section 15.5.) In order for the class `Vector` to be adapted to the

---

[1] It is actually an interface and not a class but this is of no account here.

new pattern, some of its methods have been given alternative names. The methods
`addElement` and `insertElementAt` have been named `add`, and `setElementAt`,
`elementAt`, `removeElementAt` and `removeAllElements` have been named `set`, `get`,
`remove` and `clear`, respectively. We could therefore rewrite the statements above:

```
v.clear();              // remove all elements
v.add("EEE");           // put "EEE" last
v.add("VVV");           // put "VVV" last
v.add("XXX");           // put "XXX" last
v.add(0, "JJJ");        // put in "JJJ" first
v.set(1, "AAA");        // change "EEE" to "AAA"
v.remove(3);            // remove "XXX"
String s = (String) v.get(1);  // explicit type conversion
Std.out.println(s);     // print "AAA"
v.add(v.get(1));        // copy "AAA" to the last position
```

(Please note, on lines 5 and 6, that the arguments to `add` should be given in reverse
order compared to `insertElementAt`.) In J2SDK two new iterator classes were also
introduced. Iterators of type `java.util.Iterator` or `java.util.ListIterator` can be
used to run through vectors. We could, for instance, write the following lines to print
out all elements in `v`:

```
for (Iterator i=v.iterator(); i.hasNext(); ) {
   s = (String) i.next();
   Std.out.println(s);
}
```

We can see that the method `elements` in class `Vector` is replaced by a method named
`iterator` and that the methods `hasMoreElements` and `nextElement` in class `Enu-`
`meration` are replaced by the methods `hasNext` and `next` in class `Iterator`.

In class `Vector`, an array is used internally to keep track of the components included in
the vector. The length of this array is called the vector's *capacity*. The number of
components included in the vector, that is, the vector's size, is always smaller than, or
equal to, the length of the internal array. In other words, the vector's size is always
smaller than, or equal to, its capacity. If we add so many components to an array that
the vector's capacity does not suffice, the class `Vector` will automatically allocate a
new and larger internal array and use this one instead. A vector's capacity thus
increases automatically when necessary. If nothing in particular is indicated when a
vector is created, it will, from the beginning, get a capacity of 10; every time the
internal vector does not suffice, a vector double the size will be allocated. The capacity
is, therefore, doubled. If we roughly know the capacity required by a vector, we can
indicate the vector's original capacity when we create a new vector. In this way, we can
avoid time-consuming and unnecessary memory allocations. For example, we might
write:

```
Vector v = new Vector(500); // capacity 500
```

We can also indicate the space we need each time there is not sufficient capacity.

```
Vector v = new Vector(500, 50); // increase by 50
```

When a vector has reached its final size, it is possible to save space by calling the method `trimToSize`. This reduces the vector's capacity so that it becomes equal to the vector's size.

The class `Vector` contains several methods, among them methods to search for a particular object. A compilation is given in the Revision Table.

So far, we have demonstrated that the class `Vector` can be used for dealing with objects of class `String`, but `Vector` can be used for handling any collections of objects, including heterogeneous object collections. As an example of this, we can now write a new version of the program lines that construct and output the collection of vehicles. Note that we must make an explicit type conversion to the class `Vehicle` when we read the component in the vector. Compare this with page 236:

```
Vector u = new Vector();
u.addElement(new PrivateCar("ABC123", 5));
u.addElement(new Truck("XYZ999", 10000));
u.addElement(new PrivateCar("PPP000", 6));
u.addElement(new Bike(10));

for (Enumeration e = u.elements() ; e.hasMoreElements();) {
  Vehicle ve = (Vehicle) e.nextElement(); // explicit cast
  ve.print();                             // dynamic binding
  Std.out.println();
}
```

Had one of the components not been of class `Vehicle`, or one of its subclasses, we would have got an execution error on making the type conversion. It was successful here because we only put vehicles into the vector. In heterogeneous object collections, it can sometimes be necessary to check a component's type before making the type conversion. We then use the operator **instanceof**. For example, we can write:

```
for (Enumeration e = u.elements() ; e.hasMoreElements();) {
  Object o = e.nextElement();
  if (o instanceof Vehicle)
    ((Vehicle) o).print();  // safe explicit type conversion
  Std.out.println();
}
```

The class `Vector` can be used as an alternative to arrays in order to describe multiple relations; see Section 6.10. The vector `u`, above, might then be an instance variable in a class `CarHirer`, describing the situation where the car hirer *has* a particular vehicle.

java.util.Vector	
new Vector()	new vector with a capacity of 10, is doubled when necessary
new Vector(k)	new vector with a capacity of k, is doubled when necessary
new Vector(k, d)	new vector with a capacity of k, is increased by d when necessary
setSize(n)	sets the size to n
size()	returns the size of a vector (no. of components in the vector)
isEmpty()	gives **true** if the vector contains no components
capacity()	returns the capacity
ensureCapacity(k)	ensures that the vector has a capacity of at least k
trimToSize()	sets the capacity so that it is equal to the size
addElement(x)	puts the object x last in the vector; the size is increased by 1
insertElementAt(x,i)	inserts the object x into position no. i; previous components from and including position no. i are moved to the right; size increased by 1
setElementAt(x,i)	sets the object x into position no. i; the component previously occupying this place is removed
removeElementAt(i)	removes component no. i; the components from and including position i+1 are moved to the left; the size is reduced by 1
removeAllElements()	removes all the components; the size becomes 0
firstElement()	returns the first component, return type: Object
lastElement()	returns the last component, return type: Object
elementAt(i)	returns the component in position no. i, return type: Object
contains(x)	gives **true** if the object x is in the vector
indexOf(x)	gives the index for the first occurrence of x, gives −1 if x is not there
indexOf(x,i)	as indexOf(x), but begins to search at position no. i
lastIndexOf(x)	gives the index for the last occurrence of x; gives −1 if x is not there
lastIndexOf(x,i)	as lastIndexOf(x), but searches backwards from position no. i
copyInto(a)	copies the components into the array a
clone()	gives a copy of the vector (only the references are copied)
elements()	returns an iterator; return type: Enumeration
e.hasMoreElements()	gives **true** if the vector to which the iterator e refers, contains more components; e has type Enumeration
e.nextElement()	gives the next component in the vector the iterator e refers to

From J2SDK version 1.2 there are also methods specified in the interfaces Collection and List; see Section 15.5. This means that the following methods have been given alternative names: addElement=add, insertElementAt=add, setElementAt=set, elementAt=get, removeElementAt=remove, removeAllElements=clear

7.8 Abstract classes

The method `print` for the class `Vehicle` (see page 235) is really quite meaningless since, when we call it, the only result is that we get the printout, `"A vehicle"`. However, we still defined it because we wanted to be sure that a method `print` would be available for every object in one of the subclasses of `Vehicle`. Let us suppose, for example, that we declare a new subclass, `Tram`. We shall further suppose that we forgot to define a new method `print` for class `Tram`. Objects belonging to class `Tram` will then inherit the method `print` from class `Vehicle`. The method `print` must be available to all the subclasses of class `Vehicle` for us to be able to use dynamic binding. If we have a reference variable `ve`:

```
Vehicle ve;
```

and we make the call:

```
ve.print();
```

the method `print` must be available for all the objects that `ve` might refer to.

We do not have to find a "superfluous" method for a superclass in order to be sure that all the objects will have this method. What we can do instead is to declare an *abstract method*. An abstract method will not be implemented, so we cannot call it; it is merely a marker for a real method. We will now demonstrate this by turning the method `print` in class `Vehicle` into an abstract method. The definition of class `Vehicle` looks like this:

```
public abstract class Vehicle {
   public abstract void print();
}
```

The reserved word **abstract** indicates that `print` is an abstract method. There must be no body in the method definition because the method `print` will not be implemented. Instead, a semicolon is written after the head of the method definition.

In the first line, we have indicated that all of the class `Vehicle` is to be abstract. If a class contains one or more abstract methods, we have to indicate in this way that the class is to be abstract. (We are in fact allowed to declare a class as abstract even though there are no abstract methods in it.) The peculiar thing about an abstract class is that it is not allowed to create objects of such a class, for if it were, we could create objects for with methods were not implemented. We may only create objects of non-abstract classes, where all the abstract methods have been overridden by "proper" methods. Thus, we may not create objects of class `Vehicle`, but one of the things we can do is to create objects of class `Bike` if this class, as previously, has its own version of the method `print`.

```
public class Bike extends Vehicle {
  int numGears;

  public Bike(int g) {
    numGears = g;
  }

  public void print() {  // overrides an abstract method
    Std.out.println("A bike with " + numGears + " gears");
  }
}
```

If we define a new class that is a subclass of an abstract class, we are actually allowed not to define our own versions of the superclass's abstract methods. Then the new class must also be declared as abstract and we cannot create objects of the new class. For instance, if we removed the definition of the method print in class MotorVehicle, this class would also have to be declared as abstract. Then we would not be allowed to create objects of class MotorVehicle. However, we may create objects of the subclasses of class MotorVehicle as before, since these have defined their own versions of the method print.

We create an abstract class so that it can serve as a model for its different subclasses. The abstract superclass defines the methods that must be present in all subclasses. Many of the standard classes in Java, such as the classes Component and Container, are abstract. We are not supposed to create objects of these classes, only of their subclasses.

Abstract methods and classes

A method can be declared as abstract:

```
abstract result_type m(parameters);
```

Abstract methods have no implementation. A class with one or more abstract methods must be defined as an abstract class.

```
abstract class C {
  . . .
}
```

No objects of an abstract class can be created. Subclasses that do not have their own versions of all abstract methods must also be abstract.

Let us suppose, in another example, that we work with applications where geometric figures of different kinds are to be drawn at the screen. We can then obtain an abstract superclass, Figure. Starting with this class, we can define different subclasses for different kinds of figures, for example circles, rectangles or lines. The class Figure may contain the abstract methods `draw` which draws a figure at the screen and `area` which calculates the area of a figure. But an abstract class may also contain normal methods which are not abstract. Suppose, for example, that the class `Figure` contains two instance variables `x0` and `y0` which define the starting point of a figure. If we let all subclasses of `Figure` have coordinates in relation to the point (`xo`, `yo`) then in class `Figure` we can define a non-abstract method `move` that moves a figure simply by changing the instance variables `x0` and `y0`.

Figure 7.4 demonstrates how abstract classes are described in UML. A diagram for an

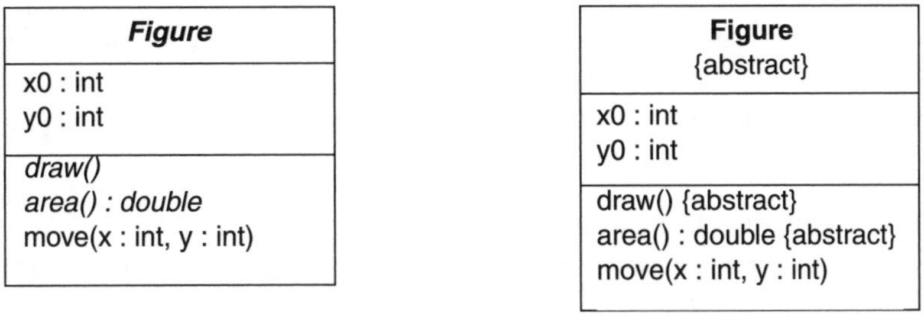

Figure
x0 : int   y0 : int
draw()   area() : double   move(x : int, y : int)

Figure   {abstract}
x0 : int   y0 : int
draw() {abstract}   area() : double {abstract}   move(x : int, y : int)

Figure 7.4 An abstract class

abstract class looks like an ordinary class diagram (see Figure 2.2 on page 37) but the class name and the abstract methods should be marked in a special way. There are two alternatives. You can either set the class name and the names of the abstract methods in italics, as in the diagram on the left in Figure 7.4, or you can use the marker {abstract} as in the diagram on the right in the figure.

7.9 Interface

The class `Bike`, which we studied in the earlier sections, is a subclass of class `Vehicle`. Now let us suppose that we want to draw bikes on the screen. One way to bring this about would be to define `Bike` as a subclass of the standard class `Canvas`. We would then be able to use all of the different standard methods to draw. However, this is not allowed in Java since a class may only have one superclass. If we were able to have more than one, we would be making use of *multiple inheritance*, a mechanism found in C++, for instance, but one that is not allowed in Java. Multiple inheritance is a powerful mechanism but it can sometimes cause technical problems, and for this reason it is not found in Java. To compensate for this, Java has something called *interface*.

As we have seen, some of the methods in an abstract class can be abstract, that is, they can lack implementation. We could say that an interface is a kind of abstract class where *all* of the methods are abstract. Because class `Vehicle` only has one method and this one is abstract, we can remake class `Vehicle` into an interface:

```
public interface Vehicle {
   public void print();
}
```

This looks like a class definition but we write the word **interface** instead of **class**. Note that we do not need to write the word **abstract** for the method `print`. In an interface, all the methods are abstract, so we do not need to indicate anything in particular. (But we can write **abstract** if we like.)

It is true that a particular class may only have one superclass but it may inherit properties from several interfaces. This is what makes interfaces so useful. We can now define class `Bike` in the following way, for instance:

```
public class Bike extends Canvas implements Vehicle {
   int numGears;

   public Bike(int g) {
      numGears = g;
   }

   public void print() {
      Std.out.println("A bike with " + numGears + " gears");
   }

   public void paint(Graphics g) {
      // draws the bike
   }
}
```

We have let `Bike` be a subclass of class `Canvas` but we have also allowed it to inherit properties from the interface `Vehicle`. When we inherit properties from an interface, we say that we *implement* the interface, and we use the reserved word **implements** to indicate this. To make this consistent with the other kinds of vehicle, we also have to redefine class `MotorVehicle` so that it implements the interface `Vehicle`, instead of being a subclass of class `Vehicle`.

```
public class MotorVehicle implements Vehicle {
   as previously
}
```

We are allowed to declare reference variables that refer to interfaces exactly as we declare reference variables that refer to classes. For instance, we can write:

```
Vehicle ve;    // reference to interface
```

However, we cannot create objects of class `Vehicle`, since an interface is like an abstract class. Consequently, the reference `ve` can never refer to an object of type `Vehicle`. But it can refer to objects of classes that implement the interface `Vehicle`. The two rules in Section 7.2 describing the relationship between references and subclasses also apply to interfaces, for which we can reformulate them:

If A *is a class and* Asub *is a subclass of* A *or if* A *is an interface and* Asub *is a class that implements* A, *then the following will apply: everywhere a value of type "reference to* A*" is required, an expression of the type "reference to* Asub*" can be given equally well. There will then be an automatic type conversion to the type "reference to* A*".*

For a reference variable r *that has the type "reference to* A*", the following will apply: if* A *is a class,* r *can refer to objects that are of class* A *or are of a subclass of* A. *If* A *is an interface,* r *can refer to objects that are of a class that implements* A.

So the following are allowed:

```
Bike  bi = new Bike(5);
Vehicle ve;
Canvas ca;
ve = bi;
ca = bi;
```

If a method in an interface is called, dynamic binding always takes place. In the call:

```
ve.print();   // dynamic binding
```

the method `print` in class `Bike` is called, since the reference variable `ve` happens to refer to a `Bike` object.

Since an interface can only contain abstract methods and never "proper" ones, a class that implements an interface will never really inherit anything, but such a class is guaranteed to have defined its own versions of all the methods enumerated in the interface. So we use interfaces to indicate that a class has certain general properties. There is, for example, an interface called `Runnable` among the Java standard classes that contains a definition of only one method, a method called `run`. Classes that implement the interface `Runnable` will have the property that they can be executed in parallel with each other. To make this possible, they merely have to define their own version of the method `run`. (We shall return to this in Chapter 9.)

A class can implement more than one interface. Let us suppose, for example, that we have defined the two interfaces `Drawable` and `Storable`:

```
public interface Drawable {
  public void draw();
}

public interface Storable {
  public void store();
}
```

If we now wanted all objects of class `Building` to be drawable and storable, we could give the definition:

```
class Building implements Drawable, Storable {
  public void draw() {

    . . .

  }

  public void store() {

    . . .

  }
  as previously
}
```

If a class implementing an interface does not contain its own definition of a method defined in the interface, the class must be declared as abstract. If we were to leave out the definition of the method `store` in class `Building`, this class would have to be declared as abstract and the method `store` would instead be defined in the subclasses of `Building`.

An interface can inherit other interfaces. The new interface will then become a *sub-interface*. We might write:

```
public interface Vehicle extends Drawable, Storable {
  public void print();
}
```

Then all the classes implementing the interface `Vehicle` have to give their own definitions of the three methods `draw`, `store` and `print`. Note that an interface can inherit several other interfaces.

We can use references to interfaces instead of references to classes when we form collections of objects. For instance, we could create an array that contains drawable objects:

```
Drawable[] r = new Drawable[100];
r[0] = new PrivateCar("ABC123", 5);
r[1] = new Truck("XYZ999", 10000);
r[2] = new Bike(10);
r[3] = new Building();
```

Interface

An interface is an abstract class that can only contain abstract methods. It may also contain constants that are **final** and **static**.

```
interface I {
  result_type m1 (parameters) ;
  result_type m2 (parameters) ;
  static final int k = constant_value ;
}
```

No objects of an interface can be created.

A class can implement an interface. The abstract methods and constants are then inherited. A class can implement several interfaces.

```
class C implements I1, I2 {
  . . .
}
```

Classes that do not have their own versions of all the abstract methods must be abstract. We can declare and work with references to interfaces in the same way as with references to classes.

This is a heterogeneous object collection, but because all the objects included in array r are of a class that implements the interface Drawable, there will be a method draw for all the objects. So we could write:

```
for (int i=0; i<r.length; i++)
  if (r[i] != null)
    r[i].draw();
```

Of course, we can also use the standard class Vector to form a heterogeneous object collection of drawable objects. We could then have written:

```
Vector v = new Vector();
v.addElement(new PrivateCar("ABC123", 5));
v.addElement(new Truck("XYZ999", 10000));
v.addElement(new Bike(10));
v.addElement(new Building());
```

We have to make an explicit type conversion to type Drawable for every object when we want to draw all of the objects in the collection. (This will be fine, since we know that all the objects that have been put into the vector are of a class that implements the interface Drawable.)

```
for (Enumeration e=v.elements(); e.hasMoreElements();) {
    Drawable dr = (Drawable) e.nextElement();
    dr.draw();
}
```

Apart from abstract methods, an interface may also contain definitions of constants and these may be defined as `final` and `static`. For instance, we can write:

```
public interface Storable {
    static final int blockSize = 1024;
    public void store();
}
```

Then all the classes implementing the interface `Storable` can make use of the constant `blockSize`.

We shall round off the discussion of interfaces by demonstrating how interfaces are described in UML. On the left in Figure 7.5 there is a diagram for the interface

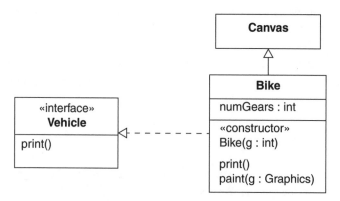

Figure 7.5 Interface diagram and interface implementation

`Vehicle`. An interface diagram looks very much like an ordinary class diagram, but the stereotype «interface» should be written above the name of the interface. Since an interface cannot have instance variables the attribute compartment may be left out. Only the compartment with operations must be shown. An interface may only contain abstract operations. Therefore, it is not necessary to mark the operations as abstract by setting their names in italic or using the marker {abstract}.

On the right in Figure 7.5 a diagram for the class `Bike` is shown. (Compare this with the definition on page 246.) The dashed line with the hollow arrow means "implements" and the arrow to the class `Canvas` means, as before, that `Bike` is a subclass of Canvas. There is another, simpler, way to represent that a class implements an interface. We can draw a little circle with the name of the interface. This is demonstrated in Figure 7.6.

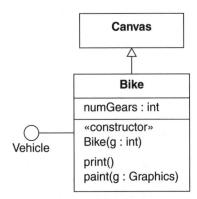

Figure 7.6 Interface implementation

If a class C uses an interface I which is implemented by one or more classes, we say that the class C is *dependent* on the interface I. If something is changed in I then the class C must also be changed. A *dependency relation* is shown in UML as a dashed line with an open arrow. Suppose, for instance, that we have a class Owner. An owner can own vehicles of different kinds and an owner must be able to call the method print to get a presentation of his vehicles. This means that the class Owner is dependent on the interface Vehicle. This is demonstrated in Figure 7.7.

Figure 7.7 A dependency relation

If we want to show that the dependent class C is dependent on another class C2 to implement a certain interface we can use the notation with the little circle. If we, for instance, want to describe that an Owner is dependent on class Bike to implement the interface Vehicle we can illustrate this as in Figure 7.8.

The dashed arrow shows the dependency. The solid line shows (as before) an association between objects of classes Owner and Bike.

251

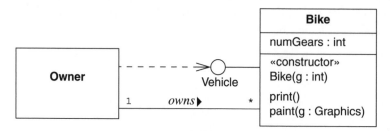

Figure 7.8 A dependency relation with association

7.10 An object-oriented example

It is now time to show a longer example constructed according to object-oriented principles. We shall write a program that allows the user to play the card game Twenty-one with the computer. The game is played in the following way: the user receives one card at a time and after each card, makes a decision whether or not to have another card. The user has to try to make the sum of a "hand" as near to 21 as possible, without exceeding this number. An ace is counted as either 1 or 14. If the number 21 is exceeded, the player loses and the computer wins. But if the player stops at a number under 21, the computer has to draw one card at a time, after each card deciding whether to continue or not. If the computer has more than 21 points or a score lower than the player's, the player wins; otherwise the computer wins. The computer, therefore, wins if both have the same number of points.

We begin by defining a class Card that describes cards. There is a constructor, so that we can initialize new cards, and methods so that we can look at a card's suit or value. In addition, there is a method toString that gives the card's value in the form of a text, for example, "Clubs Jack". The colours are represented by a whole number between 1 and 4. (1 = clubs, 2 = diamonds, 3 = hearts and 4 = spades.)

```
import extra.*;

public class Card {
  private final static String[] stab =
                    {"Clubs", "Diamonds", "Hearts", "Spades"};
  private final static String[] vtab =
                    {"Ace",  "2",  "3",  "4",  "5",  "6",  "7",
                     "8","9",  "10",  "Jack",  "Queen",  "King"};
  private int s, v;
```

```
public Card(int suit, int val) {
  if (suit < 1 || suit > 4 || val < 1 || val > 13) {
    Std.out.println("Card: illegal arguments");
    System.exit(1);
  }
  s = suit;
  v = val;
}

public int suit() {      // 1=cl, 2=di, 3=he, 4=sp
  return s;
}

public int value() {     // Ace=1
  return v;
}

public String toString() {
  return stab[s-1] + " " + vtab[v-1];
}
}
```

To describe a collection of playing cards, we then define a class Cardstack. An object of class Cardstack can describe either the cards in a player's hand, or the whole deck of cards.

```
public class Cardstack {
  private Card[] stack = new Card[52];
  private int number = 0;

  public int noOfCards() {
    return number;
  }

  public void throwCards() {
    number = 0;
  }

  public Card lookAt(int no) {
    return stack[number-no];
  }

  public void layTop(Card c) {
    stack[number++] = c;
  }

  public  Card dealTop() {
    return stack[--number];
  }
```

```
public void newPack() {
   throwCards();
   for (int s=1; s<=4; s++)
     for (int v=1; v<=13; v++)
       layTop(new Card(s,v));
}

public void shuffle() {
   for (int i=1; i<1000; i++) {
     int n1 = (int) (Math.random() * number);
     int n2 = (int) (Math.random() * number);
     Card temp  = stack[n1];
     stack[n1] = stack[n2];
     stack[n2] = temp;
   }
}
}
```

A stack of cards consists of, or "has", a maximum of 52 cards, and we put these into the array stack, which is a private instance variable. We also keep track of how many cards are currently in the stack by using the variable number. The method noOfCards gives us the number of cards currently in the stack. Because the variable number is initialized to 0, each new stack of cards will be empty from the beginning. We can call the method throwCards in order to remove all the cards from a stack.

The bottom card lies at place number 0 in the array stack, while the top card is in the position with the number number-1. In order to look at the cards without removing them from the stack, we use the method lookAt. In the parameter no of the method lookAt, 1 means the top card, 2 the next one down, and so on. To take the right card, therefore, we must pick the card with the index number-no from the stack.

To add new cards to a stack of cards, we use the method layTop, and to take cards from the pack we call the method dealTop. In the method dealTop, it is extremely important that we write --number and not number-- because the reduction in number must occur *before* we do the indexing. Similarly, it is important that in the method layTop, we write number++ and not ++number, since it is the *old* value of number we shall be indexing with.

If we want to change a stack of cards so that it contains a new deck of 52 cards, we can call the method newPack, in which we run through all the combinations of colours and values. The constructor for class Card is called once for each combination.

The method shuffle shuffles the cards in a stack, mixing them randomly. This is especially useful if the stack contains a new deck that has to be shuffled before the beginning of play. The method shuffle will run for 1000 rounds. At every round, it randomly chooses two whole numbers, n1 and n2, in the interval 0 to number-1. It then changes the places of the cards for places n1 and n2 in the stack. The standard method Math.random is called to select random numbers. When it is called, this method will return a random real number x as result, where x is in the range $0 \leq x < 1$. We multiply this result by number and convert it to type **int**. We will then get a whole number in the interval 0 to number-1. (The decimals are removed when the conversion is made to type **int**.)

Note that both Card and Cardstack are completely independent of the game that will be played. They are quite general in character and could just as easily be used to write a program for a game of Patience.

Our next class is the class Player, which describes a participant in a game of Twenty-one. This class is, of course, intended only for this game:

```
public abstract class Player {
  protected Cardstack pack;
  protected Cardstack hand = new Cardstack();
  protected int p;   // actual points

  public Player(Cardstack st) {
    pack = st;
  }

  public void newGame() {
    hand.throwCards();
    p = 0;
  }

  public Card newCard() {
    Card c = pack.dealTop();
    hand.layTop(c);

    // calculate new points
    int numAces = 0;
    p = 0;
    for (int i=1; i<=hand.noOfCards(); i++) {
      int v = hand.lookAt(i).value();
      if (v == 1) { // an ace
        p += 14;
        numAces++;
      }
      else
        p += v;
    }

    for (int j=1; j<=numAces && p>21; j++)
      p -= 13;   // count an ace as 1
    return c;     // return the new card
  }
```

```
    public int points() {
      return p;
    }

    public abstract void play();
}
```

A player has three instance variables: hand is a stack of cards that describes the cards in the hand of the player, pack is a *reference* to the pack used in the game and p is used to save a player's actual points. The variable pack is an excellent example of the relation "knows". A player must know the pack of cards used in the game to be able to draw cards from it. The variable pack is, therefore, initialized in the constructor. As parameter the constructor will get a reference to the pack to be used. In other words, when a new player is created, this player will find out about the pack to be used. It is important for both players to use the same pack, so the relation "has" would not work here. If we had written in class Player:

```
Cardstack pack = new Cardstack();   // ERROR!
```

each player would have his or her *own* pack to play with, and this would be entirely independent of the pack the other player had.

The method newGame is called every time a player is to begin a new game. Then all the cards used earlier are abandoned and the actual points are set at 0.

The method newCard is called every time the player has decided to take another card. The method draws the card at the top of the pack and puts it into the player's hand. The new points are then calculated. If the points come to more than 21, an attempt is made to calculate one or more of the aces as 1 instead of 14. The method newCard gives as result a reference to the new card drawn.

The method points is self-explanatory: it simply returns a player's actual points.

The class Player has been defined as an abstract class because it contains an abstract method, play. There are to be two kinds of players in our program, the person running the program and the computer, so we will define two subclasses of class Player, the classes Human and Computer. We define for each of the two subclasses its own variant of the method play. The subclass Human will look like this:

```
import extra.*;

public class Human extends Player {
  public Human(Cardstack st) {
    super(st);
  }
```

```
public void play() {
  boolean newCardWanted = true;
  newGame();
  while (p < 21 && newCardWanted) {
    Std.out.println("You got " + newCard() +
                    " and have " + p + " points");
    if (p < 21) {
      Std.out.print("One more card? ");
      String answer = Std.in.readLine();
      newCardWanted = answer.equals("")||answer.equals("y")||
                      answer.equals("yes");
    }
  }
}
```

The method newCard in the superclass is called in method play to draw a new card. The card and the total number of points is written out after each card. (Note that the method toString in class Card is called automatically.) After this, the human player is offered another card, the player's answer to this being read into the String variable answer. If the human player only presses the Enter key, or simply writes a single "y", or "yes", the answer will be interpreted as being in the affirmative. All other answers will be interpreted as negative.

The other subclass, the class Computer, is simpler. It looks like this:

```
import extra.*;
public class Computer extends Player {
  private Player opponent;

  public Computer(Cardstack st, Player opp) {
    super(st);
    opponent = opp;
  }

  public void play() {
    newGame();
    while (p < 21 && p < opponent.points()) {
      Std.out.println("The computer got " + newCard());
    }
    Std.out.println("The computer has " + p + " points");
  }
}
```

A new card is taken in the method play as long as the computer's points come to less than those of its opponent. For the computer and the human player to know each other's points, the two opponents must know one another. We, therefore, use another "knows" relation. The private instance variable opponent can contain a reference to the opponent. This instance variable is initialized in the constructor with a parameter that is a reference to the opponent.

Now we only have to define the class that will begin the game, and we allow this to take place in a class with the name TwentyOne. In this class there are three objects: the pack to be used, together with the two players (called you and I). Note that they are initialized so that both players will know the same pack of cards, and the computer player will know the opponent. The program begins as usual in the method main, where an object of class TwentyOne is created. The constructor is then called in which the game itself will start:

```java
import extra.*;
public class TwentyOne {
  Cardstack pack = new Cardstack();
  Human you  = new Human(pack);
  Computer I = new Computer(pack, you);

  public static void main(String[] arg) {
    TwentyOne t = new TwentyOne();
  }

  // Constructor
  TwentyOne() {
    Std.out.println("Welcome to twenty-one");
    boolean newGameWanted = true;
    while (newGameWanted) {
      pack.newPack();
      pack.shuffle();
      you.play();
      if (you.points() > 21)
        Std.out.println("You lost!");
      else if (you.points() == 21)
        Std.out.println("You won!");
      else { // the computer must play
        I.play();
        if (I.points() <= 21 && I.points() >= you.points())
          Std.out.println("You lost!");
        else
          Std.out.println("You won!");
      }
      Std.out.print("New game? ");
      String answer = Std.in.readLine();
      newGameWanted = answer.equals("") || answer.equals("y") ||
                      answer.equals("yes");

    }
  }
}
```

Finally, here is an example of what the program can look like when it is run:

```
Welcome to twenty-one
You got Diamonds Ace and have 14 points
One more card? y
You got Clubs Jack and have 12 points
One more card? y
You got Spades 10 and have 22 points
You lost!
New game? y
You got Hearts 8 and have 8 points
One more card? y
You got Clubs 6 and have 14 points
One more card? y
You got Spades 4 and have 18 points
One more card? n
The computer got Hearts 7
The computer got Clubs 10
The computer got Diamonds 6
The computer has 23 points
You won!
New game? n
```

7.11 Exercises

1. Starting with class `Person` in Exercise 2 on page 72, construct a new derived class `Student`, with appropriate members. In addition, construct a new class `Course`, relating it to class `Student` in an acceptable way.

2. Starting with class `Person` in Exercise 2 on page 72 and using the class `MotorVehicle` on page 235, define a class `CarOwner` that describes a person who can be the owner of one or more vehicles. Make use of the standard class `Vector`.

3. In the previous exercise it was assumed that the owner of a vehicle was always a natural person "of flesh and bone". Write new class definitions which allow an owner to be a person in the legal sense, that is, a corporation of some sort. A corporation has, in turn, one or more owners. Beginning with an abstract superclass `Owner` and an interface `Thing`, show whether it is possible to define the situation that certain classes, for example, persons, can be the owners of one or several things and that certain other classes, for example, persons in the legal sense of corporations (entities), can be both owned and owners at the same time.

4. Different kinds of animal can be defined using classes and inheritance. Define some animals by beginning with a class `Animal` and deriving the different animals from this class. Feel free to use such intermediate classes as `Mammal`, `Insect`, `Bird` and so on. Arrange for the class `Animal` to have an abstract method `cry` that

259

describes the sound an animal makes. Implement this method in the different subclasses.

Now declare an array of animals, writing statements to run through the array. Let all the animals in the array emit a cry.

5. Descriptions of geometric figures are often used as examples in the context of object-oriented programming. First define a class `Point` that defines a point (x, y) in a two-dimensional coordinate system. Then declare an abstract class `Figure` that contains a starting point. Let class `Figure` have an abstract method `area`.

   In addition, define a number of subclasses of the class `Figure`, for example `Circle`, `Triangle` and `Rectangle`. Give them suitable instance variables. Let each subclass have its own version of the method `Area`.

   Finally, declare an object of class `Vector` to describe a collection of figures and write the statements that are necessary to calculate and write out the area for all the figures in the collection.

6. Construct a class `Passenger` to define a passenger who travels by air. A trip can be composed of several flights (use class `Flight` on page 112). A passenger must, therefore, know these. There should be a constructor that initializes a passenger with the appropriate flight departures. Here you should check that times and flights correspond, so that the person will not take a flight which leaves before the previous flight has been completed. There should also be a method with which you can replace one flight by another. Check here, too, that times and flights correspond. If a flight is delayed, a passenger may need to change the flight that follows. Write a method that checks whether this is necessary for a particular passenger.

7. Complete the class `Cardstack`, in Section 7.10, with an operation that combines two stacks of cards into one. (Make sure that the combined stack does not contain more than 52 cards.) Now use the classes `Card` and `Cardstack` to write a program that plays the card game *Starve The Fox*. This game is played by two players. First, all the cards are dealt out so that each player gets a stack of 26 cards each. One of the players plays his top card, after which the two players take it in turns to play a card. The player who first plays a higher card of the same suit as the card first played may then take all the cards on the table and put them under his stack. If the card that is first played happens to be an ace, it is counted as 1; aces are worth 14 points otherwise. The player who loses all his cards also loses the game.

Exceptions

Writing a computer program is no mean feat and even an experienced programmer can make mistakes. Three categories of common errors can arise:

- *Compilation errors.* These are errors that arise because the rules of the language have not been followed. The compiler will discover them when an attempt is made to compile the program, and the result is normally a printout listing the various errors. Examples of ordinary compilation errors include a variable name wrongly spelt, a curly bracket omitted, a semicolon missing, or the wrong key pressed when the program has been entered.

- *Execution errors.* These are errors that arise when the program is run. The program may use the correct language and follow all of its rules but may still contain errors that prohibit its functioning normally during execution. Examples of such errors are the attempt to index outside the boundaries of an array, attempting to use a reference variable that, at the time, does not refer to an object, or attempting to open a file that does not exist.

- *Logic errors.* These are errors due to faulty program design, the root of the problem being the algorithm used. This kind of error is the most difficult to find, since the program can be both compiled and run without error printout resulting. A logic error will only reveal itself when the program has been test-run and an incorrect result is obtained. If tested data is unavailable, the programmer will find it difficult to be sure that his or her program is free from logic errors. A program may work for a particular set of input data but prove to be erroneous for another.

In this chapter we shall study errors of the second category, execution errors. Situations may arise during the execution of a program that can be regarded as exceptional. In fact, such situations are termed *exceptions*. There can be different kinds of exceptions.

When a method is being written, the algorithm should be as clear and easy to understand as possible. But if checks were inserted at each stage of the algorithm to handle every imaginable error and abnormal event, the algorithm would become very clumsy and hard to follow. In Java, there is a mechanism for handling exceptions. A method in which the error arises generates an exception which, according to predetermined rules, is passed on to other methods where the exception can be "caught" and dealt with.

Two separate stages can be distinguished when working with exceptions. In the first, an exception is generated, and in the second the exception is handled, "caught". We shall begin by describing what happens in the easier of these two stages, that is, how exceptions are generated.

8.1 Automatically generated exceptions

An exception is described by the use of an object that will belong to a subclass of the standard class `java.lang.Throwable`. There are two standardized subclasses of `Throwable`, the classes `java.lang.Error` and `java.lang.Exception`. These subclasses have in turn several different subclasses. The class `Error` and its subclasses are used by the Java interpreter to signal errors of different kinds, such as linking errors or lack of memory space, and will almost always lead to the program being interrupted.

Subclasses of `java.lang.Exception` are used to signal minor errors that can usually be caught by the program, possibly preventing program interruption. Such minor errors include so-called runtime errors, such as indexing outside array boundaries, or giving incorrect arguments for methods. Runtime errors are automatically signalled by the Java interpreter and are described with objects that are of a subclass of the class `java.lang.RuntimeException`, which in turn is a subclass of class `java.lang.Exception`. Runtime errors are usually produced by mistakes in the program itself. For example, an attempt to index outside an array's boundaries should not be found in a well-written program.

Another common type of error arises during input and output. We might try to open a non-existent file, or attempt to read from a file, in spite of the fact that *end of file* has been reached. This type of error is automatically signalled by the different classes in the package `java.io` and is described with subclasses of the class `java.io.IOException`, which also is a subclass of the class `java.lang.Exception`. Subclasses of the standard class `Exception` are shown in Figure 8.1. (There are more in other packages.)

When an exception occurs, normal execution is immediately interrupted, and control of the program is transferred to the part that catches the exception. Several activities, called threads, can be running in a Java program at the same time. (This will be

Figure 8.1 Exception classes

described in Chapter 9.) If an exception is not caught, the task in which the exception occurred will be terminated abruptly. In a normal program not making use of a graphical user interface, this usually leads to the program being interrupted. Printout is then produced informing the user of the kind of exception involved and the part of the program in which it occurred. A stack trace is also produced. This is a printout giving the order of the calls of the various methods when the exception took place. Let us suppose that we have the following program lines in a method called readAnswer:

```
Std.out.println("Do you want to continue? ");
String s = Std.in.readLine();
if (s.equals("yes")) {
   ...
}
```

Let us further suppose that the user of the program writes Ctrl-Z (or Ctrl-D) to indicate that he does not want to continue. The method readLine will then return the value

null. The variable s becomes equal to **null**, which means that we attempted to call the method equals with a empty reference. The Java interpreter will then generate an exception. Execution of the program is interrupted, producing the printout:

```
java.lang.NullPointerException
    at Extest.readAnswer(Extest.java:6)
    at Extest.main(Extest.java:17)
```

From this we can see that the error occurred in the method readAnswer, in line number 6 of the file Extest.java. We can also see that the method readAnswer was called from the method main, in line number 17 of the same file. This error is really the result of faulty programming and could have been avoided had the programmer had a little more foresight, forming the **if** statement in the following way:

```
if (s != null && s.equals("Yes"))
    ...
}
```

Let us suppose, in another example, that we define an array of whole numbers with 100 components and that we want to set the whole array to zero. We write the statements:

```
int[] a = new int[100];
for (int i=1; i<=100; i++)
    a[i] = 0;
```

When these lines are executed, the program will be interrupted, producing the error printout:

```
java.lang.ArrayIndexOutOfBoundsException: 100
    at Extest.initAll(Extest.java:12)
    at Extest.start(Extest.java:21)
    at Extest.main(Extest.java:27)
```

We have tried to index outside the array and we see from the error printout that an index value of 100 was involved. We also note that the error occurred in method initAll, in line 12. This method was called by the method start in line 21. The method start was in turn called by the method main, in line 27. Again, there is a programming error here. As we know, an array is indexed beginning at 0, which means that the last component should have the number 99 and not 100.

As a third example of automatically generated exceptions, we can look at the program FileCopy2, from page 93. The program reads in the name of the file to be copied. It then tries to connect a stream to the file with this name:

```
System.out.print("Name of the input file? ");
System.out.flush();
String name = myIn.readLine();
BufferedReader inputFile = new BufferedReader
                         (new FileReader(name));
```

Let us suppose that we are running the program and indicate the file name `mydata.txt` as input data. If there is no file of that name, the program will be interrupted with the error printout:

```
java.io.FileNotFoundException: mydata.txt
    at java.io.FileInputStream.<init>(FileInputStream.java:64)
    at java.io.FileReader.<init>(FileReader.java:43)
    at Copy2.main(Copy2.java:10)
```

In the first line, we see that the faulty file name was `mydata.txt`. Then in the second line we learn that the error occurred in the constructor (`<init>` means constructor) in the class `FileInputStream`. The third line shows that this constructor was called from the constructor in class `FileReader`, and the last line says that this constructor was in turn called from line number 10 in our program.

This example clearly shows that an exception must arise if the user indicates an incorrect file name. On the other hand, the error could have been caught and interruption of the program avoided. We shall see how this is done later in the chapter.

The exception `ArithmeticException` is generated automatically when there is an error in calculations involving whole numbers, such as an attempt to divide by zero. On the other hand, errors arising in connection with calculations involving real numbers will not generate exceptions. In order to discover such errors, we have to make use of methods `isInfinite` and `isNaN`. (See page 44.)

8.2 Exceptions generated by the programmer

As is clear from this, several common types of error are signalled automatically by the Java interpreter. We can also generate exceptions ourselves by executing a **throw** statement. This has the general form:

```
throw ex;
```

where *ex* is an object of an exception class.

All exception classes have definitions of the form:

```
public class class_name extends superclass_name {
    public class_name();
    public class_name(String s);
}
```

We see that there are two constructors, one without parameters and one that will have an argument of class `String`. We often create an exception object directly in the **throw** statement and then write an expression with one of the forms:

```
throw new E();
throw new E("a message");
```

Here, *E* will be the name of a subclass of the class `Throwable`. We normally only make use of subclasses of `Exception`. We can either indicate the name of one of the many standard classes, or of a subclass that we ourselves have defined. If we like, we can give a message as argument, and it can be read later when the exception has been caught. We can therefore use the message to insert extra information that could be useful, such as information about the reason for the exception.

If we wanted to generate an exception of the standard class `ArithmeticException`, we could write:

```
throw new ArithmeticException("x too big");
```

In Chapter 6 on page 209, we showed an applet that drew a polygon on the screen and this applet got two parameters from the HTML file. The first parameter indicated the number of corners in the polygon and the second the polygon's radius. We can now complement the method `init` in this applet with statements that check the values of the parameters:

```
public void init()
{
    String s = getParameter("number");
    n = Integer.parseInt(s);
    if (n < 3)
        throw new IllegalArgumentException("number < 3");
    s = getParameter("radius");
    r = Integer.parseInt(s);
    if (r < 0)
        throw new IllegalArgumentException("the radius < 0");
    as before
}
```

If we now give incorrect arguments to the applet, execution will be interrupted and the message will be displayed in the web browser's message line. (If `appletviewer` is run, the message is written out in the text window `appletviewer` started from.)

We can also declare our own subclasses for class `Exception`. We could give the definition:

```
public class CommunicationException extends Exception {
  public CommunicationException() {
    super();
  }
  public CommunicationException(String s) {
    super(s);
  }
}
```

We declared two constructors here to generate exceptions both with and without messages:

```
throw new CommunicationException("Timeout in reader");
throw new CommunicationException();
```

It is also possible to add instance variables in an exception class. For instance, in the class CommunicationException, we could have added an `int` that indicated the number of the actual communication channel. Then we could also have defined a third constructor enabling us to initialize the channel number. An example of an exception class with an extra instance variable is class ArrayIndexOutOfBoundsException. This has an `int` that indicates the incorrect index.

---

throw statement

```
throw new E();
throw new E("message");
```

where *E* is a subclass of Exception.
Normal execution is interrupted when a **throw** statement is executed.

8.3 Specification of exceptions

The technique of handling exceptions is based on catching exceptions occurring in the methods that have been called. Various means can be applied to deal with different kinds of exceptions. But how do we know what type of exception a method called can generate? One way of knowing this is to read the program code for the actual method but, of course, this is not possible in practice when applied to methods that are a part of large programs and which themselves call other methods. Another way is to read the documentation available about the actual method and hope that it contains information about the different kinds of exception that can be generated.

In Java this problem has been solved differently. A method declaration can contain a *specification* of the exceptions the method can generate. Suppose, for example, that we construct a method m and we know that only exceptions of type E1 and E2 can occur in this method. We can then define the method in the following way:

```
void m(parametrar) throws E1, E2 {
  ...
}
```

Last in the method head we write the reserved word **throws** followed by an enumeration of classes for the exceptions that can be generated. When we now want to make use of the method m, we will be aware of the kinds of exceptions we will have to catch. With "**throws** E1,E2,E3..." we write a "**throws** clause" but for the sake of simplicity we shall call it an *exception list*.

The exceptions that can be generated in a method are both such exceptions as the method itself generates by containing **throw** statements and those generated by other methods called by the actual method. Among these methods are methods in standard classes that can generate all the kinds of exceptions, as shown in Figure 8.1. It would therefore be inelegant, to say the least, if in every method we had to enumerate all the kinds of exceptions that this method was capable of generating. For this reason, exceptions have been divided into two categories: those that must be specified in exception lists and those that do not have to be specified. The former are called *checked* exceptions and the latter *unchecked* exceptions. Unchecked exceptions are those that belong to the class Error, or one of its subclasses, or to class RuntimeException, or one of its subclasses. Such exceptions then do not have to be enumerated in exception lists. This applies to exceptions normally generated by the system but not those generated by the programmer.

If the compiler discovers that a method might generate an exception of a kind not given in its exception list, we will get a compilation error. This means that if, in a method m1, we call another method m2 that can generate the checked exception E, then we must in m1 either ensure that the exception E is caught so that it cannot escape from m1, or include E in the exception list in m1. Let us suppose that we want to write a method readDouble that with the support of Java's standard classes will read in a real number. (Compare this with page 83.) As parameter we give the stream that we will read from. The method will look like this:

```
public static double readDouble(BufferedReader in)
                          throws IOException, ParseException {
  String s = in.readLine();
  NumberFormat nf = NumberFormat.getInstance();
  return nf.parse(s).doubleValue();
}
```

Because the call of `readLine` can generate an exception of class `IOException` and the method `parse` can generate `parseException`, both of these classes will have to be enumerated in the exception list.

If another method, for example the method `main`, now calls the method `readDouble`, then either this method must catch the two exceptions `IOException` and `parseException`, or enumerate them in its own exception list. This might look as follows:

```
static BufferedReader myIn = new BufferedReader(new
                            InputStreamReader(System.in));

public static void main (String arg[])
                            throws IOException, ParseException {
   . . .
   double d = readDouble(myIn);
   . . .
}
```

However, we must bear the following points in mind: First, if an exception of class `E` could be generated in a method, a superclass could be indicated for `E` in the method's exception list. For example, if we have a method that can generate an exception of class `FileNotFoundException`, this method's exception list might look like **throws** `IOException` since `FileNotFoundException` is a subclass of `IOException`.

Second, suppose that we have a method that overrides a method in a superclass, that is, a method that has the same name and parameters as the method in the superclass. Then for the method in the subclass, the checked exception classes indicated in its exception list must either also be found in the superclass's exception list, or be subclasses of classes in the superclass's exception list. The method in the subclass may also have fewer classes in its exception list.

Specification of exceptions

There must be an *exception list* in a method declaration where exceptions that might arise in the method without being caught are enumerated.

   return type m(*parameters*) **throws** E1, E2, E3 {

Classes `Error` and `RuntimeException` and their subclasses need not be enumerated.

Alternatively, a superclass of the class concerned may be indicated in an exception list.

8.4 Catching exceptions

So far we have only discussed how exceptions are generated but if they are not caught, the program will stop; in certain circumstances this is not acceptable. If we have a program that controls an industrial process of some sort, it is not acceptable for the program to stop abruptly when an exception occurs. The program must deal with what has happened, for example by writing a warning message to the operator, or closing down a critical process. It is also unacceptable for a program to stop because an operator happens to have entered incorrect input data into the program.

There are three levels of ambition in dealing with exceptions:

1. Take control of the exception and try to take suitable action to enable the program to continue.

2. Catch and identify the exception and pass it on to another part of the program to be dealt with.

3. Ignore the exception, in which case the program will stop.

The basic principle should be that the exception is dealt with in that part of the program where its effect can be handled most sensibly. The third level is of course the one that is easiest to apply. This is fine in the case of logic errors that have occurred while the program was being tested, before it was run properly. The right way is to deal with what has occurred outside the program, by correcting the program and so eliminating the error. We saw some examples of this type of error in Section 8.1.

We shall now write a new version of the method `readDouble`; see page 268. This is an example of ambition level 1, where we try to do something about an exception immediately. The method `readDouble` reads a real number from the stream indicated as parameter. Method `readDouble` calls the method `parse` to convert the text the user has written into a number. If there is an error in something the user has written, the method `parse` will generate an exception of type `ParseException`. When we used the former version of the method `ParseException`, the program stopped when it occurred. However, in the new version we shall catch the error and give the user another chance to write correctly.

When we call a method that can generate exceptions, we must specifically indicate that we are prepared to catch these exceptions. This we do by making use of a **try** statement, which has the general form:

```
try {
    statements
}
catch (E1 e1) {
    statements
}
catch (E2 e2) {
    statements
}
statements
```

where *E1* and *E2* represent names of exception classes and *e1* and *e2* are arbitrary parameter names. After the word `try`, a block is written which contains the statements to be performed and which might generate exceptions. (By "block" we mean a sequence of statements between curly brackets.) After this block, there should be one or more *handlers*. Each handler is introduced by the reserved word `catch` and has its own parameter, which will be of an exception class, that is, a subclass of `Throwable`.

The following things happen when the statements in the block after `try` are executed: If an exception does not occur, the statements are performed exactly as they usually are, and none of the handlers will be involved. If an exception of type *E* is generated by one of the statements after `try`, execution of this statement will be interrupted, and the program will instead jump to the first of the handlers that has a parameter of a type that matches *E*. When a handler has been found to catch the exception and the code in the handler has been executed, the exception will be cancelled. The execution process will then continue normally with the statement coming after the `try` statement, that is, with the statement that comes after the last of the handlers. Note that the program does not jump back to the statement that was interrupted inside the block. If we want to perform the statements in the `try` block again, we have to put the entire `try` statement into a repetition statement.

The rules state that when an exception of type *E* arises, control over it will be passed to the nearest handler whose type is the same as *E*, or is a superclass of *E*. By "nearest" we mean that the handler will be found in the `try` statement that was begun last, of all the `try` statements that are not yet terminated. This means that an exception is "forwarded" from the point where it arises, the interruption point, until there is a handler that can deal with it. Forwarding takes place in reverse order in respect of the path leading to the interruption. If a suitable handler cannot be found on the way back, the actual task (or thread) will be interrupted.

Incorporating use of the `try` statement, the method `readDouble` will now have the following appearance:

```
public static double readDouble(BufferedReader in)
                                        throws IOException {
  while(true)
    try {
      String s = in.readLine();
      NumberFormat nf = NumberFormat.getInstance();
      return nf.parse(s).doubleValue();
    }
    catch (ParseException pe) {
      System.out.println("Incorrect number. Try again!");
    }
}
```

The reading of input lies in a `while` statement and can be repeated time and again. If the user had written a correct number, an exception would not be generated in the method `parse`. The `return` statement would then be executed normally and the method would return the number entered. If, on the other hand, the user enters incorrect input, an exception of type `ParseException` is generated, and execution of the `return` statement is not terminated. Instead, there is a jump to the handler for exceptions of type `ParseException`, resulting in error printout. Execution of the entire `try` statement is terminated but since the try statement lies inside the `while` statement, the `try` statement will be executed once more.

Note that class `ParseException` no longer needs to be indicated in the exception list for the method `readDouble`. Because we catch all exceptions of this kind, they can never "escape" from the method. However, we have to retain `IOException`, because the method `readLine` can generate exceptions of type `IOException`, and we have not caught such exceptions. As we know, this means that all other methods that call the method `readDouble` will either have to catch exceptions of type `IOException` themselves, or enumerate `IOException` in their exception list. This is not very elegant. In addition, errors of type `IOException` are often very serious, so it is unlikely that one of the methods calling `readDouble` will itself deal with this kind of error. We shall therefore extend the method `readDouble` with a handler to catch all errors of type `IOException`. If such an error should arise, the method `readDouble` will output a stack trace and terminate the program.

```
public static double readDouble(BufferedReader in) {
  while(true)
    try {
      String s = in.readLine();
      NumberFormat nf = NumberFormat.getInstance();
      return nf.parse(s).doubleValue();
    }
```

```
    catch (ParseException pe) {
      System.out.println("Incorrect number. Try again!");
    }
    catch (IOException ie) {
      ie.printStackTrace();
      System.exit(1);
    }
  }
```

The method `printStackTrace` is defined in class `Throwable` and so is inherited by all exception classes. Another useful method in class `Throwable` is the method `getMessage`. With this we can read the message inserted when an exception object has been created. For instance, in the handler, above, we could have written:

```
System.out.println(ie.getMessage());
```

The message would then have been written out. (We did not do this because the method `printStackTrace` also writes out the message.)

---

try statement

```
try {
    statements
}
catch (E1 e1) {
    statements
}
catch (E2 e2) {
    statements
}
finally {
    statements
}
```

We can have any number of handlers (`catch` parts).

The `finally` part can be left out. (Takes place normally.)

If an exception occurs in the statements after `try`, there is a jump to the first handler (`catch` part) whose parameter matches the exception's type.

When the statements in the handler have been executed, the `try` statement is terminated and execution continues with the next statement.

There is never a jump back to the position where interruption occurred.

If there is no handler for an exception, the `try` statement is interrupted and the exception is sent on.

If there is a `finally` part, the statements in this are always executed last of all, regardless of whether an exception has arisen.

If there are several handlers in a **try** statement, it is important to place them in the right order. Because the rules say that an exception of type *E* will be dealt with by the first handler to have a parameter of type *E* or one of its superclasses, the most specific handlers should be put first. Let us suppose, for example, that we have a **try** statement that should be able to catch errors of types IOException and EOFException. Since EOFException is a subclass of IOException, we should put the handler for EOFException in front of the handler for IOException. Otherwise, we would finish in the handler for IOException, even in the case of exceptions of type EOFException.

Finally, we should mention that a **finally** part can be placed last in a **try** statement, after the handlers. This would have the form:

```
finally {
    statements
}
```

If a **finally** part is included, its statements will always be performed last of all during execution of the **try** statement. This will take place independently, whether the **try** statement has been executed normally, or an exception has occurred and we have finished in one of the **try** statement's handlers, or if an exception has occurred and has not been caught by one of the handlers.

8.5 Exercises

1. Write a method openFile that creates a new stream of class BufferedReader and connects the stream to a file. The file's name should be entered from the keyboard. If the file cannot be found, the user should get an error message and be requested to give another file name. As result, the method openFile should give a reference to the stream created.

2. In Section 5.6, on page 135, we studied the GUI program CarRent2 that read input data by making use of the auxiliary class ExtendedTextField. Complement this program to display the text "Incorrect input data" if the user enters incorrect numbers.

3. In Section 7.10, we used the classes Card and CardStack. The method System.exit is called in the constructor in class Card if the parameters are not correct. Change this so that an exception is generated instead; then insert suitable checks into methods lookAt, layTop and dealTop. (You may assume that there may be at most 52 cards in a stack of cards.) If there are errors in one of these methods, an exception will be generated. Declare your own exception class CardError and arrange for the generated exceptions to be of this class. Insert messages that explain the nature of the error.

Active objects

9

In Chapter 4, an object-oriented program was compared to a model of a real thing. An object-oriented program is built using a number of independent objects that communicate with each other by calling each other's methods. We can find active and passive things in reality, active things being ones which, on their own initiative, act or get other things to act. Passive things are ones that only do something when acted upon. If we look at traffic, for example, we could say that cars and traffic signals are active components of reality. Cars start, turn, brake and so on, while traffic signals change colour at intervals, which they themselves choose. In this context, streets or maps could be regarded as being passive, since a car drives into a street, while we can read a map. A bank account provides us with another example. A bank account is passive, while bank clerks and the bank's clients are active components, in this context.

If we are able to represent real things in an object-oriented program, we should be able to differentiate between active and passive objects. This is, in fact, a perfectly natural development in the object-oriented way of looking at things. We create a program in which some objects are active and some are passive. If we create a program in which there is more than one active object, we create a *parallel program*, a program with several execution points. We sometimes also speak of *real-time programs*. A real-time program is usually one which collaborates with its environment and changes it. It could be a program that controls the different functions in an aeroplane, or one that supervises and controls a manufacturing process. What distinguishes a real-time program from others is that it has to comply with certain time constraints in order to change its environment before it is too late. (For instance, a program for an aeroplane that does not open out the plane's landing gear in time for the plane to touch down is not worth a great deal.)

Of the better known programming languages, only Ada and Java can support the construction of parallel programs. (The other programming languages can do this but only by calling on functions in the operating system. Such programs then become affiliated with the actual operating system and cannot be moved.) Active objects in Java are described with the help of a standard class called Thread, while Ada has gone even further: special constructions for parallel programming are built into the language itself. Ada was especially intended to be used for the programming of real-time programs operating within time constraints. Because Java is interpreted, it does not lend itself to such programs but it works extremely well in programs that are free of time constraints.

9.1 Threads

It is not a novel idea to allow several activities to proceed at the same time in a computer. Operating systems that can accommodate several users at the same time, Unix for example, have always operated in this way. In operating systems of this kind, each activity is called a *process*. Actually, the computer can only execute one process at a time but by quickly changing from one process to another, it can give different users the impression that they have the computer to themselves.

When we write parallel programs containing several activities, we also alternate between activities. Each activity should be able to be described by an operating system process but to alternate between processes requires a certain amount of power from the computer. When working with parallel programs, therefore, we usually use a simpler form of process that does not require much capacity. Such a process is called a *thread*. Each separate activity in the program is described by its own thread.

In the package `java.lang`, there is a standard class called `Thread`. In a parallel Java program, every activity is described as an instance of this class. A new activity can be created by defining a `Thread` object.

```
Thread a1 = new Thread();
```

In order to start execution of a thread, we call the method `start`:

```
a1.start();
```

In class `Thread` there is a method called `run`, and this method will be called automatically when `start` is called. The method `run` is intended to describe the activity itself. The thread will exist and be active right up to the point when method `run` has finished executing. Since method `run` in class `Thread` does not do anything, we have to define our own subclass of class `Thread` when we use this technique, letting this subclass have its own version of method `run`. But there is a big disadvantage to this technique. It so happens that we often want to let our classes inherit properties from some other class but because Java does not permit multiple inheritance, a class will not be able to inherit properties from another class if it is a subclass of `Thread`. For instance, it would not be possible to define a class that described active GUI components.

We will therefore go about it in a different way. When we create a new Thread object, we can connect another object to the thread. We could write:

```
Thread a2 = new Thread(obj);
```

When we then start the thread by writing a2.start(), it is not the method run in the thread a2 that will be called but instead, the method run in the object obj. For an object to be connected in this way to a thread, it must implement the interface Runnable. The only thing defined in the interface Runnable is the method run. Every class that implements the interface Runnable must, therefore, define its own version of method run. The method run usually contains a repetition statement that is repeated time and again, so that the activity can be sustained over a long period of time.

We shall now let each class C, that will describe active objects, have an instance variable of class Thread. We could say that every active object *has* its own thread. (Instead of saying that every active object *is* a thread, as we would have done if we had allowed the class to be a subclass of class Thread.) We call this instance variable activity and write the following declaration:

```
public Thread activity = new Thread(this);
```

By giving the parameter **this**, we indicate that the thread activity will execute the code in the actual object (**this**). For this to be permitted, our class C must implement the interface Runnable and have its own version of the method run.

The following example will best illustrate this: we will begin by defining a class Writer that describes active objects. A Writer will continually write out a particular text, pausing for a certain time between each printout. When we create a new writer, we indicate the text to be written out and the time interval as parameters of the constructor. In order to create a writer to write the text Java every tenth second, for instance, we make the declaration:

```
Writer s = new Writer("Java", 10);
```

The writer is then started with the statement:

```
s.activity.start();
```

Let us now see how class Writer is defined. It will implement the interface Runnable and so must have a method called run. It will also have a constructor.

```
import extra.*;
public class Writer implements Runnable {
  public Thread activity = new Thread(this);
  private String text;
  private long interval;
```

```
// constructor
public Writer(String txt, long time) {
  text=txt;
  interval = time*1000;
}

public void run() {
  while(true) {
    try {
      Thread.sleep(interval);    // wait
    }
    catch (InterruptedException e) { }
    Std.out.print(text + " "); Std.out.flush();
  }
}
}
```

The constructor has two parameters: the text that will be written out and the time interval (indicated in seconds). When the constructor is called, the value of the parameters is kept in the instance variables `text` and `interval`. In the latter, the time interval is given in milliseconds, as a result of which the parameter will be multiplied by 1000.

The method `run` contains a continual **while** statement. The method `sleep` is called at every round, making the actual thread interrupt execution. The length of time it will pause before starting to execute again is indicated by the parameter, and this will be expressed in milliseconds. (There is another version of `sleep`, in which both milliseconds and nanoseconds can be indicated.) When the thread has been recalled to life, it will write out its text once and then pause again. The method `sleep` is a class method in the class `Thread`. We must, therefore, write the class name first. Because the method `sleep` can generate an exception of type `InterruptedException`, its call must lie in a **try** statement.

The method `interrupt` in class `Thread` can be called to interrupt an activity. For example, to interrupt the writer s, we make the statement:

```
s.activity.interrupt();
```

The actual thread will not be interrupted immediately, as we might imagine. What happens is that we request the actual thread to terminate its activity *itself* in orderly fashion.[1] Exactly what happens, when we call `interrupt`, will depend on the circumstances of the actual thread. If it has called `sleep` and is paused, `sleep` will generate an exception of type `InterruptedException`. Otherwise, an interruption flag

---

[1] In earlier versions of Java, there used to be a method `stop` that could be used to stop a thread forcibly but it has since been removed for reasons of program security.

is set, indicating that the thread has been requested to stop. In both cases it is the thread itself that must check if it is to stop and so interrupt its execution. To illustrate how this works, we shall now write a new version of method run in class Writer:

```
public void run() {
  while(!Thread.interrupted()) {
    try {
      Thread.sleep(interval);
    }
    catch (InterruptedException e) {
      break; // interrupt the while statement
    }
    Std.out.print(text + " "); Std.out.flush();
  }
}
```

Before each round in the while statement, we check that the interruption flag has not been set; this is done by using the class method interrupted in class Thread. We must also catch the exception InterruptedException that can be generated when sleep is called. If this exception arises, we interrupt the while statement.

These checks can appear inelegant when carried out in each active object, so to simplify matters, we can define our own subclass of class Thread. We place it in the package extra, so that it will be generally accessible:

```
package extra;

public class XThread extends Thread {
  public static boolean delay(long millis) {
    if (interrupted())
      return false;
    try {
      sleep(millis);
    }
    catch (InterruptedException e) {
      return false;
    }
    return true;   // the thread has not been interrupted
  }
}
```

The only contents of the new class XThread is a class method called delay, the idea here being that this method could be called instead of method sleep. Exactly as with method sleep, the method delay will have a number of milliseconds as argument. As result, delay will give a value that indicates whether or not the actual thread is to continue normally. The value **true** is then given if the actual thread has not been interrupted, and the value **false** if it has been interrupted. We can see that the method `delay` checks the interruption flag and in addition catches the exception arising in the call of `sleep`.

Through the use of class `XThread` we can now give a simpler (and final) version of the method `run` in class `Writer`. The only thing we need to do is to test whether, at each round, `delay` gives **true** as result. The whole class `Writer` will then have this appearance:

```
import extra.*;
public class Writer implements Runnable {
  public Thread activity = new Thread(this);
  private String text;
  private long interval;

  // constructor
  public Writer(String txt, long time) {
    text=txt;
    interval = time*1000;
  }

  public void run() {
    while(XThread.delay(interval)) {
      Std.out.print(text + " "); Std.out.flush();
    }
  }
}
```

To demonstrate how several active objects can execute in parallel, we shall write a program to write out the text Hocus every fifth second and the text Pocus every ninth second. The program will do this for one minute and will then be terminated. The printout will be:

```
Hocus Pocus Hocus Hocus Pocus Hocus Hocus Pocus Hocus Pocus
Hocus Hocus Pocus Hocus Hocus Pocus Hocus
```

The program will look like this:

```
import extra.*;
public class HocusPocus {
  public static void main (String arg[]) {
    Writer w1 = new Writer("Hocus", 5),
           w2 = new Writer("Pocus", 9);
    w1.activity.start();
    w2.activity.start();
    XThread.delay(60000);  // wait one minute
    w1.activity.interrupt();
    w2.activity.interrupt();
  }
}
```

The program begins by creating and starting two writers, w1 and w2. The first one will write out the text Hocus and the other, the text Pocus. The writers will execute in parallel and write out their texts for one minute. When one minute has elapsed, the program will request both writers to interrupt their activity.

When a Java program is started, a first thread is created automatically to call main. There will, therefore, be three threads in the program HocusPocus, since the two writers will each contain their own threads. Execution of a Java program will continue until all the threads created in the program have finished executing. In an ordinary, non-parallel program that only contains a single thread, the program will, therefore, terminate when main has finished executing but in a program with several threads, we cannot be sure that the program will have finished executing when main has finished. For instance, if the writers had not interrupted their activity when interrupt was called, the program would not have finished, in spite of the fact that main had finished executing.

The method sleep in class Thread (and delay in class XThread) ensure that the actual thread has to wait for a certain time. Another method in class Thread that does this is the method join. We use join when we want to wait for another thread to finish. As an example, we will complement the program HocusPocus to make it write out the number of Hocus and the number Pocus that have been written out at the end. The final printout will look like this:

```
11 Hocus and 6 Pocus have been written
```

In order to produce this result, we add a new instance variable to class Writer that will calculate the number of printouts:

```
public int number = 0;
```

(We write **public** for the sake of simplicity, so that the variable can be read from without.) We also add the following statement last in the **while** statement in the method run:

```
number++;
```

Finally, we add the following statements last of all in method main in the class HocusPocus:

```
try {
  w1.activity.join(); // wait until w1 has finished
  w2.activity.join(); // wait until w2 has finished
}
catch (InterruptedException e) {}
Std.out.println("\n" + w1.number + " Hocus and " +
                w2.number + " Pocus have been written");
```

A call of `join` must be inserted into a **try** statement, since `join` can generate an exception if the actual thread is interrupted. This technique can be used to start a computation in a separate thread in the background. Something else can then be done while waiting for the result. Note that method `join` can be found in two other versions where a time expressed in milliseconds, or milliseconds and nanoseconds, can be given as argument. These methods can be used to produce *time out*. The actual thread will then only be paused for the given time, at most.

When a Java program with several threads is executed, the Java interpreter will alternate between the different threads. Where several threads are waiting to be run, the interpreter will choose the thread with the highest priority. We can ourselves read and change a thread's priority by making use of the methods `getPriority` and `setPriority`. The lowest possible priority value is `Thread.MIN_PRIORITY`, while the highest possible priority value is `Thread.MAX_PRIORITY`. A thread will from the beginning get the same priority as the thread that created it. Unless otherwise stated, all threads get the priority `Thread.NORM_PRIORITY`. When writing a program with several threads, we should let background activities have a low priority. We should also assign a high priority to any activities in response to signals from the user.

java.lang.Thread	
new `Thread()`	creates a new thread
new `Thread(x)`	creates a new thread, connects the object x to the thread; x must belong to a class that implements `Runnable` (has a method `run`)
`t.start()`	starts the thread t; if the second constructor has been used and an object x is connected to t, the method `x.run` will be called, otherwise the method `t.run` is called
`t.interrupt()`	requests the thread t to finish executing
`interrupted()`	gives **true** if the thread executing is requested to finish
`sleep(m)` and `sleep(m,n)`	lets the actual thread wait for m milliseconds (and n nanoseconds); gives `InterruptedException` if the thread has been requested to finish
`t.join()`	waits until the thread t has been terminated
`t.join(m)`	waits until the thread t has been terminated, waits at most m milliseconds
`t.join(m,n)`	waits until the thread t has been terminated, waits at most m milliseconds and n nanoseconds
`t.getPriority()`	gives the priority for the thread t (a whole number)
`t.setPriority(p)`	changes the priority for the thread t to p (a whole number)

9.2 Dates and times

We normally have to keep track of times when we are dealing with active objects. In this section, therefore, we shall describe the Java standard classes for dealing with dates and times. In the following section, we shall construct digital clocks that can be shown on the screen.

9.2.1 The class Date

The most basic class in Java for describing times is the class Date in the package java.util. An object of class Date will describe a specific time that includes both the stroke of the clock (in Greenwich Mean Time, GMT) and the date. Times are stored with an accuracy of one millisecond. Internally in the class, they are stored as the number of milliseconds that have elapsed since 1 January 1970. We could indicate these milliseconds when creating an object of class Date but for the constructor an argument is not normally indicated. The computer's clock is then read automatically, and the new object will contain the time when it was created:

```
Date now = new Date();  // describes the actual time
```

What we get is a snapshot. The object now is not changed when the time continues but it will contain the time when it was created. In earlier versions of Java, class Date was used to convert to years, months, days, hours, etc., but class Date cannot manage to present dates and times in an international format. Instead we have to make use of the standard classes Calendar and DateFormat. We shall describe both of them but must first deal with another standard class, the class TimeZone. Like the classes Calendar and DateFormat, it lies in the package java.util.

9.2.2 The class TimeZone

It is well known that different places in the world use different time zones. In Central Europe, for example, they are one hour ahead of GMT, and on the American East Coast, they are five hours behind GMT. To read and present the time correctly, we have to know what time zone is being used. In Java we use the class java.util.TimeZone to keep track of time zones. There is always an actual time zone (default time zone). We can get the actual time zone by calling the class method getDefault:

```
TimeZone tz = TimeZone.getDefault();
```

Another class method in the class TimeZone is getTimeZone, which gives an arbitrary time zone as result. A text with the zone's designation is given as parameter. (The class method getAvailableIDs gives a list of designations that can be used.) Some examples are "GMT", "ECT" (European Central Time) and "JST" (Japanese Standard Time). For example, we can write:

```
tz = TimeZone.getTimeZone("JST");
```

The default time zone can be changed by a call of the class method `setDefault`, which should have a `TimeZone` as parameter:

```
TimeZone.setDefault(TimeZone.getTimeZone("ECT"));
```

The idea here is that an actual time zone (default time zone) will be set automatically by the Java interpreter and information retrieved from the operating system. Unfortunately, this does not always work as we would like it to, so we can insert a call of the method `setDefault` at the beginning of our program, as described above. Another solution is to use an extra parameter for the `java` command when starting the program. For instance, if the program is called `Pr`, we can give the command:

```
java -Duser.timezone=EST Pr
```

With the D parameter, we can indicate several properties for the Java interpreter. For example, we could indicate the correct language and country if the system does not do so automatically. We could write:[1]

```
java -Duser.timezone=ECT -Duser.language=fr -Duser.region=FR Pr
```

9.2.3 The class `Calendar`

The best way of describing time in Java is to make use of the class `java.util.Calendar`. An object of class `Calendar` contains a `Date` object internally, so that we do not need the class `Date` ourselves when using `Calendar`. Then to create a new `Calendar` object, we can call the class method `getInstance`:

```
Calendar cal = Calendar.getInstance();
```

The object created is initialized automatically to describe the actual time. The `Calendar` object will also keep track of the time zone concerned, an important factor when the time is to be read. The default time zone will apply if a time zone is not indicated in the call above. If we want to, we can create a `Calendar` object for another time zone. If `tz` is a `TimeZone`, as before, we can write:

```
Calendar cal = Calendar.getInstance(tz);
```

The most interesting of the methods in class `Calendar` is the method `get`, used to read the time. It gives a whole number as result. The method `get` will have an argument indicating whatever aspects of the time we wish to read. We might wish to read the year, the hour, or the number of the week, for instance. A number of constants we use as arguments are defined in class `Calendar`. We could write:

---

[1] If this is thought to be inelegant, it might be a good idea to create the command in advance. In MS-DOS, for example, we can create a BAT file, or make use of the command `doskey`. In UNIX, a script file can be created, or an alias defined.

```
int v = cal.get(Calendar.WEEK_OF_YEAR); // reads the week number
int m = cal.get(Calendar.MINUTE);       // reads minutes
int h = cal.get(Calendar.SECOND);       // reads seconds
int h = cal.get(Calendar.MILLISECOND);  // reads milliseconds
int h = cal.get(Calendar.HOUR_OF_DAY);  // reads hours
```

Examples of other constants are YEAR, MONTH, DAY_OF_MONTH and HOUR. The last one reads the hour in accordance with the 12-hour system incorporating AM and PM.

If we want a Calendar object to describe not the actual time but another time, we can call the method set, which works according to the same idea as the method get. For instance, we could set the hours to zero through the call:

```
cal.set(HOUR_OF_DAY, 0);
```

The time zone can also be changed for a Calendar object:

```
cal.setTimeZone(tz);
```

9.2.4 The class DateFormat

The last class to discuss here is the class DateFormat, which can be found in the package java.text (as against the other classes in this section, which lie in the package java.util). We use the class DateFormat when we want to convert a time into text form. (Compare this with the formatting of numbers, discussed in Section 3.1.) We first have to get a suitable instance of the class DateFormat. We can call one of the class methods getTimeInstance, getDateInstance, getDateTimeInstance and getInstance. The first one gives an object that formats a point in time as the stroke of a clock. The second one gives an object that formats the time as a date, and the last two give objects that format both the date and stroke of the clock. This is best illustrated in an example; we will begin by creating four different objects for formatting:

```
DateFormat f1 = DateFormat.getInstance();
DateFormat f2 = DateFormat.getTimeInstance();
DateFormat f3 = DateFormat.getDateInstance(DateFormat.SHORT);
DateFormat f4 = DateFormat.getDateTimeInstance
                    (DateFormat.SHORT, DateFormat.MEDIUM);
```

The class methods getTimeInstance and getDateInstance can have an extra argument that indicates formatting style. We can choose between FULL, LONG, MEDIUM, SHORT and DEFAULT. The class method getDateTimeInstance must always have two arguments, one for date and one for time.

We will now write out a time in four different ways. The conversion to text is done by the method format. It will have an object of class Date as argument and give a text as result. We will begin by creating a Date object:

```
Date now = new Date();
```

285

If we had already had a `Calendar` object `cal` and had wanted to write this out instead, we could have written:

```
Date now = cal.getTime();
```

We now call the method `format` for the four different objects, `f1`, `f2`, `f3`, and `f4`:

```
Std.out.println(f1.format(now));
Std.out.println(f2.format(now));
Std.out.println(f3.format(now));
Std.out.println(f4.format(now));
```

The formatting of the time and date will depend on the local conventions applied; see Section 3.1. If English conventions apply, the printout could be:

```
16/08/99 12:16
12:16:40
16/08/99
16/08/99 12:16:40
```

If we had instead indicated American conventions, for instance, by giving the statement:

```
Locale.setDefault(Locale.US);
```

the printout would have had the form:

```
8/16/99 5:16 AM
5:16:41 AM
8/16/99
8/16/99 5:16:40 AM
```

It is an easy matter to change the time zone without changing the default time zone. We could make the statements:

```
f2.setTimeZone(TimeZone.getTimeZone("JST"));
Std.out.println("In Japan the time is now " + f2.format(now));
```

and we would get the printout:

```
In Japan the time is now 21:16:40
```

9.3 An example – digital clocks

We shall now show an example of how active graphic objects can be constructed. We shall write a program that generates the window in Figure 9.1. In the window there are two digital clocks, one showing local time and one that gives the time in New York. Both clocks are active components that are automatically changed once per second.

We begin by defining the class `DigitalClock`. This class will describe a GUI component that can display texts. We therefore make it a subclass of class `Label`; see

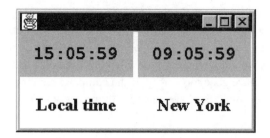

Figure 9.1

Section 5.2. But since a digital clock will also be an active object, we let the class `DigitalClock` implement the interface `Runnable`. We then declare, exactly as in Section 9.1, a thread with the name `activity` inside the class:

```java
import java.awt.*;
import java.util.*;
import java.text.*;
import extra.*;

public class DigitalClock extends Label implements Runnable {
  public  Thread activity = new Thread(this);
  private DateFormat df = DateFormat.getTimeInstance();

  public DigitalClock() {
    setFont(new Font("Monospaced", Font.BOLD, 18));
    setBackground(Color.lightGray);
    setAlignment(Label.CENTER);
    activity.start();
  }

  public DigitalClock(String zon) {
    this(); // call the parameterless constructor
    df.setTimeZone(TimeZone.getTimeZone(zon));
  }

  public void run() {
    while(XThread.delay(1000))
      setText(df.format(new Date()));
  }
}
```

There are two constructors, one without parameters and one where we can give as parameter the time zone we want. If no particular time zone is given, the default time zone will apply. The second constructor will call the parameterless constructor before it sets the time zone. Note that we started the thread `activity` inside the constructor in this class. A digital clock will, therefore, start automatically when it has been created.

9. Active objects

The method run is very simple. It will contain a **while** statement that goes one round per second. We read the computer's clock at each round by creating a new Date object. By using an object df of class DateFormat, we alter the time read to a text, calling setText to change the text for this Label object. Note that we do not tick forward the clock ourselves, as we did with class Time in earlier examples. Had we done this, our digital clock might have gone too slowly. If the computer were busy doing something else, the method run might not have started on time every second and so would have been delayed.

With the help of the class DigitalClock, we can now easily make up the program that generates the window in Figure 9.1:

```
import java.awt.*;
import java.util.*;

  class ClockDemo extends Frame {
    private DigitalClock c1 = new DigitalClock();
    private DigitalClock c2 = new DigitalClock("EST");

  public ClockDemo () {
    Label l1 = new Label("Local time", Label.CENTER);
    Label l2 = new Label("New York",  Label.CENTER);
    l1.setFont(new Font("Serif", Font.BOLD, 18));
    l2.setFont(new Font("Serif", Font.BOLD, 18));
    setSize(250,125);
    setLayout(new GridLayout(2,2,5,5));
    add(c1);
    add(c2);
    add(l1);
    add(l2);
    setVisible(true);
  }

  public static void main (String args[]) {
    ClockDemo cd = new ClockDemo();
  }
}
```

When execution begins, we know that an original thread will be there to execute the method main. When the new ClockDemo object is created, this thread will execute the constructor for class ClockDemo. The window in Figure 9.1 is made up of four GUI components, c1 and c2, which are objects of class DigitalClock, and l1 and l2, which are two simple (passive) Label objects. When the two objects c1 and c2 are created, the clocks will automatically start going. In the constructor for the object c2, we gave the parameter EST, which indicates New York's time zone. When test-running the program, we used ECT (European Central Time) as default time zone, which is the reason for the time difference of six hours in Figure 9.1.

9.4 Synchronization of threads

When working with programs with several threads, we can be faced with problems entirely different from those encountered when dealing with ordinary programs. One such problem arises when two or more threads want to make use of a particular object at the same time. To illustrate this, we can return to class `Account`, from Chapter 2. (See page 67.) This class describes bank accounts. Objects belonging to class `Account` are passive objects that do not have an activity of their own but they can be called by active objects. In class `Account` there was a method `transaction` that could be called when we wanted to credit an account or withdraw money from an account.

```
class Account {
  private double balance;
  . . .
  public void transaction(double amount) {
    if (amount<0 && balance+amount<0)   // negative amount =>
                                        // withdrawal
      System.out.println("Withdrawal not possible!");
    else
      balance = balance+amount;
  }
  . . .
}
```

Now let us suppose that we have declared an object of class `Account`:

```
Account a = new Account();
```

Let us further suppose that we have two active objects, `cash`, of class `CashpointClient`, and `giro`, that is of class `Transferor`. The first object is executed each time a client withdraws money from a cash dispenser, and the second, when automatic transfers are made to and from different accounts. There is a statement in both of these objects that looks like this:

```
a.transaction(b);
```

Let us suppose that a client withdraws $500 from a cash dispenser at the same time as an amount of $10,000 is automatically credited to his account. At the beginning, there were $13,958 in the account. The following course of events is then possible:

- The thread in the object `cash` called `a.transaction` and just had time to make the computation `balance+amount`, that is, 13,958 + (–500). The result was 13,458.
- The thread in the object `cash` is interrupted, and the thread in the object `giro` begins to execute. This calls `a.transaction` and performs the statement `balance=balance+amount`. Since the variable `cash` still has the value 13,958 before this statement is performed, the value of `cash` will be changed to 23,958.

- The thread in the object `giro` has finished executing for the moment. Execution of the thread in the object `cash` continues. This assigns its computed result of 13,458 to the variable `balance`.

The result of both these transactions will be that the balance was reduced by $500 in spite of $10,000 having been credited to the account!

To prevent this sort of thing from happening, it is sometimes necessary to make sure that only one thread at a time has access to an object. (The balance would not have been incorrect if the thread in the object `cash` had been able to finish executing the entire method `transaction` before the thread in the object `giro` had got access to the method.) This can be accomplished by indicating that certain methods are to be *synchronized*. This is done with the reserved word **synchronized**. We could write:

```
class Account {
  private double balance;
    . . .
  public synchronized void transaction(double amount) {
    if (amount<0 && balance+amount<0)   // negative amount =>
                                        // withdrawal
      System.out.println("Withdrawal not possible!");
    else
      balance = balance+amount;
  }
    . . .
}
```

When a thread calls a synchronized method, a lock is put on the object the method belongs to. If the thread in the object `cash` made the call:

```
a.transaction(b);
```

a lock would be put on the object `a`. An object will remain locked until the call of the synchronized method has finished executing. If another thread attempts to call a synchronized method for a locked object, the thread will be obliged to wait until the object is no longer locked. Note that the second thread does not have to call the *same* synchronized method for the actual object, since there can be several synchronized methods in a class.

When we define a class to be used in a program with several threads, we should declare as synchronized all the methods that *change* something in the actual object. However, methods that merely read values should not be synchronized. A constructor does not need to be synchronized, since it can only be executed a single time for a particular object and this will happen before the other methods can be called.

Class methods (static methods) can also be declared as synchronized. This results in a lock that will apply to all the class methods for the actual class.

We should mention the existence in Java of *synchronized statements*. They have the form:

synchronized (obj)
  statement;

Of course, the statement can consist of a block – a sequence of statements between curly brackets. When one of these is performed, the object obj will be locked, and other threads wanting to perform synchronized statements on the object will have to wait. It is, however, better and safer to make use of synchronized methods than of synchronized statements. It is all too easy to forget to put a vital call into a synchronized statement.

In the program examples we have seen in this chapter so far, the different threads were executed independently of one another, but it is common for the different threads in a parallel program to need to communicate with each other. For example, a thread might have to perform a computation, the result of which might be needed in another thread. Then there must be a way for the first thread to tell the second when the computation has finished and there must be a way for the second thread to read the computed value. To ensure that threads sending data to each other will not have to wait unnecessarily, we often make use of an intermediary data buffer. The thread producing a result leaves it in the buffer, and the thread needing the result collects it from the buffer.

We will now give an example of this type of program. Let us suppose that we have a number of threads that compute results. We call these threads *producers*. These producers place their results in a buffer that functions like a queue. Each new result is placed last in the queue. Let us further suppose that there are threads wanting to read the computed values. These threads are called consumers. These consumers will collect the values from the buffer. Each time a value is collected, the value that is first in the queue is taken. This is shown in Figure 9.2, where we have drawn 3 producers and 2 consumers.

We begin by defining a class that describes a queue. We can easily construct a class of this kind as a subclass of the standard class Vector, which we discussed in Section 7.7.

```
import java.util.*;
public class Queue extends Vector {

  public synchronized void putLast(Object obj) {
    addElement(obj);
    notify();
  }
```

Producers   Consumers

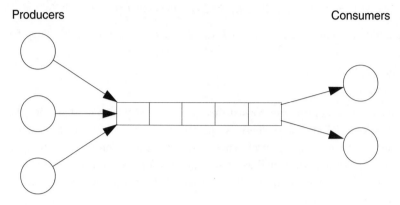

Figure 9.2

```
public synchronized Object getFirst() {
   while (isEmpty())
      try {
         wait();
      }
      catch (InterruptedException e) {
         return null;
      }
   Object obj = elementAt(0);
   removeElementAt(0);
   return obj;
   }
}
```

A queue is quite simply a `Vector`. To the subclass we have added two new methods, `putLast`, which puts an object last in the queue, and `getFirst`, which gets the object lying first in the queue. Both of these methods have been declared as synchronized, so that only one thread at a time can put in or take out objects in the queue.

The method `putLast` has as parameter the object that is to be put last in the queue. It is an easy matter to put the object there. We simply call the inherited method `addElement`, which puts an object last into a vector. The call of the method `notify` is interesting. This method is defined in the class `Object` and so is available for all classes. When `notify` is called, a signal is generated that says that something has happened to the actual object. In this case, we say that something has happened to the queue, which is that a new object has been inserted last in it.

The method `getFirst` gets and returns the first object from the queue but for it to go to collect something, the queue must have something in it. The method `isEmpty`, inherited from class Vector, will test whether a Vector is empty. If the queue is empty, we call the method wait. As with the method notify, this is defined in class Object and is available to all classes. When wait is called, execution of the actual thread is momentarily interrupted, while at the same time, the lock on the actual object is opened. In this way, threads other than the actual thread can execute synchronized methods. The interrupted thread is called to life again when another thread has called the method notify for the actual object. We then again test whether the condition we were waiting for has been fulfilled. In this case we were waiting for the queue not to be empty. Note that we shall always carry out this test in a **while** statement, so that we can wait again in case the condition has not been fulfilled. (There may be other causes for the waiting thread to have been awakened.) Note, too, that the call of wait must always lie in a **try** statement, since it can generate an exception. The inherited methods elementAt and removeElementAt are used last in the method getFirst to read and take away the first object (the one with the index number 0) from the queue.

Several threads can call wait for a particular object. They will then be passive and wait to be alerted again. When another thread then calls notify for the actual object, one of the the the waiting threads will be notified. There is also a method notifyAll that notifies all the threads waiting on the actual object concerned.

We shall now see how a queue can be utilized. The data that can be placed in a queue is of type Object, which means that we can put data of any class into a queue. We can also have different kinds of data. (Compare this with Section 7.7.) We begin by defining a class that produces data to be put into a queue. For the sake of simplicity, we will let this data be of class String. A producer is an active object that, time and again, puts a particular text into a queue. The producer will wait for a certain time between each bout of activity. The text and the time interval are given as parameters of the constructor, which also gets as parameter a reference to the queue to be used. The class Producer will then look like this:

```
import extra.*;

public class Producer implements Runnable {
  public Thread activity = new Thread(this);
  private String text;
  private long interval;
  private Queue q;

  public Producer(String txt, long time, Queue k) {
    text=txt;
    interval = time*1000;
    q = k;
  }
```

```
  public void run() {
    while(XThread.delay(interval))
      q.putLast(text);
  }
}
```

The class Consumer is built up according to the same model, although it takes texts from the queue. This activity, too, is punctuated by time intervals. The texts that are collected are written out on the screen. The time interval and a reference to the queue to be used are given as parameters for the constructor:

```
import extra.*;

public class Consumer implements Runnable {
  public Thread activity = new Thread(this);
  private long interval;
  private Queue q;

  public Consumer(long time, Queue k) {
    interval = time*1000;
    q = k;
  }

  public void run() {
    while(XThread.delay(interval)) {
      Std.out.print(q.getFirst() + " "); Std.out.flush();
    }
  }
}
```

We shall now bring everything together by writing a demonstration program that creates a queue, together with an arbitrary number of consumers and producers. When the program starts, it asks the user to indicate the number of producers and consumers there are to be. The user also has to indicate the texts that the producers will generate and the time intervals to be used. When the program is run it might look like this:

```
Number of producers? 3
Producer no.1:
   Time interval? 5
   Text? Ole
Producer no.2:
   Time interval? 7
   Text? Dole
Producer no.3:
   Time interval? 9
   Text? Doff
Number of consumers? 2
Consumer no.1:
   Time interval? 4
```

```
Consumer no.2:
   Time interval? 8
Ole Dole Doff Ole Dole Ole Doff Ole Dole Ole Doff Dole Ole Ole
Dole Doff Ole Dole Ole Doff Dole
Number left in the queue: 4
```

The principal thread in method main starts the producers and consumers, then waits for a minute. After this time, the principal thread comes in again, reads and writes out the actual length of the queue, then interrupts the program forcibly by calling System.exit. (It could also have called the method interrupt for all the producers and consumers.) The method size, inherited by class Queue from class Vector, is called to find out the length of the queue. The thread in main raises its priority so that it will be certain of coming in before the other threads after one minute has elapsed. The program looks like this:

```
import extra.*;

public class OleDoleDoff {
  public static void main (String arg[]) {
    Queue buffer = new Queue();

    // read input data
    Std.out.print("Number of producers? ");
    Producer[] p = new Producer[Std.in.readInt()];
    for (int i=0; i<p.length; i++) {
      Std.out.println("Producer no. " + (i+1) +":");
      Std.out.print("   Time interval? ");
      int time = Std.in.readInt();
      Std.out.print("   Text? ");
      String s = Std.in.readLine();
      p[i] = new Producer(s, time, buffer);
    }

    Std.out.print("Number of consumers? ");
    Consumer[] c = new Consumer[Std.in.readInt()];
    for (int i=0; i<c.length; i++) {
      Std.out.println("Consumer no. " + (i+1) +":");
      Std.out.print("   Time interval? ");
      int time = Std.in.readInt();
      c[i] = new Consumer(time, buffer);
    }

    // start activities
    Thread.currentThread().setPriority(Thread.MAX_PRIORITY);
    for (int i=0; i<p.length; i++)
      p[i].activity.start();
    for (int i=0; i<c.length; i++)
      c[i].activity.start();
```

```
    // wait
    XThread.delay(60000);
    Std.out.println("\nNumber left in the queue: " + buffer.size());
    System.exit(0);
  }
}
```

9.5   Threads in applets

Applets can contain threads too. We will recall, from Section 1.7, that the method main should not be included in the program when we use applets. An applet can be understood in two different ways: we can either think of it as a program that only begins a little differently from an ordinary program, or it can be regarded as a GUI component (or possibly several) that is/are displayed on a web page. In the first case we might imagine that when it is initialized, an applet could create and activate a number of threads that executed in parallel, exactly as the method main in an ordinary program. If instead we understood an applet as being a GUI component, we could make it active by following the same model as we did in the earlier chapter. We shall, therefore, allow the applet to contain a thread and connect it to the applet concerned. An applet that is an active GUI component could, for example, be used to draw moving pictures on a web page. We shall see examples of this in the following section.

We begin with a discussion of how an applet is initialized and terminated. An applet is normally created by a web browser. As soon as the applet has been created, the web browser will call the method init for the applet. The method init is, therefore, only called once for a particular applet, and in this method we are meant to perform what we would otherwise carry out in a constructor. In the method init we can initialize and start the threads we want to execute during the entire life of the applet.

When the web browser has called the method init, it calls the method start for the applet. (Note that we are dealing with the method start in class Applet, and not the method start in class Thread.) This is done each time the web page with the applet concerned begins to be displayed. So it can occur several times for any applet. If an applet contains a thread we want to be active only when the applet is displayed on the screen, this thread will be activated in the method start. An example of such a thread is one that draws a moving figure.

When the web page with the applet is no longer displayed, the browser will automatically call the method stop in the applet. If an applet has a thread that displays a moving figure, this thread should be interrupted in the method stop. Unless this is done, the thread will continue to execute.

Another useful method in class `Applet` is the method `destroy`. This method is called by the browser when the applet is to be destroyed. This is an opportunity to do some "cleaning up", to close some files perhaps, or interrupt background threads that the applet has started.

It should be pointed out that the methods `init`, `start`, `stop` and `destroy` are particular to applets. As we know, for ordinary objects we use a constructor instead of `init`, and the method `finalize` roughly corresponds to the method `destroy`; see Section 7.6.

Initialization and termination of applets
`init`   is called when the applet is created, corresponds to a constructor for ordinary objects
`start`   is called each time the web page with the applet begins to be displayed
`stop`   is called each time the web page with the applet ceases to be displayed
`destroy` is called when the applet will cease to exist, corresponds to `finalize` for ordinary objects

We normally regard an applet as being a GUI component. We can give the applet the following structure if we want it to be active:

```java
import java.awt.*;
import java.applet.*;
import extra.*;

public class ActiveApplet extends Applet implements Runnable {
    private Thread activity;
    other instance variables

    public void init() {
        initialize instance variables, etc.
    }

    public void start() {
        if (activity == null) {
            activity = new Thread(this);
            activity.start();
        }
    }

    public void stop() {
        if (activity != null) {
            activity.interrupt();
            activity = null;
        }
    }
```

```
public void run() {
  while (XThread.delay(time interval)) {
    make changes
    repaint();
  }
}

public void paint(Graphics g) {
  draw the applet again
}
}
```

The interesting things here are the methods `start` and `stop`, which are called automatically when the applet begins and ceases to be displayed on the web page. The threads in the applet are started and stopped in these methods. (The methods are so constructed that it will not matter if they are called twice in succession.) As usual, the method `run` describes the component's activity.

9.6 Moving figures

We can construct an active object that draws a figure repeatedly at regular time intervals. If the figure is altered slightly when it is drawn again, it can be made to look as though it is moving. We shall describe this in this chapter by showing an example with an active applet.

In Section 6.9, we designed an applet that drew a polygon on the screen. We will now remake this applet so that the polygon moves, rotating in a clockwise direction. When the applet is run, it can look as in Figure 9.3. We will recall that in Section 6.9 we indicated, in the HTML file, the number of corners the polygon was to have and the size the radius was to be, as parameters for the applet. (By "radius" was meant the radius of a circle in which the polygon was inscribed.) In the example in Figure 9.3, we indicated that the polygon was to have five corners and its radius was to be 40 pixels.

We shall let the applet have the structure that was shown in Section 9.5. In the earlier version of the applet (see page 209), we had the instance variables n, r, x0, y0 and angle, which described the number of corners of the polygon, its radius, the circle's centre point and the angle between the corners in the polygon. In addition, we had two arrays x and y that contained the coordinates of the circle's corners. We still need all of these instance variables; in addition, we need a constant variable dv that will indicate how many degrees the polygon is to move after each unit of time, together with a variable turn that will indicate the degrees that the polygon has turned. Finally, of course, we need the variable activity. The applet will, therefore, have the following instance variables:

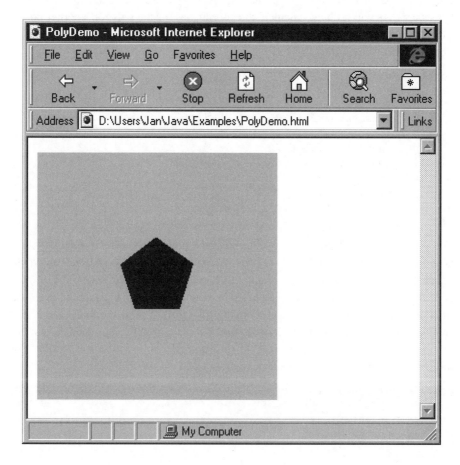

Figure 9.3

```
private Thread activity;
int n, r, x0, y0;
double angle;
int[] x, y;
final double dv = 5*2*Math.PI/360;  // 5 degrees
double turn = 0;
```

Here we have supposed that the polygon will be turned 5 degrees at each time interval and that it has not been turned from the beginning. All angles are, as before, measured in radians.

The method `init` will look almost the same as it did on page 209. It will get parameters that indicate the number of corners and the radius, calculate the circle's

9. Active objects

centre and the angle between the corner points. It will also create the arrays x and y. However, init will not now calculate the coordinates for the polygon's corner points, since these will be changing constantly. This will instead be done in the method paint. The method init will look like this:

```
public void init() {
    String s = getParameter("number");
    n = Integer.parseInt(s);
    s = getParameter("radius");
    r = Integer.parseInt(s);
    x0 = getSize().width/2;
    y0 = getSize().height/2;
    x = new int[n];
    y = new int[n];
    angle = 2*Math.PI/n;
}
```

The variable turn will indicate by how much the polygon is to be turned when it is next drawn. There is a continual **while** statement in the method run. At each round, the variable turn is increased by dv radians (this corresponds to 5 degrees). If the polygon is then turned by more than a full circle (more than 2π radians), the variable turn will be shortened by 2π radians, so representing a full circle. The method repaint is then called; as a result, the polygon is drawn again. We shall await the lapse of a certain unit of time between each round in run; in this example, this will correspond to 100 milliseconds. The method run then becomes:

```
public void run() {
  while (XThread.delay(100)) {
    turn = turn + dv;
    if (turn>2*Math.PI)
      turn -= 2*Math.PI;
    repaint();
  }
}
```

The method paint will be called whenever the polygon has to be redrawn. (This is done by repaint.) The new coordinates for the polygon's corner points will then be computed and placed in the arrays x and y. The computation will be done with the same formulae as on page 209, the only difference now being that we must remember that the polygon has been turned. As before, we divide a complete revolution into n equal angles and from the resulting angle, we subtract the angle turn. (We subtract turn instead of adding it because angles are measured in an anti-clockwise direction when the methods sin and cos are called. If we added the angle turn, the polygon would have moved in an anti-clockwise direction.) The drawing of the polygon takes place as before with the standard method fillPolygon. The method paint will look like this:

300

```
public void paint(Graphics g) {
  // compute new corner points
  for (int i=0; i<n; i++) {
    double v = i*angle - turn;
    x[i] = x0 + (int)Math.round(r * Math.cos(v));
    y[i] = y0 - (int)Math.round(r * Math.sin(v));
  }
  // draw new picture
  g.fillPolygon(x, y, n);
}
```

We can now put together the whole applet.

```
import java.awt.*;
import java.applet.*;
import extra.*;
public class PolyDemo extends Applet implements Runnable {
  private Thread activity;
  int n, r, x0, y0;
  double angle;
  int[] x, y;
  final double dv = 5*2*Math.PI/360;   // 5 degrees
  double turn = 0;

  public void init() {
    String s = getParameter("number");
    n = Integer.parseInt(s);
    s = getParameter("radius");
    r = Integer.parseInt(s);
    x0 = getSize().width/2;
    y0 = getSize().height/2;
    x = new int[n];
    y = new int[n];
    angle = 2*Math.PI/n;
  }

  public void start() {
    if (activity == null) {
      activity = new Thread(this);
      activity.start();
    }
  }

  public void stop() {
    if (activity != null) {
      activity.interrupt();
      activity = null;
    }
  }
```

```
public void run() {
  while (XThread.delay(100)) {
    turn = turn + dv;
    if (turn>2*Math.PI)
      turn -= 2*Math.PI;
    repaint();
  }
}

public void paint(Graphics g) {
  // compute new corner points
  for (int i=0; i<n; i++) {
    double v = i*angle - turn;
    x[i] = x0 + (int)Math.round(r * Math.cos(v));
    y[i] = y0 - (int)Math.round(r * Math.sin(v));
  }
  // draw new picture
  g.fillPolygon(x, y, n);
}
}
```

9.7   Reduction of flicker

It is true that if we test-run the applet in Section 9.6, we will get a turning polygon appearing on the screen but there will be some unpleasant flicker. This is a common problem in the design of objects that draw moving figures. We can make use of three different techniques to try to reduce flicker:

- do not bother to efface the component
- cut out part of the component and only draw this part again
- use double buffering

These techniques can be used independently but also in conjunction with each other. In the following section, we shall discuss these different techniques.

9.7.1   Do not efface the component

When we call the method `repaint` for a graphics component, the method `paint` is not called directly. Instead, the call goes through yet another method called `update`. This method is defined in the class `Component` and looks roughly like this:

```
public void update(Graphics g) {   // standard version
  g.setColor(getBackground());
  g.fillRect(0, 0, getSize().width, getSize().height);
  g.setColor(getForeground());
  paint(g);
}
```

The method `update` effaces the entire component by filling it with background colour, and only then is the method `paint` called to draw the component once more. The flicker is caused by the whole component being effaced and if this could be avoided, the flicker would be diminished.

In some cases, the component does not have to be effaced. This is true where the method `paint` will draw over *everything* that needs to be redrawn. What we can do then is to redefine the method `update` in the class concerned. This is easy to do but the easiest way of going about it is to define a method that looks like this:

```
public void update(Graphics g) { // own version
   paint(g);
}
```

But we have to be careful. If `paint` does not redraw the entire component, it will draw on top of the component's old contents. For instance, if we redefined `update` in this way in our class `PolyDemo`, from Section 9.6, a black circle would gradually be displayed on the screen.

9.7.2   Only redraw what is necessary

To every component belongs an object of the class `java.awt.Graphics`. The parameter that the methods `repaint`, `update` and `paint` will get is simply a reference to this `Graphics` object. A `Graphics` object is, as we have seen, a kind of toolbox containing a number of tools that make it possible for us to draw on the screen. Besides these tools, class `Graphics` contains a method `setClip`, with which we can define an area, a scrapbook area, that is a subset of the total drawing area. If we wanted, the `Graphics` object could ignore all commands that entailed drawing outside this scrapbook area, and, as a result, methods `update` and `paint` would only change whatever lay inside the scrapbook area. If this is small in relation to the area for the whole component, then redrawing will naturally go much faster, reducing flicker.

It is very easy to define a scrapbook area in our applet `PolyDemo`. We merely insert the following statement last in the method `init`:

```
getGraphics().setClip(x0-r, y0-r, 2*r, 2*r);
```

First, the method `getGraphics` is called, and this returns a reference to the `Graphics` object used by the component. (It is a reference to the same object given as parameter for the methods `repaint`, `update` and `paint`.) The method `setClip`, which defines the scrapbook area, is then called for this `Graphics` object. Its parameters will indicate a rectangle. The first two parameters indicate the rectangle's upper left-hand corner and the other two the rectangle's width and height, respectively. In this example, we have defined a rectangle that is just big enough to encompass the circle in which the polygon is inscribed.

303

In our applet, it is relatively easy to define a scrapbook area, since the polygon's dimensions have been known from the beginning and the polygon is not going to move. We can, therefore, define the scrapbook area once and for all and put the call of setClip into the method init. If we are dealing with active components that draw figures moving on the screen, we shall have to gradually change the scrapbook area. We shall then use the figure's actual position on the screen to determine this area. Now a complication arises, however. We cannot be certain that every call of the method repaint will lead to calls of update and paint. If the call of repaint comes so quickly as to catch the Java interpreter unawares, it could skip a number of calls of update and only carry out the latest one. This means that we must be careful not to change the scrapbook area so that those parts of the moving figure not yet effaced finish up outside it and remnants of the figure remain on the screen. The program code that has to be written to avoid this problem can become quite complicated. When dealing with moving figures, therefore, it is much simpler to use double buffering, which we shall describe in the next section.

9.7.3 Double buffering

When we use double buffering, we do not draw directly onto the screen. Instead, we draw an invisible picture "on the side". Only when we have finished drawing the invisible picture will we copy it onto the visible screen, in one operation. As a result, the flicker will more or less disappear. To be able to use double buffering, we must declare and create an invisible picture. This will be an object of the standard class Image. In addition, a Graphics object, that is, a toolbox with graphics tools, must be connected to the invisible picture. (The class Image is defined in the package java.awt, as is class Graphics.) We therefore add the following two instance variables to our applet PolyDemo:

```
Image picture2;
Graphics g2;
```

We also add these initializations in method init:

```
picture2 = createImage(getSize().width, getSize().height);
g2 = picture2.getGraphics();
```

The method createImage will create a new, invisible picture. The dimensions the picture will have are given as parameters. We make this invisible picture exactly as large as the visible one on the screen. (The call of getSize is really a call of **this**.getSize and so will give the actual Applet object's size.)

In method paint, we draw our figure onto picture2, instead of drawing directly onto the screen; to achieve this, we use the Graphics object g2, instead of g. When the new coordinates of the corner points have been computed, this call is then made:

```
g2.fillPolygon(x, y, n);        // draw a new figure onto picture2
```

The invisible picture is then copied onto the screen and becomes visible through the call:

```
g.drawImage(picture2, 0, 0, this); // copy to the screen
```

The Graphics object g is connected to the visible screen, which is why we call the method drawImage for the object g. The first parameter for drawImage will be the picture to be drawn, and the next two will indicate where in the visible picture picture2 will begin to be drawn. We shall begin drawing in the upper left-hand corner and indicate the coordinates (0,0). The last parameter will be a reference to an object that can supervise the drawing of the picture. This object will belong to a subclass of Component. The easiest way is to allow the actual object to be the "supervisor"; so we write this.

For this to work properly, we must also redefine the method update. In the standard version (see page 302), the visible picture is effaced before the method paint is called. It was this effacing of the picture that caused the flicker. We do not have to efface the visible picture now, however, because a completely new picture is copied to the screen each time the above call is made. Instead, we have to efface the invisible picture picture2 each time, before we draw a new figure onto it. The new version of update will therefore have the following appearance. We have simply been effacing the invisible picture with the Graphics object g2, instead of the visible picture with g:

```
public void update(Graphics g) {   // our own version
   // efface picture2
   g2.setColor(getBackground());
   g2.fillRect(0, 0, getSize().width, getSize().height);
   g2.setColor(getForeground());
   paint(g);
}
```

Graphics objects need a large number of resources. We therefore recommend that these resources be released as soon as they are no longer required. One way of doing this is to call the method dispose. In our program, we should release the object g2. As we know, when an applet ceases to exist, the method destroy is called automatically. We can write our own version of this when we add a call of dispose:

```
public void destroy() {
   g2.dispose();
}
```

These are all the changes necessary to ensure that the applet PolyDemo will produce a picture relatively free of flicker. We shall show the complete code for the applet, but to make it a little more enjoyable and to demonstrate that double buffering works even for pictures moving on the screen, we will make a few additions to the method run. We

305

will let the rotating polygon move both horizontally and vertically on the screen. We first declare two new instance variables that will indicate the number of pixels the polygon will move each time the figure is redrawn.

```
int xStep=4, yStep=3;
```

We then add the statements, below, to the method run. The variables x0 and y0 indicate, as before, the polygon's centre point. We let these variables be increased by xStep and yStep, respectively, with each call of run. If xStep has a positive value, the polygon will move to the right of the screen, and if xStep has a negative value, the polygon will move to the left. For yStep, positive values result in a movement downwards, and negative values in a movement upwards. If the polygon happens to reach the edge of the drawing area, we change the sign of xStep or yStep. The polygon will then "rebound" and begin to move in the other direction.

```
if (x0-r+xStep < 0 || x0+r+xStep > getSize().width)
  xStep = -xStep;   // at the edge, change direction
x0 += xStep;
if (y0-r+yStep < 0 || y0+r+yStep > getSize().height)
  yStep = -yStep;   // at the edge, change direction
y0 += yStep;
```

We can now put together our new version of the applet, which we will call PolyMove:

```
// an applet that displays a rotating and rebounding polygon
import java.awt.*;
import java.applet.*;
import extra.*;

public class PolyMove extends Applet implements Runnable {
  private Thread activity;
  int n, r, x0, y0;
  double angle;
  int[] x, y;
  final double dv = 5*2*Math.PI/360;   // 5 degrees
  double turn = 0;
  Image picture2;          // picture for double buffering
  Graphics g2;
  int xStep=4, yStep=3;

  public void init() {
    String s = getParameter("number");
    n = Integer.parseInt(s);
    s = getParameter("radius");
    r = Integer.parseInt(s);
    x0 = getSize().width/2;
    y0 = getSize().height/2;
    x = new int[n];
    y = new int[n];
```

306

```
    angle = 2*Math.PI/n;
    picture2 = createImage(getSize().width, getSize().height);
    g2 = picture2.getGraphics();
}

public void start() {
  if (activity == null) {
    activity = new Thread(this);
    activity.start();
  }
}

public void stop() {
  if (activity != null) {
    activity.interrupt();
    activity = null;
  }
}

public void run() {
  while (XThread.delay(100)) {
    turn = turn + dv;
    if (turn>2*Math.PI)
      turn -= 2*Math.PI;
    if (x0-r+xStep < 0 || x0+r+xStep > getSize().width)
      xStep = -xStep;  // at the edge, change direction
    x0 += xStep;
    if (y0-r+yStep < 0 || y0+r+yStep > getSize().height)
      yStep = -yStep;  // at the edge, change direction
    y0 += yStep;
    repaint();
  }
}

public void update(Graphics g) {
  // efface picture2
  g2.setColor(getBackground());
  g2.fillRect(0, 0, getSize().width, getSize().height);
  g2.setColor(getForeground());
  paint(g);
}

public void paint(Graphics g) {
  // compute new corner points
  for (int i=0; i<n; i++) {
    double v = i*angle - turn;
    x[i] = x0 + (int)Math.round(r * Math.cos(v));
    y[i] = y0 - (int)Math.round(r * Math.sin(v));
  }
```

```
    g2.fillPolygon(x, y, n);    // draw new figure onto picture2
    g.drawImage(picture2, 0, 0, this); // copy to the screen
  }

  public void destroy() {
    g2.dispose();
  }
}
```

9.8 Exercises

1. Write a program to keep track of when a person has to take medicine. Whenever it is time to take medicine, a message such as "Take a Javacyl tablet now" should be produced. An active object will be necessary for each medical element. When the program is started, the different medicines and information about how often they are to be taken should be input.

2. Construct an applet with a digital clock that will show the duration of the user's visit to the actual website.

3. Complement class Queue, in Section 9.4, with operations that make it possible for objects to be placed in order of priority into a queue. Objects with a higher priority will be put in front of objects with a lower priority. The priority of an object will be determined by the priority of the thread inserting the object.

4. Complement the applet PolyMove, on page 306, so that it emits a metallic sound every time the polygon touches a side.

5. Construct an applet that displays a set of traffic lights with red, yellow and green lights. The traffic lights should change colour automatically at regular intervals. The time interval is given as a parameter for the applet.

6. Construct an active object displaying a red ball that is released from the top of the drawing area. The ball should rebound against the bottom of the drawing area. At every rebound, the ball will lose some of its height, finally coming to rest. If the program flickers when you test-run it, you should make use of double buffering.

7. Construct an active object that displays an analogue clock with an ordinary clockface having hour, minute and second hands. The clock will move forward once per second. Use the formulae in the applet PolyDemo to calculate the angle the different hands are to have.

Event-driven programs   10

The computer world entered a new phase in the 1980s. An ever-increasing number of programs began to use graphical user interfaces (GUIs) and programs started to look much as they do today. Menus and buttons are an integral part of programs and we communicate with programs using a mouse. Prior to this, programs communicated with the user through a terminal similar to a typewriter. The program wrote out text at this terminal and the user entered text at the keyboard. Even if modern computer systems have a graphical user interface, they still retain these typewriter-like terminals in a simulated form. For example, we can open a terminal window in a Unix system and an MS-DOS prompt in Windows systems.

The transition from terminal-based communication to GUIs revolutionized and simplified the use of computers and made it possible for new categories of users to make use of them. A GUI program is event-driven and is constructed quite differently from a program that communicates through a terminal. Programmers had to learn new techniques. GUI programs are also more complex. To construct a GUI program within a reasonable time, we have to utilize libraries with ready-made functions, for example, Xlib and Motif in Unix and Win API (Application Programming Interface) in Windows. It is important for programmers not only to master the programming language, but also the many sets of ready-made functions.

This is why we have made use of GUIs from the very beginning of the book, describing their construction at the same time as discussing the more traditional basic programming techniques. In Chapter 5, where we discussed GUI components, we saw the first examples of event-driven programs, and we employed so-called listeners. In this chapter, we shall be looking at events and listeners in a little more detail. We shall also describe events that are generated by the user clicking with the mouse, or pressing a key at the keyboard.

10.1 Events and listeners

10.1.1 Program structure

In a traditional program that communicates with the user via a terminal, we say that the reading of input data is *program-driven*. The program decides when it is time to read input data. It then outputs a request to the user. The program will wait until the user has written input data before it continues. The program `CarRent`, on page 86, was an example of this type of program. The program only contains one activity (a thread), and when this has finished executing, the program is terminated. In Java, this means that there is only one thread executing the method `main`. When `main` has reached its conclusion, the program has finished.

A GUI program has a completely different structure. We say that such a program is event-driven. Execution of an event-driven program takes place in two phases. The first is the initialization phase; we enter this phase as soon as the program starts. In Java, the initialization phase is executed by the thread that executes the method `main`. In the initialization phase, we declare and initialize the different GUI components that will be used by the program. We also define what are called *callback functions*, which will deal with the events that interest us. In Java, these callback functions are defined as methods in special *listeners*.

When the initialization phase is over, the program goes into its *waiting phase*. In most systems, this transition occurs at the end of the initialization phase, when we call a special wait function. In Java it is easier still, since it is completely automatic, without calls of any kind. In GUI programs, the Java interpreter starts a new thread in the background that takes care of the execution of the waiting phase. The initialization phase in Java ends when the thread that executed `main` comes to an end. We will remember from the previous chapter that a Java program executes until all the threads running have finished executing, so if there were no more threads, apart from the thread in `main`, the program would stop when `main` had finished.

The program remains in the waiting phase until *events* outside it occur. When we speak of outside events, we mean, for example, that the user clicks with the mouse, or presses a key. With the occurrence of an event of this kind, the callback function is called (in Java it is the listener) that was defined to deal with the event. It is, therefore, the user and not the program that will decide when it is time to enter data into the program. So we say that the program is event-driven.

An event-driven program, therefore, consists not of connected programs but of an initialization part and a number of callback functions (listener methods). The callback functions are never called in the ordinary way in a program. Instead, they are always called automatically when the corresponding event occurs.

10.1.2 Event classes

In Java, different events are described by making use of special *event classes*. When an event occurs, an object of the class that describes the event is created. A method is then called in the listener defined to listen to that type of event. The created event object is then given as parameter for the method in the listener. All event classes have a common subclass with the name EventObject. This class lies in the package java.util. Classes that describe events connected to the package java.awt have the subclass AWTEvent. This will apply to events connected to Java's standard GUI classes. The class AWTEvent is defined in the package java.awt and is a subclass of class EventObject. All the other classes that describe events in connection with Java's AWT can be found in a special package with the name java.awt.event. These classes are shown in Figure 10.1.

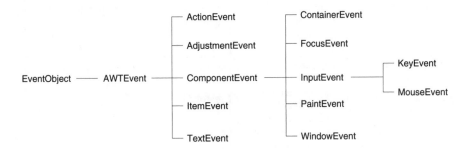

Figure 10.1 Event classes

There is for each event a GUI component in which the event has occurred. To get a reference to this component, we can call the method getSource, defined in class EventObject, which all the event classes inherit. Alternatively, we can call the method getComponent for subclasses of class ComponentEvent, the method getContainer for class ContainerEvent and the method getWindow for the class WindowEvent. The class AWTEvent has a method called getID, with which we can find out exactly what kind of event is involved. But it is simpler to define a special listener method for each kind of event, rather than to call getID. A compilation of the event classes used to describe different kinds of events is given in Table 10.1.

A particular event class can be used to describe several similar events. For example, the class FocusEvent is used both for the event focusGained and for focusLost.

Event Class	Events	Can be generated by
ActionEvent	actionPerformed	Button — button pressed List — double-click MenuItem — alternative chosen TextField — text change terminated
AdjustmentEvent	adjustmentValue-Changed	Scrollbar — scrollbar changed
ItemEvent	itemStateChanged	Checkbox, CheckboxMenuItem, Choice, List — alternative chosen
TextEvent	textValueChanged	TextComponent (text changed)
ComponentEvent	componentHidden componentMoved componentResized componentShown	Component — component hidden, moved, resized or shown
ContainerEvent	componentAdded componentRemoved	Container — a component added or removed
FocusEvent	focusGained focusLost	Component — the component gained or lost focus
PaintEvent		*is used internally by the system*
WindowEvent	windowActivated windowClosed windowClosing windowDeactivated windowDeiconified windowIconified windowOpened	Window — the window is opened, closed, is closing, is iconified, or restored
InputEvent	*see subclasses*	*see subclasses*
KeyEvent	keyPressed keyReleased keyTyped	Component — a key has been pressed or released
MouseEvent	mouseClicked mouseEntered mouseExited mousePressed mouseReleased	Component — mouse button pressed or released, the mouse moved into or out of the component
	mouseDragged mouseMoved	Component — mouse dragged or moved

Table 10.1 Events

Note that for classes `Button` and `MenuItem` (see Chapter 11), we can call the method `setActionCommand` to give each button or menu option a unique name. (This does not have to be the same text as on the button or menu option.) We can then call the method `getActionCommand` in class `ActionEvent` to find out the name of the button or menu option that caused the event. This can be useful if we do not have access in the listener to the variable names of the buttons or menu options.

10.1.3 Listener classes and listener interfaces

To catch an event we create a *listener*, an object of a *listener class*. We should define listener classes ourselves. Such a class must contain special methods that the system will call automatically when an event occurs. For every one of the event classes there is an interface defined in the package `java.awt.event` that the listener class must implement. These listener interfaces have the same names as their corresponding event classes but with the suffix `Listener`, instead of `Event`. For class `FocusEvent`, there is, for example, an interface with the name `FocusListener`, and for the event class `KeyEvent` an interface `KeyListener`. The only exception to this rule is the class `MouseEvent`. It has an interface with the name `MouseListener` as well as one with the name `MouseMotionListener`.

The methods the listener class must have are defined in the interface. The names of these methods are the same as the event names in the second column of Table 10.1. For instance, the methods `focusGained` and `focusLost` are defined in the interface `FocusListener`. A listener class for the event class `FocusEvent` must therefore have the structure:

```
class MyListener implements FocusListener {
  public void focusGained(FocusEvent e) {
    . . .
  }
  public void focusLost(FocusEvent e) {
    . . .
  }
}
```

As parameter, a listener method will always get an object of the actual event class. The methods `focusGained` and `focusLost` have a parameter of type `FocusEvent`.

The class `MouseEvent` is, as mentioned above, an exception, as it has two different listener interfaces. The methods `mouseClicked`, `mouseEntered`, `mouseExited`, `mousePressed` and `mouseReleased` are defined in the interface `MouseListener`. The interface `MouseMotionListener` contains definitions of the methods `mouseDragged` and `mouseMoved`. If we want to define our own listener classes for `MouseEvent`, we might have to define two different listener classes, one for each interface.

A listener must be registered. We do this by calling the method `add?Listener` for the component the listener is to be connected to. The character `?` is then replaced by the name of the event. For example, if we wish to connect a listener of type `MyFocusListener` to the actual component, we can write:

```
FocusListener fl = new MyListener();
addFocusListener(fl);
```

In the examples we showed in Chapter 5, we made it easy for ourselves by allowing the class describing the surrounding component to be a listener class as well. For example, when we wanted to listen to events of the type `actionPerformed`, we made our program have the structure:

```
class C extends C0 implements ActionListener {

  public void actionPerformed(ActionEvent e) { // listener method
    ...
  }

  // constructors and other methods in C
  C() {
    addFocusListener(this); // register the listener
    ...
  }
  ...
}
```

However, generally it is better to define a separate listener class because. (This makes it possible to use adapter classes, as will be demonstrated in Section 10.1.4.) When we define a listener class, we normally define it *inside* the class where it is to be used, because we are allowed to define classes inside other classes in Java. We employ this procedure when we want to use a local class as an auxiliary class for another. When we have defined the listener class, we can create a listener from it. This might look as follows:

```
class C extends C0 {

  class MyListener implements FocusListener {  // listener class
    public void focusGained(FocusEvent e) { // listener method
      ...
    }

    public void focusLost(FocusEvent e) {    // listener method
      ...
    }
  }

  MyListener l = new MyListener(); // listeners
```

```
  // constructors and other methods in C
  C() {
    addFocusListener(l); // register the listener
    ...
  }
  ...
}
```

One way of shortening this is by making use of something called an *anonymous class*. We can then create an object with the required properties directly, without declaring a class name. An alternative way of writing the above might be:

```
class C extends C0 {

  FocusListener l = new FocusListener() {  // anonymous class
    public void focusGained(FocusEvent e) {

      ...

    }

    public void focusLost(FocusEvent e) {

      ...

    }
  };

  // constructors and other methods in C
  C() {
    addFocusListener(l); // register the listener
    ...
  }
  ...
}
```

Note that the definition of the anonymous class is included in the initialization by the variable l and that initialization will be terminated by a semicolon.

10.1.4 Adapter classes

In Table 10.1 we saw that there were several event classes for which there was more than one event. The class WindowEvent, for example, has seven different events. A method is defined for each kind of event in the corresponding listener interface WindowListener. If we are to define our own listener class for WindowEvent, we will, therefore, have to define seven different listener methods in it. We might only wish to deal with a couple of kinds of event, in which case it would be inelegant to have to define listener methods for all the events that did not concern us. In order to avoid this, we have recourse to *adapter classes*, found in the package java.awt.event. There is an adapter class for every event class having more than one event. An adapter class is an abstract class that implements corresponding interfaces. An adapter class has the same name as the corresponding event class but with the suffix `Adapter`, instead of `Event`. Consequently, there is an adapter class with the name `WindowAdapter` for class `WindowEvent`, and this class implements the interface `WindowListener`. All the listener methods in an adapter class are implemented with empty method bodies. In other words, nothing will happen if one of these listener methods is called, enabling us to construct our own listener classes as subclasses of the corresponding adapter class. In this way we can inherit all the methods and only have to redefine the methods that concern us. We can also use the technique of using anonymous classes when we inherit adapter classes.

As an example, let us look at the class `ExtendedFrame`, which we defined in Section 1.9. This class has a listener that is only interested in listening to `windowClosing` events, generated when the user clicks a window's closure box. Class `ExtendedFrame` will not be interested in other events concerning the window, such as the window being iconified. Class `ExtendedFrame` will look as follows (note that the technique involving anonymous classes has been used but that we have written **new** `WindowAdapter` instead of **new** `WindowListener`):

```java
package extra;
 import java.awt.*;
 import java.awt.event.*;

 public class ExtendedFrame extends Frame {
    private static boolean first = true;
    private boolean isFirst = first;

    public ExtendedFrame() {
      addWindowListener(theListener);
      first=false;
    }

    WindowAdapter theListener = new WindowAdapter() {
      public void windowClosing(WindowEvent e) {
        dispose();
        if (isFirst)
          System.exit(0);
      }
    };
 }
```

10.2 Mouse

In this section, we shall be discuss the implications of clicking on a mouse button, or performing some other kind of operation with the mouse. The different kinds of events that can take place are listed in Table 10.1. If we wish to track events of the type mouseDragged or mouseMoved, we use a listener that implements the interface MouseMotionListener, or one that belongs to a subclass of the class MouseMotionAdapter. If we wish to track one or more of the other mouse events, we should use a listener that implements the interface MouseListener, or that belongs to a subclass of the class MouseAdapter. In both cases, the listener methods will get a parameter of class MouseEvent, and this parameter will contain information about what has taken place.

The following example will best illustrate this: we will construct a program that displays an empty window. Each time we click in the window, the program will write out which mouse button was used, whether it was a single click, double click, or a multiple click (three or more clicks). The printout will also tell us where in the window we clicked. Printout from the program will not be displayed in the window but will be displayed in a text window, at the side. The output might look as follows:

```
Single click with the left-hand button at (72,123)
Single click with the right-hand button at (148,78)
Double click with the left-hand button at (38,126)
Single click with the left-hand button at (146,168)
    Shift pressed
Single click with the right-hand button at (41,140)
    ALT pressed
```

As can be seen from the last few lines, the program will also recognize whether the Shift or Alt key was pressed when the mouse was clicked. This is the program:

```java
import java.awt.*;
import java.awt.event.*;
import extra.*;
class MouseTest extends Frame {

  MouseTest() {
    addMouseListener(l);
    setSize(200,200);
    setVisible(true);
  }

  MouseListener l = new MouseAdapter() {
    public void mouseClicked(MouseEvent e) {

      // how many clicks?
      String click;
      if (e.getClickCount() == 1)
        click = "Single click";
      else if (e.getClickCount() == 2)
        click = "Double click";
      else
        click = "Multiple click";
```

```
      // which mouse button?
      String button;
      if (e.isControlDown())
        button = "middle button";
      else if (e.isMetaDown())
        button = "right-hand button";
      else
        button = "left-hand button";
      Std.out.println(click + " with the " + button +
                         " at (" + e.getX() + "," + e.getY() +")");

      // was Alt or Shift pressed?
      if (e.isAltDown())
        Std.out.println("     ALT pressed");
      if (e.isShiftDown())
        Std.out.println("     Shift pressed");
    }
  };
  public static void main (String arg[]) {
    MouseTest m = new MouseTest();
  }
}
```

What interests us here is the definition of the listener 1. It has been defined as a subclass of the class MouseAdapter, because we have not defined methods for all of the mouse events, only for the event mouseClicked.

We begin by checking if there was a single click, a double click, or a multiple click. We can get this information by calling the method getClickCount for the actual event. The method will return a whole number indicating the number of clicks.

Now we find out which mouse button the user clicked with. Some of the methods contained by the class InputEvent, a superclass of class MouseEvent, are isControlDown, isMetaDown, isAltDown and isShiftDown. These are normally used to check whether the corresponding keys were pressed when the event occurred. In relation to mouse events, however, the methods isControlDown and isMetaDown are used not to indicate whether the keys were pressed but to see which mouse button the user had pressed. The method isControlDown returns the value **true** if the middle button (in a mouse with three buttons) was pressed, while the method isMetaDown will similarly indicate whether the right-hand mouse button was pressed. If both of these methods return the value **false**, it will mean that the left-hand button was pressed.

To find out where in the window the user clicked, we call the methods getX and getY, which are defined in the class MouseEvent. We could also have called the method getPoint, which returns an object of the standard class Point; see Section 2.8.

Finally, the methods `isAltDown` and `isShiftDown` are called in the listener to see whether the Alt key or the Shift key (or both of them) were pressed. Note that we cannot find out whether the Ctrl key or the Meta key was pressed, as the corresponding methods are used to indicate the mouse button the user has pressed.

java.awt.event.MouseEvent	
`getX()`, `getY()`	gives the x- and y-coordinates, respectively, of the mouse's position
`getPoint()`	gives a `Point` object that indicates the mouse's position
`getClickCount()`	indicates the number of times the user has clicked
`getComponent()`	gives the GUI component in which the mouse finds itself
`isControlDown()`	indicates whether the user pressed the middle button
`isMetaDown()`	indicates whether the user pressed the right-hand button
`isAltDown()`	indicates whether the user held down the Alt key
`isShiftDown()`	indicates whether the user held down the Shift key

We will now give an example to demonstrate how other kinds of mouse events are dealt with. We shall write a simple drawing program that will allow the user to draw lines. The program will look like Figure 10.2 when it is run. When the user is to draw a line, he puts the mouse where the line is to start and presses the mouse button. Then he holds the mouse button pressed and moves (drags) the mouse to the point where the line is to stop. He then releases the mouse button.

We shall use the standard class `Point`. We have to write our own class `Line`, because there is no standard class for lines. We define a line with two points, its end points. This class `Line` will look as follows. (Do not worry about why `implements Serializable` has been written here. This will be explained in Chapter 13.)

```java
package extra;
import java.awt.*;
import java.io.*;
public class Line implements Serializable {
  public Point p1, p2;

  public Line() {
    p1=new Point();
    p2=new Point();
  }

  public Line(Point a, Point b) {
    p1=new Point(a);
    p2=new Point(b);
  }
```

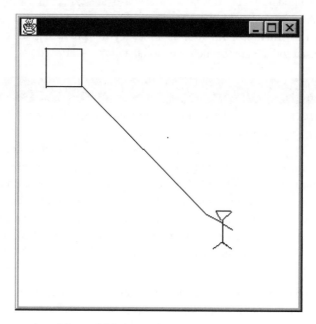

Figure 10.2 A simple drawing program

```
public void draw(Graphics g) {
   g.drawLine(p1.x, p1.y, p2.x, p2.y);
  }
}
```

There are two constructors, one that is parameterless, and one that has two points as parameters. We will also let the class Line have a method that draws a line on the screen; as parameter for this method we give a Graphics object that can be used for drawing.

We now use a vector to describe the lines we have drawn:

```
Vector lines = new Vector();
```

An instance variable newL of class Line is used to describe the line as it is being drawn. We let newL refer to a new line each time the user presses a mouse button. The line is initialized from the beginning, where the start and end points are the same, that is, giving the position of the mouse when the user first presses the mouse button.

```
newL = new Line(e.getPoint(), e.getPoint());
```

(Here, e is, as usual, the parameter of the listener.) When the user releases the mouse button, the mouse's position is read and the end point is changed in the line newL.

```
newL.p2 = e.getPoint();
```

The new line is then placed last in the vector:

```
lines.addElement(newL);
```

As usual, the method `paint` is called automatically each time the window has to be redrawn. We run through all of the lines of the vector in this method and draw them one by one. To do this, we make use of an iterator, described in Section 7.7, on page 239.

```
for (Enumeration e=lines.elements(); e.hasMoreElements(); )
  ((Line) e.nextElement()).draw(g);
```

The method `nextElement` gives as result a value of type `Object`, and so we have to make an explicit type conversion to type `Line`.

The different parts can now be combined into a complete class, with the name `Draw1`. We let `Draw1` be a subclass of class `ExtendedFrame` instead of class `Frame`. We can then terminate the program by simply clicking in the window's closure box:

```
import java.awt.*;
import java.awt.event.*;
import java.util.*;
import extra.*;

public class Draw1 extends ExtendedFrame {
  Vector lines = new Vector();
  Line newL;

  Draw1() {
    addMouseListener(l1);
    setSize(300,300);
    setVisible(true);
  }

  public void paint(Graphics g) {
    for (Enumeration e=lines.elements(); e.hasMoreElements(); )
      ((Line) e.nextElement()).draw(g);
  }

  MouseListener l1 = new MouseAdapter() {
    public void mousePressed(MouseEvent e) {
      newL = new Line(e.getPoint(), e.getPoint());
    }

    public void mouseReleased(MouseEvent e) {
      newL.p2 = e.getPoint();
      lines.addElement(newL);
      repaint();
    }
  };
```

```
public static void main (String arg[]) {
  Draw1 d = new Draw1();
}
}
```

We let the listener for the mouse listen to the two events that occur when the mouse is pressed and released. Note that `repaint` is called last in the method `mouseReleased`. All the lines in the window are then drawn, including the new line.

This drawing program serves its purpose but it has a major weakness: the line we are drawing cannot be seen until we have finished drawing it and release the mouse button. Let us, therefore, make a new, improved version and call it `Draw2`.

In `Draw2` we will use a technique called *XOR mode*. In a window, there is normally a background colour and a foreground colour; when a drawing command is given, everything is drawn with the colour in the foreground. In XOR mode, the drawing colour alternates between two different colours, the actual colour in the foreground and another one, the XOR colour, which we ourselves can specify. If we make several passes with the mouse in the same position on the screen, whatever is drawn will be displayed in these two, alternating colours. If we now choose the XOR colour so that it is the same as the background colour and we draw in the same place on the screen, we will be drawing with the foreground and background colours alternating: whatever we draw will, therefore, appear and disappear alternately. In XOR mode, therefore, we can erase a line we have just drawn by drawing it again.

To indicate that XOR mode is to be used, we call the method `setXORmode` for the `Graphics` object used. The XOR colour is given as parameter. If we want the actual background colour to be used as the XOR colour, we write:

```
g.setXORMode(getBackground());
```

To return to the normal situation and drawing as usual, we make the call:

```
g.setPaintMode();
```

In the new version of the drawing program, we change over to XOR mode each time the user presses a mouse button and begins to draw a new line. We add a listener that listens to the mouse when it has been dragged, that is, moved with the button pressed. When this has been done, we read the mouse's actual position and update the line `newL` so that it will describe a line from `p1` (the point at which the mouse button was pressed) to the actual mouse position, point `p2`. We then draw the line `newL`. However, before we change `newL`, we redraw it. Because drawing takes place in XOR mode, the old line will be erased. When the program is run, it will look as though the line that is being drawn remains at its starting point `p1`, while the end point follows the movements of the mouse for as long as the mouse button is pressed. When the mouse button is released, we leave the XOR mode and begin to draw normally again. The new line is then drawn in its final version.

When all of this is combined, we will get the following program. Note that the new listener will be a subclass of MouseMotionAdapter, since it listens to a mouseDragged event:

```java
import java.awt.*;
import java.awt.event.*;
import java.util.*;
import extra.*;

public class Draw2 extends ExtendedFrame {
  Vector lines = new Vector();
  Line newL;
  Graphics g;

  Draw2() {
    addMouseListener(l1);
    addMouseMotionListener(l2);
    setSize(300,300);
    setBackground(Color.white);
    setVisible(true);
    g = getGraphics();
  }

  public void paint(Graphics g) {
    for (Enumeration e=lines.elements(); e.hasMoreElements(); )
      ((Line) e.nextElement()).draw(g);
  }

  MouseListener l1 = new MouseAdapter() {
    public void mousePressed(MouseEvent e) {
      newL = new Line(e.getPoint(), e.getPoint());
      g.setXORMode(getBackground());  // change over to XOR mode
    }

    public void mouseReleased(MouseEvent e) {
      newL.p2 = e.getPoint(); // set the end point
      lines.addElement(newL);
      g.setPaintMode();      // return to normal drawing
      newL.draw(g); //the line is finished, now draw it properly
    }
  };
```

```
MouseMotionListener l2 = new MouseMotionAdapter() {
  public void mouseDragged(MouseEvent e) {
    newL.draw(g);                // erase the line
    newL.p2 = e.getPoint();  // change the end point
    newL.draw(g);                // redraw the line
  }
};

public static void main (String arg[]) {
  Draw2 d = new Draw2();
}
}
```

Note that we no longer need to call `repaint` to get the new line drawn. In this way, we avoid unnecessary flicker. The method `paint` must still be retained, since it is called in case the window is hidden. All the lines then have to be redrawn.

10.3 Keyboard

When the user presses a key on the keyboard, events described by the type `KeyEvent` are generated. These events are guided by the system to the GUI component that is in *focus* for the present. The component in focus is determined by the user, by clicking with the mouse or by using the Tab key (or Ctrl-Tab) in order to change between components. A component that is in focus is usually marked in some special way; it might be through a different colour or a change in its edges. For a component to be in focus, it must lie in the *active window*. The active window's frame is usually shown in a different colour. (In Windows, for example, the frame of an active window is often dark blue, while frames of non-active windows are grey.) The user will determine which window is to be active by clicking on it (Windows), or by moving the mouse to it (Unix).

A window will recognize when it has become active by defining a listener that listens to `WindowActivated` events. In addition, there is a method `getFocusOwner` in class `Window` that returns a reference to the component in the actual window in focus. The method returns the value `null` if no component is in focus, which will happen if the window is not active. A particular component can expressly request to be in focus by calling the method `requestFocus`. For this request to succeed, the window in which the component lies must be the active window. A particular component can also define a listener that listens to the events `focusGained` and `focusLost` to find out when it comes into focus.

The component currently in focus can listen to all keyboard events, that is, events of class `KeyEvent`. To track such events, we have to create a listener that implements the interface `KeyListener`, or one that belongs to a subclass of class `KeyAdapter`. There are three different kinds of keyboard events: `keyPressed`, `keyReleased` and `keyTyped`. The first two are always generated when a key is pressed or released. The event `keyTyped` is generated if a key (or a combination of keys), which would have produced a visible character in an ordinary text window, is pressed. Note that `keyPressed` and `keyReleased` are always generated, even if the event `keyTyped` is also generated.

To demonstrate how this works, we shall construct a listener `l` that listens to all the kinds of key events. We connect this listener to a component with the statement:

```
addKeyListener(l);
```

In the listener, we will use the following methods defined in the class `KeyEvent`. The method `getKeyCode` gives a key number, a whole number that is unique for each key. This key number is called a "virtual key code". The method `getKeyCode` can be used when we track events such as `keyPressed` and `keyReleased` to find out which key was involved. There are also a number of whole number constants with different key numbers defined in class `KeyEvent`. All of these have a name beginning with `VK_`, for example, `VK_SPACE`, `VK_F3`, `VK_J` and `VK_9`, corresponding to a space, F3, the J key and the 9 key. We can use these constants when we wish to check which key was pressed or released. For instance, to check whether the user pressed the Enter key or the Tab key, we can write:

```
if (e.getKeyCode() == KeyEvent.VK_ENTER ||
       e.getKeyCode() == KeyEvent.VK_TAB)
```

(`e` is the parameter of the listener method here, that is, an object of class `KeyEvent`.) There is also a class method called `getKeyText` in the class `KeyEvent`. This gets a key number as parameter and translates this to a text with the name of the keys.

The method `getKeyCode` cannot be used for `keyTyped` events. The user may, of course, need to press two or more keys to generate a particular key character. (For instance, we use the Shift key and a letter key to generate a capital letter.) For `keyTyped` events, on the other hand, we can use the method `getKeyChar`. This will return a **char** indicating which key character was generated by pressure on the keys.

The methods `isAltDown`, `isControlDown`, `isMetaDown` and `isShiftDown`, inherited from class `InputEvent`, can be used to check whether one of the control keys was pressed.

We can now look at our listener `l`. It will display a message in the text window for every keyboard event and this will continue until the user presses the Esc key or Alt-q. The program will then be terminated.

---

java.awt.event.KeyEvent

Events of class `KeyEvent` are guided to the component that has focus.
This component must be found in the active window.
A component can call the method `requestFocus` to get focus.

`getKeyCode()`	gives the key number (virtual key code) upon `keyPressed` and `keyReleased` events.
`VK_name`	constant with the key number for the key *name*
`getKeyText(n)`	translates the key number `n` to a text
`getKeyChar()`	gives a generated character (a `char`) upon `keyTyped` events
`getComponent()`	gives the GUI component in which the mouse finds itself
`isAltDown()`	indicates whether the user held down the Alt key
`isControlDown()`	indicates whether the user held down the Ctrl key
`isMetaDown()`	indicates whether the user held down the Meta key
`isShiftDown()`	indicates whether the user held down the Shift key

```
KeyListener l = new KeyListener() {
  public void keyPressed(KeyEvent e) {
    Std.out.println("The key " +
      KeyEvent.getKeyText(e.getKeyCode()) + " was pressed.");
    if (e.getKeyCode() == KeyEvent.VK_ESCAPE ||
      (e.getKeyCode() == KeyEvent.VK_Q && e.isAltDown()))
      System.exit(0);
  }

  public void keyReleased(KeyEvent e) {
    Std.out.println("The key " +
      KeyEvent.getKeyText(e.getKeyCode()) + " was released.");
  }

  public void keyTyped(KeyEvent e) {
    Std.out.println("The character " + e.getKeyChar() +
                    " was generated.");
    if (e.isAltDown())
      Std.out.println("    ALT down");
    if (e.isControlDown())
      Std.out.println("    Ctrl down");
    if (e.isMetaDown())
      Std.out.println("    Meta down");
    if (e.isShiftDown())
      Std.out.println("    Shift down");
  }
};
```

Let us suppose that the user does the following: presses the PgUp key, presses the 7 key, holds the Shift key down and presses the 5 key, holds the Alt key down and presses the G key, presses the F5 key and presses the Q key while holding down the Alt key. Then the following text will be written out when the program is run.

```
The Page Up key was pressed.
The Page Up key was released.
The 7 key was pressed.
The 7 character was generated.
The 7 key was released.
The Shift key was pressed.
The 5 key was pressed.
The % character was generated.
   Shift down
The 5 key was released.
The Shift key was released.
The Alt key was pressed.
The G key was pressed.
The g character was generated.
   Alt down
The G key was released.
The Alt key was released.
The F5 key was pressed.
The F5 key was released.
The Alt key was pressed.
The Q key was pressed.
```

From this we can see that we should listen to `keyPressed` and `keyReleased` events if we are interested in key presses and key releases and to `keyTyped` events when we are interested not in the key presses themselves but in the characters they generate.

10.4 An advanced example – a game of tennis

In order to demonstrate how we can use listeners in a program employing multiple threads and displaying moving figures, we will construct a program that plays a game very much like tennis. The program will display a window that looks like Figure 10.3.

The game is played by two players, each of whom wields a racket, indicated by the black vertical lines on the short sides. Each player can move his or her racket up or down. The player on the right will use the keys ↑ and ↓, and the player on the left will use the A and Z keys as "up" and "down" keys.

A red ball bounces back and forth (and up and down) in the playing area, and each player has to hit the ball with the racket so that the ball does not touch the player's short side. If this does happen, the opponent gets a point. The point is displayed at the side of the playing area. When play begins, the ball travels relatively slowly from the

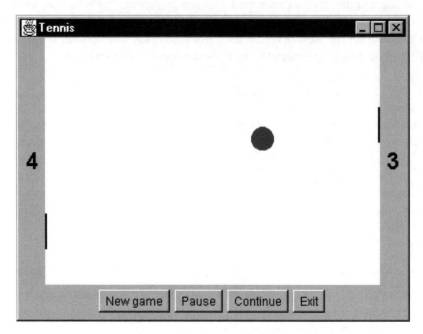

Figure 10.3 A game of tennis

left but every time a player is able to hit the ball, its speed increases, making it more difficult to hit. The speed of the ball increases until one of the players misses it and it bounces against one of the short sides. The ball then returns to the speed it had at the beginning of the game. The game begins when we click on the "New game" button. A game is interrupted automatically when one of the players has reached 10 points. A game can be temporarily interrupted if the "Pause" button is clicked and continued when the "Continue" button is clicked. The actual game played can be interrupted and a new game begun instead, by clicking on the "New game" button.

There is an aspect of the program that is not obvious from the figure. The playing area's width and length can be changed at any time by dragging on the window. So the game can be made easier or more difficult, and play will be adjusted automatically to continue on the altered "court".

We will begin by describing the class Tennis, which will construct the window itself. The window contains four basic components: two Label objects that display the points, an object of class TennisCourt and a panel. The panel in turn contains four buttons. BorderLayout is used in the window. The Label objects are placed in the east and west positions, the panel is placed in the south, and the "court" in the centre.

We have defined the class TennisCourt ourselves. It is a subclass of the standard class Canvas and, in addition, describes an active object. It has four methods called from without. The first one is the method init, which must be called before the first game is begun. It will have two arguments, references to the Label objects that will display the points. The other three methods are newGame, which sets the points to zero and starts a new game, stopGame, which temporarily stops the game, and startGame, which restarts a game that has been stopped. We shall return to class TennisCourt soon.

A listener is needed in class Tennis for the event actionPerformed, which occurs when the players click on a button with the mouse. As usual, we arrange for the class itself to be the listener class and define the method actionPerformed. The methods in class TennisCourt are called in this method. Note that requestFocus is called when the user has clicked on a button, so that the "court" will be in focus. This is important as otherwise we could not be certain that the court would recognize when the players pressed the keys.

```java
import java.awt.*;
import java.awt.event.*;
import extra.*;

public class Tennis extends ExtendedFrame
                    implements ActionListener {
  TennisCourt court = new TennisCourt();
  Label points1  = new Label("0", Label.CENTER);
  Label points2  = new Label("0", Label.CENTER);
  Panel buttons = new Panel();
  Button b1 = new Button("New game");
  Button b2 = new Button("Pause");
  Button b3 = new Button("Continue");
  Button b4 = new Button("Exit");

  public Tennis() {
    setTitle("Tennis");
    court.setSize(350,250);
    court.setBackground(Color.white);
    points1.setFont(new Font("SansSerif", Font.BOLD, 24));
    points2.setFont(new Font("SansSerif", Font.BOLD, 24));
    points1.setBackground(Color.lightGray);
    points2.setBackground(Color.lightGray);
    buttons.setBackground(Color.lightGray);
    buttons.setLayout(new FlowLayout());
    buttons.add(b1); buttons.add(b2);
    buttons.add(b3); buttons.add(b4);
    b1.addActionListener(this); b2.addActionListener(this);
    b3.addActionListener(this); b4.addActionListener(this);
    setLayout(new BorderLayout());
```

```
      add("Center", court);
      add("West", points1); add("East", points2);
      add("South", buttons);
      pack();
      court.init(points1, points2);
      setVisible(true);
   }
   public void actionPerformed(ActionEvent e) {
      court.requestFocus();
      if (e.getSource() == b1)
        court.newGame();
      else if (e.getSource() == b2)
        court.stopGame();
      else if (e.getSource() == b3)
        court.startGame();
      else if (e.getSource() == b4)
        System.exit(0);
   }
   public static void main(String[] arg) {
      Tennis s = new Tennis();
   }
}
```

The class `TennisCourt` is a little more complicated. Let us begin by showing it in its entirety and only then give a commentary.

```
class TennisCourt extends Canvas implements Runnable {
   Thread activity;     // executes the method run
   Label points1, points2; // to display points
   int p1, p2;          // actual points
   int xMax, yMax;      // the court's highest x- and y-coordinates
   int r, x0, y0;       // the ball's radius and centre point
   int xStep, yStep;    // the ball's "step" length
   int v, v0 = 5;       // the ball's speed
   int rLeft, rRight,   // the y-coordinate for the racket's
                        // upper edge
        rL, rStep; // the racket's length and "step" length
   Image image2;   // assigns double buffering
   Graphics g2;         // is used for image2

   public void init(Label l1, Label l2) {
      points1 = l1; points2 = l2;
      xMax = getSize().width-1;
      yMax = getSize().height-1;
      r  = yMax/20;   // compute the ball's radius
      rL = 3*r;       // compute the racket's length
      rStep = r;      // compute the racket's "step" length
```

```
    addKeyListener(kl);          // listen to the keyboard and
    addComponentListener(cl);    // changes in the court's size
    image2 = createImage(xMax+1, yMax+1);
    g2 = image2.getGraphics();
    clear();
  }

  private void clear() {
    p1 = p2 = 0;  // set points to zero
    points1.setText("0"); points2.setText("0");
    xStep = yStep = v = v0 = 5; // speed at the beginning
    x0 = r + 1;                 // set the ball on the left side
    y0 = yMax/2;                // in the middle of the short side
    rLeft = rRight = yMax/2-rL/2; // place the rackets in the middle
  }

  public void startGame() {
    if (activity == null) {
      activity = new Thread(this);
      activity.start();
    }
  }

  public void stopGame() {
    if (activity != null) {
      activity.interrupt();
      activity = null;
    }
  }

  public void newGame() {
    stopGame();
    clear();
    startGame();
  }

  public void run() {
    while (XThread.delay(100)) {
      if (x0-r <= 0)  { // is the ball at the side on the left?
        if (y0<rLeft || y0>rLeft+rL) { // a miss?
          Toolkit.getDefaultToolkit().beep();   // beep
          points2.setText(String.valueOf(++p2));
          if (p2 == 10)
            stopGame();
          v = v0;  // return to the speed at the beginning
        }
        else       // a hit
          v++;     // increase the speed
        xStep = v; // move to the right next time
      }
```

```
      else if (x0+r >= xMax)      // is the ball at the side
                                  // on the right?
        if (y0<rRight || y0>rRight+rL) { // a miss?
          Toolkit.getDefaultToolkit().beep();    // beep
          points1.setText(String.valueOf(++p1));
          if (p1 == 10)
            stopGame();
          v = v0;  // return to the speed at the beginning
        }
        else          // a hit
          v++;        // increase the speed
        xStep = -v; // move to the left next time
      }
      if (y0-r<=0 || y0+r>=yMax) // at upper or lower edge?
        yStep = -yStep;            // change vertical direction

      x0 += xStep;   // move the ball horizontally
      y0 += yStep;   // move the ball vertically
      if (x0 < r)    // did the ball land too far to the left?
        x0 = r;
      else if (x0 > xMax-r)  // did the ball land too far
                             // to the right?
        x0 = xMax-r+1;
      if (y0 < r)              // did the ball land too far up?
        y0 = r;
      else if (y0 > yMax-r)  // did the ball land too far down?
        y0 = yMax-r+1;
      repaint();
    }
  }

  public void update(Graphics g) {
    g2.setColor(getBackground());
    g2.fillRect(0, 0, xMax+1, yMax+1);   // erase image2
    g2.setColor(getForeground());
    paint(g);
  }

  public void paint(Graphics g) {
    g2.setColor(Color.red);
    g2.fillOval(x0-r, y0-r, 2*r, 2*r); // draw the ball
    g2.setColor(Color.black);
    g2.fillRect(0, rLeft, 2, rL);          // draw the racket on
                                           // the left
    g2.fillRect(xMax-1, rRight, 2, rL);  // draw the racket on
                                           // the right
    g.drawImage(image2, 0, 0, this);      // copy to the screen
  }
```

```
KeyListener kl = new KeyAdapter() {
  public void keyPressed(KeyEvent e) {
    // a key has been pressed
    if (e.getKeyCode() == KeyEvent.VK_A)        // left up
      rLeft = Math.max(0, rLeft-rStep);
    else if (e.getKeyCode() == KeyEvent.VK_Z)   // left down
      rLeft = Math.min(yMax-rL, rLeft+rStep);
    if (e.getKeyCode() == KeyEvent.VK_UP)       // right up
      rRight = Math.max(0, rRight-rStep);
    else if (e.getKeyCode() == KeyEvent.VK_DOWN) // right down
      rRight = Math.min(yMax-rL, rRight+rStep);
  }
};

ComponentListener cl = new ComponentAdapter() {
  public void componentResized(ComponentEvent e) {
    // the size of the court has been changed
    xMax = e.getComponent().getSize().width-1;
    yMax = e.getComponent().getSize().height-1;
    image2 = createImage(xMax+1, yMax+1);
    g2.dispose();
    g2 = image2.getGraphics();
    e.getComponent().requestFocus();
    repaint();
  }
};
}
```

Since we are dealing with a moving game, we let the court be an active object. The class TennisCourt will therefore follow the model from Chapter 9 and implement the interface Runnable. This means that there is an instance variable activity that describes the thread itself. Class TennisCourt must also have a method called run that is executed by the thread. As usual, this method will contain a continual repetition statement, where the ball is moved at every round. The instance variables xStep and yStep indicate the number of pixels the ball will move each time.

Similarly, the instance variable rStep indicates the number of pixels a racket can move up or down each time a player presses an "up" or a "down" key.

All the initializations that only have to be done once, each time the program is run, are made in the method init. For instance, the size of the ball and the rackets are computed from the size of the court. The reason for using a method init and not a constructor to carry out these initializations, is that we must be able to read the size of the court. This cannot be done in a constructor, since the size is still unknown.

The method clear is called before each new game. The points for both of the players are set at zero, and the two rackets are put in the middle of the short sides.

The methods startGame and stopGame are simple. They are constructed in exactly the same way as the methods start and stop in the applets discussed in Section 9.5. Accordingly, we interrupt the active thread when a game is stopped, and when it is to start again, we create a new thread and connect it to the actual court object. The method newGame is easy to construct. It only has to stop a game in session, set the points to zero and then start the game.

The method run is the most complicated one here. It is in this method that the activity takes place. New coordinates are computed for the ball every hundredth millisecond. A check is made to see whether the ball has reached one of the sides before it is moved. First, the sides on the left and the right are checked; if the ball is on one of these sides, there are two cases to consider. In the first case, the racket is not at the place where the ball hits the side. The opponent then gets a point, and the ball is given the speed it had at the beginning. To indicate clearly that one of the players has missed the ball, the program will emit a "beep". If, however, the racket is at the place where the ball hits the side, the speed of the ball is increased by one pixel per "step". If the ball hits the side, its direction must also be changed so that it is made to bounce.

When the method run has checked whether the ball is to be found at one of the sides, it changes the ball's x- and y-coordinates. When these changes have been carried out, a small adjustment has to be made if parts of the ball should finish up outside the court. In this case, the ball is placed so that it is precisely at the side. Each round of the method run is terminated with the method repaint being called so that the court can be redrawn with the ball in its new position.

Double buffering is used to avoid flicker, and we do exactly as we did in Section 9.7.3 on page 304. The drawing takes place in an invisible picture that we call image2. This picture has been initialized so that it will be exactly the same size as the court. To image2 we connect the Graphics object g2, which is used for the drawing itself. As we know, the method repaint will automatically call the method update. We have written our own version of update, and, in this version, we erase image2 instead of the court. The method update, in its turn, calls the method paint, in which we draw the ball and the two rackets in image2. The rackets are drawn as rectangles, with a width of 2 pixels and not as lines, so that they can be viewed more easily. The method paint is terminated in that the whole of image2 is copied to the screen in a single operation.

Two listeners are needed in class TennisCourt. The listener k1 listens to events generated by keys being pressed. We use the technique of anonymous listener classes and define the method keyPressed, which is called when a key is pressed. (We shall not worry about when keys are released.) A check is made in this method to see whether the key pressed is one of the four used as "up" and "down" keys. If it is, the corresponding racket is moved a step up or down. However, we have to be careful that we do not move a racket either above or below the court. This is most easily done using the methods max and min, in the standard class Math; see page 70.

We have defined the method componentResized in the other listener c1. This is called automatically if the user drags on the window, so that the size of the actual component, that is, the court, is changed. If this happens, the two instance variables xMax and yMax must be updated. The invisible picture that the variable image2 refers to will now be useless, as it will be the wrong size, so we have to create a new, invisible picture with the new size. We shall also release the resources for the old Graphics object and create a new object that will be connected to the new picture.

This concludes our description of the tennis program. Of course, it was a little complicated but this was because we used several different techniques and combined them. The program makes use of GUI components, active objects, double buffering and listeners. We trust that it will serve as a model for other, similar programs.

10.5 Exercises

1. Let us suppose that you have a class F that is a subclass of the class Frame. An object of class F can, therefore, contain other components. Further suppose that first, one of these components, must always finish up in focus each time the actual window becomes active. Construct a listener for the class F that ensures that the component first always gets in focus when the window becomes active. Then construct a listener for the component first that automatically makes the component's background colour blue each time the component is in focus.

2. Write a listener that can be connected to a button, a Button object, which will make the button's background colour turn red automatically when the mouse is on the button.

3. The class Component has a method setCursor that can be used to alter the appearance of the mouse pointer. As argument, this method will have an object of the class Cursor, which is also defined in the package java.awt. In class Cursor, there is a class method getPredefinedCursor that returns a Cursor object. As argument, getPredefinedCursor will have a whole number that will indicate the appearance chosen for the mouse pointer. There are a number of pre-defined whole number constants in class Cursor that can be used. Some examples are TEXT_CURSOR, HAND_CURSOR, WAIT_CURSOR and DEFAULT_CURSOR.

   Construct a listener that will automatically change the appearance of the mouse pointer, so that each time the mouse is moved to the component, it will look like a hand.

4. Add to the program Draw2, on page 323, so that the user can reconsider when he or she has drawn a line. If the keys Ctrl-Z are pressed, the last line to be drawn will be removed.

5. A number of improvements spring to mind in connection with the tennis program in Section 10.4. For example, when a new game is begun, the ball is always to be found in the middle, on the left. It then moves diagonally towards the bottom of the opposite side. Change the situation so that the ball can land at the right or left side of the court and be played arbitrarily up or down. The ball's vertical position should also be arbitrary.

6. Another improvement to the tennis program, apart from that of exercise 5, might be the following. Change the program so that instead of one button with the text "New game", there will be two buttons, one with the text "One player" and one with the text "Two players". When the user clicks on the button "Two players", the game will function as before but when the user clicks on the button "One player", the player on the left will be replaced by the computer. The program will then automatically move the left-hand racket so that it always hits the ball. Because the human player will never get any points, it will not matter that these are not shown; instead, the right-hand Label object should be allowed to display the number of times the human player has succeeded in hitting the ball before he or she loses by 10:0. A player's skill can then be judged by the number of hits made.

Windows, dialog boxes and menus

11

All the examples we have studied so far have only made use of one window on the screen. However, we sometimes deal with programs that require the use of more than one window. A text editor, for instance, may need to edit several text files at the same time. This is easy to do in Java, and we will be discussing how in this chapter. One special sort of window is a dialog box, which a program can temporarily display to leave a message, or to ask the user to answer a question or enter input data.

In Chapter 5 we discussed many different kinds of standard GUI components but we did not deal with menus. We have waited until now because they are special kinds of components. They do not belong to a subclass of the standard class `Component` and have rather special properties.

11.1 The class `Window`

The class `java.awt.Window` describes standalone windows. All GUI components that can be displayed as their own windows on the screen are subclasses of class `Window`. This applies to the classes `Dialog`, `FileDialog` and `Frame` (see Figure 5.1, on page 118). A component of the class `Window` has no frame. We therefore seldom use class `Window` directly but instead define objects of its subclasses. These subclasses inherit several interesting methods from class `Window`. One example is the method `pack`, which we have used in different programs. A compilation of some of the methods in class `Window` is given in the Revision Table.

Events are generated when a window is opened, closed or iconified, and the class `WindowEvent` describes these events. The many different kinds of events that may occur were given in Table 10.1, on page 312. The event `windowActivated` occurred, for example, when a window became activated through the user moving the mouse to it and highlighting it. The event `windowClosed` occurred when the window was closed by the program through a call of `dispose`, or `setVisible(false)`, and `WindowClosing` occurred when the user clicked in the window's closure box or a similar icon. We

java.awt.Window	
`dispose()`	removes the window and releases all the system resources it uses
`setVisible(b)`	displays or hides the window; b has type **boolean**
`isShowing()`	indicates whether or not the window is visible
`getFocusOwner()`	gives the component in the window that is in focus (or **null**)
`pack()`	places the window's sub-components and sets its size
`show()`	makes the window visible and puts it at the top of the screen
`toBack()`	puts the window at the bottom of the screen
`toFront()`	puts the window at the top of the screen
`addWindowListener(1)`	indicates that the listener 1 will deal with events described by class `WindowEvent`

showed an example, on page 316, of how events of the type `WindowClosing` could be dealt with.

11.2 The class `Frame`

The class `Frame` describes a window that has a frame and that can have menus. The first window in a standalone GUI program usually belongs to this class (or is of a subclass of it, as in the case of `ExtendedFrame`). We have seen several examples of this. New windows can easily be generated in a program by creating new `Frame` objects. As an example of this, we will make a new version of the drawing program from Section 10.2. We showed the latest version of this program on page 323. The class `Draw2` was a subclass of class `ExtendedFrame` and so also of class `Frame`. We will retain class `Draw2` as it is, without changing it at all. We now write a new program that looks like this:

```java
import java.awt.*;
import java.awt.event.*;
import extra.*;

public class FrameDemo extends ExtendedFrame
                implements ActionListener {
  Button newButton  = new Button("New window");
  Button exitButton = new Button("Exit");
  int n;  // the number of windows created

  // constructor
  public FrameDemo() {
    setLayout(new FlowLayout());
    add(newButton); add(exitButton);
    newButton.addActionListener(this);
    exitButton.addActionListener(this);
```

```
    pack();
    setVisible(true);
  }

  // listeners
  public void actionPerformed(ActionEvent e) {
    if (e.getSource() == newButton) {
      Frame f = new Draw2();
      f.setTitle("Draw #" + ++n);
      Point p = getLocationOnScreen();
      p.translate(30*n, getSize().height+30*(n-1));
      f.setLocation(p);
    }
    else if (e.getSource() == exitButton)
      System.exit(0);
  }

  public static void main (String arg[]) {
    FrameDemo fd = new FrameDemo();
  }
}
```

When the program is started, the small, upper window of Figure 11.1 is displayed. Every time we click on the button "New window", a new window is opened on the screen. From the figure we can see the resulting appearance when we have clicked on the button three times. Windows for drawing work quite independently of each other, and we can draw lines in them exactly as we demonstrated in Section 10.2. Note that we start the program by giving the command:

```
java FrameDemo
```

Execution will then begin in method main, in the class FrameDemo. Of course, there is a method called main in class Draw2 as well but it will never be called if we start the program in this way.

The two buttons are arranged in the constructor in class FrameDemo, and the FrameDemo object is itself registered as listener, in the usual way. An interesting thing now occurs in the listener: the program will create a new object of class Draw2 when the user has clicked on the button "New window". When a new Frame object is created, it will be invisible from the beginning but because the constructor in class Draw2 makes the call setVisible(true), the new window will become visible. When the new window has been created, the method setTitle is used to indicate the text that will be in the window's frame. Here we use the whole number variable n as counter. It will be increased by one each time we create a new window.

When a new window is made visible, it is placed far up in the left-hand corner on the screen, unless otherwise indicated. Because we do not want windows to land directly

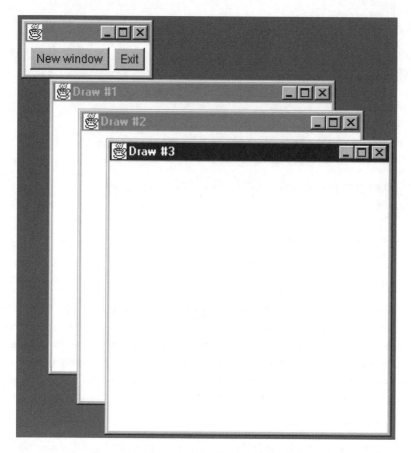

Figure 11.1 A program with several windows

on top of each other, we indicate explicitly where each new window is to be placed. We can do this by calling the method `setLocation`, which determines where the window's upper left-hand corner is to be placed. There are two variants of this method. We can either give the x- and y-coordinates as arguments or, as we have done here, give an argument of the standard type `Point` (see page 65). The point will be determined on the basis of the position of the window with the buttons. We can read the position of this window by using the method `getLocationOnScreen`, which returns a `Point` object. The method `translate` moves a point to another position. The two parameters will indicate the adjustment in the x and y directions, respectively. We want window number 1 to be placed directly under the small window and somewhat to the right (30 pixels), and we will move the other windows another 30 pixels towards the bottom, to the right.

Because all the windows in our program are of class ExtendedFrame, we can close them by clicking in the closure box (or equivalent). If we look at the listener in class ExtendedFrame, on page 316, we will see that this is done through calls of the method dispose, inherited from class Window. This method will not interrupt the program, however, and we will not want it to do so when we close the windows. On the other hand, it is quite reasonable for the program to be interrupted if we click the closure box in the small window, as this is the program's main window. This also happens automatically, because the listener in class ExtendedFrame will check whether the window to be closed is the first one we created. If this is so, the method System.exit is called and the program interrupted.

java.awt.Frame	
new Frame()	creates a new window, invisible from the beginning
new Frame(*text*)	creates a new window, invisible from the beginning, with the title *text*
setTitle(*text*)	sets the title in the window frame to *text*
getTitle()	reads the window's title
setLocation(x,y)	indicates where the window's upper left-hand corner is to be placed
setLocation(p)	indicates where the window's upper left-hand corner is to be placed; p is of class Point
getLocationOnScreen()	reads the window's position; gives a Point object
setResizable(*bool*)	determines whether the window's size can be changed
isResizable()	reads whether the window's size can be changed
setMenuBar(*mb*)	indicates that the window should have the menu bar *mb*
getMenuBar()	gives a reference to the window's menu bar
remove(*mb*)	removes the menu bar *mb* from the window
setIconImage(*im*)	indicates that the picture *im* will be the window's icon image
getIconImage()	gives a reference to the window's icon image
setState(s)	s could be Frame.ICONIFIED or Frame.NORMAL
getState()	gives Frame.ICONIFIED or Frame.NORMAL
getFrames()	gives an array with the Frame objects that have been created by the program

A compilation of some of the methods in class Frame is given in the Revision Table. The methods setLocation and getLocationOnScreen are actually defined in class Component but since we use layout managers to arrange ordinary components these two methods are most useful when it comes to arranging windows on the screen.

11.3 The class `Dialog`

In GUI programs, dialog boxes are often used to leave messages for the user, or to put questions to the user. Some dialog boxes can be visible at the same time as the user is busy with other things in the program. They will not obstruct the functioning of the program generally, and the program will not depend on whether the user has responded to its questions or filled in the boxes with input data. This kind of dialog box is called a *non-modal dialog box*. A couple of examples of this are shown in Figure 11.2.

Figure 11.2 Non-modal dialog boxes

However, we most often make use of *modal dialog boxes*. As long as it is open, a modal dialog box will obstruct all other input to the program. For instance, the user will not be able to click on other windows in the program. A modal dialog box can contain an important message to the user, or a question that the user must respond to immediately for the program to proceed. Examples of modal dialog boxes are shown in Figure 11.3. Modal dialog boxes may also contain text arrays into which the user has to write input data. An example of this is a dialog box with names and a password.

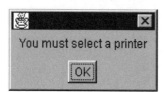
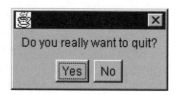

Figure 11.3 Modal dialog boxes

The class `Dialog` is used in Java to create dialog boxes of both the modal and non-modal variety. Because class `Dialog` is a subclass of class `Window`, dialog boxes can be shown as independent windows on the screen. We shall begin by showing how the dialog box on the left in Figure 11.2 is generated:

```
import java.awt.*;
import java.awt.event.*;

public class DialogTest extends Frame implements ActionListener
{
  Dialog info = new Dialog(this);   // non-modal
  Button OKButton = new Button("OK");

  // constructor
  DialogTest() {
    info.add("Center", new Label("This is a demo version"));
    info.add("South", OKButton);
    OKButton.addActionListener(this);   // register listener
    info.pack();   // arrange the components
    other initializations
  }

  public void showInfo() {
    info.show();                     // display dialog box
  }

  // listener
  public void actionPerformed(ActionEvent e) {
      if (e.getSource() == OKButton) {
        info.setVisible(false);      // close the dialog box
        do anything else that may need to be done because
        the user has clicked in the dialog box
      }
  }

  other methods
}
```

Here we are dealing with a class `DialogTest`, which describes the window the dialog box will be opened from. A reference to the window the dialog box is opened from, the dialog's *parent window*, must always be indicated in the constructor of a dialog. Therefore `this` is written on the fifth line. The initializations of the dialog box have been placed in the constructor of the class `DialogTest`. Because class `Dialog` is a subclass of class `Container`, it can contain other components. These are arranged in the usual way with the method `add`. Note that, unless otherwise indicated, `BorderLayout` will be used, exactly as for class `Frame`.

In order to display a dialog box, we call the method `show`. In this example, we have put the call in a special method with the name of `showInfo`. The dialog box is not closed automatically when the user clicks on the OK button. We ourselves have to connect a listener to the button and close the box by making the call `setVisible(false)`.

If nothing in particular is indicated when a `Dialog` object is created, it will be a non-modal dialog. In our example, the dialog `info` will be non-modal, meaning that it can

343

be visible while other things are being done in class `DialogTest`. If we had instead written:

```
Dialog info = new Dialog(this, true);   // modal
```

`info` would have been a modal dialog. If we then had showed the dialog box, nothing could have happened in the program until the user had clicked on the OK button. The method `actionPerformed` would then have been called and we could close the dialog box in that method.

The class `Dialog`, of course, inherits all the methods in its superclasses `Component`, `Container` and `Window` but there are also methods characteristic of class `Dialog`. These are shown in the Revision Table. (The methods `setLocation` and `getLocation OnScreen` are defined in class `Component`, however.)

java.awt.Dialog

In the first three forms of the constructor, *parent* can either be a `Frame` or a `Dialog`. In the fourth of these forms, *parent* will be a `Frame`.

new `Dialog`(*parent*)	creates a non-modal dialog box without a title
new `Dialog`(*parent, t*)	creates a non-modal dialog box with the title *t*
new `Dialog`(*parent, t, modal*)	creates a dialog box with the title *t*, *modal* is **boolean**
new `Dialog`(*parent, modal*)	creates a dialog box without a title; *modal* is **boolean**
`show()`	displays the dialog box and places it at the top of the screen
`setTitle`(*text*)	sets the title in the dialog box to *text*
`getTitle()`	reads the title of the dialog box
`setLocation(x,y)`	indicates where the dialog box's upper left-hand corner is to be placed
`setLocation(p)`	indicates where the dialog box's upper left-hand corner is to be placed; `p` is of class `Point`
`getLocationOnScreen()`	reads the position of the box; gives a `Point` object
`setResizable`(*bool*)	determines whether the size of the dialog box can be changed
`isResizable()`	reads whether the size of the dialog box is changeable
`setModal`(*bool*)	determines whether the dialog box will be modal
`isModal()`	reads whether the dialog box is modal

In our example, we used a `Label` object to display the message in the dialog box. `Label` objects are easy to use but they have a big disadvantage: they can only display a single line and we often want to display longer messages in dialog boxes. To make our task a little easier, we define our own class `MessageDialog`, which is a subclass of class `Dialog`. When we construct a dialog using this class, we will indicate three parameters for the constructor: the parent window, the message to be displayed and a **boolean** that will indicate whether or not the dialog is to be modal. We use the end-of-line character \n to indicate where we will begin a new line. The character \n will not be written after the last line. (This means that the end-of-line character will not be used for messages that can be written on a single line.) For instance, the dialog box on the right in Figure 11.2 is created by the declaration:

```
MessageDialog about = new MessageDialog(this,
   "SuperJavaTools\nVersion 1.1\nCopyright Miss Java", false);
```

The class `MessageDialog` also contains a method `setTextFont` that can be used to indicate fonts and font size for the text in messages. The definition of `MessageDialog` looks like this:

```
package extra;
import java.awt.*;

public class MessageDialog extends Dialog {
   private Panel text = new Panel();  // panel with Labels

   public MessageDialog(Frame parent, String m, boolean modal) {
      super(parent, modal);
      initText(m);
   }

   public MessageDialog(Dialog parent, String m, boolean modal) {
      super(parent, "", modal);
      initText(m);
   }

   private void initText(String m) {
      text.setLayout(new GridLayout(0,1));
      add("Center", text);
      int i=0, j; // index for the first and last character in a line
      // remove one line at a time from the message
      while ((j=m.indexOf('\n', i)) >= 0) {
         text.add(new Label(m.substring(i,j), Label.CENTER));
         i = j+1;
      }
      // remove the last line
      text.add(new Label(m.substring(i), Label.CENTER));
      pack();
   }
```

```
public void setTextFont(Font f) {
    text.setFont(f);
    pack();
}
}
```

We placed class `MessageDialog` in the package `extra` so that it would be generally accessible. A panel is created so that the message can be displayed in several lines, and as many `Label` objects as there are lines are then placed in it. These `Label` objects are created in the private method `initText`. In the panel, `GridLayout` is used, with 1 column. A zero for the number of lines means that there can be an arbitrary number. The `Label` objects arranged in the panel will, therefore, land under each other. In the method `initText` we run through the text `m` that contains the message and look for the end-of-line character `\n`. Every time we come upon one of these, we remove the text up to the character, creating a new `Label` object with this text. The last line has to be specially handled since it does not terminate with an end-of-line character.

Let us now discuss modal dialogs. We can, of course, use these for important messages, as in the left-hand dialog box in Figure 11.3, but it is more common for a dialog box to contain a question for the user to answer. Looking at the right-hand dialog box in Figure 11.3, for example, we might ask ourselves what the best way might be to transfer the answer to the part of the program that opened the dialog box. There are several variants here. The first thing we might think of doing is to put the listener listening to events in the dialog box into the part of the program that opens the dialog box. As an example, let us suppose that we write a program that will be used to carry out course evaluations. In one part of the program we want to display the dialog box in Figure 11.4. In order to carry out a statistical analysis of the answers from participants in the course, we shall assign points for the various answers: "Bad" gets 1 point, "Acceptable" gets 2 points, and so on.

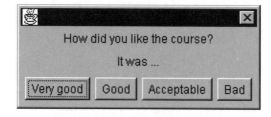

Figure 11.4 A modal dialog box with several alternative answers

We can begin by defining the dialog box and the buttons according to the usual model. We let the dialog box be a subclass of our new class, `MessageDialog`. It will then be a simple matter to get two lines in the message:

```
int points;
String  question = "How did you like the course?\n" +
                   "It was ...";
MessageDialog d = new MessageDialog(this, question, true);
Panel buttons = new Panel();
Button b1 = new Button("Very good");
Button b2 = new Button("Good");
Button b3 = new Button("Acceptable");
Button b4 = new Button("Bad");
```

Of course, the buttons then have to be put into the dialog box and the listener registered. As usual, we let the actual object itself be the listener:

```
buttons.add(b1); buttons.add(b2);
buttons.add(b3); buttons.add(b4);
d.add("South", buttons);
d.pack();
b1.addActionListener(this); b2.addActionListener(this);
b3.addActionListener(this); b4.addActionListener(this);
```

We call the method `show` when it is time to display the dialog box:

```
d.show();
System.out.println(points + " points");
```

Only now can the user click in the dialog box. In addition, the thread in the program that makes the call of `show` is stopped, and execution of the thread will not continue until the dialog box has been closed.

We must also define the listener that will indicate that the user has clicked on one of the buttons in the dialog box. We assign the right value to the variable `points` in this listener and close the dialog box.

```
public void actionPerformed(ActionEvent e) {
  if (e.getSource() == b1) {
    points = 4;
    d.setVisible(false);
  }
  else if (e.getSource() == b2) {
    points = 3;
    d.setVisible(false);
  }
  else if (e.getSource() == b3) {
    points = 2;
    d.setVisible(false);
  }
```

```
  else if (e.getSource() == b4) {
    points = 1;
    d.setVisible(false);
  }
}
```

Execution of the statements after the call of show can continue when the dialog box has been closed, and we can then make use of the variable points, by now initialized.

This construction of the program gets quickly into the essentials. The only problem is that it would be somewhat inelegant to have to do this for all the dialog boxes in a program. So we introduce another technique. We shall create our own new dialog class with the name QuestionDialog, which will describe modal dialog boxes containing a question and an arbitrary number of buttons with different answers. We let the new class be a subclass of class MessageDialog so that we can have questions displayed on several lines. We shall give the complete definition of class QuestionDialog presently but first let us see how the part of the program looks where the dialog box is opened and where we wish to receive the answer. As an example, we shall again look at the dialog box in Figure 11.4.

Three arguments will be given to the constructor when an object of class QuestionDialog is created. The first argument is, as usual, a reference to the parent window, and the second argument is the text with the question. We will use the end-of-line character \n if there are several lines, exactly as with class MessageDialog. The third argument will be an array with texts. There will be as many components in the array as there are buttons, and the different components will contain the text appearing on the buttons. To create the Dialog object that describes the box in Figure 11.4, we write the following program lines:

```
String  question = "How did you like the course?\n" +
                   "It was ...";
String[] answer = {"Very good", "Good", "Acceptable", "Bad"};
QuestionDialog d = new QuestionDialog(this, question, answer);
```

When it is time to display the dialog box, we will call the method show, as usual. This will temporarily stop execution of the thread. Execution will continue with the statements after the call of show when the user has clicked on one of the buttons in the dialog box, and we will be able to read the answer the user has given. There is a method called getAnswer, in class QuestionDialog, which will give as result a text identical to the text on the button that the user has clicked on. For example, if the user has clicked on the button "Good", then getAnswer will return the text "Good". We can now write the lines where we display the dialog box and read the answer:

```
 d.show();
 for (int i=0; i<answer.length; i++)
   if (d.getAnswer().equals(answer[i]))
     points = answer.length-i;
System.out.println(points + " points");
```

This is all that needs to be done! We do not have to write in a listener, nor do we have to create and arrange the buttons.

Our own class `QuestionDialog` is obviously very useful. We shall, therefore, put it into the package `extra`. The definition looks like this:

```
package extra;
 import java.awt.*;
 import java.awt.event.*;

 public class QuestionDialog extends MessageDialog
                             implements ActionListener {
   private Panel buttons = new Panel();
   private String answer;

   private void initButtons(String[] answers) {
     for (int i=0; i<answers.length; i++) {
       Button b = new Button(answers[i]);
       buttons.add(b);   // FlowLayout
       b.addActionListener(this);
     }
     add("South", buttons);
     pack();
     setResizable(false);
     addWindowListener(wl);
   }

   public QuestionDialog(Frame parent, String question,
                         String[] answers) {
     super(parent, question, true);
     initButtons(answers);
   }

   public QuestionDialog(Dialog parent, String question,
                         String[] answers) {
     super(parent, question, true);
     initButtons(answers);
   }

   public String getAnswer() {
     return answer;
   }
```

```
public void actionPerformed(ActionEvent e) {
  answer =e.getActionCommand(); //gives the text on the button
  setVisible(false);
}

WindowListener wl = new WindowAdapter() {
  public void windowActivated(WindowEvent e) {
    // lets the left-hand button come into focus
    buttons.getComponents()[0].requestFocus();
  }
};
}
```

The buttons are created and arranged in the private method `initButtons` that is called from the constructors. The actual `QuestionDialog` object is itself registered as listener for every button, so we will come to the method `actionPerformed` when the user has clicked on one of the buttons. In this method we call the method `getActionCommand`, defined in class `ActionEvent`. This will return a text that is connected to the component that caused the event. If we ourselves have not initialized this text and the component is a button, the method `getActionCommand` will give the text on the button as result. We will make use of this here. (We could connect another text to a component ourselves. This would be done with the method `setActionCommand` in class `Component`.) The button's text is copied to the variable `answer`, which can be read by using the method `getAnswer`.

When a dialog box is displayed, the user can press the Tab key and Shift-Tab to alternate between the buttons and can press the space bar (possibly the Enter key, too) to choose a particular alternative. We have defined yet another listener in the class `QuestionDialog` so that the button lying furthest to the left will automatically come into focus each time the dialog box becomes active. It will listen to the event `windowActivated`. The buttons lie in the panel `buttons`, first among its components being the button lying furthest to the left.

The most common type of modal dialog box is one that only contains a message and an OK button, or one that has buttons with the answers "Yes" and "No" and perhaps "Cancel". Therefore, to make things really easy for the programmer, we will define the subclasses `OKDialog`, `YNDialog` and `YNCDialog`.

```
package extra;
 import java.awt.*;
 public class OKDialog extends QuestionDialog {
   public OKDialog(Frame parent, String message) {
     super(parent, message, new String[] {"OK"});
   }
 }
```

```
package extra;
import java.awt.*;
public class YNDialog extends QuestionDialog {
  public YNDialog(Frame parent, String question) {
    super(parent, question, new String[] {"Yes", "No"});
  }
}
```

```
package extra;
import java.awt.*;
public class YNCDialog extends QuestionDialog {
  public YNCDialog(Frame parent, String question) {
    super(parent, question,
          new String[] {"Yes", "No", "Cancel"});
  }
}
```

Using these subclasses, it will be extremely easy to produce modal dialog boxes as those in Figure 11.3. For example, we could make the definitions:

```
OKDialog  d1 = new OKDialog (this, "You must select a printer");
YNDialog  d2 = new YNDialog(this,"Do you really want to quit?");
```

The right-hand box in Figure 11.3 is displayed with the following program lines. If the user clicks on the "Yes" button, the program will be interrupted:

```
d2.show();
if (d2.getAnswer().equals("Yes"))
  System.exit(0);
```

A modal dialog box can contain more components than a text and buttons with different alternatives. It can contain different input components. For instance, there may be one or more `TextField` components in which the user can enter text. The technique we used in constructing class `QuestionDialog` can also be used in dealing with dialog boxes of this kind. We create a subclass of the class `Dialog` (or `MessageDialog`) and let this class arrange the components and contain the listeners it needs. We also define one or more methods that we can call from without to read the input data, or answers that the user has entered into the program; see Exercise 4 on page 368.

A word must be said here about applets. An applet can have dialog boxes, exactly like a standalone GUI program. We are presented with a little problem, however. When we create a dialog box, an argument of class `Frame` that refers to the window our application is running in has to be given as parameter to the constructor. An applet is not a subclass of class `Frame`, so we cannot give the parameter **this**, as we have done in examples in this section. However, an applet always executes inside a window, either the web browser's window, or the window that is started by `appletviewer`. There is a

351

method getParent in class Component, which as result gives the Container object the actual component has been put into. Because both Applet and Container are subclasses of Component, we can call getParent again and again until we gradually get a reference to the window in which the applet is executing. This window will be of class Frame. The reference we then get can be used as parameter when we create our dialog windows. We show how this can be done in the following program lines, which we will assume lie in an applet:

```
Container c = getParent();       // the applet's parent
while (!(c instanceof Frame))
    c = c.getParent();           // go upwards until c is in Frame
Dialog d = new Dialog((Frame) c);
```

11.4 The class FileDialog

There is a very useful subclass of class Dialog in java.awt. This is the class FileDialog, which is used to create dialog boxes where the user can indicate a file name. It is extremely easy to use class FileDialog in a program. We might make the following declaration in order to create a dialog box that we can use when we open a file:

```
FileDialog fd = new FileDialog(this, "Open");
```

The second argument indicates the title we want to have in the frame of the dialog box. As usual, we call the method show when we want to display the dialog box. We then get a modal dialog box that will have the typical appearance of boxes in the system being used. In Windows this may look like Figure 11.5.

When in the usual way the user has marked the file to be opened, the method getFile can be called to find out the name of the chosen file. The method getFile returns a value of type String. Had the user clicked on the button "Cancel", method getFile would have returned the value null. The method getDirectory can be called to find out the name of the directory the chosen file is in.

As an example we show how to open a text file. As in Section 3.3.2 on page 92, let us suppose that we have declared a stream of class BufferedReader:

```
BufferedReader inFile;
```

When the file is to be opened, we shall do the following:

```
fd.show();
String name = fd.getDirectory()+fd.getFile();
if (fd.getFile() != null)
    try {
        inFile = new BufferedReader(new FileReader(name));
    }
```

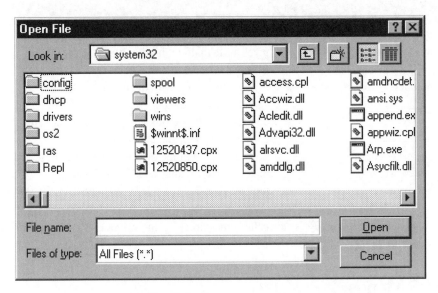

Figure 11.5 The dialog box generated by `FileDialog`

```
catch (FileNotFoundException e) {
   (new OKDialog(this, "Cannot find " + name)).show();
}
```

Note that we cannot be sure that the file given as result from the file dialog really exists. The user might, of course, have written the file name instead of clicking. The constructor for class `FileReader` generates the exception `FileNotFoundException` if the given file cannot be found. An exception of this kind must be handled. In this example, we have made use of the class `OKDialog` from the previous section to inform the user that the file does not exist.

If instead we wish to save a file, we can make use of the fact that class `FileDialog` has a constructor with a third argument. We could write:

```
FileDialog fd2 = new FileDialog(this, "Save", FileDialog.SAVE);
```

We then get a dialog box that is suitable for saving files. In Figure 11.5, for example, "Save" would be on the upper button, instead of "Open".

The class `FileDialog` has another two methods we should be familiar with. These are `setFile` and `setDirectory`. Both of them have a single argument, a `String`. The method `setFile` indicates the file name to be displayed as default when the dialog box is opened, while `setDirectory` indicates the directory that the dialog box will initially

java.awt.FileDialog	
new FileDialog (*parent*)	gives a file dialog intended for the reading of files
new FileDialog (*parent,t*)	gives a file dialog with the title *t*, for the reading of files
new FileDialog (*parent,t,m*)	gives a file dialog with the title *t*; *m* can be FileDialog.LOAD or FileDialog.SAVE
show ()	displays the dialog box and places it at the top
getFile ()	gives the name of the chosen file
getDirectory ()	gives the name of the directory with the chosen file
setFile (*name*)	indicates the file that will be the default
setDirectory (*name*)	indicates the directory to be displayed

display. (If setDirectory is not called, the directory the program started in will be displayed.)

11.5 Menus

We can construct menus with a collection of standard classes that can be found in java.awt. Menus can be placed either in the usual way in a bar at the top of the window, or as standalone pop-up menus that are displayed when a particular button on the mouse is pressed (or special keys on the keyboard). Every menu can have an arbitrary number of alternatives, and any one of these alternatives can in turn be a submenu. It is also possible to define shortcuts so that pressing certain keys, such as Ctrl-C or Ctrl-X, will entail the choice of a particular menu alternative. The classes used to describe menus are shown in Figure 11.6. The class MenuComponent is an abstract superclass that contains a number of methods common to all menu classes. The most important of these is the method setFont.

Figure 11.6 Menu classes

11.5.1 Menu bars, menus and menu alternatives

As an example, we will construct the menu "Options" in this section. This menu is shown in Figure 11.7. Using this menu, we should be able to change the size of the text

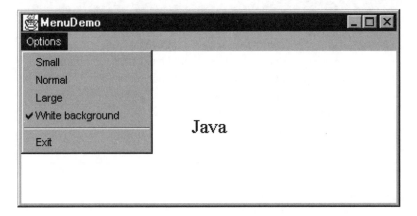

Figure 11.7 A window with a menu

in the window. We should also be able to determine whether we shall have a white or grey background.

A menu bar can be placed in a window. This is done by first declaring a `MenuBar` object and then connecting it to the window. An arbitrary number of menus can be placed on a menu bar. We will begin by defining the menu bar and the menu itself:

```
MenuBar mb = new MenuBar();
Menu optMen = new Menu("Options");
```

The following statements then put the menu bar in the window and connect the menu to the menu bar:

```
setMenuBar(mb);
mb.add(optMen);
```

These statements have to be executed in a constructor or a member function in the `Frame` object where the menu is to be found. A particular window can only have one menu bar but several menus can be arranged on the menu bar by several calls of the method `add`. The menus are then arranged from left to right. Instead of using the method `add` to place a help menu at the extreme right of the window, we can use the method `setHelpMenu`.

When we deal with a menu, we can arrange a number of menu alternatives in it. These alternatives are described by the class `MenuItem`. We demonstrate below how the alternatives are arranged in the menu "Options", in Figure 11.7. The menu alternatives themselves are declared first:

java.awt.MenuBar	
new MenuBar()	creates a menu bar
add(*m*)	places the menu *m* on the bar (from left to right)
setHelpMenu(*m*)	places the menu *m* at the extreme right on the bar
getMenuCount()	gives the number of menus on the bar
getMenu(*i*)	gives menu number *i*
getHelpMenu()	gives the help menu
remove(*i*)	removes menu number *i*
remove(*m*)	removes menu *m*

```java
MenuItem small   = new MenuItem("Small");
MenuItem normal  = new MenuItem("Normal");
MenuItem large   = new MenuItem("Large");
CheckboxMenuItem backgr = new CheckboxMenuItem
                                ("White background", true);
MenuItem exit    = new MenuItem("Exit");
```

The alternative `backgr` is an object of class `CheckboxMenuItem`, which is a subclass of `MenuItem`. Menu alternatives of this kind have a little marker that indicates whether or not the alternative is marked. Each time this alternative is chosen, it will alternate between being marked and not being marked. We can indicate the situation from the beginning, in the constructor.

The menu alternatives can then be placed in the menu with the following statements:

```java
optMen.add(small); optMen.add(normal); optMen.add(large);
optMen.add(backgr);
optMen.addSeparator();
optMen.add(exit);
```

We would like to have a horizontal line between the last two alternatives, as shown in the figure, and we can do this by calling the method `addSeparator`.

This concludes the menu itself, as shown in Figure 11.7. The next step is to define what will happen when the user chooses the different alternatives. As usual, this is done by using listeners. Listeners of type `ActionListener` are connected to menu alternatives of class `MenuItem`, while listeners of type `ItemListener` are connected to menu alternatives of class `CheckboxMenuItem`. The following statements will do this. As usual, we use the object itself as listener.

```java
small.addActionListener(this);
normal.addActionListener(this);
large.addActionListener(this);
backgr.addItemListener(this);
exit.addActionListener(this);
```

---

java.awt.Menu

new Menu (*rubr*)	creates a menu with the rubric *rubr*
add (*alt*)	places the alternative *alt* in the menu
add (*text*)	places the text *text* in the menu
addSeparator ()	places a horizontal line in the menu
insert (*alt*, *i*)	places the alternative *alt* in the menu, in position number *i*
insert (*text*, *i*)	places the text *text* in the menu, in position number *i*
insertSeparator (*i*)	places a horizontal line in the menu, in position number *i*
getItemCount ()	gives the number of alternatives on the bar
getItem (*i*)	gives the alternative number *i*
remove (*i*)	removes the alternative number *i*
remove (*alt*)	removes the alternative *alt*
removeAll ()	removes all alternatives

---

java.awt.MenuItem

new MenuItem (*text*)	creates a menu alternative with the text *text*
new MenuItem (*text*, *sh*)	creates a menu alternative with the text *text* and the shortcut *sh*
addActionListener (*al*)	connects the listener *al* to the menu alternative
setEnabled (*bool*)	determines if the menu alternative is to be active
getEnabled ()	reads whether the menu alternative is active or not
setLabel (*text*)	changes the text in the menu alternative
getLabel ()	reads the text in the menu alternative
setActionCommand (*text*)	connects a text to the menu alternative
getActionCommand ()	reads the text that is connected to the menu alternative
setShortcut (*sh*)	connects the shortcut *sh* to the menu alternative
getShortcut ()	reads the shortcut of the menu alternative

---

java.awt.CheckboxMenuItem

new CheckboxMenuItem (*text*)	creates a menu alternative with the text *text*
new CheckboxMenuItem (*text*, *bool*)	creates a menu alternative with the text *text* and a certain initial state
addItemListener (*il*)	connects the listener *il* to the menu alternative
setState (*bool*)	places the menu alternative in a certain state
getState ()	reads the state

Other methods are inherited from the class MenuItem.

We have to extend our example a little to be able to define the listener methods. Let us suppose that everything we have done up to now lies in the class MenuDemo. This has the following structure:

```
import java.awt.*;
import java.awt.event.*;

public class MenuDemo extends Frame
                      implements ActionListener, ItemListener {
    Label l = new Label("Java", Label.CENTER);
    Font smallFont  = new Font("Serif", Font.PLAIN, 10);
    Font normalFont = new Font("Serif", Font.PLAIN, 20);
    Font largeFont  = new Font("Serif", Font.PLAIN, 30);
    declarations of menu bar, menu and menu alternatives (as above)

    // Constructor
    public MenuDemo() {
        arrangement of the menu and menu alternatives, connection of listeners
        (as above)
        setTitle("MenuDemo");
        setSize(400,200);
        add("Center", l);
        l.setFont(normalFont);
        setVisible(true);
    }

    public static void main(String[] arg) {
        new MenuDemo();
    }

    definitions of listener methods
}
```

A Label object with the text "Java" is placed in the window. Because BorderLayout is used and the Label object is placed in the centre, it will fill out the whole window.

We will need two listener methods: actionPerformed and itemStateChanged. We get to the first one when the user chooses one of the menu alternatives described by the class MenuItem. We get to the second when the user chooses the alternative "White background", described by the class CheckboxMenuItem. The method actionPerformed will have the appearance:

```
public void actionPerformed(ActionEvent e) {
    if (e.getSource() == small)
        l.setFont(smallFont);
    else if (e.getSource() == normal)
        l.setFont(normalFont);
    else if (e.getSource() == large)
        l.setFont(largeFont);
```

```
   else if (e.getSource() == exit)
     System.exit(0);
}
```

The class CheckboxMenuItem has a method with the name getState. This can be called to find out whether the menu alternative is marked or not. We will use this information in the second listener:

```
public void itemStateChanged(ItemEvent e) {
  if (e.getSource() == backgr)
    if (backgr.getState())
      l.setBackground(Color.white);
    else
      l.setBackground(Color.lightGray);
}
```

Note that changes to the font and background colour will be made for the Label object l, since it fills out the whole window. If we had made these changes for the MenuDemo object itself, they would have had no effect.

11.5.2 Shortcuts

A shortcut can be connected to a menu alternative, either in the constructor, or with the help of the method setShortcut. Let us suppose, for example, that we want to be able to use the shortcuts Ctrl-S, Ctrl-N and Ctrl-L, so that we have something looking like Figure 11.8.

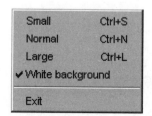

Figure 11.8 Menu with shortcuts

We can then define the three first menu alternatives in the following way. The extra parameter will be an object of the class MenuShortcut:

```
MenuItem small  = new MenuItem("Small",
                               new MenuShortcut(KeyEvent.VK_S));
MenuItem normal = new MenuItem("Normal",
                               new MenuShortcut(KeyEvent.VK_N));
MenuItem large  = new MenuItem("Large",
                               new MenuShortcut(KeyEvent.VK_L));
```

When an object of the class MenuShortcut is created, a key number will be given as parameter. This is the same key number that is used by class KeyEvent; see Section 10.3. We can, therefore, use the constants VK_? defined in this class. The shortcuts will be included automatically in the text of the menu alternative. Note that we only indicated the "pure" letters S, N and L in the definitions. The control key in question will depend on the system. In Windows, it is Ctrl. If we like, we can indicate that the Shift key must also be pressed. We could write:

```
new MenuShortcut(KeyEvent.VK_S, true)
```

11.5.3 Sub-menus

A menu alternative can, in turn, contain a whole menu, a sub-menu. The sub-menu will be displayed when the user chooses this alternative. To demonstrate how sub-menus are constructed, we will extend the menu in Figure 11.7 so that it will look as in Figure 11.9. A new menu alternative "Colour" has been added. When it is chosen, a sub-menu will come up in which the user can indicate the colour to be used when the text is displayed in the window.

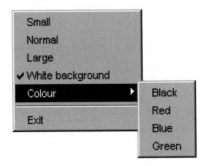

Figure 11.9 Menu with sub-menu

We begin by defining the sub-menu and the alternative menus it will contain. When defining the alternatives, the program can often be simplified if we use an array instead of declaring each alternative individually; this technique is used here:

```
Menu colourMen = new Menu("Colour");
MenuItem[] colour={new MenuItem("Black"), new MenuItem("Red"),
                   new MenuItem("Blue"),new MenuItem("Green")};
```

The next step is to place the sub-menu "Colour" as an alternative in the original menu "Options". This is done with the following statement that is placed in the constructor, in the demonstration class `MenuDemo`:

```
optMen.insert(colourMen, 4);
```

The alternative "Colour" is inserted as alternative number 4. (As usual, numbering starts from 0.) The alternatives will then be arranged in the sub-menu. A simple **for** statement can do this, since we have used an array. In this statement we can also connect a listener to each alternative.

```
for (int i=0; i<colour.length; i++) {
  colourMen.add(colour[i]);
  colour[i].addActionListener(this);
}
```

All that remains now is to supplement the listener method `actionPerformed` so that it will also deal with the events arising when the user has chosen one of the alternatives in the new sub-menu. It will look like this:

```
public void actionPerformed(ActionEvent e) {
  if (e.getSource() == small)
    l.setFont(smallFont);
  else if (e.getSource() == normal)
    l.setFont(normalFont);
  else if (e.getSource() == large)
    l.setFont(largeFont);
  else if (e.getSource() == exit)
    System.exit(0);
  else if (e.getSource() == colour[0])
    l.setForeground(Color.black);
  else if (e.getSource() == colour[1])
    l.setForeground(Color.red);
  else if (e.getSource() == colour[2])
    l.setForeground(Color.blue);
  else if (e.getSource() == colour[3])
    l.setForeground(Color.green);
}
```

11.5.4 Pop-up menus

Pop-up menus are menus that are not fixed to a menu bar. They can pop up anywhere in a window. We can normally open a pop-up menu by pressing a particular mouse button (usually the right-hand button), but we can also open one by using a particular combination of keys.

We shall now make another change to the menus in class MenuDemo. This time we let the "Options" menu regain its original appearance as given in Figure 11.7 and construct a pop-up menu that will be displayed each time the user presses the mouse's right-hand button somewhere in the window. This will look as in Figure 11.10. The pop-up menu will be displayed at the point in the window where the mouse pointer is.

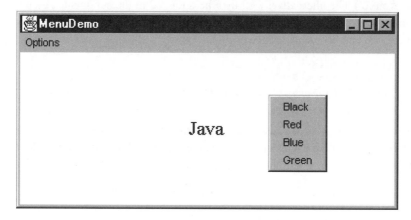

Figure 11.10 A window with a pop-up menu

A pop-up menu will be an object of class PopupMenu, and the menu alternatives can be defined as an array, exactly as in the previous section:

```
PopupMenu colourPopup = new PopupMenu();
MenuItem[] colour={new MenuItem("Black"), new MenuItem("Red"),
                   new MenuItem("Blue"),new MenuItem("Green")};
```

The alternatives will then be connected to the pop-up menu in the constructor, in class MenuDemo. We can use a simple repetition statement:

```
for (int i=0; i<colour.length; i++) {
  colourPopup.add(colour[i]);
  colour[i].addActionListener(this);
}
```

At the same time, we connect a listener to each menu alternative.

The pop-up menu will be connected not to a menu bar but to the graphics component through which it will be displayed. In class Component there is a method add, which can be used to make this connection. In fact, pop-up menus can be connected to all

362

kinds of graphics components. The method add will have a pop-up menu as argument. Because our pop-up menu will be displayed through the Label object 1 in class MenuDemo, we make the call:

```
1.add(colourPopup);
```

(Note that simply to write add(colorPopup) would not work, as the pop-up menu would be connected to the MenuDemo object itself, while the Label object 1 fills the entire window.) To ensure that the user's action of pressing the right-hand mouse button will be recognized, a listener must be connected to the component through which the pop-up menu is to be displayed:

```
1.addMouseListener(ml);
```

All that now remains is to define the listener ml. The event class MouseEvent describes several kinds of event but we are only interested in the event MousePressed, so we let the listener ml belong to a subclass of the class MouseAdapter. This will look as follows:

```
MouseListener ml = new MouseAdapter() {
  public void mousePressed(MouseEvent e) {
    if (e.isMetaDown())   // The right-hand button
      colourPopup.show(1, e.getX(), e.getY());
  }
};
```

The class PopupMenu has its own version of the method show. It has three parameters. The first parameter will be a reference to the component through which the pop-up menu will be displayed. The last two parameters indicate the x- and y-coordinates of the point on the screen that will accommodate the menu's upper left-hand corner.

java.awt.PopupMenu	
new PopupMenu()	creates a pop-up menu
show(*co, x, y*)	shows the menu through the component *co* in position (*x, y*)
Other methods are inherited from the class Menu	

11.6 An example – a text editor

In conclusion, we now show a new, improved version of the text editor we discussed in Section 5.15. In this version we shall use most of the building blocks dealt with in this chapter: modal dialog boxes, file dialog boxes and menus. In this example, we would like to show how these building blocks work together, in a larger and more realistic

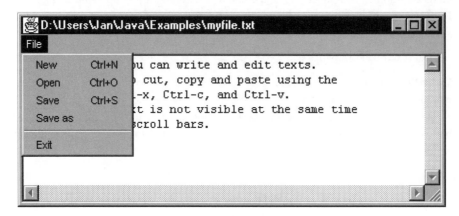

Figure 11.11 A text editor

example. How this might look when the new version of the text editor is run is shown in Figure 11.11.

The buttons from Section 5.15 have been replaced by a menu with familiar headings, and some of the menu alternatives have shortcuts. When one of the alternatives, "Open", or "Save as" is chosen, a file dialog is displayed where the name of the file has to be indicated, in the normal way. (One of these file dialogs may look as in Figure 11.5.) If we try to open a file that does not exist, a modal dialog box is displayed with a message. Each time we indicate that we want to edit a new text, or read in a new file, the program will check to see whether the actual text has been changed. If it has, we will get a question, displayed in a dialog box, asking whether the text is to be saved. The program will allow files in different directories to be edited. The complete name of the file being edited will be displayed throughout in the window frame.

The class `TextArea`, which is used to create the editing area in the window, allows cutting and pasting, using shortcuts in the normal way. In this way, the program will do a fairly good job as a text editor. (The most important things missing are the commands to search and carry out global changes throughout the text; but it is easy to add another menu with these functions.)

Handling of the file itself is carried out in the same way as in the earlier version; see Section 5.15. We use our own class `ExtendedReader` to make this as easy as possible. Treatment of the text area inside the window is also carried out in the same way as in the earlier version of the program. We shall now show the program in its entirety. It does not contain any constructions that have not been dealt with before, so it is now left to the reader to go through the program text and note its construction.

364

```
import java.awt.*;
import java.awt.event.*;
import extra.*;

 class TextEdit extends Frame implements ActionListener {
   private MenuBar mb = new MenuBar();
   private Menu fileMen = new Menu("File");
   private MenuItem[] fileItem = {
        new MenuItem("New", new MenuShortcut(KeyEvent.VK_N)),
        new MenuItem("Open", new MenuShortcut(KeyEvent.VK_O)),
        new MenuItem("Save", new MenuShortcut(KeyEvent.VK_S)),
        new MenuItem("Save as"),
        new MenuItem("Exit")};
   private TextArea area = new TextArea(10,60);
   private FileDialog openD = new FileDialog(this, "Open");
   private FileDialog saveD = new FileDialog(this, "Save as",
                                          FileDialog.SAVE);
   private String currentFile = "noName";
   private boolean changed = false;
 // constructor
 public TextEdit() {
    area.setFont(new Font("Monospaced", Font.PLAIN, 12));
    // build the menu
    setMenuBar(mb);
    mb.add(fileMen);
    for (int i=0; i<fileItem.length; i++) {
      fileMen.add(fileItem[i]);
      fileItem[i].addActionListener(this);
    }
    fileMen.insertSeparator(4);
    add("Center", area);
    pack();
    setTitle(currentFile);
    area.addKeyListener(kl); // to note whether the text has
                             // been changed
    setVisible(true);
  }

  private KeyListener kl = new KeyAdapter() {
    // the user has pressed a key in the text window
    public void keyPressed(KeyEvent e) {
      changed = true;
    }
  };
```

```java
public void actionPerformed(ActionEvent e) {
  // check which menu alternative the user has chosen
  if (e.getSource() == fileItem[0]) {        // New
    saveOld();
    area.setText("");  // empty the text area
    currentFile = "noName";
    setTitle(currentFile);
    changed = false;
  }
  else if (e.getSource() == fileItem[1]) {  // Open
    saveOld();        // save the edited text first
    openD.show();  // ask for the file name
    if (openD.getFile() != null) {
      // make sure that both file dialogs are in the same
      // directory
      saveD.setDirectory(openD.getDirectory());
      // open the file and read it
      loadFile(openD.getDirectory()+openD.getFile());
    }
  }
  else if (e.getSource() == fileItem[2])    // Save
    saveFile(currentFile);
  else if (e.getSource() == fileItem[3]) { // Save as
    saveD.show();  // ask for the file name
    if (saveD.getFile() != null) {
      // make sure that both file dialogs are in the same
      // directory
      openD.setDirectory(saveD.getDirectory());
      // save the file
      saveFile(openD.getDirectory()+saveD.getFile());
    }
  }
  else if (e.getSource() == fileItem[4]) { // Terminate
    saveOld();     // save the edited text first
    System.exit(0);
  }
}

private void saveOld() {
  if (changed) {
    YNDialog d = new YNDialog(this,
                 "Save" + currentFile + "?");
    displayDialog(d);
    if (d.getAnswer().equals("Yes"))
      saveFile(currentFile);
  }
}
```

```
private void loadFile(String fName) {
  ExtendedReader inFile=ExtendedReader.getFileReader(fName);
  if (inFile != null) {    // was the file there?
    currentFile = fName;
    setTitle(currentFile);
    area.setText("");    // empty the text area
    String s;
    while ((s=inFile.readLine()) != null) //read line by line
      area.append(s + "\n");               //add the line
    inFile.close();
    changed = false;
  }
  else {  // the file does not exist
    Toolkit.getDefaultToolkit().beep();  // give a beep
    displayDialog(new OKDialog(this,
              "Cannot find " + fName));
  }
}

private void saveFile(String fName) {
 ExtendedWriter outFile=ExtendedWriter.getFileWriter(fName);
  outFile.print(area.getText());  // write out the whole of
                                  // the text area
  outFile.close();
  currentFile = fName;
  setTitle(currentFile);
  changed = false;
}

private void displayDialog(Dialog d) {
  // compute the dialog box's start point so that it
  // lands in the middle above the text editor's window
  Point p = getLocationOnScreen();
  p.translate((getSize().width-d.getSize().width)/2,
              (getSize().height-d.getSize().height)/2);
  d.setLocation(p);
  d.show();
}

public static void main (String[] arg) {
  new TextEdit();
}
}
```

11.7 Exercises

1. Reconstruct class `CarRent2` on page 135 so that several computations can be done in different windows at the same time. Add a button that can be pressed if we wish to start a new computation in parallel with the current one.

2. Make changes to class `TextEdit` in Section 11.6 so that a new editing window is opened automatically when the user chooses the alternative "New". The text in the existing window should not be erased, therefore. Ensure that the new window does not completely cover the old one but is instead moved slightly to one side.

3. Make your own versions of the dialog classes `YNDialog` and `YNCDialog` in some other language than English.

4. Construct a general class to describe a modal dialog box that contains a message and a `TextField` that the user will fill out. The dialog box should contain an OK button that the user can click on when finished. Alternatively, the Enter button can be pressed. There should be a method `getAnswer` that can be called when the box has been closed to read the user's answer. Use class `MessageDialog` in Section 11.3 as a model.

5. Reconstruct the applet `CircleDemo3` on page 146 so that the radio buttons will be displayed in a separate non-modal dialog box. Only the circle should be displayed in the applet's window.

6. Rewrite the program `Twentyone` in Section 7.10 so that it uses dialog boxes to communicate with the user.

7. In solving Exercise 3 on page 217, let the program have a graphical user interface and make use of class `FileDialog` to get the file's name for the program.

8. Supplement the drawing program `Draw2` on page 323 so that it will contain a help menu with one alternative. When the user chooses this alternative, a box should pop up explaining how we go about drawing a picture.

9. Supplement the drawing program `Draw2` on page 323 so that it will contain a menu with the alternatives "Open", "Save" and "Exit". When "Open" or "Save" is chosen, the program should display a file dialog in which the user can indicate a file name. We shall be able to save a figure that has been drawn by writing out the start and end points of the lines to a text file.

10. Add yet another menu to the class `TextEdit` in Section 11.6. The new menu should have the heading "Edit" and contain the alternatives "Search" and "Search/ Change". The first alternative is used to search for a particular text, and the second to search for and change a text.

Sounds and images

12

In Java, it is relatively easy to produce sounds and display images. This is often used to make applets more entertaining but it can also work to excellent effect in independent applications. We now begin by discussing how images can be generated in applets.

12.1 Images in applets

In an applet, it is easy to read in a file containing an image. Java can handle image files stored in GIF and JPEG format. For security reasons, an applet cannot read and write files in a computer other than the one in which the applet is to be found (that is, the computer from which the applet has been loaded). This also applies to image files, which must be in the same computer as the applet. In an applet, it is easy to find out the web address of the applet itself. We simply call a method with the name `getCodeBase`. This will give as result a URL (Uniform Resource Locator) object, which represents a unique address on the Internet. `getCodeBase` will give us the address of the applet's `class` file. There is also a similar method called `getDocumentBase`, which will give as result a URL object with the address of the HTML file the applet is started from.

The method `getImage` is used to read in an image file to an applet. This method will give as result an object of class `Image` (the same class we used when we were dealing with double buffering). The version of the method `getImage` suitable for using in an applet has two parameters. The first is a URL object and the second is an address relative to the first parameter. This address will be a text. We can quite simply call `getCodeBase` (or `getDocumentBase`) to get the value of the first parameter of method `getImage`. If the image file is called `image1.gif`, for example, and lies in the same directory as the applet, an image can be read in to the applet with the following line:

```
Image im = getImage(getCodeBase(), "image1.gif");
```

If we wanted to keep image files in a separate directory, it would, of course, be fine to indicate the corresponding search path when making the call of `getImage`. If, for example, the image is kept in a directory called `image_directory` we could write:

369

```
theImage = getImage(getCodeBase(), "image_directory/image1.gif");
```

In both cases, the applet can be moved in the file system, provided that the file image1.gif is moved with it. The method getImage will return the value **null** if there is no file with the name indicated.

We shall begin by studying a very simple applet that gets the name of an image file as parameter and retrieves and displays the image. The applet can look as shown in Figure 12.1 when it is executed in a web browser. The HTML file the applet is started from will have the following structure:

```
<html>
  <head><title>ImageDemo</title></head>
  <body>
  <applet code=ImageDemo.class width=208 height=198 align=right>
    <param name=imageName value=dog.gif>
  </applet>
  <H1>Welcome to the
  <br>
  Java Gallery</H1>
  </body>
</html>
```

The applet will read the name of the image file when it is initialized. It then retrieves the image for an Image object with the name image. The only thing that then has to be done is to redefine the method paint, so that the image that has been read in can be drawn. This looks like this:

```
import java.applet.*;
import java.awt.*;

public class ImageDemo extends Applet {
  Image image;

  public void init() {
    String name = getParameter("imageName");
    image = getImage(getCodeBase(), name);
  }

  public void paint(Graphics g) {
    g.drawImage(image, 10, 10, this); // begin in (10,10)
  }
}
```

Printout of the image takes place using the method drawImage, exactly as before, when we were dealing with double buffering. The image, together with the x- and y-coordinates for the image's upper left-hand corner, are indicated as parameters. (The last parameter will always be included, as before.) The method drawImage exists in

Figure 12.1 An applet that displays an image

several different versions. One of these has two other parameters that indicate the width and height of the image when it is printed out. We can resize the image using this method. The original image's size can be read with the methods `getWidth` and `getHeight`. To cut the image down to half its size, for instance, we can write:

```
g.drawImage(image, 10, 50, image.getWidth(this)/2,
                           image.getHeight(this)/2,this);
```

Note that the methods `getWidth` and `getHeight`, as well as method `drawImage`, will have a reference to a `Component` object as parameter. We will generally use `this`.

As we know, it can take quite a long time to retrieve an image over the Internet. This is certainly the case when using a telephone modem. The method `getImage` does not wait until the whole image is transferred but starts a parallel thread that carries on with the transfer in the background. As a result, the whole image may not yet be accessible when we return from the call of `getImage`. The method `drawImage` also works well for incomplete images. It will draw only as much as is available.

We can watch the transfer of an image, if we want to. This is done using the class `MediaTracker` in the package `java.awt`. We first create an object of class

Images in applets	
`getDocumentBase()`	gives a URL object with the address of the HTML file's directory
`getCodeBase()`	gives a URL object with the address of the `class` file's directory
`getImage`(*url, filename*)	initializes the transfer of an image with the name *filename,* given the corresponding URL address *url*
`im.getWidth(this)`	gives the width for the image `im`
`im.getHeight(this)`	gives the height for the image `im`
`g.drawImage(im,` *x,y,***this**`)`	draws the image `im`, beginning in position (x,y)
`g.drawImage(im,` *x,y,w,h,***this**`)`	draws the image `im`, beginning in position (x,y), resized to a size of $w \times h$
`g.drawImage(im,` *x,y,c,***this**`)`	as above but with the background colour c
`g.drawImage(im,` *x,y,w,h,c,***this**`)`	as above but with the background colour c
`g.drawImage`	also exists in versions where we can draw, resize and rotate part of an image (see documentation on the class `Graphics`)

`MediaTracker`. A reference must be given to the actual object as parameter for the constructor. So we write:

```
MediaTracker mt = new MediaTracker(this);
```

We then use a method with the name `addImage` to register the images we want to watch. In addition to the image, the method will have an ID number, which will be a whole number that we ourselves can determine. If, for example, we want the image to have the number 0, we write:

```
mt.addImage(image, 0);
```

Then there is a collection of methods that can be used to check the state of transfer of the image. The method `checkID` will indicate, for example, whether the transfer of a particular image has finished. (See also the Revision Table, where the most important methods have been shown.) Especially interesting is the method `waitForID` that can be used to wait until the transfer of a particular image is finished. We shall supplement our applet `ImageDemo` with a number of statements indicating that we shall defer drawing the image until the whole image has been transferred. So we rewrite the method `init`:

```
public void init() {
    String name = getParameter("imageName");
    image = getImage(getCodeBase(), name);
    showStatus("Loads " + name);
    MediaTracker mt = new MediaTracker(this);
    mt.addImage(image, 0);
```

```
try {mt.waitForID(0);}
catch(InterruptedException e){}
showStatus("Loading finished");
}
```

As before, we initialize the transfer of the image by calling the method `getImage`. Then we use the method `showStatus` to inform the user of what is happening. The method `showStatus` is defined in the class `Applet`. When this method is called, the message given as parameter is displayed in the web browser's message line, normally at the bottom of the frame.

We then create a `MediaTracker` object and register that the image should be watched. We give the image the ID number 0. The method `waitForID` is then called to wait until the transfer is finished. The ID number of the image we are waiting for is given as parameter. The call must be placed in a **try** statement because the method `waitForID` could generate an exception of type `InterruptedException`.

java.awt.MediaTracker	
new MediaTracker(**this**)	creates a MediaTracker object
addImage(im,n)	registers that the image im with the ID number n is to be watched
removeImage(im)	registers that the image im is no longer to be watched
checkAll()	gives **true** if all the watched images have been loaded
checkID(n)	gives **true** if the image with the ID number n has been loaded
isErrorID(n)	gives **true** if the loading of image number n has been unsuccessful
isErrorAny()	gives **true** if the loading of any image has been unsuccessful
waitForID(n)	wait until the loading of image number n is finished
waitForID(n,ms)	as above but wait at most ms milliseconds
waitForAll()	wait until all the images have been loaded
waitForAll(ms)	as above but wait at most ms milliseconds

12.2 The class URL and images in standalone applications

Images can also be displayed in standalone GUI programs, and we do not have the limitations that apply to applets. A standalone program can retrieve images from any computer. However, the methods we used in the previous section, `getImage`, `getDocumentBase` and `getCodeBase`, cannot be used in standalone programs as they have only been defined for applets. Instead, we have first to create a URL object. As we

java.net.URL	
new URL (*addr*)	creates a URL object with the address *addr*
new URL (*prot, host, file*)	creates a URL object with the address *prot+host+file*
new URL (*prot, host, portno, file*)	creates a URL object with the address *prot+host+portno+file*
new URL (u, *file*)	creates a URL object on the basis of the URL object u and the corresponding address *file*
getContent()	gives whatever the URL object refers to; return type: Object
openConnection()	gives a URLConnection object
openStream()	gives whatever the URL object refers to; return type: InputStream
getHost()	gives the host name
getFile()	gives the corresponding file name
getProtocol()	gives the protocol that is used
getPort()	gives the port number
toExternalForm()	gives the complete address as a text

noted in the previous section, the class URL describes a unique Internet address. Class URL has been defined in the package java.net. Class URL has several different constructors; see the Revision Table. In the most straightforward of these, we can simply indicate the address as a text. We could write:

```
URL u = new URL("http://www.xyz.se/pub/Java_dir/image1.gif");
```

There can be several parts to a URL address. The first part will always contain the name of a *protocol* that will indicate how we communicate with the distant computer. After this comes a name that can contain the host name. There may also be a port number. The most common protocol for web browsers is http. Another common protocol is file; this can be used when we want to refer to a file on our own computer. For example, if we are running Windows, we can write:

```
URL u = new URL("file:C:\\own\\images\\myimage.gif");
```

When we have created a URL object in our program, we can load whatever the URL object refers to. In class URL there are three different methods that can be used for it: getContent, openConnection and openStream. The simplest of the three is getContent; we shall be using it here to read in image files. The other two will be dealt with in Chapter 14. The method getContent gives as result an object that contains whatever the URL object refers to. The result type is Object, because a URL object can refer to any kind of object at all on the Internet. If the URL object refers to a file with an image, the method getContent will return an object of class java.awt.image.ImageProducer. We can therefore convert the result type from the call to this class as follows:

```
ImageProducer ip = (ImageProducer) u.getContent();
```

Once we have an ImageProducer object, it is easy to create an image. We use the method createImage in class Component, which we used when we created images for double buffering. Then, we gave as parameters the new image's width and height. We shall now use another version of createImage. This will have an ImageProducer object as parameter. We can then simply write:

```
Image im = createImage(ip);
```

In class java.awt.Toolkit there are two other versions of createImage. These could be used instead of the version defined in class Component. The first of these other version has a parameter of type URL and therefore no ImageProducer-object is needed. If the variable u is defined as before we can write:

```
Image im = Toolkit.GetDefaultToolkit().createImage(u);
```

The second version of createImage in java.awt.Toolkit can be used when we want to show a picture that is stored on our own computer. Then the file name is given as parameter:

```
Image im = Toolkit.GetDefaultToolkit().
            createImage("C:\\own\\images\\myimage.gif");
```

Irrespective of which version of createImage has been used, we can draw the image using method drawImage, exactly as we did in applets in the previous section. Of course, the methods getWidth and getHeight can be used as well.

As an example, we shall look at a simple, standalone GUI program with the name ImageDemo2. It will retrieve an image from another computer and display it on the screen. As usual, we start the program in a text window. We indicate the image to be displayed as parameter to main; see Section 6.8. If we start the program with the command:

```
java ImageDemo2 http://www.cs.chalmers.se/~skanshol/Java_eng/vase.jpg
```

the image in Figure 12.2 will be displayed. The program looks as follows:

```
import java.awt.*;
import java.awt.image.*;
import java.io.*;
import java.net.*;

public class ImageDemo2 extends Frame {
  URL u;
  Image image;
```

www.cs.chalmers.se/~skanshol/Java_eng/vase.jpg

Figure 12.2 A standalone application displaying an image

```
public ImageDemo2(String name) {
  try {
     u = new URL(name);
  }
  catch (MalformedURLException e) {
    System.out.println("Incorrect URL: " + name);
  }
  try {
    image = createImage((ImageProducer) u.getContent());
  }
  catch (IOException e) {
    System.out.println("Error at reading of: " + name);
  }
  setSize(400,210);
  setTitle(u.getHost()+u.getFile());
  setVisible(true);
}

public void paint(Graphics g) {
  g.drawImage(image, 10, 25, this);
}

public static void main(String[] arg) {
  new ImageDemo2(arg[0]);
}
}
```

Note that the constructor for class URL can generate the exception
MalformedURLException. Similarly, the getContent can generate the IOException.
We therefore have to enclose the calls of these methods in **try** statements.

12.3 Images as GUI components

As we have seen, the method `drawImage` requires the x- and y-coordinates to be indicated for the image to be positioned in the window. We sometimes would like to be able to insert an image into a window with such GUI components as texts and buttons. It is then better to enclose the image in a `Canvas` object so that the layout manager can put the image in a suitable position. To facilitate this, we shall construct a class `ImageCanvas` that is a subclass of class `Canvas`. The new class will ensure that an image will be a GUI component that can be handled in the same way as other GUI components. We shall begin by showing the class `ImageCanvas` in its entirety:

```java
package extra;
import java.awt.*;
import java.awt.image.*;
public class ImageCanvas extends Canvas  {
  private Image im;
  private boolean scale;

  // constructors
  public ImageCanvas() {}

  public ImageCanvas(Image img) {
    setImage(img);
  }

  public void setImage(Image img) {
    im=img;
    repaint();
  }

  public Image getImage() {
    return im;
  }

  // indicate whether the image will be resized to the size of
  // the drawing area
  public void setScale(boolean b) {
    scale=b;
    repaint();
  }

  // wait until the whole image has been loaded
  public void waitForImage() {
    if (im.getWidth(this) < 0 || im.getHeight(this) < 0) {
      MediaTracker mt = new MediaTracker(this);
      mt.addImage(im, 0);
      try {mt.waitForID(0);}
      catch(InterruptedException e){}
    }
  }
```

```
// change the size of the drawing area so that it will be
// the same size as the size of the image
public void adjustSize() {
  waitForImage();
  if (im.getWidth(this) > 0 && im.getHeight(this) > 0)
    setSize(im.getWidth(this), im.getHeight(this));
  repaint();
}

public void paint(Graphics g) {
  if (im != null)
    if (scale)
      g.drawImage(im, 0, 0, getSize().width,
                              getSize().height, this);
    else
      g.drawImage(im, 0, 0, this);
}
}
```

The instance variable `im` contains the image to be drawn. This variable can either be initialized in one of the constructors, or in the method `setImage`. Since class `ImageCanvas` is a subclass of class `Canvas`, its size can be indicated in the same way as for other GUI components. We can call the inherited method `setSize`, or we can use a layout manager that sets the size automatically. (If, for instance, a `Canvas` object is put into the `"Center"` position when `BorderLayout` is used, the `Canvas` object will automatically be big enough to fill out all the accessible space in the window.) If we have not called `setSize` or used a layout manager to set the size automatically, we will know from previous discussions that a `Canvas` object will have a size of 0×0. In both these cases we can make use of the method `adjustSize` for our new class. This method will set the size of the `Canvas` object so that it makes just enough space for the enclosed image. We will remember from Section 12.1 that a condition for being able to know the size of an image is that the whole image should have been loaded into the application. The method `adjustSize` will, therefore, in turn call the method `waitForImage`, which uses a `MediaTracker` object, to wait until the image has been loaded in its entirety.

Instead of adjusting the `Canvas` object's size to the size of the image, we can do things the other way round, that is, let the image's size be adjusted so that it fills out the whole of the `Canvas` object. We do this by calling, in the method `paint`, the version of method `drawImage` that has two extra parameters for height and width. The method `setScale`, which will have an argument of type **boolean**, is used to indicate whether we want the image to be resized in this way or not. As default, the image is not resized but keeps its original size. The variable `scale` is used internally in the class `ImageCanvas` to keep track of whether the image is to be resized or not. This variable will control, in the method `paint`, the version of `drawImage` to be used.

We will now look at a slightly more advanced applet that uses the new class `ImageCanvas`. When this applet is run, it will look as in Figure 12.3. The applet can display a number of different images. The user will determine the image to be displayed by pressing one of the radio buttons on the left. The images are flanked by scrollbars so that all the parts of an image can be seen, even when the image happens to be bigger than its frame.

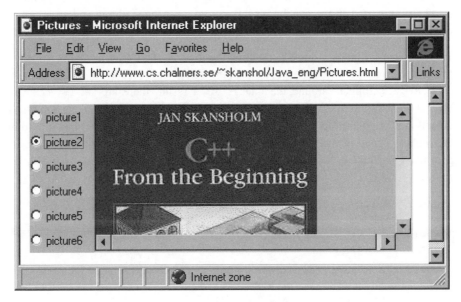

Figure 12.3 An applet that uses images as components

When the applet is started, two parameters will be given in the HTML file. The first one, `number`, indicates the number of images that the user will be able to choose from and the second, `fileName`, indicates the names of the image files. These must have names of the form `fileNamei.jpg`, where *i* will be a number beginning with 1. If, for example, `number` has the value 3 and `fileName` the value `"picture"`, the image files will have the names `picture1.jpg`, `picture2.jpg` and `picture3.jpg`. The applet in Figure 12.3 started from an HTML file looking like this:

```
<html>
  <head>
    <title>Pictures</title>
  </head>
```

379

```
<body>
  <applet code=Pictures.class width=400 height=150>
    <param name=number value=6>
    <param name=fileName value=picture>
  </applet>
</body>
</html>
```

The window is built in the applet with the use of two panels, one with radio buttons and one that displays the images. BorderLayout is used. The panel with the radio buttons is placed in the "West" position and the image panel in the "Center" position. GridLayout is used in the panel with the buttons, with one column and an arbitrary number of lines.

The class ImageCanvas is used to describe the images. An object is created for each image. Every ImageCanvas object is placed in its own ScrollPane object (see Section 5.13) to get scrollbars around the images. As a result, there are six ImageCanvas objects and six ScrollPane objects in the example in the figure. The ScrollPane objects are then placed in the image panel. CardLayout (see Section 5.14.4) is used in the image panel. This will mean that only one ScrollPane object, with its accompanying image, will be shown at a time. The applet Pictures will look as follows:

```java
import java.applet.*;
import java.awt.*;
import java.awt.event.*;
import extra.*;

public class Pictures extends Applet implements ItemListener {
  Panel picturePanel = new Panel();
  Panel buttonPanel  = new Panel();
  CheckboxGroup buttonGroup = new CheckboxGroup();
  CardLayout manager;

  public void init() {
    // determines Layout
    setLayout(new BorderLayout());
    buttonPanel.setLayout(new GridLayout(0,1));
    picturePanel.setLayout(new CardLayout());
    manager = (CardLayout) picturePanel.getLayout();
    add("West", buttonPanel);
    add("Center", picturePanel);
    // read parameters
    int n = Integer.parseInt(getParameter("number"));
    String fileName = getParameter("fileName");
```

```
    for (int i=1; i<=n; i++) {
      String name = fileName+i;  // name for file number i
      // create button number i
      Checkbox button = new Checkbox(name, false, buttonGroup);
      buttonPanel.add(button);
      if (i==1)
        button.setState(true); // button number 1 pressed from
                               // the beginning
      button.addItemListener(this);
      // load image number i
      ScrollPane  pane = new ScrollPane(
                      ScrollPane.SCROLLBARS_ALWAYS);
      ImageCanvas image = new ImageCanvas(
                      getImage(getCodeBase(), name+".jpg"));
      showStatus("Loading " + name);
      image.adjustSize();            // set the image object's size
      pane.add(image);   //place the Image object in a Scrollpane
      picturePanel.add(name,pane);  // place the pane in the
                                     // image panel
    }
    showStatus("Finished");
    // display image number 1 from the beginning
    manager.show(picturePanel,
              buttonGroup.getSelectedCheckbox().getLabel());
    setVisible(true);
  }
  // listeners for button pressure
  public void itemStateChanged(ItemEvent e) {
    if (e.getSource() instanceof Checkbox) {
      Checkbox c = (Checkbox) e.getSource();
      manager.show(picturePanel, c.getLabel()); //display image
    }
  }
}
```

Most of this is done in the method init. The parameters are read when the layout for the window has been initialized. A loop is run through for every image in the **for** statement. We first create a radio button and place it in the button panel. All of the radio buttons must belong to a group so that only one button at a time will be able to be pressed. We must ensure that button number 1 is pressed from the beginning. A listener is connected to each button and the applet object itself is used as the listener.

An image is read in at each loop of the **for** statement. When we load an image, the method adjustSize is called, and this will wait until the image has been read in its entirety. The ImageCanvas object, in which the image can be found, is then placed in a new Scrollpane object. Finally, the Scrollpane object is put into the image panel. As we will remember from Section 5.14.4, each component is given a unique name when `CardLayout` is used. The variable `manager` refers to the `CardLayout` manager that arranges the components in the image panel. When the **for** statement has finished, it is instructed to display the image that has the same name as the button pressed.

The listener method `itemStateChanged` is called when the user has pressed one of the radio buttons. The button's name is read in this method using the method `getLabel`. This name will then be used to instruct the layout manager in the image panel to display a particular image.

12.4 Moving images

In Chapter 9 we looked at the means of using active objects to produce moving figures. Active objects can also be used when we work with images. In fact, the same technique is used for ordinary films. Changing images are displayed in the same place on the screen. If the subject of the images changes only slightly between each image and images are changed at a predetermined time interval, we shall obtain a kind of moving film. We shall show how this can be done. Images can, of course, be shown directly in an applet or the start window of a standalone application but to make the case more general, we begin by constructing a class `Movie`. Instances of this class will be active objects that can display moving images. We arrange for class `Movie` to be a subclass of class `Canvas`. The objects that are created of this class can then be arranged in the window in the usual way by using a layout manager.

We use the same technique as in Chapter 9 to construct active objects. We let class `Movie` have an instance variable that is a `Thread` object. This thread is connected to the actual object. The class `Movie`, therefore, has to implement the interface `Runnable` and have a method `run`, in which the actual execution of the thread will take place. In class `Movie` we shall also define the methods `start` and `stop`.

There are two constructors in class `Movie`, and both will have an array of images as parameter. The images in this array are the frames of the film to be shown. When the activity is started, the film will be shown time and again. One constructor will have another parameter that is a whole number, used to indicate the time interval required between each display of the film frames. Time is indicated in milliseconds. (If we make use of the first constructor, where we cannot indicate a time interval, this interval will automatically be set to 500 ms.) The class `Movie` will look as follows:

```
import java.awt.*;
import extra.*;
public class Movie extends Canvas implements Runnable {
   private Thread activity;
   private Image[] filmFrames;
```

```java
  private int interval;
  private int no;   // no. of the next frame to be displayed

  // constructors
  public Movie(Image[] filmFrames) {
    this(filmFrames, 500);
  }

  public Movie(Image[] filmFrames, int interval) {
    this.filmFrames = filmFrames;
    this.interval = interval;
    // wait until all the frames have been loaded
    MediaTracker mt = new MediaTracker(this);
    for (int i=0; i<filmFrames.length; i++)
      mt.addImage(filmFrames[i], i);
    try {mt.waitForAll();}
    catch (InterruptedException e){}
    // make the film screen as large as the frames
    setSize(filmFrames[0].getWidth(this),
            filmFrames[0].getHeight(this));
  }

  public void run() {
    while (XThread.delay(interval)) {
      repaint();
      no = (no+1) % filmFrames.length;
    }
  }

  public void update(Graphics g) {   // own version that
    paint(g);                        // does not erase
  }

  public void paint(Graphics g) {
    g.drawImage(filmFrames[no], 0, 0, this);
  }

  public void start() {
    if (activity == null) {
      activity = new Thread(this);
      activity.start();
    }
  }

  public void stop() {
    if (activity != null) {
      activity.interrupt();
      activity = null;
    }
  }
}
```

The method `run` contains an eternal top that will make one turn per time interval. At each turn, `repaint` is called so that the component can be redrawn. The whole number variable `no` is used to keep track of the frame waiting to be displayed. The variable is increased by 1 at each turn. By making use of the `%` operator, we ensure that `no` will automatically be equal to 0 when `no+1` is equal to the number of frames.

We will recall from Chapter 9 that the method `repaint` in turn calls the method `update`. The standard version of `update` will erase the entire component but this is not necessary, as we will draw a new image to fill the entire component in any case. To avoid flicker, we redefine the method `update` so that it will not erase.

Note that we could have done the drawing ourselves in the method `run` and would not have had to define the methods `update` and `paint`, but we chose to do things as we did, to be consistent and to follow the same pattern as we had before. Then again, this version works better in the places where `repaint` is automatically called, that is, when the window has been completely or partially hidden.

We should now show how the class `Movie` can be used. We write an applet `Animation`, which will show a moving film. The HTML file that the applet will start from might look like this:

```
<html>
  <head>
    <title>Animation</title>
  </head>
  <body>
    <applet code=Animation.class width=300 height=150>
      <param name=number value=10>
      <param name=fileName value=film>
    </applet>
  </body>
</html>
```

As parameters, the applet will both have a number of frames and a text indicating the names of the image files. This will work in the same way as our example on page 379. If the second parameter, as in this example, has the value `film`, the frames will lie in image files with the names `film1.gif`, `film2.gif`, and so on.

Now comes the applet `Animation`. We cannot show a picture of how it will look, as moving images are a little difficult to show in a book. (If the reader would like to test-run it, he or she can make use of the two image files `T1.gif` and `T2.gif`, which can be found in the demonstration example `Animator`, in J2SDK.)

```
import java.awt.*;
import java.applet.*;
```

```
public class Animation extends Applet {
  private Movie m;

  public void init() {
    int n = Integer.parseInt(getParameter("number"));
    String fileName = getParameter("fileName");
    Image[] frames = new Image[n];
    for (int i=0; i<n; i++)
      frames[i] =getImage(getCodeBase(), fileName+(i+1)+".gif");
    m = new Movie(frames);
    add(m);
  }

  public void start() {
    m.start();
  }

  public void stop() {
    m.stop();
  }
}
```

12.5 Sounds in applets

Handling sound in Java is similar in many respects to handling images, except that it is rather easier. Java only used to be able to deal with sound files in the au format but since the appearance of J2SDK version 1.2, we can also handle files formatted in AIFF, WAW, TYPE 0 MIDI and TYPE 1 MIDI. Everything to do with sound is defined in the package `java.applet`. A sound sequence is represented by the class `AudioClip`. We load a sound file in an applet in the same way as we load an image file, except that we use the method `getAudioClip`, instead of `getImage`. For instance, to read in the sound file `beep.au`, we write:

```
AudioClip a = getAudioClip(getCodeBase(), "beep.au");
```

Sound files, too, must be in the same computer as the applet. We can, therefore, use the form of `getAudioClip` where the first parameter is a URL address and the second one is a text that describes the corresponding file name.

Class `AudioClip` is a very simple one. It contains only three methods: `play` is used to start the sound file playing once, `stop` interrupts playing and `loop` starts the sound file playing again and again. For example, to start the file `beep.au` playing, we can now write:

```
a.play();
```

But if we want the sound file to start playing only once, we can do this rather more simply in class `Applet`. We use the method `play` and write, for example:

```
play(getCodeBase(), "beep.au");
```

Sound methods in the class Applet	
newAudioClip *(url)*	a class method that gives the sound file with the URL address *url*
getAudioClip *(url, filename)*	gives the sound file with the name *filename*, given in relation to the URL address *url*
play *(url, filename)*	plays the sound file with the name *filename*, given in relation to the URL address *url*

java.awt.AudioClip	
Describes a sound file	
play()	starts the sound file playing
stop()	stops the sound file playing
loop()	plays the sound file repeatedly

We now show an applet that gets a name in a sound file as parameter. The applet retrieves the file and starts it playing over and over again. The file's name is displayed in the window as follows:

```java
import java.awt.*;
import java.applet.*;

public class SoundDemo extends Applet {
  AudioClip a;
  String fileName;

  public void init() {
    fileName = getParameter("fileName");
    a = getAudioClip(getCodeBase(), fileName);
    a.loop();
    add(new Label("Playing " + fileName));
  }

  public void start() {
    a.loop();
  }

  public void stop() {
    a.stop();
  }
}
```

Note that we start the playing in the method `start` and stop it in the method `stop`. This means that the sound file will automatically begin to play when the actual web page is displayed in the browser. As soon as another page is shown, the sound will stop. If we had not stopped the sound in method `stop`, the sound file would have continued to play, even when we changed pages in the browser.

12.6 Sounds in standalone applications

It is easy to play sound files also in standalone applications. We make use of the class method `newAudioClip`. For practical reasons, the method has been defined in class `Applet`, although it has nothing whatever to do with applets. As parameter the method `newAudioClip` will have a URL object that gives the web address of the sound file to be played. (Because it is a standalone application, this file could be placed anywhere on the Internet.) So we have to begin by defining a URL object. For instance, we can write:

```
URL u = new URL("http://www.xyz.se/pub/Java_dir/noise.au");
```

We can then load the sound file.

```
AudioClip a = Applet.newAudioClip(u);
```

Here we have a standalone application that corresponds to the applet `SoundDemo` from the previous section. The sound file's name will be given as parameter for `main` when the program is started:

```
import java.awt.*;
import java.applet.*;
import java.net.*;

public class SoundPlayer extends Frame {
  URL u;
  AudioClip a;

  SoundPlayer(String fileName) {
    try {
      u = new URL(fileName);
    }

    catch (MalformedURLException e) {
      System.out.println("Illegal URL: " + fileName);
    }
    a = Applet.newAudioClip(u);
    a.loop();
    setSize(400,200);
    add(new Label("Playing " + fileName));
    setVisible(true);
  }
```

```
public static void main (String arg[]) {
  new SoundPlayer(arg[0]);
}
}
```

As before, the constructor for class URL can generate an exception of type MalformedURLException. Therefore, a **try** statement must be used.

12.7 Exercises

1. Extend the applet ImageDemo in Section 12.1 so that it will not draw the picture before it has been loaded in its entirety. Instead, a little rectangle should be drawn in the same position as the picture will occupy, while it is being loaded.

2. Write, with the assistance of class ImageCanvas, a program to load images and display them. Apart from the image, there should be a TextField component in the window in which the user can write in the URL address for the image to be displayed. Each time the user writes in a new address, the old image should be removed and the new one loaded and displayed instead.

3. Develop the program in Exercise 2 so that a scrollbar (of the class Scrollbar), graduated from 0.5 to 2, will be shown in the window. With the scrollbar the user will be able to zoom the picture so that it becomes larger or smaller. Every time a new picture begins to be displayed, the scrollbar should be automatically set to 1, so that the picture will be displayed in its original size.

4. Develop the program in Exercise 2 to include yet another TextField component. In this component the user should be able to indicate the URL address of a sound file that will be played continuously in the background.

5. Develop class Movie, on page 382, with a method that will make it possible to show a film only once.

6. Develop class Movie, on page 382, so that it can show sound films. Make new constructors with an AudioClip object as parameter. Then use your developed version of Movie to make a new version of the applet Animation on page 385. In the new version, the name of a sound file should also be given as parameter in the HTML file.

7. Extend the applet PolyMove, on page 306, with an appropriate background sound. (Look in your own computer for one or more sound files that can be used.)

Streams and files

13

In Chapter 3 we discussed how we could read and write texts in a text window. We also saw how we could read and write files containing text. To do this we used streams. It is now time to generalize the description of streams so that we can put into context what we learnt so far. In this chapter we shall also discuss binary files, that is, files that do not contain text. We will be looking at sequential files, which can be described by using streams, and direct access files, which are handled by a special class.

A stream is a kind of communication path for data from a *source* to a *destination*. When data flows into a program, we speak of an *input stream*, and of an *output stream* when data flows out of the program. As we saw in Chapter 3, the source or destination of a stream can be anything, a file, for example, or a distant computer. Streams are used in a program so that data can be handled uniformly, regardless of what the source or destination might be.

In the package `java.io` there are several classes that describe streams with different characteristics. There are many different classes of streams; they fall into two distinct categories: *byte streams* and *char streams*. In byte streams, data is transferred in the form of bytes, that is, in groups of 8 bits. Groups of this kind are described most easily by the built-in type `byte`. In char streams, data is transferred in Unicode format (see Section 6.1) of 16 bits, and this kind of data is described by the built-in type `char`. Char streams are intended to handle data containing text, while byte streams are meant to take care of the other kind of data, binary data. When Java was first created, it only used byte streams but char streams were introduced in Version 1.1 because it was found that byte streams could not handle Unicode characters properly. It is easy to differentiate between the classes that describe byte streams and those that describe char streams. All the classes that describe byte streams contain the word `Stream` in their names, while all those describing char streams have the word `Reader` or `Writer` in their names.

When char streams were introduced, a couple of the classes in earlier versions of Java became obsolete (or *deprecated* as it is called in the literature). These were the classes

389

StringBufferInputStream and LineNumberInputStream. We will not be discussing these classes. The class PrintStream could have been included with these two but it has been retained for historical reasons. (This is discussed further in Section 13.3.10.)

All the examples in this chapter deal with files called for standalone programs because, for security reasons, applets cannot read and write files on a local computer. In addition, they cannot discover information about files or directories.

13.1 An overview

Streams can be connected in much the same way we connect hoses and the flow of data from one stream can be input directly into another. In Figure 3.1 on page 80, for example, we saw how three streams were connected to transmit input data from the keyboard to the program. Streams can be connected in many different ways. It is, actually, quite complex and confusing. So we shall try to introduce some order by presenting two "connection charts" that will demonstrate how different streams are connected. Properties unique to streams, methods for instance, will be discussed later in the chapter.

13.1.1   Byte input streams

To describe complicated classes, a diagram showing their inheritance structure is useful. In this way, we can see that all classes involved in the reading of byte streams are subclasses of the class InputStream. Perhaps more interesting is to see how streams can be connected. We shall, therefore, study a connection chart instead; see Figure 13.1. The chart is divided into two parts. Byte streams are described in the upper half, and char streams in the lower half. We shall begin by looking at byte streams.

Data flows from left to right in the chart. The source of this flow is on the extreme left, while the program that reads data from the stream is furthest to the right. There are four classes describing streams that can be connected to a source: InputStream, FileInputStream, ByteArrayInputStream and PipedInputStream. The class InputStream describes a general input stream, and the type of source is not specified. It is an abstract class, which means that it is not possible to create instances of it. One way of gaining access to a stream of this class is to call a special method giving a stream as result. For example, the class URL, which we studied in Section 12.2, has a method with the name openStream that can be used to create a stream whose source is a file on another computer.

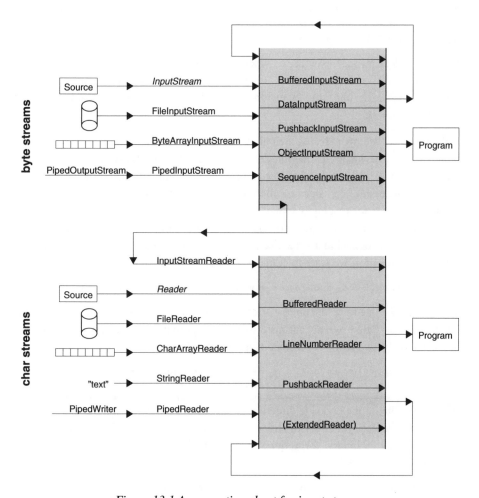

Figure 13.1 A connection chart for input streams

The class `FileInputStream` is used when the source of the flow is a file. In other words, we want to read from a file, and the name of the file can be indicated directly when the stream is created.

```
FileInputStream fin = new FileInputStream(file_name);
```

The class `ByteArrayInputStream` can be used when we want to retrieve data from an array of bytes. By using a stream, we can "read" from the array just as if the data came from a file. We write this in the following way:

```
byte[] a = new byte[1000];
...  // here input data is placed in a
ByteArrayInputStream bin = new ByteArrayInputStream(a);
```

We use the class `PipedInputStream` when we want two objects to communicate with each other. We arrange for one object to enter an output stream of class `PipedOutputStream` and the other one to read from an input stream of class `PipedInputStream`.

In Figure 13.1, the upper shaded area gives the streams that can be connected to a byte input stream. The arrow at the top (the one without text) illustrates that it is not necessary to make any connection at all, since the program will read directly from the original input stream here. Because the four classes to the left in the figure only have primitive methods for reading, we may often want to connect to another stream. In the shaded area, we can see that there are five different classes to choose from. For instance, we can connect to a stream of class `BufferedInputStream` to make reading a little more efficient. If we want to connect a buffer to the stream `fin`, we can write:

```
BufferedInputStream bufin = new BufferedInputStream(fin);
```

When we now come to read from the stream `bufin`, this stream will, in turn, read from the stream `fin`. Often, we do not need to access the first stream directly. We do not then need to give it a name but instead can write:

```
BufferedInputStream bufin = new BufferedInputStream
                            (new FileInputStream(file_name));
```

The arrow going in the opposite direction at the top of Figure 13.1 tells us that we can connect to an arbitrary number of streams in this way. If we wanted to be able to read numerical data in binary form quickly, we could connect to a stream of class `DataInputStream` like this:

```
DataInputStream din = new DataInputStream(bufin);
```

The classes `BufferedInputStream`, `DataInputStream`, `PushbackInputStream` and `ObjectInputStream` have in common a constructor in which we indicate the input stream that the new stream is to be connected to. The class `SequenceInputStream`, however, is somewhat special. It enables us to connect two or more input streams to a single stream. We shall show in Section 13.2.14 how this is done.

13.1.2   Char input streams

Input streams used for the reading of Unicode characters are given in the lower half of Figure 13.1. All of these classes are subclasses of class `Reader`. Class `Reader` describes a general input stream, where data flowing into the stream is of type **char**. The source type is not specified. Class `Reader`, like class `InputStream`, is abstract, so we cannot create our own objects of this class. Instead, we shall use one of the other classes indicated at the bottom on the left, in Figure 13.1.

The most important of the non-abstract classes is class `InputStreamReader`. With it, we can create a char input stream that, in turn, will read from a stream of class `InputStream`. We could write:

```
InputStream s = initialized in some way;
InputStreamReader r = new InputStreamReader(s);
```

When we read from stream `r`, stream `r` will, in turn, read from stream `s`. The data flowing in stream `s` is in the form of bytes of 8 bits, because `s` is a byte stream but the data read from stream `r` will be in the form of Unicode with 16 bits. To deal with this in class `InputStreamReader`, a *translation* is made from 8-bit bytes to 16-bit Unicode. We shall discuss in Section 13.2.3 how this is done. Class `InputStreamReader` is, effectively, a bridge between byte streams and char streams; see Figure 13.1.

The class `FileReader`, a subclass of class `InputStreamReader`, enables us to read directly from a file. `FileReader` also makes translations from 8-bit bytes to 16-bit Unicode.

Perhaps the simplest of these classes are `CharArrayReader` and `StringReader`. These are used to connect a stream to an array of **char** or a `String` object. The stream will then enable us to "read" from the array or `String` object. These classes function in the same way as the stream `ByteArrayInputStream`. No conversions will be necessary, as data in a **char** array and a `String` object will already exist in Unicode format.

Like the class `PipedInputStream`, class `PipedReader` is used in a program when we want two active objects to communicate with each other through a stream.

The lower shaded area in Figure 13.1 gives the connections that can be made in a char stream. We can read directly from an original char stream, as indicated by the arrow at the top of this section, or we can connect to streams of one of the classes indicated. The arrow pointing in the opposite direction illustrates that we can connect an arbitrary number of streams. Connections are made in the same way as for byte streams, that is, we indicate the stream we want to connect to, in the constructor.

We have included our own auxiliary class `ExtendedReader`, shown in Figure 13.1 in brackets, which we introduced in Section 13.2.2. We included this class to show that it follows the same pattern as the other classes. Note, however, that it is not a standard class. As we saw in Chapter 3, class `ExtendedReader` contains a set of methods that helps the programmer when entering data in the form of text. This class is a subclass of class `BufferedReader`, so we do not have to connect an extra buffer when we use it. If `r`, as above, is a stream of class `Reader`, we can write directly:

```
ExtendedReader er = new ExtendedReader(r);
```

13.1.3 Byte output streams

In the chart in Figure 13.2 we show how output streams are connected. Output streams, containing data in the form of 8-bit bytes, are shown in the upper part of the figure. The program writing to a stream is shown furthest to the left, and on the extreme right we find the different destinations this stream can have. We shall begin by discussing the classes for those streams connected to a destination, that is, the classes indicated furthest to the right.

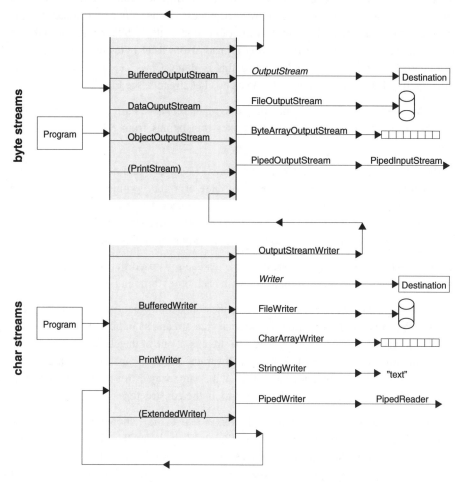

Figure 13.2 A connection chart for output streams

The class OutputStream is an abstract class that is a superclass of all the classes handling byte output streams and describes a general output stream. The destination of this stream is not specified. We cannot create our own instances of this class. However, we can call special methods that give a stream of this kind as result. (For example, the method getOutputStream in class Socket, to be discussed in Chapter 14, gives an OutputStream that we can write in when we want to send data to another computer.)

If we want to write data to a file, we can use the class FileOutputStream. We can indicate the file's name directly when we create the stream:

```
FileOutputStream fout = new FileOutputStream(file_name);
```

We can also let the destination be an array of bytes and "write" to the array by using the stream, exactly as we might write in a file.

We use class PipedOutputStream when we want to be able to send data through a stream from one active object to another. The active object that sends the data will use a stream of class PipedOutputStream, and the active object that receives the data will make use of class PipedInputStream.

The shaded area at the top of Figure 13.2 shows the connections that can be made to a byte output stream. The difference, when compared to input streams, is that a connection is made *in front of* the stream connected to a destination. For example, if we wanted to use a buffer when outputting data, we could connect a stream of class BufferedOutputStream.

```
BufferedOutputStream bout = new BufferedOutputStream(fout);
```

The arrow in the opposite direction indicates, as before, that several streams can be connected in this way. If we wanted to write out numerical data in binary form in a file using buffering, we could write the following stream:

```
DataOutputStream dout = new DataOutputStream(bout);
```

13.1.4 Char output streams

How we connect char output streams is shown in the lower part of Figure 13.2. The classes furthest to the right are those that describe streams that can be connected directly to a destination. The abstract class Writer is a superclass of all the classes that describe char output streams. The most important of the non-abstract classes is OutputStreamWriter. This is a link between char streams and byte streams. When we write in a stream of class OutputStreamWriter, the 16-bit Unicode characters we write are translated into a sequence of 8-bit bytes so that they can be output in the byte stream that the OutputStreamWriter stream is connected to. (This translation process is described in Section 13.3.2.) If `fout`, as above, is a stream of class `FileOutputStream`, we could create the stream:

```
OutputStreamWriter ow = new OutputStreamWriter(fout);
```

Then the data we wrote would be translated into bytes and stored in the file the stream `fout` is connected to. If we want to write to a file in this way, however, we could simplify things somewhat by using a stream of class `FileWriter` instead.

We use the classes `CharArrayWriter` and `StringWriter` when we want to utilize a stream to "write" to a char array or a `String` object. As we saw earlier, the class `PipedWriter` is employed when two active objects are to make use of char streams to communicate with each other.

The connections that can be made in a char output stream are shown in the lower shaded area of Figure 13.2. Several streams can be connected in sequence in this way, and connections are made in the same way as for byte streams.

The class `PrintWriter` contains methods, `println`, for example, which are useful when writing out data of the simple, built-in types, with printout in text form.

In Figure 13.2, class `ExtendedWriter` has also been included, in spite of the fact that we ourselves constructed it and it is not a standard class. It was included to show that it fits into the chart and follows the same pattern as the other classes of char output streams. As we saw in Section 3.2.2, the class `ExtendedWriter` is a subclass of class `PrintWriter`. It will, therefore, contain methods for the printout of different forms of data into text form. The difference, when compared with class `PrintWriter`, is that the data we output can be edited. As we saw in Chapter 3, we were able to control the number of positions and decimals we wanted to have in the printout.

Two arrows are, in fact, missing from Figure 13.2. Both the class `PrintWriter` and its subclass `ExtendedWriter` can also be connected to an `OutputStream` but we did not want to further complicate the chart.

13.2 Streams for inputting

We shall now discuss, in a little more detail, the different classes used to describe streams. Many of the methods and constructors can generate exceptions of class `IOException` (or of one of its subclasses). We will, therefore, assume that such exceptions have been dealt with by using a **try** statement or through writing **throws** `IOException`.

Let us begin with streams for inputting. There are similar streams for byte streams and char streams, so we can describe the two different categories of streams in parallel.

Input streams of the classes `DataInputStream` and `ObjectInputStream` must be discussed together with their corresponding output streams. We will not deal with them in this section, therefore, but later on in this chapter.

13.2.1 `InputStream`

The class `InputStream` is a superclass for all the classes handling the inputting of byte streams. The class is abstract, so we cannot create our own instances of it. It defines the fundamental methods for reading that all of its subclasses must have. The most important of these methods is `read`, which exists in three versions. The simplest form of `read` reads a single byte. This method will wait until there is a byte to read from the stream, or until the stream has finished. The value read is then given as result by the call. If the stream has finished, a value of –1 will be returned. Let us suppose that we have a byte input stream `s`. We can then read the stream with the following statements:

```
byte b;
int i;
while((i = s.read()) != -1) {  // read until end of stream
  b = (byte) i;  // type conversion from int to byte
  // do something with b
  ...
}
```

We should note an important point here: the method `read` returns not a value of type **byte** but one of type **int**. If we want to have the value read in the form of a **byte**, we must make an explicit type conversion, as shown in the example.

The two other versions of read have an array of bytes as parameter and can read more than one byte at a time. One of these versions has three parameters: an array of bytes that we can read to, a start index in the array and the maximum number of bytes to be read. A call of this method can look like this:

```
numberRead = s.read(a, startPos, maxNumber);
```

We suppose that `a` is an array of type **byte**[] and that `numberRead`, `startPos` and `maxNumber` are variables of type `int`. This call of `read` essentially reads `maxNumber` bytes from the stream `s` and places the values read into the array `a`, beginning in the position `startPos`. The call will give the number of bytes read as result. If the stream completes, the value –1 is given as result. This version of `read` reads as many bytes as are immediately accessible in the stream and will then return. However, it will never read more bytes than the maximum number indicated. So it will not wait until there are at least `maxNumber` bytes available. If no data is available when the call is made, `read` will wait until at least one byte is available. So we cannot be sure that this version of `read` will always read the number of bytes given as parameter.

The third version of `read` only has one parameter, the byte array that we will read to. The start position will then be equal to zero and the maximum number of bytes equal to the length of the array. The call `s.read(a)` is, therefore, the same thing as `s.read(a,0,a.length)`. By using the third version of `read`, we can obtain a more efficient reading from the stream `s` than in the example, above, when we only read one byte at a time.

```
byte[] a = new byte[1024];
int n;
while ((n = s.read(a)) != -1) { // read until end of stream
    // do something with bytes number 0 to n-1 in the array a
    ...
}
```

It is the job of the subclasses to make their own versions of the method `read` to ensure it works as efficiently as possible.

If we would like to test the number of bytes that can be read from a stream in advance without having to wait, we can call the method `available`. It must also be redefined in the subclasses, as the variant in class `InputStream` will always give a value of 0 as result.

If we want to skip a certain number of bytes in an input stream, we can call the method `skip`. As parameter it will have the number of bytes we want to skip and as result it will give the number of bytes it actually skipped. If the stream completes, a value of –1 will be returned. The result value has type **long**. So we can write:

```
long numberSkipped = s.skip(n);
```

We may sometimes have to go back to data in a stream. We might have to read for a while to see what kind of input data is coming and then go back to deal with it as we would like to. We might then want to use the methods `mark` and `reset`. The method `mark` is used to mark the place to which we will want to return. As parameter this method will have the maximum number of bytes we can read before we go back. To return to the place in the stream last marked, we then use the method `reset`. Note that we cannot go back in this way with all streams. To test whether a particular stream supports the methods `mark` and `reset`, we can call the method `markSupported`. This may look like this:

```
if (s.markSupported()) {
    s.mark(512); // remember this place in the stream
    // read at most another 512 bytes
    ...
    s.reset();  // return to the marked place
}
```

The last method in class InputStream is the method close, which is called to close the stream and return all the resources associated with it:

```
s.close();
```

The class InputStream		The class Reader	
int	read()	int	read()
int	read(byte[] b)	int	read(char[] b)
int	read(byte[] b, int off, int len)	int	read(char[] b, int off, int len)
long	skip(int n)	long	skip(int n)
int	available()	boolean	ready()
boolean	markSupported()	boolean	markSupported()
void	mark(int limit)	void	mark(int limit)
void	reset()	void	reset()
void	close()	void	close()

13.2.2 Reader

The class Reader is an abstract class that is superclass to all of the classes involved in the inputting of char streams. Class Reader directly corresponds to class InputStream, and the two classes have, with a minor exception, exactly the same methods. The exception here is that the method available does not exist for class Reader. Instead, there is a method with the name ready that we can call to check whether there is a character directly available in a stream, without our having to wait. The method ready gives a **boolean** as result. If we have a **char** stream r, we can write, for example:

```
if (r.ready()) {
    ...
```

The only other difference, when compared to class InputStream, is that the two versions of the method read that can read several characters at a time will have an array of **char** as parameter, instead of an array of **bytes**. The first, simplest version of read will return, as before, an **int** but we have to make a type conversion of this **int** to a **char**, instead of to a **byte**. This might look as follows:

```
char c;
int i;
while((i = r.read()) != -1) { // read until the stream finishes
    c = (char) i;  // type conversion from int to char
    // do something with c
    ...
}
```

13.2.3 `InputStreamReader`

The class `InputStreamReader` is, as we saw on page 393, a link between byte streams and char streams. It is used when we want to read a byte stream and translate the bytes we read into characters in the Unicode format. As we know, Java uses 16-bit Unicode internally in the program but we cannot be sure that this format is used externally to store text. If, for example, we want to read in data stored in a text file, this information is usually held in ASCII or LATIN_1 format, with 8 bits for each character that can be written. And we cannot be sure either that each character will be represented by an equal number of bytes. An example of a code where the different characters can be represented by a different number of bytes is the UTF 8 code, where a character is represented as one byte, or several bytes in succession.

When we create a stream of class `InputStreamReader`, we can indicate how the bytes that will be input data for the stream are to be coded. There are two constructors. We can write either:

```
new InputStreamReader(input_stream)
```

or

```
new InputStreamReader(input_stream, "code_name")
```

The inputting stream indicated as parameter will be of class `InputStream`. If we choose the first version, the translation will take place from the code that is the default for the conventions in use. (This is controlled by the default `Locale` that applies.) In English installations, this code is the same as LATIN_1. If we want to translate from another code, we should use the other form of the constructor. The code name is a text. For example, UTF 8 code is called `"UTF8"`, LATIN_1 is called `"8859_1"`, and the code in MS-DOS that corresponds most closely to LATIN_1 is called `"Cp850"`. (We can see which codes are available if we read the documentation for the command `native2ascii` included in J2SDK.) If we want to know the coding that is the default for the installation we are using, we can call the standard method `getProperty`.

```
String code = System.getProperty("file.encoding");
```

13.2.4 `FileInputStream`

We use this class when we want to create a byte stream that reads from a file. There are three different constructors:

```
new FileInputStream(file_name)   // file_name has type String
new FileInputStream(file)        // file has type File
new FileInputStream(fd)          // fd has type FileDescriptor
```

The first constructor will simply have as parameter the file name in the form of a `String`. In the second constructor, we indicate the file to be read by giving as parameter an object of the standard class `File`. This is a class with which we can get information on files and directories. Each `File` object will describe a file or a directory. We shall discuss this class in Section 13.6. The third constructor has as parameter an object of class `FileDescriptor`. This is a standard class that is a kind of reference to a file at a low level. We do not need to use this class.

13.2.5 `FileReader`

This class is a subclass of class `InputStreamReader`. It therefore translates a stream of bytes to a stream of **char**. We use this class when we want to read a text file, that is, a file that contains text, which will be coded in the standard format applicable to the actual installation. If the text is coded in some other way, we instead have to use class `InputStreamReader` and connect it to an object of class `FileInputStream`. Class `FileReader`, just like `FileInputStream`, has three different constructors, where a file name, a `File` object or a `FileDescriptor` object can be indicated as parameter. The first form:

```
new FileReader(file_name)    // file_name has type String
```

is equivalent to:

```
new InputStreamReader(new FileInputStream(file_name))
```

13.2.6 `ByteArrayInputStream` **and** `CharArrayReader`

On page 392 we saw that we could use a stream of class `ByteArrayInputStream` when we wanted to read input data from an array of bytes. If we have declared an array:

```
byte[] a = new byte[1000];
```

then we can create a stream that reads from this array:

```
ByteArrayInputStream s = new ByteArrayInputStream(a);
```

There is also an alternative form of constructor where we can indicate that only a certain part of an array will constitute the input data to the stream:

```
new ByteArrayInputStream(array, startpos, number)
```

When we read from a stream of this kind, it looks just as though we were reading from a file or some other external source.

We use the class `CharArrayReader` when we want to create a char stream that reads data from a char array. No conversions are necessary since the array will already contain data in Unicode format. We proceed as we would for class `ByteArrayInputStream`, the only difference being that the array will be of type **char**[] instead of **byte**[].

13.2.7 StringReader

This class functions in the same way as class CharArrayReader. The only difference is that input data will come from a String object instead of from a **char** array. There is only one constructor, and it will have an object of class String as parameter:

```
new StringReader(text)   // text has type String
```

13.2.8 PipedInputStream **and** PipedReader

These classes are used together with the classes PipedOutputStream and PipedWriter when two active objects communicate through streams. We will be giving examples of how they are used in Section 13.3.7.

13.2.9 FilterInputStream **and** FilterReader

The classes FilterInputStream and FilterReader describe input streams that can be connected after another input stream. As their names suggest, they will be used to describe streams which in some way "filter" the data entered. (Class FilterInputStream is superclass for classes BufferedInputStream, DataInput Stream and PushbackInputStream and class FilterReader is superclass for class PushbackReader.) The filter classes FilterInputStream and FilterReader have a single constructor that as parameter has another input stream named in. What happens, when one of the methods in the filter classes is called, is that the corresponding method in the stream in is called. If a FilterInputStream or a FilterReader were connected to a stream, therefore, data would flow straight through without being changed.

We should, of course, define our own subclasses of the filter classes. (The class FilterReader is, in fact, an abstract class and cannot be used directly.) In these subclasses we can redefine methods as required. Of course, it would be interesting to redefine the different versions of the method read so that read first read from the input stream in and then in some way changed or "filtered" the data that had been read. The method read can be found in all three versions (see Section 13.2.1) in class FilterInputStream, and these should be redefined in a subclass. We need to redefine only two versions of method read in subclasses of FilterReader but the version with only a **char** array as parameter does not have to be redefined.

We shall now give an example of how we can create our own filter class. The following class, a subclass of the filter class FilterReader, describes a filter that translates all the capitals in a char stream to lower-case letters:

```
import java.io.*;

public class ToLowerCaseReader extends FilterReader {
```

```
// constructor
public ToLowerCaseReader(Reader r) {
  super(r);
}
// redefine the methods read
public int read() throws IOException {
  int i = in.read();
  if (i == -1)
    return -1;
  else
    return (int) Character.toLowerCase((char) i);
}
public int read(char[] cbuf, int off, int len)
                                    throws IOException {
  int n = in.read(cbuf, off, len);
  for (int i=off; i<off+n; i++)
    cbuf[i] = Character.toLowerCase(cbuf[i]);
  return n;
}
}
```

There are a couple of things here to note. The first is that we have to call the superclass's constructor in the constructor so that the input stream in can be correctly initialized. The other is that the input stream in is inherited by our subclass and is directly accessible in all methods.

We have used the method toLowerCase in the wrapper class Character (see page 176) to do the job of translating. This method will leave unchanged all characters that are not capital letters.

Here is an example of how our new filter class can be used when we want to read text from the keyboard and output the text entered, with all the capitals changed to lower-case letters:

```
import java.io.*;
import extra.*;

class FilterDemo {
  public static void main(String[] arg) throws IOException {
    BufferedReader r = new BufferedReader
                       (new ToLowerCaseReader
                       (new InputStreamReader
                       (System.in, "Cp437")));
    String s;
```

```
    while ((s=r.readLine()) != null)
        Std.out.println(s);
    }
}
```

Data flows in from the keyboard through the standard stream `System.in`, which is a stream of type `InputStream`. In order to translate the 8-bit bytes in this stream to 16-bit `char`, an `InputStreamReader` is used. We have supposed here that the program will be run in an MS-DOS window. The LATIN_1 coding is not used in MS-DOS, so we have indicated in the constructor of the intermediate `InputStreamReader` stream that "Cp437" coding is to be used.

When in the program we call the method `readLine` (defined in the class `BufferedReader`), this method will in turn call the method `read` in class `ToLowerCaseReader`. All the capitals will then be translated into lower-case letters.

13.2.10 `BufferedInputStream` **and** `BufferedReader`

It can be very inefficient, when reading from an external source such as a file, to read only one **byte** or one **char** at a time. Data transfer will go much more quickly if we can read whole blocks at a time; we can do this with the classes `BufferedInputStream` and `BufferedReader`. They will disengage internal reading from external reading by using a buffer where data that has been read is stored temporarily. When we call the method `read` in a buffered stream, the stream can read in advance and fill the buffer. It is useful to use a buffered stream that is directly connected to the first input stream. There will be two constructors. The first has as its only parameter the input stream from which the buffered stream will read. The second also has, apart from this stream, a whole number that indicates the number of bytes or char for which the buffer will have space. (When we use the first of these constructors, we use a default value.) If `rin` is an input stream of class `Reader`, we can write, for instance:

```
BufferedReader br = new BufferedReader(rin, 1024);
```

The classes `BufferedInputStream` and `BufferedReader` contain all the methods that were defined in classes `InputStream` and `Reader`. Class `BufferedReader` also contains a new method that is very useful, the method `readLine`, which can read a whole line at a time. This method is so useful that a stream of class `BufferedReader` is often used simply to gain access to it. The method `readLine` is demonstrated in Sections 3.3.1 and 3.3.2.

13.2.11 `ExtendedReader`

In spite of the fact that there are so many standard classes for handling streams, oddly enough, there is no standard class that makes it possible for the programmer to read data of different types from a char stream with ease. The class `BufferedReader` has, as we stated above, the method `readLine` but that is the only one. If we want to read numerical data from a char stream, putting it into normal numerical variables, for example, in variables of type `int` and `double`, then there are no ready-made aids at hand. We must, as we saw in Section 13.2.1, first enter data in text form, then make type conversions using a wrapper class or an object of class `NumberFormat`. (Another alternative is to use an object of class `StringTokenizer` and connect this object to the input stream. This is general but a bit complicated.)

For this reason, we have chosen in this book to construct and use our own class `ExtendedReader`. This is a subclass of the class `BufferedReader` and has all of its properties. It has the same constructors, for instance. The stream `std.in`, which we used when reading from the keyboard, is a stream of class `ExtendedReader`. It is declared in the following way in class `std`:

```
public static final ExtendedReader in = new ExtendedReader
                        (new InputStreamReader(System.in, code), 1);
```

The variable `code` is a `String` that contains the code's name. If we are running a PC with an English version of Windows, `code` will contain the text `"Cp437"`. (To find out which platform and language will apply, the calls `System.getProperty("os.name")` and `System.getProperty("user.language")` are made in the class `std`.) The "one" in the constructor means that the buffer will contain only one character. We chose such a small buffer because `std.in` is essentially intended for interactive inputting. So it will work better if the buffer contains only the one character.

As we stated in Section 3.2.2, there is a set of methods in class `ExtendedReader` that makes it easier for the programmer to read different types of data from an input stream. There are also methods that can facilitate inputting in other ways; see the Revision Table on page 84.) Class `ExtendedReader` is accessible through the Internet on the home page of this book.

13.2.12 LineNumberReader

This class is a subclass of class `BufferedReader`. It will, therefore, have all the properties of `BufferedReader`. An extra property is that it can keep track of line numbers. There are two new methods. The method `getLineNumber` lacks parameters and gives as result the actual line number. The method `setLineNumber` has a whole number as parameter and assigns a number to the actual line. If `lno` is a stream of class `LineNumberReader`, the following call will give the actual line the number 100. Consecutive lines will then get the numbers 101, and so on:

```
lno.setLineNumber(100);
```

13.2.13 PushbackInputStream and PushbackReader

Sometimes we may need to read a little bit ahead to see the type of data coming in a stream. Depending on the kind of data, we might then want to handle it in different ways; for instance, we might want to read this data in a different part of our program. We can then make use of the classes PushbackInputStream and PushbackReader, which will allow us to push back data that has already been read into the input stream so that this data can be read again. There are two constructors. The first has only an input stream as parameter. We could write:

```
PushbackReader pr = new PushbackReader(rin);
```

If we use this constructor, we will be able to push back only a single character or byte into the stream. The other constructor includes another parameter. By using this one, we can indicate the maximum number of characters or bytes we want to push back:

```
PushbackReader pr = new PushbackReader(rin, 100);
```

Apart from all the methods inherited from the classes InputStream and Reader, classes PushbackInputStream and PushbackReader also have a method with the name unread. There are three variants of this method. The first one has only one parameter, and this will indicate the **byte** or **char** to be pushed back into the stream. In the following example, for instance, we read one character. If this should turn out to be a letter, the character will be the beginning of a name. We then push back this character into the stream and call another method to read in and deal with the whole name:

```
char c = (char) pr.read();
if (Character.isLetter(c)) {
  pr.unread(c);
  dealWithName(pr);
}
```

The two other variants of unread allow us to push back more than one byte or character. They have an array of bytes and a char, respectively, as parameter. In one variant, all the data in the array is pushed back into the stream and in the other variant, a sub-interval can be indicated in the array; then only the data in this sub-interval will be pushed back. For example, we can write:

```
char[] a = new char[50];
pr.unread(a);           // all 50 characters are pushed back
pr.unread(a, 10, 5);    // characters 10-14 are pushed back
```

13.2.14 SequenceInputStream

We use this class when we want to connect several streams to form one stream. To connect two input streams s1 and s2 into one, we can write, for example:

```
SequenceInputStream s = new SequenceInputStream(s1, s2);
```

When we then read from the stream s, all the data in stream s1 will be read first, followed by all the data in stream s2. If we want to connect more than two streams, we can give as argument for the constructor an iterator that refers to a data collection consisting of several input streams. For example, we can use the class Vector to create a collection of three input streams s1, s2 and s3.

```
Vector v = new Vector();
v.addElement(s1);
v.addElement(s2);
v.addElement(s3);
```

We can then create a SequenceInputStream that connects the three streams.

```
SequenceInputStream t = new SequenceInputStream(v.elements());
```

When we then read from the stream t, stream s1 will be read first, then stream s2 and finally stream s3.

13.3 Streams for outputting

In this section we shall look rather more closely at the streams that are used with outputting. We shall discuss byte streams and char streams in parallel, as they have similar classes. But we shall not discuss the classes DataOutputStream and ObjectOutputStream until Section 13.4.

13.3.1 OutputStream **and** Writer

These two classes are abstract. OutputStream is superclass for all classes that describe byte output streams while Writer is superclass for all the classes that describe char output streams. The methods write, flush and close, available for all output streams, are defined in the classes OutputStream and Writer.

The method write can be found in several different versions. The simplest of these writes out a single byte or char to a stream. Let us suppose that out is a reference to an output stream and d a simple variable of type **byte** or **char** (depending on whether a byte or char stream is involved). Then we can make the call:

```
out.write(d);
```

The next two versions of write will write out several bytes or char to a stream at a time. These versions will have an array as parameter. We can either write out the whole of the array to the stream, or only a part of it. If we suppose that a is an array of **byte** or **char**, we could make the statements:

```
out.write(a);  // writes out the entire array
out.write(a, startpos, number); // writes out a sub-array
```

We have supposed that `startpos` and `number` are of type `int`.

There are two other versions of the method `write` for class `Writer` (but not for `OutputStream`), with which we can write out a `String` or part of a `String`. If `w` is a stream of class `Writer` and `txt` a `String` object, we could for instance make the statements:

```
w.write(txt);  // writes out a text
w.write(txt, startpos, number); // writes out part of a text
```

When we write to an output stream, we cannot be entirely certain that the data we write will immediately reach the stream's destination. If, for instance, we wrote to a file, we could not be certain that the data would immediately land in the file. This is because the stream may use a buffer in which the data might be temporarily stored. If we want to be certain that data will really be written out, we can call the method `flush`. This will empty any buffers and output data to the stream's destination. We simply make the statement:

```
out.flush();
```

We saw earlier that it was important to use `flush` when we were dealing with interactive programs that wrote out questions in a text window.

The last method in the classes `OutputStream` and `Writer` is `close`, which closes a stream and releases all its resources. This method normally calls the method `flush` to empty all the buffers before the stream is closed.

The class OutputStream	The class Writer
`void flush()`	`void flush()`
`void close()`	`void close()`
`void write(int b)`	`void write(int b)`
`void write(byte[] b)`	`void write(char[] b)`
`void write(byte[] b,` `        int off, int len)`	`void write(char[] b,` `        int off, int len)`
	`void write(String str)`
	`void write(String str,` `        int off, int len)`

13.3.2 `OutputStreamWriter`

As we saw on page 396, the class `OutputStreamWriter` is used to translate a char output stream to a byte output stream. The 16-bit Unicode characters in the char stream will be translated into a sequence of 8-bit bytes. These can then be sent on to their destination, which might be a file for storing them.

When we create a stream of class `OutputStreamWriter`, we can indicate how the bytes, which will be output data from the stream, are to be coded. There are two constructors.

We can write either:

```
new OutputStreamWriter(output_stream)
```

or

```
new OutputStreamWriter(output_stream, "code_name")
```

The outputting stream indicated as parameter will be of class `OutputStream`. If we use the first constructor, translation will take place to the default code for the conventions being used. In English installations this code is the same as LATIN_1. (Available codes are given in the documentation of the command `native2ascii` in J2SDK.)

13.3.3 `FileOutputStream`

We use this class when we want to store a byte stream in a file. There are four different constructors:

```
new FileOutputStream(file_name)          // file_name has type String
new FileOutputStream(file_name, append)  // file_name has type String
new FileOutputStream(file)               // file has type File
new FileOutputStream(fd)                 // fd has type FileDescriptor
```

The first and second constructors will have as parameter a file name in the form of a `String`. In the second constructor, the parameter *append* is a **boolean** that indicates whether we are to write over an existing file or add new data at the end of the file. The value **true** means that new data has been added to the end of the file. In the third constructor, we indicate the file to be written by giving as parameter an object of the standard class `File`; see Section 13.6. The third constructor has as parameter an object of class `FileDescriptor`. This class gives a reference to a file at a low level.

13.3.4 `FileWriter`

This class is a subclass of the class `OutputStreamWriter`. It will therefore translate a stream of **char** to a stream of bytes. We use this class when we want to store text in a file. The text in the file will be coded in the standard format applying to the actual installation. If we want the text to be coded in some other way, we must use the class `OutputStreamWriter` and connect it to an object of class `FileOutputStream`. The class `FileWriter`, like class `FileOutputStream`, has four different constructors in which we can indicate as parameter a file name, a file name and a **boolean**, a `File` object, or a `FileDescriptor` object. We could write:

```
new FileWriter(file_name)   // file_name has type String
```

which would be equivalent to:

```
new OutputStreamWriter(new FileOutputStream(file_name))
```

13.3.5 `ByteArrayOutputStream` **and** `CharArrayWriter`

We use these two classes when we want to "write out" data in an array. This array will exist as a buffer inside the stream object itself. When we use a stream of class `ByteArrayOutputStream`, the buffer is of type **byte**[], while the buffer will, of course, be of type **char**[] when an object of class `CharArrayWriter` is used. The buffer will automatically increase in size as new data is written out.

It is quite easy to create a stream of one of these classes. We simply write:

```
ByteArrayOutputStream bas = new ByteArrayOutputStream();
CharArrayWriter       caw = new CharArrayWriter();
```

The constructors can also be found in an alternative form, where a size can be indicated for the internal buffer at the outset:

```
ByteArrayOutputStream bas = new ByteArrayOutputStream(size);
CharArrayWriter       caw = new CharArrayWriter(size);
```

Streams of these classes contain the methods that all output streams have. For instance, we could write data using the method `write`:

```
bas.write(b);
```

To find out the number of data elements (**bytes** or **char**) actually in the internal buffer, we can call the method `size`, which will give a whole number as result. We could make the call:

```
bas.size()
```

Of course, we will want to have access to the buffer when we have written data to a stream. Then we can use the method `toByteArray`, or `toCharArray`. For example, we could write:

```
byte[] ba = bas.toByteArray();
char[] ca = caw.toCharArray();
```

The method `toString`, which translates data in the internal buffer to a `string` object, is also available for both classes:

```
String s1 = bas.toString();
String s2 = caw.toString();
```

This translation is self-evident in the case of a stream of class `CharArrayWriter`, since the buffer will already contain components of type **char**. If we have a stream of class `ByteArrayOutputStream`, translation must take place from a sequence of bytes to a text. This is the same problem that arose when we had to read from a byte stream and translate the stream to a char stream. There are therefore two different versions of the method `toString` in class `ByteArrayOutputStream`. The first, which was used above, lacks parameters, making the translation in accordance with the default code for the actual installation. The second version of toString has a code name as parameter, exactly like the constructor of class InputStreamReader. We can then indicate how the bytes in the buffer should be decoded. We could write:

```
String s3 = bas.toString("UTF-8");
```

The last of the new methods in classes ByteArrayOutputStream and CharArrayWriter is the method reset. New printout will begin in the internal buffer in the stream – the old content will, of course, be destroyed – if we make the following call:

```
bas.reset();
```

13.3.6 StringWriter

This class may remind us of the class CharArrayWriter but the internal buffer is not of type **char**[]. It is an object of the standard class StringBuffer. We have not discussed StringBuffer but it suffices to say that like class String, it can contain text. The difference, when compared to class String, is that the text in a StringBuffer object can be changed.

The class StringWriter has two constructors, one with no parameters, where a default value is used for the initial size of the internal buffer, and one where the buffer size is given as a parameter:

```
StringWriter sw = new StringWriter();
StringWriter sw2 = new StringWriter(size);
```

We can, of course, write to a stream of type StringWriter with the method write.

```
sw.write("Java");
```

To access the text written in the buffer, we can call the method toString.

```
String s = sw.toString();
```

There is also a method with the name getBuffer that can be used to access the internal buffer. The result will be an object of type StringBuffer.

The class StringWriter is useful when we want to use the aids offered by streams for editing text, without having to write out the text to a file or a text window. Let us suppose, for example, that in a graphics program we want to show a Label object containing a current balance. This will look as in Figure 13.3.

When we create a Label object, we will indicate, as parameter for the constructor, a String object containing the desired text. We can create this String object by writing in a stream of class StringWriter. To edit the text, we first connect a stream of class ExtendedWriter. This might look as follows:

Figure 13.3 An example of the use of StringWriter

```
double balance;
...  // compute balance
// edit the text
StringWriter    sw = new StringWriter();
ExtendedWriter out = new ExtendedWriter(sw);
out.print("Balance:");
out.setFillChar('*'); out.print(balance,15,2); out.flush();
// display the text
add(new Label(sw.toString()));
```

13.3.7 PipedOutputStream **and** PipedWriter

We can let two active objects send data to each other through streams. Here we will show a schematic example to demonstrate how this is done. Let us suppose that we have two active objects, obj1 and obj2. When obj1 is executing, it sometimes requires a computation to be done. It will therefore send input data for computation to obj2, which carries out the computation and returns the answer to obj1. We let obj1 and obj2 be objects of the classes C1 and C2, respectively. These classes will have the following structure:

```
class C1 implements Runnable {
  private Thread activity = new Thread(this);
  InputStream in;
  OutputStream out;

  public C1(InputStream in, OutputStream out) {
    this.in = in;
    this.out = out;
    activity.start();
  }

  public void run() {
    while (true) {
      byte b;
      ... // put input data in b
```

```
        // send input data to obj2
        out.write(b);
        ... // do something else
        // read the answer from obj2
        byte answer = (byte)in.read();
        ...
    }
  }
}
```

```
class C2 implements Runnable {
  private Thread activity = new Thread(this);
  InputStream in;
  OutputStream out;

  public C2(InputStream in, OutputStream out) {
    this.in = in;
    this.out = out;
    activity.start();
  }

  public void run() {
    int inputData;
    while ((inputData = in.read()) != -1) {
      byte result;
      ...  // compute the result
      out.write(result);
    }
  }
}
```

We see that internally, both of these classes have their input streams and output
streams. These are initialized in the constructors. We will be using two communication
streams, stream A, going from `obj1` to `obj2`, and stream B, going in the opposite
direction. To achieve this, we will have to create four stream objects, two going in each
direction:

```
PipedOutputStream outA = new PipedOutputStream();
PipedInputStream  inA  = new PipedInputStream(outA);
PipedOutputStream outB = new PipedOutputStream();
PipedInputStream  inB  = new PipedInputStream(outB);
```

Stream `outA` is the stream in which `obj1` will write. This will be connected to `inA`,
which is the stream `obj2` will read from. We connect two streams of this kind by giving
the one stream as parameter of the other's constructor. (We could just as well have put
the declarations in the reverse order and given `inA` as parameter for the constructor of
`outA`.) The streams `outB` and `inB` are similarly connected. There is another way to
connect streams. Both streams can be created without arguments for the constructor,

and the method `connect` is then called for one of the streams; the other stream is then given as parameter.

When two streams have been connected correctly, we merely have to declare the two active objects `obj1` and `obj2` and let them start:

```
C1 obj1 = new C1(inB, outA);
C2 obj2 = new C2(inA, outB);
```

We used classes `PipedInputStream` and `PipedOutputStream` in this example but `PipedReader` and `PipedWriter` work in exactly the same way.

13.3.8 `FilterOutputStream` **and** `FilterWriter`

The classes `FilterOutputStream` and `FilterWriter` describe output streams that can be connected in front of another output stream. They can be used to create streams that "filter" data before they are output. (The class `FilterOutputStream` is a superclass of the classes `BufferedOutputStream`, `DataOutputStream` and `PushbackOutputStream`.) The filter classes have a single constructor that has another output stream as parameter. This output stream is called `out`. When one of the methods in the filter classes is called, the corresponding method in stream `out` will also be called.

We have to define our own subclasses of the filter classes so that data can be changed in a filter stream. The different versions of the method `write` should be redefined in the subclasses, so that they will first "filter" data, then write out the filtered data in the output stream `out`. The three versions of method `write`, which was defined in the superclass `OutputStream` (see Section 13.3.1), can be found in the class `FilterOutputStream` and these should be redefined in a subclass. In subclasses of `FilterWriter` we only have to redefine the following three versions of method `write`:

```
write(c)                    // writes out a char
write(a, startpos, number)  // writes out part of a char array
write(s, startpos, number)  // writes out part of a string
```

13.3.9 `BufferedOutputStream` **and** `BufferedWriter`

Writing one **byte** or one **char** at a time to an external destination such as a file often wastes time. It is much quicker to output entire blocks of data. The classes `BufferedOutputStream` and `BufferedWriter` collect data in an internal buffer and write it out in blocks. It can often be useful to use a buffer stream that is connected directly in front of the last output stream. To connect a buffer before printout to a char stream that writes in a file, we might for instance make the declaration:

```
BufferedWriter bw = new BufferedWriter(new FileWriter(file_namee));
```

There are two different constructors in the classes `BufferedOutputStream` and `BufferedWriter`. Both have as parameter the output stream the buffer stream will write to. We can also indicate, in the second constructor, the number of bytes or char the buffer will hold. (A default value is used in the first constructor.) If `fout` is an output stream of class `FileOutputStream`, we might write:

```
BufferedOutputStream bos = new BufferedOutputStream(fout, 1024);
```

The classes `BufferedOutputStream` and `BufferedWriter` contain all the methods that were defined in classes `OutputStream` and `Writer`. Apart from these, there is a method `newLine`, in class `BufferedWriter`, which writes out an end-of-line marker. As we will remember from Section 6.1, an end-of-line marker can look different on different platforms. The single character '\n' is used in a Unix system, while in MS-DOS, the two characters '\r' and '\n' are employed. If we use the method `newLine`, instead of writing out these characters ourselves, the combination of characters that apply in the actual platform will be written out. We can then move the program we have constructed between different platforms.

13.3.10 `PrintStream` **and** `PrintWriter`

The class `PrintStream` was defined in Version 1.0 of Java. It was intended to be used for writing out texts in an ordinary 8-bit character format, to a text window, for example, or to a text file, but `PrintStream` could only write out text correctly when LATIN_1 coding was used. When char streams were introduced in Java 1.1, therefore, it was a good time to remove class `PrintStream`. It was replaced by class `PrintWriter`, which can handle character codes properly. Class `PrintStream` was spared the fate of being made obsolete by the pre-defined streams `System.out` and `System.err`, both of which are of class `PrintStream`. So the class was allowed to remain.

The classes `PrintStream` and `PrintWriter` are unusual in that they have the methods `print` and `println`. These have a single parameter and write out the value of the parameter in text form. The methods `print` and `println` are defined in several versions. The parameter can be of any of the simple built-in types, of class `String`, or a char array. There is also a version that has a parameter of class `Object`. When we call `print` or `println`, the parameter will be translated from its internal, binary form to text. If class `PrintStream` is used, we get a sequence of 8-bit characters, while the use of `PrintWriter` will result in a sequence of 16-bit **char**. We have seen several examples in the book where methods `print` and `println` were used when we wrote to the streams `System.out` and `Std.out`. Note, however, that versions of `print` and `println` with more than one parameter are not defined in either `PrintStream` or `PrintWriter`; they are defined in our own class `ExtendedWriter`; see next section.

Class PrintStream has no accessible constructor but class PrintWriter has no fewer than four of them. The first two have an output stream as their only parameter, and this can be either of class Writer or of class OutputStream. If bw is a stream of class BufferedWriter and bos a stream of class BufferedOutputStream we could write:

```
PrintWriter pw1 = new PrintWriter(bw);
PrintWriter pw2 = new PrintWriter(bos);
```

The two other constructors have one more parameter. This is a **boolean** that will indicate whether flush should be called automatically when the method println is used. We could write, for example:

```
PrintWriter pw3 = new PrintWriter(new BufferedWriter
                         (new FileWriter(file_name)),true);
```

13.3.11 ExtendedWriter

Naturally, the classes PrintStream and PrintWriter are valuable when outputting data in text form. However, as we mentioned in Section 3.2.2, they are incomplete, as there is no simple way of formatting printout. For instance, we cannot determine the number of decimals when we write out a real number and neither can we decide whether we want the printout in the English form, with a decimal point, or with a decimal comma, as used in other countries. This was why we defined our own class ExtendedWriter.

Class ExtendedWriter is a subclass of class PrintWriter and has the same four constructors as this class. All the versions of print and println in class PrintWriter can also be found in class ExtendedWriter. Some have been directly inherited, while others have been redefined. In addition to these methods, there are also a number of new methods with which output can be formatted. A set of instance methods in class ExtendedWriter was given in the Revision Table on page 85, and in Section 3.2.2 we showed examples of how some of them were used.

Class ExtendedWriter also contains a set of useful class methods that can be used to format text without the text having to be written in a stream. These methods will instead return a String that contains the formatted text. A set of these methods was given in the Revision Table on page 89. We shall now give an example of another way of producing text; see Figure 13.3 on page 412. We wrote to a stream of class StringWriter before but this can be simplified by using the class method formatNum, in the class ExtendedWriter.

```
double balance;
...  // compute the balance
// edit the text
String s= ExtendedWriter.formatNum(balance,15,2,'*');
```

```
// display the text
add(new Label(s));
```

The streams `Std.out` and `Std.err` are of class `ExtendedWriter`. `Std.out` is initialized in the following way in class `Std`:

```
public static final ExtendedWriter out = new ExtendedWriter
                (new OutputStreamWriter(System.out, code), true);
```

A char stream is connected to the pre-defined stream `System.out`. The code that will be used in the translation is indicated by the `String` variable `code`. (Compare this with the declaration of the stream `std.in` in Section13.2.11.) The parameter `true` indicates that `flush` will be called automatically with every call of `println`.

13.4 Streams with binary data

Our discussions up to now have mainly concerned the reading and writing of streams containing text. The original source or the final destination of a stream has been a text file or a text window. Text files and text windows are usually intended for communication with people. On the other hand, when a program produces output data to be read by another program, it is not necessary to store data in text form. It is generally more efficient to store the data in the same binary format as it has been in the program. For instance, if we wish to store an `int` variable in a file, we can use 32 bits, or 4 bytes, instead of decoding the variable and representing it by a sequence of character codes. Files containing data stored in this binary format are usually called *binary files*.

There are two ways in Java of handling streams with binary data. If we only have to deal with simple data such as can be described by Java's simple, built-in types, we can use the classes `DataInputStream` and `DataOutputStream`. If we are handling more complicated data, data described by classes, we shall have to use the classes `ObjectInputStream` and `ObjectOutputStream`. We can also store simple data in binary form in direct access files, in which case we do not use streams but instead make use of the class `RandomAccessFile`. We shall discuss this in Section 13.5.

Apart from the classes we have named here, there are four interfaces: `DataInput`, `DataOutput`, `ObjectInput` and `ObjectOutput`. All the methods in class `DataInputStream` are defined in the interface `DataInput`. The class `DataInputStream`, therefore, implements the interface `DataInput`. Similarly, the class `DataOutputStream` implements the interface `DataOutput`, the class `ObjectInputStream` the interface `ObjectInput`, and the class `ObjectOutputStream` the interface `ObjectOutput`. The interfaces have been defined in parallel with the classes because it will then be possible to define other classes that implement the interfaces. The class `RandomAccessFile` is

417

an example of this. It does not describe a stream but it still implements both the interface DataInput and the interface DataOutput.

13.4.1 DataInputStream **and** DataOutputStream

These two classes are subclasses of FilterInputStream and FilterOutputStream, respectively. They can be connected to a stream when we want to read or write simple data in binary form. The different methods in these classes are shown in the Revision Table. Those methods with a direct equivalent in both classes are shown in the upper part of the table. If we output data with one of the printout methods and then input with the corresponding input method, we will get exactly the same data as we printed out. We see that there is an input method, together with its corresponding output method, for each one of the 8 simple, built-in types. In addition, there are the methods writeUTF and readUTF that print out and read in texts coded in UTF 8 code. (The parameters for several of the write methods, for example, writeShort, have type **int** but we can make calls with a value of the actual type.) Note that the methods readChar and writeChar read and write 16-bit **char** values.

There are three methods in the interface DataOutput that lack an equivalent in the interface DataInput. The method writeChars writes out all the characters in a text of 16 bits per character, while the method writeBytes writes out a text of 8 bits per character. The three methods with the name write write out a single byte, or several bytes, from an array. We discussed how these functioned in Section 13.3.1 in connection with the class OutputStream. The method size indicates the total number of bytes that have been written to the stream.

Some methods in the interface DataInput also lack equivalents in the interface DataOutput. There are integer types in the programming languages C and C++ that are "unsigned". A variable of this type can only contain numbers that are greater than, or equal to, zero. There are no "unsigned" integer types in Java, but the methods read UnsignedByte and readUnsignedShort can be used to input data of this kind. The result type will then be an **int**.

The two methods readFully function in the same way as the methods read, inherited from the class InputStream; see Section 13.2.1. The difference is that the methods readFully always wait until *all* data has been input to the array given as parameter. As we saw earlier, the methods read did not always do this. They only waited until at least one byte could be read. The method skipBytes skips over a number of bytes in the input stream. It differs from the method skip in class InputStream in that it waits until *all* the bytes needing to be skipped have been skipped.

The method readLine is a remnant from Java 1.0. It has been eliminated from the class DataInputStream as char streams should be used to read text. As we saw earlier, there is an equivalent method in the class BufferedReader.

The interface DataInput	The interface DataOutput
`boolean readBoolean()`	`void writeBoolean(boolean v)`
`char    readChar()`	`void writeChar(int v)`
`byte    readByte()`	`void writeByte(int v)`
`short   readShort()`	`void writeShort(int v)`
`int     readInt()`	`void writeInt(int v)`
`long    readLong()`	`void writeLong(long v)`
`float   readFloat()`	`void writeFloat(float v)`
`double  readDouble()`	`void writeDouble(double v)`
`String  readUTF()`	`void writeUTF(String s)`
`int    readUnsignedByte()`	`void writeChars(String s)`
`int    readUnsignedShort()`	`void writeBytes(String s)`
`void readFully(byte[] b)`	`void write(int b)`

`void readFully(byte[] b,`
`               int off, int len)`
	`void write(byte[] b)`
	`void write(byte[] b,`
	`               int off, int len)`

`void skipBytes(int n)`	`int size()`
`String readLine()`	

By way of an example, we will show how an array of `double` can be stored in a binary file. We will suppose that the file's name has been given as parameter for `main`:

```
DataOutputStream out = new DataOutputStream
                        (new FileOutputStream(arg[0]));
double a[] = new double[100];
... // compute data and store in the array
// write out the array to the file
out.writeInt(a.length);
for (int i=0; i<a.length; i++)
  out.writeDouble(a[i]);
out.close();
```

Note that we first write out the array's length as an `int`, then all the components in the array. We can now write another program that reads in the file and re-creates the array:

```
DataInputStream in = new DataInputStream
                        (new FileInputStream(arg[0]));
int n = in.readInt(); // read the array's length
double z[] = new double[n];
// read in the array's components
for (int i=0; i<z.length; i++)
    z[i] = in.readDouble();
```

Note that data is stored in the file in binary format. If we tried to read the file as text, in a text editor, for instance, we would only get a lot of gobbledegook on the screen.

13.4.2 `ObjectInputStream` **and** `ObjectOutputStream`

To write out and read in binary data of the simple, built-in types is relatively straightforward. Each value written will always have a definite length. For example, an `int` is always four bytes long. We only need a moment's thought to realize that it must be a much more complicated matter to write out data objects described by classes, when much of the data is considerably more complex. We also have to store information about the object so that it can be re-created. In addition, a particular object can have instance variables referring to other objects, and these other objects will have to be written out. Then these objects can, in turn, contain references to other objects that must be written out, and so on. An object that contains references to other objects forms a kind of tree structure in a system's primary memory and when this tree is written out to a stream, it has to be "flattened out". In Java, we say that we *serialize* the object. In spite of all of this, it is surprisingly straightforward to read whole objects in Java. This is because the classes `ObjectInputStream` and `ObjectOutputStream` are extremely sophisticated and will do the whole job. We really only have to use two methods: `readObject` and `writeObject`. Classes `ObjectInputStream` and `ObjectOutputStream` also implement the interfaces `DataInput` and `DataOutput`, respectively, so that all the methods in the Revision Table on page 419 will also be available.

We can create streams of the classes `ObjectInputStream` and `ObjectOutputStream` in the usual way. As parameter for the constructor, we indicate another stream to which the new stream will be connected. So, if `sin` and `sout` are of classes `InputStream` and `OutputStream` respectively, we can write:

```
ObjectInputStream  in  = new ObjectInputStream(sin);
ObjectOutputStream out = new ObjectOutputStream(sout);
```

There is one requirement that must be satisfied if we are to be able to write out an object `obj` in a stream: the class `C` that `obj` belongs to must implement the interface `Serializable`, or the interface `Externalizable`. This does not only apply to class `C`. If `obj` contains a reference to another object, the class of this object must also implement one of these interfaces. The interface `Externalizable` is used when we want full control over the input and output processes. We shall not go further into this here but will content ourselves with a discussion of the interface `Serializable`. This is a particularly simple interface. It contains no methods and is merely a sort of marker indicating that we are allowing objects of the class to be serialized. We could declare our own class `C`:

```
public class C implements Serializable {
  the usual definitions of variables and methods
}
```

If we indicate that a class is to be serializable, this will also apply to all of the class's subclasses. Many of the standard classes in Java will implement the interface `Serializable`. This is true for class `Component`, so it follows that all GUI components can be serialized. The class `Vector` is another example of a standard class that implements the interface `Serializable`.

Let us now suppose that we have an object `obj` of the class `C`. We can then write out `obj` to the stream `out` with the following simple statement:

```
out.writeObject(obj);
```

To read in and re-create an object is almost as simple. We write:

```
obj = (C) in.readObject();   // explicit type conversion
```

The method `readObject` returns a reference of type `Object`. To assign this to the variable `obj`, we have to make an explicit type conversion to the class concerned. Both methods, like all other inputting and outputting methods, can generate an exception of class `IOException`. The method `readObject` can, in addition, give an exception of class `ClassNotFoundException`.

In certain types of application programs, text editors or GUI programs, for instance, the user can save his or her work, loading it later to continue with it. A number of games also offer this possibility. When constructing such programs, the classes `ObjectInputStream` and `ObjectOutputStream` might be very useful. If there is an object in the program that describes the actual condition, we can save this condition simply by writing out the object to a file. The object can be read from the file later. For example, in Section 10.2, we wrote a program in which we could draw lines. To keep track of the lines that went into a figure, we used a vector; see class `Draw2` on page 323.

```
Vector lines = new Vector();
```

Into this we put objects of class `Line`; see page 319. Each time the user drew a new line, we added a new `Line` object to the vector. We can save the whole figure the user drew by writing out the object `lines` in a file.

When we are to save and load an object in this type of application program, we can use the two class methods `storeObject` and `loadObject`, shown below. Both will get a file name as parameter. The method `storeObject` will in addition get as parameter a reference to the object to be saved. Both of these methods will catch any exceptions that might arise:

```
public static void storeObject(Object obj, String name) {
  try {
    ObjectOutputStream out = new ObjectOutputStream
                               (new FileOutputStream(name));
    out.writeObject(obj);
    out.close();
  }
  catch (IOException ie) {
    ie.printStackTrace(); System.exit(1); }
}
```

```
public static Object loadObject(String name) {
  Object obj = null;
  try {
    ObjectInputStream in = new ObjectInputStream
                             (new FileInputStream(name));
    obj = in.readObject();
    in.close();
  }
  catch (IOException ie) {
      ie.printStackTrace(); System.exit(1); }
  catch (ClassNotFoundException ce) {
      ce.printStackTrace(); System.exit(2); }
  return obj;
}
```

The method `loadObject` returns a reference to class `Object`. So we must use an explicit type conversion when we call it. For example, to read in a saved vector v from the file `saved`, we can make the statement:

```
v = (Vector) loadObject("saved");
```

By way of an example, let us return to class `Draw2` on page 323. Let us now suppose that we want to be able to save the figures we have drawn in a file so that we can return to load our work and carry on working with the figures we saved earlier. In our program we can then add a menu that contains the options, "New", "Open" and "Save":

```
private MenuBar mb = new MenuBar();
private Menu fileMen = new Menu("File");

private MenuItem[] fileAlt = { new MenuItem("New"),
                               new MenuItem("Open"),
                               new MenuItem("Save") };
```

We will also define two file dialogs that are displayed when the user chooses the file that will be read in, or in which the figure is to be saved:

```
private FileDialog openD = new FileDialog(this, "Open");
private FileDialog saveD = new FileDialog(this, "Save",
                                            FileDialog.SAVE);
```

When the user chooses one of the options in the menu, we will come to a listener. This could look as follows. We get the name of the file we will use to save to, or read from, from the file dialogs by calling the methods getDirectory and getFile:

```
public void actionPerformed(ActionEvent e) {
  if (e.getSource() == fileAlt[0]) {   // New
    lines.removeAllElements();
    repaint();
  }
  else if (e.getSource() == fileAlt[1]) { // Open
    openD.show();
    if (openD.getFile() != null)
      lines = (Vector) loadObject(openD.getDirectory() +
                                    openD.getFile());
    repaint();
  }
  else if (e.getSource() == fileAlt[2]) {   // Save
    saveD.show();
    if (saveD.getFile() != null)
    storeObject(lines, saveD.getDirectory() +
                      saveD.getFile());
  }
}
```

We conclude this section by showing how we can have a little more control over what is written out and read in when we use the methods writeObject and readObject. We will start with an example. In Section 6.10, we discussed how we could have references in an object to several other objects, and on page 212 we defined the class Person:

```
class Person {
  private String name, address;
  private Person husbOrWife;
  private Person[] children = new Person[20];
  private int numberOfChildren = 0;

  various methods
}
```

Each person had an array with space for at most 20 children, and in this array we placed references to the children. The variable numberOfChildren was used to keep track of the number of children a person had or, in other words, the number of components in the array children that were used. If we want to save information about many persons in a file, we can use the method writeObject and write out the persons one after another in a stream of the class ObjectOutputStream. It is unusual for one person to have 20 children and therefore it is pointless to write out 20 components for each person. It is more efficient to write out only the number of components used; we can achieve this if, before we output, we remake the array children, so that it contains only the number of components required. It will also be superfluous to write out the value of the variable numberOfChildren to the file, as the number of children will be equal to the length of the array. We will now make these changes.

If we do not want a variable to be written out when writeObject is called, we can write the reserved word **transient** in the variable declaration. In this way, we can ensure that the variable numberOfChildren is not written out by changing the declaration in the following way:

```
private transient int numberOfChildren = 0;
```

A variable marked as **transient** will not be read in calls of readObject. We must initialize it ourselves, therefore, after an input is made.

We can define two methods with the names readObject and writeObject when we define a class that implements the interface Serializable. If we do this, the first lines in their definitions must always look exactly like this:

```
private void readObject(ObjectInputStream in)
                    throws IOException, ClassNotFoundException
private void writeObject(ObjectOutputStream out)
                    throws IOException
```

Note that the word **private** must appear first and the exceptions must be specified. If we have declared a writeObject method in a class C, we will come to this method every time writeObject is called for an output stream and an object of class C has been indicated as parameter. In this way, the object can be adjusted before output takes place. We can then allow output to proceed as usual by calling the method defaultWriteObject for that output stream. A similar procedure applies to input. If we have defined a readObject method in a class C, we will come to this method every time input of an object of class C takes place. We can now call the method defaultReadObject for the input stream to carry out input in the normal way and make our adjustments.

We will now change the class Person so that it functions like this. We let it implement the interface Serializable, we declare numberOfChildren as **transient**, and we define the two methods readObject and writeObject:

```
import java.io.*;
class Person implements Serializable {
  private String name, address;
  private Person husbOrWife;
  private Person[] children = new Person[20];
  private transient int numberOfChildren = 0;

  private void writeObject(ObjectOutputStream out)
      throws IOException {
    Person[] temp = children;
    children = new Person[numberOfChildren]; // make the array
                                             // shorter
    System.arraycopy(temp,0,children,0,numberOfChildren);
    out.defaultWriteObject();      // write out
  }

  private void readObject(ObjectInputStream in)
      throws IOException, ClassNotFoundException {
    in.defaultReadObject();    // read in
    numberOfChildren = children.length;  // initialize
                                         // numberOfChildren
    Person[] temp = children;
    children = new Person[20];    // extend the array
    System.arraycopy(temp,0,children,0,numberOfChildren);
  }
  various methods
}
```

In the method writeObject, we change the variable children so that it refers to a new array that is precisely as long as it has to be. The variable temp refers to the old array, and we have to copy all the children from the old array to the new one. We do exactly the opposite in the method readObject. Here we read in a short array. We let the variable temp refer to the short array and then change the variable children so that it refers to a long array that can accommodate 20 children. We then copy the children from the short array to the long one.

13.5 Direct access files

When we read data from a file or write data to a file by using streams, we have to read or write in a sequence from beginning to end. However, we may sometimes want to be able to move back and forth in a file, more or less as we do when indexing in an array. We can do this by using the class RandomAccessFile. This class does not describe a stream but implements both of the interfaces DataInput and DataOutput. It will, therefore, have all the methods that were defined in the Revision Table on page 419. In addition, there are three versions of read defined in class InputStream; see the

Revision Table on page 399. This means that data can be read and written by using class `RandomAccessFile` in exactly the same way as is done with the classes `DataInputStream` and `DataOutputStream`. Note that class `RandomAccessFile` handles binary data seen as a sequence of bytes. There is no "char version" of `RandomAccessFile`.

When we create an object of class `RandomAccessFile`, we will give two parameters. The first, which can either be a `String` with a file name or an object of class `File`, will indicate the file concerned. The second is a text that must be equal to `"r"` or `"rw"`. It will indicate whether we only want to read from the file, or want to be able to both read and write. To create a `RandomAccessFile` object that makes it possible for us to both read and write the file `"diverse.dat"`, we can write, for instance:

```
RandomAccessFile f = new RandomAccessFile("diverse.dat", "rw");
```

What is interesting about direct access files is that the class `RandomAccessFile` will automatically keep track of an actual position in the file. The actual position is the place in the file where the next byte will be read from or written to. This actual position is automatically moved forward when we read or write in the file. The actual position is represented by a whole number of type **long** that will give the number of bytes from the beginning of the file. Numbering will take place from 0. There are four interesting methods: `getFilePointer`, `seek`, `length` and `setLength`. The methods `getFilePointer` and `length` are the simplest ones. They lack parameters and give as result the actual position and the file's total length expressed in number of bytes, respectively. The method `seek` moves the actual position to the place indicated by the parameter. If we wanted to move back the actual position by 10 bytes, we could write:

```
f.seek(f.getFilePointer() - 10);
```

The last method, `setLength`, is used to change a file's total length. The required length is given as parameter. To shorten the file `f` by 100 bytes, for example, we can write:

```
f.setLength(f.length() - 100);
```

If we indicate as parameter a length that is greater than the old length, the file will be lengthened, and the new part will consist of bytes with an undefined content.

Direct access files are often used to store databases of different kinds. Booking programs, programs that keep track of booked and available places, for example, in hotels and at concerts, often make use of direct access files. Stock-keeping programs, which will keep track of the number of articles in a stock, are another example. What distinguishes this type of program from others is that direct access files are used to store *entries*. A file will contain a number of entries of the same kind. An entry is a group of data that belongs together. It may describe a particular room in a hotel, for instance, or a certain article in a stock-keeping program. Entries are stored in binary

---

java.io.RandomAccessFile

new RandomAccessFile(*name*,*mode*)	*name* is a String or a File object
	mode is `"r"` (read) or `"rw"` (read/write)
getFilePointer()	gives actual position
seek(pos)	moves actual position
length()	gives the file's length
setLength(n)	changes the file's length

In addition, all the methods in the interfaces DataInput and DataOutput are included.

---

form in a file, so there will be *no* conversion to characters. Data in the file will have exactly the same appearance as in the system's primary memory. When we read and write entries from and to files, we normally transfer a whole entry at a time.

In Java, we shall, of course, describe entries using classes. A class that will describe an entry must be very simple, however. It must contain only simple data. In addition, all the entries in a direct access file must have the same length if we are to locate them easily. This will pose problems, for example, if a class contains String objects, for then we have to be sure that these will always contain the same number of characters. If necessary, spaces have to be filled out with blank characters, or text has to be cut out. As an example, we shall show the class Account, which describes bank accounts. We will let this class have four instance variables: account number, balance, the account holder's name and address. Simple data types can describe the account number and balance (**long** and **double**, respectively) but the name and address will be objects of class String. We therefore have to ensure that these will have the same lengths for all accounts. We will make the name consist of 20 characters and the address of 30 characters. To keep track of these lengths, we define the constant class variables nameL and addrL. We shall also define a constant class variable that gives the length of the whole entry. Since the account number and the balance consist of 8 bytes each (see the Revision Table on page 41), the total length will be equal to 8+8+nameL+addrL. The class variables will not be included in this, as we will not be storing them in the entries. The class Account will look as follows:

```java
import java.io.*;
import extra.*;

public class Account {
  public long    number;
  public double  balance;
  public String name = "";
  public String addr = "";
```

```
public final static int nameL = 20;
public final static int addrL = 30;
public final static int length = 8 + 8 + nameL + addrL;

public void write(DataOutput out) throws IOException {
  // writes entries with a fixed length
  out.writeLong(number);
  out.writeDouble(balance);
  out.writeBytes(ExtendedWriter.toFixedLength(name,nameL));
  out.writeBytes(ExtendedWriter.toFixedLength(addr,addrL));
}

public void read(DataInput in) throws IOException {
  // reads entries with a fixed length
  number = in.readLong();
  balance = in.readDouble();
  byte[] nameBuf = new byte[nameL];
  in.readFully(nameBuf);
  name = new String(nameBuf);
  byte[] addrBuf = new byte[addrL];
  in.readFully(addrBuf);
  addr = new String(addrBuf);
}
}
```

In this class we have defined two methods that are used when we want to read and write Account entries. They will get as parameter a reference to the interfaces DataOutput and DataInput and can therefore be called with an object of class RandomAccessFile as parameter, as this class implements both these interfaces. We can also give parameters of the classes DataOutputStream and DataInputStream, respectively, if we wish to write or read Account entries sequentially. The method write writes out the four components. The texts are adjusted before the account holder's name and address are written out, to ensure they will be precisely 20 and 30 characters long, respectively. This can easily be done using the class method toFixedLength, in the class ExtendedWriter. The method read will do the opposite. It first reads the two simple components and then reads in exactly 20 bytes and 30 bytes, respectively, placing them in two arrays having these lengths. These arrays are then remade into String objects and put into the object.

We shall now look at a class AccountDatabase that keeps track of a bank account. Information about the different accounts lies stored in a direct access file. When we create an object of class AccountDatabase, we give the file's name as the only parameter of the constructor. The class AccountDatabase contains the methods open, close, finalize and transaction. The method open creates an object of class RandomAccessFile. This object is then used internally in class AccountDatabase to read and write in a file. The method close calls close for the object file. The method finalize is called automatically when an AccountDatabase object ceases to exist. The most interesting method here is transaction. Before dealing with this method, we shall first show the class AccountDatabase:

```java
import java.io.*;
public class AccountDatabase {
  private RandomAccessFile file;
  private String fileName;
  private Account record = new Account();

  // constructor
  public AccountDatabase(String fileName) throws IOException {
    this.fileName = fileName;
    open();
  }

  public void open() throws IOException {
    if (file == null)
      file = new RandomAccessFile(fileName, "rw");
  }

  public void close() throws IOException {
    if (file != null) {
      file.close();
      file = null;
    }
  }

  public void finalize() throws Throwable  {
    close();
    super.finalize();
  }

  public synchronized boolean transaction(long accounNo,
            double amount, Account result) throws IOException {
    // binary search
    boolean found = false;
    long recordNo = 0, first = 0,
         last = file.length()/Account.length-1;
    while (!found && first <= last) {
      recordNo = (first+last)/2; // the middle of the interval
      file.seek(recordNo*Account.length);   // move to the middle
      record.read(file);            // read the entry in the middle
      if (accounNo < record.number)
        last = recordNo-1;      // search in the half on the left
      else if (accounNo > record.number)
        first = recordNo+1;     // search in the half on the right
      else
        found = true;           // the entry is found
    }
```

```
      if (!found) {
        result.number = -1;
        return false;
      }
      // the account exists,
      // give account information in the parameter result
      result.number  = record.number;
      result.balance = record.balance;
      result.name = record.name;
      result.addr = record.addr;
      if (amount>0 || record.balance+amount>=0) {
        // deposit or permitted withdrawal
        record.balance += amount;
        // update the file
        file.seek(recordNo*Account.length);
        record.write(file);
        result.balance  = record.balance;
        return true;
      }
      else
        return false;
  }
}
```

The method `transaction` is called when we want to carry out a transaction (a withdrawal or a deposit) on a particular account. It has three parameters: an account number, an amount and an object of class `Account`. The first two are input parameters for the method. The account number, of course, indicates the account on which the transaction is made, and the amount will indicate the sum to be deposited or withdrawn. The amount will be positive for deposits and negative for withdrawals. The third parameter is an output parameter with the name `result`, which will be a reference to an object of class `Account`. When the transaction has been carried out, the method `transaction` will fill in the result in the output parameter `result`. The method `transaction` also returns a value of type **boolean** that will indicate whether the transaction has been successful or not. A transaction may be unsuccessful for two reasons: firstly, an account with the given account number may not exist, in which case the method will put the value –1 in the place for the account number in the output parameter `result`; secondly, if the transaction involves a withdrawal of more money than is in the account. Then the withdrawal will be refused, and the account will remain unchanged in the database.

Note that the method `transaction` is defined as **synchronized**. This means that only one thread at a time can execute this method. There is therefore no risk of information for an account in the database being incorrect when we have a program of several threads, with some of these attempting to update the account at the same time.

Let us now see how the method transaction functions internally. The instance variable file is used to handle the direct access file with the account entries. Let us suppose that the file entries have been sorted in numerical order. The entries in the file are numbered from 0 upwards. Since all the entries are of equal length, we can calculate the initial position in the file for a particular entry by multiplying the entry's number by its size. A binary search is used to find a particular entry in the file; compare this with our discussion on page 202. Since the file's length is calculated in bytes, the number of entries in the file can be calculated by dividing the file's length by the size of the entry. The length of the file is obtained by calling the method length, while the entry's size is given by the class variable length in class Account. The variable recordNo contains the number of the next entry to be read from the file. It will be set from the beginning to the number of the file's most central entry. The method seek is used to move to the correct place in the file. When we call this method, we have to multiply by the size of the entry, since the position in the file is indicated in bytes.

The instance variable record is declared in class AccountDatabase. This variable is of class Account and is used when we are going to read and write entries in the file. We read or write a whole entry at a time with the methods read and write, which we defined in class Account.

If we do not find the entry with a binary search, we put the value –1 into the account number in the output parameter result and then return the value **false** to indicate that the search has been unsuccessful. If the entry was found, we copy the information in the file to the output parameter result. We then try to carry out the transaction, and if a withdrawal is involved, we check to see whether there is enough money in the account. If there is not, we will return the value **false**.

We will now show a small demonstration program that uses the class AccountDatabase. Let us suppose that the account is run by a bank clerk. Whenever there is a new client, the program will ask for an account number and an amount. A positive amount will mean a deposit and a negative amount a withdrawal. The program will then look for the entry in the database containing the account number indicated. If there is an entry with this number, the program will carry out the given transaction and update the actual account entry in the database. Here is an example of how this might look when the program is run:

```
Account no? 123456
Amount? -50
Elisabeth Bergman
1 Coffee Lane, Longdale
New balance: 434.00
```

```
Account no? 178520
Amount? 100
Incorrect account no

Account no? 234567
Amount? -500
Charles Wilson
19 Bean Road, Notown
Balance: 224.50
Withdrawal cannot be done!
```

The program has the following appearance. We will suppose that the account file is called accounts:

```java
import java.io.*;
import extra.*;

public class BankDemo {

  public static void main(String[] arg) throws IOException {
    AccountDatabase  b = new AccountDatabase("accounts");
    Account acc = new Account();      // output parameter
    while(true) {
      Std.out.print("Account no? ");
      if (!Std.in.more())
        break;
      long no = Std.in.readLong();
      Std.out.print("Amount? ");
      if (!Std.in.more())
        break;
      double amount = Std.in.readDouble();
      boolean transOK = b.transaction(no, amount, acc);
      // the result can be found in the acc
      if (acc.number > 0) {  // account number OK
        Std.out.println(acc.name);
        Std.out.println(acc.addr);
        if (transOK) {
          Std.out.print("New balance: ");
          Std.out.println(acc.balance, 1, 2);
        }
        else {
          Std.out.print("Balance: ");
          Std.out.println(acc.balance, 1, 2);
          Std.out.println("Withdrawal cannot be done!");
        }
      }
    }
```

```
    else
      Std.out.println("Incorrect account no");
      Std.out.println();
    }
  }
}
```

This concludes our description of direct access files. We might perhaps ask ourselves if it would not have been possible to use the classes `ObjectOutputStream` and `ObjectInputStream`, writing and reading whole entries to a file, instead of constructing our own methods `read` and `write` in class `Account`. There are two problems here: the first is that when we use `ObjectOutputStream` more information than the values of the instance variables is stored, taking up a lot of extra space in the file, which is not a good thing if the file has to hold a great number of entries; the other problem is that all the entries have to be of the same length if we are to be able to search properly in a direct access file. However, there is one way of solving this second problem, enabling us to combine the flexibility of classes `ObjectOutputStream` and `ObjectInputStream` with the quick search a direct access file allows. Two direct access files can be used: one where the different objects are stored sequentially and one where we only store the object's search key (for example, the account number) for every object, together with its position and length in the first file. We shall leave this task for an exercise.

13.6 The class `File`

The class `File` is used when we want to access information about individual files or directories. It also contains methods to remove files, change the names of files and create new files and directories. Note that the class `File` is not used to read or write to a file. For this we have to make use of the stream classes discussed earlier in this chapter. Of course, we can also use the class `RandomAccessFile`. The class `File` contains a number of methods. A list of these is given in the Revision Table. The names of these methods will usually explain what they do. We will only give examples of how some of the methods are used; for a complete description of all their details we refer the reader to the online documentation.

As we can see, there are three constructors. We indicate the file's name as a text in the first one. The name can either be relative or absolute. A relative file name is indicated in relation to the *current directory* the program is executing in, while an absolute file name contains the complete *path* of the file. In the second constructor, the name of the directory is indicated as first parameter and the file's relative name as second parameter. In the third constructor, we use another `File` object to indicate the directory in question. For example, we can write:

java.io.File	
`File(String path)`	`boolean mkdir()`
`File(String path, String name)`	`boolean mkdirs()`
`File(File dir, String name)`	`boolean createNewFile()`
	`boolean delete()`
`String   getName()`	`boolean renameTo(File dest)`
`String   getPath()`	`boolean equals(Object obj)`
`String   getAbsolutePath()`	`int compareTo(File file)`
`String   getCanonicalPath()`	`int compareTo(Object o)`
`String   getParent()`	`String toString()`
`File      getAbsoluteFile()`	`URL       toURL()`
`File      getCanonicalFile()`	`String[] list()`
`File      getParentFile()`	`String[] list`
`void      deleteOnExit()`	`          (FilenameFilter filter)`
`boolean exists()`	`File[] listFiles()`
`boolean canWrite()`	`File[] listFiles`
`boolean canRead()`	`          (FilenameFilter filter)`
`boolean setReadOnly()`	`int hashCode()`
`boolean isFile()`	
`boolean isDirectory()`	`static File createTempFile`
`boolean isAbsolute()`	`(String prefix, String suffix)`
`boolean isHidden()`	`static File createTempFile`
`long      lastModified()`	`(String prefix, String suffix,`
`boolean setLastModified()`	` File dir)`
`long      length()`	`static File[] listRoots()`
	`static separator`

```
File f1 = new File("Diverse");
File f2 = new File("C:\\Diverse\\my_file.txt");
File f3 = new File(f1, "Demo.java");
```

Note that there does not have to be a real file with the given name for us to be able to create a `File` object. We might, for instance, want to create a `File` object to use later for the creation of a new directory of that name, or to rename a file. The full file name can be either relative or absolute and will depend not on the constructor we have used but the parameters we have given for it. We can use the method `isAbsolute` to check whether a `File` object contains an absolute or a relative file name. The method `getName` will give the simple file name without the name of the directory, while the method `getPath` gives the file's name, including the name of the directory. The method `getAbsolutePath` will give the file's name in its absolute form. If we want to compose our own file names, we can make use of the class variable `separator`, which contains the character (or possibly, characters) that will appear between the file names in an absolute name. For example, if we are running Windows, separator will contain the character \. In Unix, the character would be /.

We now give an example of a program that will write out the name of the current directory. A list of the names of all the files in this directory is then given and the length of each file is indicated. Every file that is a directory is indicated by the character /, which appears first in the name. To find the name of the current directory, the class method `System.getProperty` is called, with `"user.dir"` as parameter. The method `list` is called to get a list of all the files in the directory.

```
import java.io.*;
public class FileDemo {
  public static void main(String[] arg) {
    String name = System.getProperty("user.dir");
    File f = new File(name);      // describes current directory
    System.out.println(f.getAbsolutePath());
    String[] l = f.list();
    System.out.println("Number of files: " + l.length);
    for (int i=0; i<l.length; i++) {
      File g = new File(l[i]);    // describes a file in the
                                  // directory
      if (g.isDirectory())
        System.out.print("/");
      else
        System.out.print(" ");
      System.out.print(l[i]);
      System.out.println("   " + g.length());
    }
  }
}
```

We can also show an example of how we can create new directories. The following program lines will create two new directories. The directory `new_directory` will land in the current directory and the directory `example` will end up in the directory `C:\temp`:

```
File d1 = new File("new_directory");
d1.mkdir();
File d2 = new File("C:\\temp\\example");
d2.mkdir();
```

It is also a simple matter to change the names of file or directories or to remove them. The following lines will change the name of the directory `new_directory` to `newDirectory` and remove a file called `old.txt`:

```
File d3 = new File("newDirectory");
d1.renameTo(d3);
File f4 = new File("old.txt");
f4.delete();
```

The method `list` in an earlier example gave a list of *all* the files in the current directory, but this method exists in an alternative version that we can use if we only want to have a list of certain files in a directory. For instance, we might want a list of all the files containing Java programs, in which case this list would only contain files with the suffix ".java". This alternative version of the method list has as parameter a reference to an object that implements the interface FilenameFilter. There is only one method defined in this interface, that is, the method accept, with the definition:

```
public boolean accept(File dir, String name);
```

Every class that implements the interface FilenameFilter must, therefore, have its own version of this method. When the method list is to create a list of files, it calls the method accept for each file. If accept returns the value **true**, the actual file will be included in the list, otherwise it will not be included. The method accept has two parameters. The first is a File object that describes the directory the file lies in, and the second is the name of the file.

There are no ready-made standard classes that implement the interface FilenameFilter. We have to define such interfaces ourselves. We will now show a class of our own that can be useful for filtering out files with certain suffixes. We call the class SuffixFilter. It has a single constructor that has as parameter the suffix we want to filter out. To get a list with all the file names that contain Java programs, for instance, we can make the statements:

```
SuffixFilter filter = new SuffixFilter("java");
String[] = f.list(filter);
```

We shall now show what the class SuffixFilter looks like. It only contains one constructor and its own version of the method accept. For every file, a check is made to see whether its name ends with the desired suffix. If so, we check to see whether we can read the file. To do this, we create a new File object that describes the file. Since class SuffixFilter can be generally useful, we have put it in our package class **extra** together with the other general classes:

```
package extra;
import java.io.*;

public class SuffixFilter implements FilenameFilter {
  public String suffix;

  public SuffixFilter(String suffix) {
    this.suffix = suffix;
  }

  public boolean accept(File dir, String name) {
    return name.endsWith("." + suffix) &&   // ends with suffix?
           (new File(dir, name)).canRead(); // can be read?
  }
}
```

Finally, the class `FileDialog`, which we looked at in Section 11.4, has a method with the name `setFilenameFilter`. We can call this to control the files that will be shown in the dialog box. If we have defined a `FileDialog` object with the name `openD` and only want to see files with the suffix `txt`, we can make the statement:

```
openD.setFilenameFilter(new SuffixFilter("txt"));
```

13.7 Exercises

1. We have saved a secret message in a text file with the name `secret.txt`. The message has been encoded so that no unauthorized person may easily read it. Each letter in the message has been coded to another letter by using the following table:

    ```
    code letters:    guwyrmqpsaeicbnozlfhdkjxtv
    original text:   abcdefghijklmnopqrstuvwxyz
    ```

    If, for example, the file contains the text "inybrt jgshsbq jrybrfygt rsqph oc", the decoded message will be "rodney waiting wednesday eight pm". Write a program to read the file with the secret message and write it out in plain language. The program should begin by reading in the code (the first line in the above table) from the terminal.

2. A command that is often used in the Unix operating system is one called `cat`. The task here is to write your own version `Cat` of this program. Feel free to use the class `SequenceInputStream`. We should be able to use the program `Cat` to combine files but could also use it to write out the contents of one or more files at the terminal. The command to run the program should have the form:

    ```
    java Cat f1 f2 f3 ...
    ```

    An arbitrary number of file names are, therefore, given as parameters for `main`. If no parameters are given, the program should read from standard input. The program should write out the files one at a time to standard output. If we want to concatenate files, standard output can be redirected. For example, the following command will mean that `fc` will contain a copy of `fa` concatenated with `fb`.

    ```
    java Cat fa fb > fc
    ```

    Note that a redirection is not an argument that is sent to `main`, so the program will only get `fa` and `fb` as arguments on this line.

3. In Section 7.7 we worked with a class `Vehicle` that had several subclasses and on page 241, we showed how we could describe a collection of different kinds of vehicle by using class `Vector`. The exercise now is to write the program lines necessary for such a vector to be saved in a file. In addition, write program lines to

enable us later to read in information about all vehicles and store them in a vector. Use the classes ObjectOutputStream and ObjectInputStream.

4. Information about a number of persons has been collected in a file as part of some statistical research. Each person is described by an object of a class Person (which you must define yourself), and information is stored using the class ObjectOutputStream. A person's name, height, weight, shoe size, age and civil status are included in this class Person. To deal with the data in the file properly, you will also have to know a person's sex but this information has not been stored.

Write a program that will read the file and create two new files, one containing only women and one only men. For every person in the file, the program will ask the operator whether the person is a woman or a man. A person will be described in the new files by a new class that also contains a person's sex.

5. Extend the class AccountDatabase in Section 13.5 with a method that opens a new account. The account holder's name and address will be given as parameters for the method, which should give as result the number the new account has got. The method should choose account numbers arbitrarily. Having checked that an account number is available, the method should then create a new entry, putting it into the correct position in the direct access file to ensure that this file remains sorted.

6. When we handle files, they are usually sorted. (The direct access file with the bank account, in Section 13.5, was an example of this.) Some particular component among the entries, for instance a civic registration number, or a car registration number, is normally chosen to institute the sort procedure. This component is called the *sort key*. A problem can occur if there are two sorted files with entries of the same type and a new, sorted file has to be made containing the entries of both files. The new file should also be sorted. We say that the two original files have been *merged*. Write a program that merges two files containing entries of the same length that define cars. The sort key is the car registration number. You may decide what the other entries are to be.

7. Let us suppose that the time of day is defined by a text string in the format "hh.mm.ss". Write a class method that updates a time of day by adding a certain number of seconds (which can be greater than 60). The method should have two parameters: a string object that contains a time of day and a whole number that will indicate the number of seconds to be added. As result, the method should give a string object that describes the updated time. *Hint*: Use the technique of connecting streams to texts.

8. It is difficult to use the technique of serialization together with direct access, since the objects stored in a file will have different lengths. A trick we can use to find the stored objects quickly is to use two direct access files. In one of the files – let us call it the data file – all of the objects are stored in serialized format. The file is not

sorted. In the other file, the index file, we store entries of equal length. There is an entry for every object stored in the data file. Every entry in the index file contains three pieces of information: the object's search key, the object's initial position in the data file and the number of bytes that the object will occupy in the data file. The index file is sorted. We shall, of course, use the classes ObjectInputStream and ObjectOutputStream when we are to read and write in the data file, but we cannot connect streams directly to a direct access file. What we can do is to use byte arrays. When we read from the data file, we read the number of bytes that the active object occupies. We then use a ByteArrayInputStream and an ObjectInputStream to read the array. We reverse this process when outputting to the data file.

Let us now suppose that information about the different kinds of motor vehicles has been stored in this way. (The class definitions in Section 7.7 can be used.) Your task is to write a method that will find a motor vehicle with a particular registration number and to write out information about this vehicle on the screen. The registration number is given as parameter for the method.

Communication

14

The many examples in this book have shown us that it is relatively easy to write GUI programs in Java. We have even been able to produce programs with moving pictures and sound. It may come as something of a surprise, therefore, to learn that the best is yet to come – the resources we have in Java for communications. It is very easy to write Java programs that can communicate with other computers in various ways. This opens new vistas for "ordinary" programmers who are not experts in data communication. In this chapter, we shall be looking at the different ways of communicating. We will see how we can examine and retrieve a file from another computer, how we can send quick messages in the form of datagrams, how we can use multicast to send messages to several computers at the same time and how we can establish a connection and write client–server programs. For security reasons, certain restrictions apply to applets. For this reason, most of the examples in the chapter have been worked out as independent applications. Communication in applets will be discussed in a separate section.

14.1 URL connections

In Section 12.2 we discussed the class URL. A URL object will identify a particular file on the Internet. We saw how we could give a file's complete address when we created a URL object. For instance, we could write:

```
URL u = new URL("http://www.xyz.xx/pub/Java/filename");
```

Naturally, we could make this more general by giving a variable as parameter. If the file name has been given as the first parameter for main, we could write:

```
URL u = new URL(arg[0]);
```

In Chapter 12 we saw how easy it was to download the actual file by making use of the method getContent in class URL. If we wish to have a little more control over what is happening, we can open a URL connection. In class URL, there is a method with the name openConnection that is used for this purpose. This will give as result a reference to an object of class URLConnection. For instance, we can write:

```
URLConnection uc = u.openConnection();
```

When we have created the connection, we can indicate how we want it to be used. If we only want to read the file on the distant computer, we can write:

```
uc.setDoInput(true);
```

There is also a corresponding method with the name setDoOutput that indicates whether we want to write in the file or not.

Then we can establish the connection with the command:

```
uc.connect();
```

When this has been done, we can access the distant file and read its properties. If we want to know how long the file is, for example, we can write:

```
int length = uc.getContentLength();
```

To read the file, we call the method getInputStream that connects a stream to the file:

```
InputStream in = uc.getInputStream();
```

Similarly, we can use the method getOutputStream if we want to write to the file. (Actually, the methods setDoInput and connect are superfluous in this example, as the default value is **true** for setDoInput, and the method getInputStream will itself call connect if this has not already been done.)

We can then read the stream in the usual way to copy the file to our own computer. If we want to do this to a new file on our computer, we will first have to create an output stream that we can copy to. This can be done by the declaration:

```
FileOutputStream out = new FileOutputStream(arg[1]);
```

(We suppose that the name of the new file has been given as the second parameter for main.) We can now copy the distant file to our own computer with the program lines:

```
int i, n = 0;
while ((i=in.read()) >= 0) {
       out.write((byte) i);
       n++;
}
Std.out.println(n + " bytes copied");
```

Note that this could be done rather more easily if we merely wanted to read the file, without reading its properties. Then we would not have to create a URLConnection object but could instead directly get an input stream connected to the file on the distant computer by calling the method getFile in the class URL. We simply write:

java.net.URLConnection	
url.openConnection()	gives a URLConnection object for the URL object url
setDoInput(*bool*)	indicates whether or not we wish to read the file
setDoOutput(*bool*)	indicates whether or not we wish to write to the file
connect()	makes the connection
getInputStream()	gives an input stream that is connected to the file
getOutputStream()	gives an output stream that is connected to the file
getContent()	same as the method getContent in the class URL
getContentLength()	gives the file's length
getContentType()	gives a text that describes the file's type
getDate()	gives the file's date of creation
getLastModified()	gives the date when the file was last modified

A point in time *t* is returned as the number of milliseconds since 1 January 1970 and can easily be converted to a Date object: **new** Date(*t*). (See page 283.)

```
InputStream in = u.openStream();
```

Since the file in the above example will be copied exactly as it is, we have been able to read it with a byte stream and copy one byte at a time. We will now give another example where a text file will be copied. Let us suppose that, on some central computer, we have a text file containing information about current temperatures in different locations. The reading of every temperature can be found in its own line in the file, where each line contains the name of the location, the temperature read and the time a temperature was reported. The program we will now be looking at will download the file from the central computer and present the current temperatures in a window on the screen. When the program is run, it could look as in Figure 14.1. The file is written out in a TextArea component. At the bottom, in a Label object, we can see the time when the downloaded file was last updated in the central computer. There is also a button on which the user can click to download a new, more current copy from the central computer. We make use of BorderLayout and place the text area in the "Center" position. The Label object and the "Update" button are put into a panel, which in turn is placed in the "South" position in the window. When we start the program, we give the URL address as parameter for main. This might look as follows:

```
java TemperatureDisplay http://www.weather.xx/pub/temperatures
```

Here is the program:

```
import java.awt.*;
import java.awt.event.*;
import java.net.*;
import java.io.*;
import java.util.*;
```

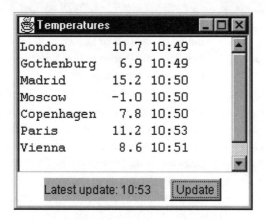

Figure 14.1 Downloading a text file

```java
import java.text.*;
import extra.*;

public class TemperatureDisplay extends ExtendedFrame
                              implements ActionListener {
 TextArea ta = new TextArea("",0,0,
                           TextArea.SCROLLBARS_VERTICAL_ONLY);
  Panel  p  = new Panel();
  Label  la = new Label();
  Button up = new Button("Update");
  URL u;

  public TemperatureDisplay(String address) {
    try {
      u = new URL(address);
      update();  // download the file
    }
    catch (MalformedURLException e) {
      e.printStackTrace();
    }
    setTitle("Temperatures");
    ta.setEditable(false);
    ta.setFont(new Font("Monospaced", Font.PLAIN, 14));
    ta.setBackground(Color.white);
    la.setBackground(Color.lightGray);
    add("Center", ta); add("South", p);
    p.add(la); p.add(up);
    up.addActionListener(this);
    setSize(250,200);
```

```
    setVisible(true);
  }
  private void update() { // download and display the file
    try {
      // open a connection, connect a text stream to the file
      URLConnection c = u.openConnection();
      BufferedReader in = new BufferedReader
                    (new InputStreamReader(c.getInputStream()));
      // read in the file to the text newText, line by line
      String newText = "", line;
      while ((line = in.readLine()) != null)
        newText += line + '\n';   // insert \n after each line
        // display the new file in the window
      ta.setText(newText);
      in.close();
      // read in, format and display the updated date
      Date d = new Date(c.getLastModified());
      DateFormat f = DateFormat.getTimeInstance
                    (DateFormat.SHORT);
      la.setText("Latest update: "+ f.format(d));
    }
    catch (IOException e) {
      e.printStackTrace();
    }
  }

  public void actionPerformed(ActionEvent e) {
    // when the user has clicked on the button
    if (e.getSource() == up)
      update();
  }

  public static void main(String[] arg) {
    // the address is given as parameter
    new TemperatureDisplay(arg[0]);
  }
}
```

As usual, the configuration of the window is done in the constructor, and initialization of the URL object referring to the file of temperatures is also done there. Note that the constructor for class URL can generate an exception of type MalformedURLException, and this must be dealt with or sent on.

The real work is done in the method update. This is called both from the constructor, when the file is to be downloaded for the first time, and from the listener when the user has clicked on the button. We have to connect a char stream to the input stream, as the file to be downloaded is a text file. We use a stream of class BufferedReader, as this class has the method readLine, which reads a line at a time. As we will remember, a stream of class BufferedReader cannot be directly connected to a stream of class InputStream without the use of an intermediary stream of class InputStreamReader. One line is then read at a time and placed last in the text newText. An end-of-line character is inserted after each line. The new text in the TextArea object is displayed when all the lines have been read in.

The method getLastModified gives a time in the form of a whole number value of type **long**, and this value is used as parameter of the constructor for the class Date. We will then get a Date object that describes the time. We will make use of a DateFormat object to display this value in the desired form, exactly as we did in Section 9.2.

14.2 Ports and sockets

As we know, a URL address describes the address of a file on the Internet. A computer can not only have files on the Internet, it can also offer different kinds of services. One of these is the opportunity to send and receive data by using HTTP protocol; another, to give the exact time and date for the computer. To keep track of the different kinds of services, we use something called a *port*. Each service is assigned a particular port, identified by a whole number. For instance, port number 80 is used for HTTP communication, port number 21 for FTP communication, and port number 13 gives the exact time and date. If we want to have a particular service from a certain computer, we have to indicate both the computer's name on the Internet and the port number we wish to use. Port numbers are whole numbers in the interval 0 to 65,535. Numbers up to 1024 are reserved for different forms of standard service, while those over 1024 can be freely used when programs providing a service are written. We can think of a port as a connection point on a computer, a sort of "virtual input". (Compare this with the input points on the back of a computer, TV or stereo amplifier.)

When we want to get on the Internet to communicate with other computers through a program, we have to connect a "virtual line" through the "virtual input" out to the Internet. This "virtual line" is called a *socket*. So a socket is a kind of channel for data. Only one socket is usually drawn through a particular port but it is possible to have several sockets running through a port. A program can also make use of several ports and sockets. Figure 14.2 gives a diagrammatic view of ports and sockets.

We shall utilize ports and sockets in the following sections in order to communicate through programs. There are two main principles according to which communication can proceed. We can either send *datagrams*, independent packets of data that contain the address of their destination, or we can set up a *connection* between two computers and send data through this connection. In the first case, that is, when we use datagrams,

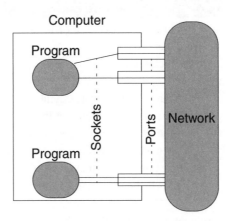

Figure 14.2 Ports and sockets

we have the option of using *multicast*, a means of sending data packets at the same time to several connected members of a particular group.

14.3 Datagrams

A datagram is a packet of data sent over the Internet. It will contain the address of both the sender and the receiver, where this address is indicated as the computer's address with the port number added. Sending a datagram can be compared to sending an ordinary letter through the post. There is no guarantee that it will actually reach the receiver, and if several datagrams are sent, we cannot be certain that they will arrive in the same order as they are sent.

Datagrams in Java are described by the class `java.net.DatagramPacket`. One of the things a datagram will contain is the receiver's Internet address. Internet addresses are described by the class `java.net.InetAddress`. This class has no constructors. Instead we create an `InetAddress` object by calling one of the class methods `getLocalHost` and `getByName`. The first lacks parameters and gives the Internet address of our own computer. The method `getByName` has a text as parameter. This text will contain the Internet address either as a symbolic name, for example `www.xyz.pqr.com`, or as an IP address, such as `206.26.48.100`. For example, we can write:

```
InetAddress toAddr = InetAddress.getByName("www.xyz.pqr.com");
```

If we have given an incorrect address as parameter, we will get an exception of type `UnknownHostException`.

java.net.InetAddress	
`getLocalHost()`	class method that gives an `InetAddress` to one's own computer
`getByName(name)`	class method that gives an `InetAddress` to the computer *name*
	name can be indicated as a symbolic name or an IP address
`getHostName()`	gives the computer name for this `InetAddress`
`getHostAddress()`	gives the IP address for this `InetAddress`
`isMulticastAddress()`	indicates whether this `InetAddress` can be used to send multicast messages (messages to several receivers)
`equals(iAddr)`	checks whether this `InetAddress` is the same as `iAddr`

A datagram will of course contain the data that is being sent, and this will be in the form of an array of bytes. The data to be sent must, therefore, be converted into this form. For instance, if we want to send a text of type `string`, the text can be converted to an array of bytes with the method `getBytes`:

```
String message = "Hello";
byte[] data = message.getBytes();
```

We can now put together a datagram by creating a new object of the class `DatagramPacket`:

```
DatagramPacket packet = new DatagramPacket(data, data.length,
                                           toAddr, toPort);
```

As we can see, the length of the byte array must also be given as parameter. The last parameter is a whole number that indicates the port number of the receiving computer.

When we have created a datagram, we can send it. To do this, we have to create a socket on the sender computer, that is, a "line" to an appropriate port to send it through. The class `DatagramSocket` describes such a socket, which is very easy to create. We simply write:

```
DatagramSocket socket = new DatagramSocket();
```

Alternatively, we can indicate a port number as parameter for the constructor. If we do not do this, the constructor will automatically choose a vacant port. The constructor for the class can generate an exception of type `SocketException` if something goes wrong.

Everything is now ready to send the message. This is done with the method `send`.

```
socket.send(packet);
```

If for some reason the transmission is not successful, an exception of type
`IOException` is generated.

We can combine all of this into a small program that sends a number of messages to an
arbitrary receiver. The receiver's Internet address and port number are given as
parameter for `main` when we start the program. For example, we can write:

```
java MessageSender www.xyz.pqr.com 15318
```

We then enter in the messages we want to send, one message to each line. The program
will look as follows:

```
import java.net.*;
import java.io.*;
import extra.*;

public class MessageSender {
  public static void main(String[] arg) throws
          UnknownHostException, SocketException, IOException {
    InetAddress toAddr = InetAddress.getByName(arg[0]);
    int toPort = Integer.parseInt(arg[1]);
    // create a socket to send through
    DatagramSocket socket = new DatagramSocket();
    while (true) {
      // read in the message from the keyboard
      Std.out.print("? ");
      String message = Std.in.readLine();
      if (message == null)
        break;
      // convert the message from a String to a byte array
      byte[] data = message.getBytes();
      // prepare a data packet and send it
      DatagramPacket packet = new DatagramPacket(data,
                                 data.length, toAddr, toPort);
      socket.send(packet);
    }
  }
}
```

Now it is time to take a look at what is happening at the receiving end. The receiver
must also create a socket, that is, a "line" to the program from the socket the messages
will come through. This is done by the creation of a `Socket` object. This time we must
use the form of the constructor where we explicitly indicate the port to be used. For
example, we write:

```
DatagramSocket socket = new DatagramSocket(15318);
```

The next step is to create an object of class `DatagramPacket`. The incoming datagram
will be placed in this object. We do not indicate an Internet address or port number

when we create it, as it will be used for reception of the datagram. However, we must indicate as parameter an array of bytes in which the incoming message will be placed. The size of the array must also be given.

```
DatagramPacket packet = new DatagramPacket(data, data.length);
```

For example, the array `data` is declared in the following way:

```
byte[] data = new byte[256];
```

When we want to receive a datagram, we simply call the method `receive`. The listener in the actual port and program will wait until the datagram comes through the port.

```
socket.receive(packet);
```

This method can generate an exception of type `IOException` if reception is unsuccessful.

java.net.DatagramSocket	
`new DatagramSocket(port)`	creates a socket through the port `port`
`new DatagramSocket()`	creates a socket through a vacant port
`send(pack)`	sends the datagram `pack`
`receive(pack)`	receives the datagram `pack`
`setSoTimeout(ms)`	indicates that `receive` will wait at most `ms` milliseconds gives `InterruptedIOException` at time out
`close()`	breaks the connection
`getLocalPort()`	gives the number for the port the socket is tied to

java.net.DatagramPacket	
`new DatagramPacket(data, len, iAddr, port)`	creates a datagram with the content `data` (a byte array) of length `len`; will be sent to the port `port` at `iAddr`
`new DatagramPacket(data, len)`	creates a datagram for reception, `data` is a byte array of length `len`
`getData()`	gives data that has been sent (or will be sent)
`getLength()`	gives the length of data that has been (or will be) sent
`getAddress()`	gives the sender's `InetAddress` (on reception)
`getPort()`	gives the sender's port number (on reception)

When the datagram has been received, it can be examined with the methods getData, getLength, getAddress and getPort. The first two will give the byte array received and its length. The other two will give the sender's InetAddress and port number. Data received will be in the form of an array of bytes, so this array must be converted to the type we want the message to have. For example, if the received message should be a text, we can use the constructor for class String that initializes a String with part of a byte array. The first parameter will be the array, the second the start index in the array and the third the number of bytes we want to include. For example, we can write:

```
String message = new String(packet.getData(), 0,
                               packet.getLength());
```

We will combine this into a program that can execute in the receiving computer. When we start the program, we give as parameter the number of the port we want to listen to:

```
java MessageReceiver 15318
```

Here is the entire program:

```
import java.net.*;
import java.io.*;
import extra.*;

public class MessageReceiver {
   public static void main(String[] arg)
                              throws SocketException, IOException {
      int myPort = Integer.parseInt(arg[0]);
      // create the socket that will listen at the port
      DatagramSocket socket = new DatagramSocket(myPort);
      byte[] data = new byte[256];
      while (true) {
         // create a datagram to receive the next message in
         DatagramPacket packet =
                          new DatagramPacket(data, data.length);
         // wait for the next message
         socket.receive(packet);
         Std.out.println("Message from " +
                     packet.getAddress().getHostName());
         // convert the message from bytes to String
         String message = new String(packet.getData(), 0,
                               packet.getLength());
         Std.out.println(message);
      }
   }
}
```

Let us look at another example of communication through datagrams. This time, communication in both directions will be shown, and we will be making use of time out. In Section 14.1, we wrote a program that retrieved information about temperatures from a file in a central computer. We will now look at how we can read temperatures at different stations and report these temperatures to a central computer which will receive the information and store it in a file. We begin by discussing the stations where the temperatures are read. The program TemperatureReader is run at each station. When it is run, a window is displayed like the one in Figure 14.3. The user fills in the

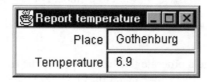

Figure 14.3 Reporting temperatures

name of the location together with the current temperature, and every time he or she presses the Enter key, this information will be sent to the central computer.

When the program is started at a station, the name and port number of the central computer are given as arguments. This can have the appearance:

```
java TemperatureReader www.weather.se 9963
```

We will now show the whole program, followed by the commentary:

```
import java.awt.*;
import java.awt.event.*;
import java.net.*;
import java.io.*;
import extra.*;

public class TemperatureReader extends ExtendedFrame
                                implements ActionListener {
    final int placeLen=10;
    final int temLen=6;
    TextField          place = new TextField(10);
    ExtendedTextField tem = new ExtendedTextField();
    InetAddress       iaddr;
    DatagramSocket socket;
    int port;

    public TemperatureReader(String toAddress, int portNo)
                throws UnknownHostException, SocketException {
```

```java
      // creates a socket for sending and receiving
      iaddr = InetAddress.getByName(toAddress);
      port = portNo;
      socket = new DatagramSocket();
      socket.setSoTimeout(10000);

      // prepare the window's layout
      setTitle("Report temperature");
      setLayout(new GridLayout(2, 2));
      add(new Label("Place ", Label.RIGHT));        add(place);
      add(new Label("Temperature ", Label.RIGHT)); add(tem);
      place.addActionListener(this);
      tem.addActionListener(this);
      pack();
      setVisible(true);
   }
   private void report(String where, double temp) {
     // read the location and temperature from the window
     String mess = ExtendedWriter.toFixedLength(where,placeLen)+
                   ExtendedWriter.formatNum(temp, temLen, 1);
    byte[] data = mess.getBytes(); // convert the text into bytes

     for (int i=1; i<=3; i++) {      // make three attempts to send
       // create a datagram with the message
       DatagramPacket packet = new DatagramPacket(data,
                                      data.length, iaddr, port);
       try {
         socket.send(packet);
         socket.receive(packet); // wait until an answer has come
         // convert the received bytes into a String
         String answer = new String(packet.getData(), 0,
                               packet.getLength());
         if (answer.equals("OK"))
           return;    // the attempt to send was successful
       }
       catch(IOException ie) {} // time out or error
     }
     // all attempts to send were unsuccessful
     System.out.println("Communication error");
   }

   public void actionPerformed(ActionEvent e) {
     // the user has pressed the Enter key
     if (e.getSource()==place || e.getSource()==tem)
       report(location.getText(), tem.getDouble());
   }
```

```
public static void main(String[] arg)
                throws UnknownHostException, SocketException {
   // retrieve the Internet address and port number from the
   // arguments
   new TemperatureReader(arg[0], Integer.parseInt(arg[1]));
}
}
```

A socket is created in the constructor for the sending and reception of datagrams. The method `setSoTimeout` is called to set the time out at reception to 10 seconds. When we then call the method `receive` to receive datagrams at the socket, an exception of type `TimeoutError` will be generated if no datagram has arrived within 10 seconds.

The different components of the window are also created in the constructor. Because a temperature is read as a number, we will use a GUI component of our own class `ExtendedTextField` to read the temperatures into. This means that we get an automatic check on whether the user has read in the correct figures.

When the user has written data in the window and pressed the Enter key, the method `actionPerformed` is called. This in turn calls the method `report`. Every time this method is called, input information will be retrieved from the window and sent to the central computer in the form of a datagram. This datagram will contain text and have a fixed length. The location will be indicated in 10 characters and the temperature in 6 characters. The temperature will be given with one decimal. The class methods `toFixedLength` and `formatNum` in class `ExtendedWriter` (see page 89) are used to format data into this form. Conversion from type `String` to an array of bytes is then done, as before, with the method `getBytes` in class `String`.

When the message has been formatted and converted, it is sent as a datagram to the central computer. Because datagrams are a little unreliable, the method `report` will wait until the central computer sends a datagram with the text `"OK"` as a receipt for the message. Note that we can use the same socket and datagram packet for both sending and receiving. If a receipt does not come within 10 seconds, the message is sent once more. The method `report` will make a maximum of three attempts at sending. If all of these are unsuccessful, an error message is given. The class `TimeoutError` that is generated at time out is a subclass of the class `IOError`. All the errors can therefore be caught in the same handler.

Let us now turn to the central computer where the program `TemperatureCentral` is executed. This program will be listening for incoming messages from the different stations. When a message comes, the program will update the file that contains the temperatures. The line applying to the station in question will be updated. We give two arguments when we start the program. The first is the name of the file and the second is the number of the port the program will listen at. We can write:

```
java TemperatureCentral /pub/temperatures 9963
```

The program consists of two main parts, a constructor and the method `store`. The program listens in the constructor at the receiving port, receives the messages and sends the receipt. Every time a message is received, a check is made to see that it has the correct length. If it has, the method `store` is called to store the message in the file.

The program will look as follows:

```java
import java.net.*;
import java.io.*;
import java.text.*;
import java.util.*;
import extra.*;

public class TemperatureCentral {
  final int placeLen=10;
  final int temLen=6;
  String fileName;
  DateFormat f = DateFormat.getTimeInstance(DateFormat.SHORT);

  public TemperatureCentral(String fileName, int portNo)
                                      throws SocketException {
    this.fileName=fileName;
    // create a socket for receiving and sending
    DatagramSocket socket = new DatagramSocket(portNo);
    // create a bytes array for receiving and sending
    byte[] data = new byte[placeLen+temLen];
    byte[] OKData = "OK".getBytes();
    while (true)
      try {
        // create a datagram to receive messages
        DatagramPacket packet =
                    new DatagramPacket(data, data.length);
        socket.receive(packet);  // wait for a message
        // create a datagram to send receipts
        DatagramPacket OKPacket =
              new DatagramPacket(OKData,OKData.length,
                      packet.getAddress(), packet.getPort());
        socket.send(OKPacket);       // send a receipt
        // check that the message has the correct length
        if (packet.getLength() == placeLen+temLen)
          store(packet.getData()); // store in the file
      }
      catch (IOException e) {}
  }

  private void store(byte[] data) throws IOException {
    // translate the name of the location from bytes to String
    String place = new String(data, 0, placeLen);
```

```
    // open the file of temperature
    RandomAccessFile file = new RandomAccessFile(fileName,"rw");
    // search the file for the current location
    String line;
    long pos = 0;   // actual position in the file
    while ((line = file.readLine()) != null) {
      if (line.substring(0,placeLen).equals(place)) {
        // line found
        file.seek(pos);   // go back to the line's start position
        break;
      }
      pos =file.getFilePointer(); //remember the line's position
    }
    // write over the old line
    file.write(data); // data contains both location and temp.
    // write date
    file.writeBytes(" " + f.format(new Date()) + "\n");
    file.close();
  }
  public static void main(String[] arg)
                    throws SocketException {
    // retrieve the file name and port number from the arguments
    new TemperatureCentral(arg[0], Integer.parseInt(arg[1]));
  }
}
```

The method store handles the file as a direct access file and, therefore, uses a stream of class RandomAccessFile to update the file. Because a RandomAccessFile is a binary file, data in the file is stored as a sequence of bytes, and when the datagram is received it will be in this form.

Lines are of a fixed length in the file. All lines will therefore be of equal length. The file will look as in Figure 14.1. To update the file, we have to find the line that contains data about the current location, overwriting this line with the new information. The file will be read line by line until the correct line has been found. Before a line is read, the method getFilePointer is called to see where in the file the line began. When the correct line has been found, we only have to call the method seek to go back to the beginning of the line. If a line does not already exist in the file for the current location, a new line will be added at the end of it.

When the old line is overwritten (or a new line written at the end), we can write out the message from the datagram directly, as this message will have the correct form (an array of bytes). The current date is written out last in the line. To format the time properly, we will use an editor of class DateFormat (see page 285).

14.4 Multicast

It might be the case that, in certain applications, we will want to send messages to several receivers at a time. Instead of sending a message to a specific receiver, then, we will send it to a group of receivers. A message of this kind is called a *multicast message*, and the group of receivers is known as a *multicast group*. The sender of a multicast message is normally included in a multicast group but this is not necessarily so. When we want to send or receive multicast messages in Java, we create a socket of class `MulticastSocket`, which is a subclass of the class `DatagramSocket`. As parameter, we indicate the port to be used.

```
MulticastSocket so = new MulticastSocket(16718);
```

A multicast message is sent in the form of a datagram. As we know, one of the things a datagram contains is the receiver's Internet address. When we send a multicast message, we do not indicate an Internet address for some particular receiver. Instead, we use an imaginary *multicast address* that all the receivers in the group know and listen to. This type of multicast address will be an IP address in the interval `224.0.0.1` to `239.255.255.255`. Every receiver wanting to belong to a particular multicast group must report this by calling the method `joinGroup` in class `MulticastSocket`. If the imaginary multicast address is `234.235.236.237`, we can write, for example:

```
iaddr = InetAddress.getByName("234.235.236.237");
so.joinGroup(iaddr);
```

The method `joinGroup` will have a parameter of type `InetAddress` so, as in the last section, we will have to use the class method `getByName` to convert the text with the IP address to an `InetAddress` object. In order to leave a multicast group, we will call the method `leaveGroup`.

Methods can then be sent and received, as for ordinary datagrams, with the methods `send` and `receive`.

java.net.MulticastSocket	
`new MulticastSocket(port)`	creates a multicast socket through the port `port`
`send(pack)`	sends the datagram `pack`
`receive(pack)`	receives the datagram `pack`
`joinGroup(iaddr)`	joins the multicast group with the multicast address `iaddr` (of class `InetAddress`)
`leaveGroup(iaddr)`	leaves the multicast group with the multicast address `iaddr` (of class `InetAddress`)
`close()`	breaks the connection

In order to demonstrate the use of multicast, we will construct a so-called chat program. This is a program where we can get connected to the net and chat with several people at the same time. When our chat program is run, a window is displayed that could look like the one in Figure 14.4.

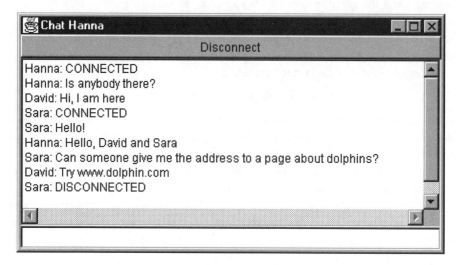

Figure 14.4 A chat program

The program is extremely simple to run. In the middle of the window there is a text area in which all the messages, even those we write ourselves, are displayed. At the bottom, there is a text field where we can write our own messages. To terminate the program, we click on "Disconnect". This program is called `chat`. When we start it, we can indicate as parameter what we want to call ourselves. If we write nothing, we will be assigned the name "Anonymous". To start the program that will generate Figure 14.4 we write:

```
java Chat Hanna
```

The program makes use of two parallel threads. The normal thread (the one that is active when the program starts) deals with the messages the user writes in the text field and sends them out to all of the other members of the multicast group. An active object, which reads in multicast messages from the Net and displays them in the text area, is used in parallel with this thread. The two threads execute in parallel and will not affect one another. A user's name is automatically inserted first when a message is sent out. Automatic messages are also generated when we connect and disconnect. We will also receive our own messages, as a multicast message is sent to all the members in a multicast group.

Let us begin by looking at the class that describes the active object that deals with the reception of multicast messages. The constructor has two parameters, the socket that we will read from and the text area that the messages will be displayed in. Because the receiver will be an active object, it will have a thread in the usual way, started in the constructor. The work itself is done in the method run, which uses a repetition statement that reads a message at every loop. Every message read in is displayed in the text area. The method run will execute until IOException occurs, which will happen when the socket from which it is reading is closed. Here is the class Receiver:

```java
import java.awt.*;
import java.awt.event.*;
import java.net.*;
import java.io.*;

class Receiver implements Runnable {
  Thread activity = new Thread(this);
  MulticastSocket so;
  TextArea  txt;

  // constructor
  Receiver(MulticastSocket sock, TextArea txtAr) {
    so = sock;
    txt =txtAr;
    activity.start();
  }

  public void run() {
    byte[] data = new byte[1024];   // space for received data
    while (true)
      try {
        // create a datagram for reception
        DatagramPacket packet =
                        new DatagramPacket(data, data.length);
        // wait for next message
        so.receive(packet);
        // convert the message to a String
        String mess = new String(data, 0, packet.getLength());
        txt.append(mess + "\n");   // display the message
      }
      catch (IOException e) {break;} //occurs when so is closed

  }
}
```

The rest of the program is composed of the class Chat which prepares the window's layout and deals with the sending of messages. Execution will begin, as usual, in the method main and this will in turn call the constructor. The parameters given are the name the user has chosen, a multicast address in the form of an IP address and the port number to be used. For the sake of simplicity, we have used the fixed IP address 234.235.236.237 and the port number 9876. The class Chat looks like this:

```
public class Chat extends Frame implements ActionListener {
    String name;        // the name the user has chosen
    InetAddress iaddr;  // the multicast address
    int port;
    MulticastSocket so;
    TextArea  txt   = new TextArea();   // displays the messages
    TextField writeField = new TextField();// for our own messages
    Button stop = new Button("Disconnect");

    // constructor
    public Chat(String userName, String groupAddr, int portNo)
                                        throws IOException {
        // deal with the parameters
        name = userName;
        iaddr = InetAddress.getByName(groupAddr);
        port = portNo;
        // create socket and start communication
        so = new MulticastSocket(port);
        so.joinGroup(iaddr);
        new Receiver(so, txt);   // create and start reception
        sendMessage("CONNECTED");
        // prepare layout for the window
        setTitle("Chat " + name);
        txt.setEditable(false);
        add("North", stop);
        add("Center", txt);
        add("South", writeField);
        stop.addActionListener(this);
        writeField.addActionListener(this);
        pack();
        setVisible(true);
    }

    private void sendMessage(String s) {
        // convert the message to an array of bytes
        byte[] data = (name + ": " + s).getBytes();
        // create and send a datagram packet
        DatagramPacket packet =
                new DatagramPacket(data,  data.length, iaddr, port);
        try {so.send(packet);}
        catch (IOException ie) {}
    }
```

```java
public void actionPerformed(ActionEvent e) {
  if (e.getSource() == writeField) {
    // the user has written his/her own message
    sendMessage(writeField.getText());
    writeField.setText("");
  }
  else if (e.getSource() == stop) {
    // the user has pressed the "Disconnect" button
    sendMessage("DISCONNECTED");
    try {so.leaveGroup(iaddr);}
    catch (IOException ie) {}
    so.close();      // close the socket
    dispose();       // remove the window
    System.exit(0);  // terminate the program
  }
}

public static void main(String[] arg) throws IOException {
  String name = "Anonymous";
  if (arg.length > 0)
    name = arg[0];
  new Chat(name, "234.235.236.237", 9876);
}
}
```

All our own messages are sent in the method sendMessage which gets the message as parameter. Note that the method sendMessage will put the user's name first in the datagram sent.

14.5 Establishing client–server connections

Communicating by means of datagrams has the advantage of being quite simple. The disadvantage is the lack of security. As we pointed out earlier, we cannot be certain that when we send a datagram, it will really reach the receiver; neither can we be certain that the datagrams we send will arrive in the same order as they were sent. In many applications, this is not terribly important. In our example concerning temperature readings, it would not have been a catastrophe if one reading were lost. In the chat program, too, one message missing would not have meant a great deal. In certain applications, however, it is important to know that we can count on the means of communication. If this is the case, we cannot make use of datagrams. Instead, we have to establish a virtual connection between the two parties that are to communicate. This works much as when we use an ordinary telephone. First the connection is made and then, when contact has been established, communication takes place on the line. The information sent on an established line does not, like a datagram, need to be divided into packets containing sender and receiver addresses. Instead, information is transferred as a continual flow of data. This idea is illustrated in Figure 14.5. What we do is to extend the "virtual line", that is, the socket, of the calling party so that it goes through the port of the receiving computer straight to the program with which the caller is to communicate.

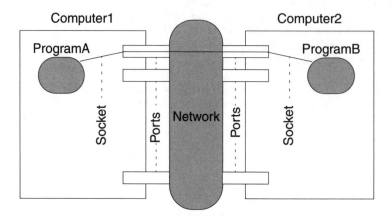

Figure 14.5 Established connections

In this section we shall demonstrate the establishment of connections in relation to the client–server technique. When this technique is used, there is a computer, or *server*, which provides a service. Other computers, or *clients*, can be associated with the server to gain access to this service. A server can often handle several clients at the same time. An example of an ordinary client–server system is that of databases, where current information is available at a centrally situated computer. An example is a database that contains information concerning the booking of seats on an aeroplane. Clients can be connected to the database to find out about available seats and to make bookings. In this kind of system, it is very important for the server to deal with several different clients so that a seat is not booked more than once. It is also important for communication between a server and its clients to be reliable.

A client who wants to connect to a server will create a new socket, where the server's address and port number are indicated. We can write:

```
Socket s = new Socket("www.xyz.serv.se", 13781);
```

Note that we use the class `Socket` (not `DatagramSocket`). The constructor generates an exception of class `IOException` or `UnknownHostException` (a subclass of `IOException`) if a connection is unsuccessful.

When the connection is ready, we call the methods `getInputStream` and `getOutputStream` in class `Socket` to get access to two streams in the connection, one for each direction of communication. These streams are of the fundamental classes `InputStream` and `OutputStream`. We can, of course, connect other streams to them, in the way discussed in Chapter 13. If we want to be able to read and write simple data in binary form, we can connect, for example, streams of the classes `DataInputStream` and `DataOutputStream`, respectively.

```
DataInputStream  in =new DataInputStream(s.getInputStream());
DataOutputStream out=new DataOutputStream(s.getOutputStream());
```

java.net.Socket
Created by a client
`new Socket(addr, port)` connects to the port `port` in the server `addr` (a `String`)
`getInputStream()` gives a stream to read data from the other computer
`getOutputStream()` gives a stream to send data to the other computer
`getInetAddress()` gives the other computer's `InetAddress`
`close()` breaks the connection

This is all that needs to be done in the client to establish the connection. Let us now turn to the server. The server must be listening to discover whether there is a client wishing to make a connection. This is done by means of a special `ServerSocket` that can be created in the following way:

```
ServerSocket listenerSock = new ServerSocket(13781);
```

As parameter for the constructor we give the number of the port we will be listening to. The method `accept` is then called in order to wait for a client, and we do not return from this method until a client has been connected. The method `accept` will then give as return value the socket the client uses to communicate in. This can have the following appearance:

```
Socket clientSock = listenerSock.accept();
```

The server, just like the client, can now use the methods `getInputStream` and `getOutputStream` to create two streams of the classes `DataInputStream` and `DataOutputStream` if simple data in binary form has to be read and written.

```
DataInputStream  in  = new DataInputStream
                              (clientSock.getInputStream());
DataOutputStream out = new DataOutputStream
                              (clientSock.getOutputStream());
```

java.net.ServerSocket

Created by a server

new ServerSocket (port)	gives a socket that will listen in the port port
accept ()	waits until a client has been connected;
	returns the Socket created by the client
close ()	breaks the connection

There is a small difficulty here, however. Because several clients will normally join the connection to a server, it is not a good idea to let the server get stuck with one client. We shall therefore create a new active object (with its own parallel thread) for each client connected. Meanwhile, the original thread can continue to listen at the port to see whether there is another client wishing to be connected. The server will then have the structure:

```
while (true) {
    // wait until the next client gets connected
    Socket clientSock = listenerSock.accept();
    // create a new active object,
    // give the client's socket as parameter
    new ActiveObject(clientSock);
}
```

The class *ActiveObject* is a class we define ourselves. We can establish the two communication streams in class *ActiveObject* by means of the client's socket, which is given as parameter for the constructor.

We shall now study the client–server technique in a rather simplified, yet complete, example. We shall set up a system for deposits and withdrawals on a bank account. Clients of the bank will be able to make deposits and withdrawals at different branches far apart from each other by communicating with a central computer through a network. The local computer at each branch is tended by a clerk, who uses a program to book the deposits and withdrawals that clients wish to make. Naturally, the clerk will also be able to check that there is enough money in an account to enable a withdrawal to be made. In the central computer, which represents the server in our example, there is a database that keeps track of clients' accounts. When the distant computers connect to the system and want to carry out various transactions, the server will use its database to enter the transactions. It will then send the result back to the distant computers.

Our example will be a little simpler than one that would be required of a real system. For example, we do not require the bank clerk to communicate with the central computer by means of a special password. We also let the program executed by the branches use a simple text window to communicate with the bank clerk. (Although it would not be difficult to put on a GUI, we do not do so in this example, because the principles of communication are clearer in a program that uses a simple text window.)

We shall deal with the server first. In Section 13.5, which dealt with direct access files, we constructed on page 429 a class AccountDatabase, which described a simple database that kept track of bank accounts. In this example, we will use class AccountDatabase in the server, and nothing needs to be changed. This class will function exactly as before. We remember from Section 13.5 that we made use of a direct access file in which information about the accounts was stored. When we created an object of class AccountDatabase, we were asked to give the name of the file as parameter for the constructor. Then, to perform transactions in the database, we were asked to use the method transaction. This method was to have three parameters: an account number, an amount and an object of class Account. The first two were input parameters, and the third was an output parameter that was a reference to an object of class Account (defined on page 427). When the transaction had been carried out, the method transaction filled in the result in the Account object. The method transaction also returned a value of type **boolean**, which indicated whether the transaction was successful or not.

The server in our example is made up of two classes. The first is the class BankServer, which listens for new clients. It is constructed according to the model that we sketched above. The only method in class BankServer is main. When we start the server, we give as parameter for main the number of the port the server will listen to. The class BankServer has the following appearance:

```java
import java.io.*;
import java.net.*;
import extra.*;

public class BankServer {
  public static AccountDatabase dbase;

  public static void main(String[] arg) throws IOException {
    int listenerPort = Integer.parseInt(arg[0]);
    // create a socket to listen for new clients
    ServerSocket listenerSock = new ServerSocket(listenerPort);
    Std.out.println("Server running. Port no " + listenerPort);

    // open the database for the account
    dbase = new AccountDatabase("accounts");
```

```
    while (true) {
        // wait until the next client gets connected
        Socket clientSock = listenerSock.accept();
        Std.out.println(clientSock.getInetAddress().getHostName()
                        + " connected");
        // create a new active object
        new ClientHandler(clientSock);
    }
  }
}
```

The class `BankServer` creates the `AccountDatabase` object that handles the file with the accounts. To ensure that all the `ClientHandler` objects can gain access to this `AccountDatabase` object, a reference to it is put as a class variable (static variable) in class `BankServer`.

A new active object of class `ClientHandler` is created every time a new client gets connected to the server. This object will then take care of the new client.

The class `ClientHandler` is relatively simple. The constructor will get as parameter a reference to the client's socket, and it will use this socket to create the two streams required to communicate with the client.

```
class ClientHandler implements Runnable {
  public Thread activity = new Thread(this);
  Socket so;
  DataInputStream  streamIn;
  DataOutputStream streamOut;

  // constructor
  public ClientHandler(Socket s) throws IOException {
    so = s;
    // open streams to the client
    streamIn  = new DataInputStream (so.getInputStream());
    streamOut = new DataOutputStream(so.getOutputStream());
    activity.start();
  }

  public void run() {
    Account acc = new Account();
    while (true)
      // new transaction
      try {
        // retrieve account number and amount from the client
        long no       = streamIn.readLong();
        double amount = streamIn.readDouble();
        // perform the transaction
        boolean transOK = BankServer.dbase.
                          transaction(no, amount, acc);
```

```
        // send the answer to the client
        streamOut.writeBoolean(transOK);   // result value
        acc.write(streamOut);              // output parameter
      }
      catch(IOException e) {break;} //when the client disconnects
    Std.out.println(so.getInetAddress().getHostName() +
                    " disconnected");
    try {so.close();}
    catch (IOException e) {}
  }
}
```

The transactions are performed in the method run. In this, there is a repetition statement that executes one loop per transaction. The repetition is interrupted if we get an IOException. This will happen if, for instance, the client breaks the connection. Input data sent by the client is retrieved first in every transaction. This will apply to the account number and the amount of the transaction. Note that we use streams of the classes DataInputStream and DataOutputStream, so data will be transferred in binary form. The methods readLong and readDouble are called to read the input data the client has sent. When the transaction has been carried out in the database, the result is sent back to the client. The result value, of type **boolean**, is sent first, followed by the Account object that contains the output data. The method write, which is defined in class Account, is used to output the contents of the Account object to the stream.

This is all we need to have in the server. Let us now look at the client programs executing at the various bank branches. We define a class BankClient. This looks almost exactly like the class BankDemo on page 432. The class BankDemo called the account database directly to perform the different transactions but in class BankClient, these calls will take place through the server. The server's address and port number are given as parameters for main when we start the program. For example, we write:

```
java BankClient www.bank.serv.se 17916
```

When the program BankClient is run, it will look exactly the same as when we run the BankDemo program. The class BankClient will look like this:

```
import java.io.*;
import java.net.*;
import extra.*;
public class BankClient {
  public static void main(String[] arg) throws IOException{
    String toComputer = arg[0];
    int toPort = Integer.parseInt(arg[1]);
```

```
// try to connect to the server
Socket so = new Socket(toComputer, toPort);
Std.out.println("Connecting to " + toComputer +
                " port no " + toPort);
// create streams to the server
DataInputStream  streamIn  = new DataInputStream
                                (so.getInputStream());

DataOutputStream streamOut = new DataOutputStream
                                (so.getOutputStream());
while(true) {
  // read input data for transaction
  Std.out.print("Account no? ");
  if (!Std.in.more())
    break;
  long accountNo = Std.in.readLong();
  Std.out.print("Amount? ");
  if (!Std.in.more())
    break;
  double amount = Std.in.readDouble();

  // ask the server to perform the transaction
  streamOut.writeLong(accountNo);
  streamOut.writeDouble(amount);

  // read answer from the server
  boolean transOK = streamIn.readBoolean();
  Account acc = new Account();
  acc.read(streamIn);

  // analyze the result
  if (acc.number > 0) {  // account number OK
    Std.out.println(acc.name);
    Std.out.println(acc.addr);
    if (transOK) {
      Std.out.print("New balance: ");
      Std.out.println(acc.balance, 1, 2);
    }
    else {
      Std.out.print("Balance: ");
      Std.out.println(acc.balance, 1, 2);
      Std.out.println("Withdrawal cannot be done!");
    }
  }
  else
    Std.out.println("Incorrect account no");
  Std.out.println();
}
```

```
    so.close();
  }
}
```

Input data for the transaction is sent in binary form in the output stream to the server. The answer will then return in the input stream. The result value from the method transaction (a value of type **boolean**) will come first, followed by the Account object that has been filled up. The method read in class Account is used to read the account number in binary form from the stream.

14.6 Applets and communication

We will remember that an applet is not allowed, for security reasons, to use a local file system. There are also a number of restrictions that apply to communication through applets. Briefly, we can say that an applet may only establish a connection to the computer from which it has been downloaded. The client–server relationship may be used in an applet if the applet is the client and the server is in the computer from which the applet has been downloaded. When we want to create a connection in an applet to a server, we can write, for instance:

```
Socket so = new Socket(getCodeBase().getHost(), 9876);
```

This enables us to construct web pages with applets which, when they are downloaded to another computer, can be connected back to the host to get different kinds of services.

We will now show another form of communication that can be used in applets. For every applet, there is an environment provided by the web browser or appletviewer the applet started from. This environment is described by the class AppletContext, in the packet java.applet. If in an applet we want to access the AppletContext object that describes the actual environment, we can call the method getAppletContext.

The class AppletContext contains several interesting methods. We have already discussed some of them, for example showStatus, as they are also available to the class Applet. An interesting method in the class AppletContext is showDocument, used to request the web browser to download and display a particular web page. This method exists in two variants. The first has one parameter, a URL object that describes the web address for the web page we wish to display. For example, we can write:

```
URL webURL = new URL("http://www.awl-he.com");
getAppletContext().showDocument(webURL);
```

Then the page displayed in the web browser will be replaced by the page indicated by the URL address. The second variant of showDocument has two parameters: the first parameter is, as before, a URL object; the second is a text that indicates how the page chosen is to be displayed. This text can be one of the following: "_self", which indicates that the page containing the applet will be replaced, "_top", which indicates that the web browser's top window will be replaced, "_blank", which indicates that the given page will be displayed in a new top window (without a name) and "_parent", which indicates that the window that is parent to the applet's window will be replaced. We can also give a text with a name as second parameter. The page will then be displayed in a window of this name. If there is no window with the given name, a new window will be created at the top. For instance, we can write:

```
getAppletContext().showDocument(webURL, "_blank");
```

We will now make use of this to construct an applet that displays an arbitrary picture. When the user clicks on the picture, a certain given web page will be displayed in a new window. The picture and the web page to be displayed will be indicated as parameters of the applet in the HTML file the applet started from. This file might look like this:

```
<html>
    <head>
      <title>PictureDemo</title>
    </head>
    <body>
      <applet code=PictureDemo.class width=400 height=150>
        <param name=pictureName value=pic1.gif>
        <param name=wwwPage value=http://www.awl-he.com>
      </applet>
    </body>
  </html>
```

This applet will be an extended version of the one that was discussed in Section 12.1. We must add a listener that listens for mouse clicks. When a mouse click occurs, we will check to see whether the mouse is inside the picture. If it is, the method showDocument is called to display the web page indicated.

We use the standard class Rectangle (in the packet java.awt) to simplify the task of finding out whether the mouse is in the picture. We construct a rectangle that is exactly as big as the picture and placed in the same position. It is easy to create a rectangle. We indicate only the coordinates of the rectangle's upper left-hand corner and the rectangle's length and width. We use the class Rectangle because this class has a method with the name contains that checks to see whether a certain point, of the standard class Point, lies in the rectangle or not.

We also take this opportunity to reveal a little trick that we have only touched on in an exercise. When the user moves the mouse so that the mouse's cursor lands inside the picture, we will let the cursor change its appearance so that it looks like a pointing hand. If the cursor is moved outside the picture, it will resume its standard appearance. To produce this effect, we use the method setCursor, defined in the class Component and thus accessible in all GUI components. As argument, setCursor will have an object of class Cursor, which is also defined in the packet java.awt. There is a class method getPredefinedCursor in class Cursor that returns a Cursor object. As argument, getPredefinedCursor will have a whole number that indicates the appearance we want for the mouse cursor. In class Cursor there are a number of predefined whole number constants that can be used. Some examples are TEXT_CURSOR, HAND_CURSOR, WAIT_CURSOR and DEFAULT_CURSOR.

With these additions, the applet will have the following appearance:

```java
import java.applet.*;
import java.awt.*;
import java.awt.event.*;
import java.net.*;

public class PictureDemo extends Applet {
    Image im;
    int x0 = 10, y0 = 50;
    Rectangle r;
    URL webURL;

    public void init() {
        // retrieve the name of the file with the picture
        String name  = getParameter("pictureName");
        // begin to load the picture
        im = getImage(getCodeBase(), name);
        showStatus("Loading " + name);
        // wait until the picture has been loaded
        MediaTracker mt = new MediaTracker(this);
        mt.addImage(im, 0);
        try {mt.waitForID(0);}
        catch(InterruptedException e){}
        showStatus("Loading finished");
        // create a rectangle that describes the picture's surface
        r = new Rectangle(x0, y0, im.getWidth(this),
                                  im.getHeight(this));
        // retrieve the address of the desired web page
        String wwwPage = getParameter("wwwPage");
        try {
            webURL = new URL(wwwPage);
        }
        catch(MalformedURLException e) {
            showStatus("Illegal parameter: " + wwwPage);
        }
```

```
      // listen to mouse clicks and movements
      addMouseListener(l1);
      addMouseMotionListener(l2);
   }

   // listeners called when the mouse is clicked
   MouseListener l1 = new MouseAdapter() {
      public void mouseClicked(MouseEvent e) {
         if (!e.isControlDown() && !e.isMetaDown())
           // the left-hand button
           if (r.contains(e.getPoint()))
             // the user has clicked on the picture
             // request the web browser to display a new window
             // with the indicated page
             getAppletContext().showDocument(webURL, "New page");
      }
   };

   // listeners called when mouse is moved
   MouseMotionListener l2 = new MouseMotionAdapter() {
      public void mouseMoved(MouseEvent e) {
         // check whether mouse is in the picture or not
         // and choose appropriate cursor
         if (r.contains(e.getPoint()))
           setCursor(Cursor.getPredefinedCursor
                       (Cursor.HAND_CURSOR));
         else
           setCursor(Cursor.getPredefinedCursor
                       (Cursor.DEFAULT_CURSOR));
      }
   };

   public void paint(Graphics g) {
     g.drawImage(im, x0, y0, this);
   }
}
```

14.7 Exercises

1. Reconstruct our system involving temperature readings in Sections 14.1 and 14.3 to exclude the idea of a central computer that keeps track of all the temperatures. The stations should instead send out multicast messages containing the current temperatures to all interested parties. Every computer that is interested will then keep track of all the temperatures itself.

2. Construct a client–server system for customer support. Customers will be able to run a program that connects them to a server and will be able to put questions to and receive answers from someone at customer service running the server

program. Both the customer program and the server will use a graphical user interface where we can enter our own text and see what our correspondent writes to us. The server program should open a new window for every new customer joining the connection. The window should close when a customer breaks the connection.

3. On a certain web page, we want to give the user the possibility of leaving a message for the web page's owner. To this end, we put an applet on the page that can send a message back to the computer from which the web page was downloaded. The applet should contain a button with the text "Leave message". If we click on this button, a new window should pop up with a text area in which we can write a message. The message should be sent automatically when we have finished writing it. Now construct the applet!

4. Construct the server program required to receive such messages as are generated by the applet in Exercise 3. Messages received should be written out.

A bit of everything

15

In this last chapter we shall deal with some language constructs that we did not need in the earlier chapters of the book but which we should know to get a more complete picture of Java. We shall also be looking at some more useful standard classes.

15.1 Comments and documentation

All our programs call for some kind of comment. Comments fall into two categories. The first is for those who will be reading the program code itself and possibly making changes to it. These comments are intended to make the program easier to read and understand. They can also be of a technical nature, their aim being to clarify complex constructions in the code. The other category is for those who will want to use ready-made classes or methods but are not interested in knowing what the code looks like inside these classes or methods. This type of comment might describe the parameters a method has.

In Java, there are three types of comment. We have constantly used one type, the kind that is introduced by the pair of parallel lines, //. Everything on the *same* line after this can be understood to be a comment:

```
...    // This is a comment
```

Another kind of comment is introduced by the characters /* and is terminated by the characters */. A comment of this kind can extend to several lines:

```
/* This is a comment
   that continues for several lines */
```

The final pair of characters should not be forgotten. If they are, the rest of the program will be understood to be a comment. This kind of comment is useful for long explanations. We can also use them when we are testing a program and want to exclude part of the program temporarily. We can then make this part a comment.

We provide the first two types of comment for whoever would like to study the program code itself. The third type is provided as an aid for the use of ready-made classes and is therefore called a *documentation comment*. This is introduced by the character combination `/**` and is terminated by the combination `*/`. Like the second type of comment, a documentation comment can comprise several lines:

```
/** This is a documentation comment.
  * We often begin each line with the character *
  * so that the comment will be clear
  * but this is not necessary.
  */
```

Comments of the form `/*...*/` and documentation comments appear exactly the same to the Java compiler. They only contain text, and the compiler will skip this. The interesting thing about documentation comments is that they can be used with the program `javadoc`, included in J2SDK. The `javadoc` program can be started by the command:

```
javadoc parameter1 parameter2 parameter3 ...
```

In this way we can indicate an arbitrary number of parameters. Each parameter can be either the name of a Java package or the name of a file that contains a Java program. If it is a file, the file name must end with `.java`. (We can also indicate different options in front of the parameters; see the J2SDK documentation for details.) The `javadoc` program reads the program code for the packages or files given as parameters and produces a set of HTML files containing documentation on all the classes, interfaces, methods, constructors and variables that are marked as **public** or **protected**. An HTML file is produced for every file with program code. `javadoc` also produces an HTML file that displays inheritance structure and one that contains an index with all the methods and variables. The files that are generated will land in the same directory we are in when we give the command. (However, this can be changed if we use the options.) We can read the generated HTML files with a web browser, Netscape or Internet Explorer, for instance. The `javadoc` program is extremely useful. For instance, the HTML files in J2SDK that contain documentation on all the standard classes were produced by `javadoc`.

What does this have to do with comments? When `javadoc` produces HTML documentation files, the documentation comments in the program listings are put into the files. The idea is to put a documentation comment in front of every class, interface, constructor, variable or method that is to be documented. These documentation comments can be arbitrarily long but first there should always be a sentence, terminated by a period, describing what is being documented. The first sentence will be included in the general summary of the class in question. The text in a documentation comment can contain simple HTML commands such as `<i>`, which indicates that the text will be in italics, or <code>, which signals that the font for program listings will be used. HTML commands that affect the structure of the document may not be used, however.

Special *tags* can also be inserted in a documentation comment. These tags always begin with the character @ and must be written at the beginning of the line (or directly after an introductory asterisk, *). Some examples of tags are:

```
@author the name of the author
@version text
@see class
@see class# attribute
@param parameter name parameter description
@return description of return value
@exception class name description
```

When javadoc discovers a tag, it generates documentation in a standardized format. For an exception tag, for example, it will generate a "Throws" section, where the exceptions that can be generated will appear.

To give a more complete example of what this might look like, we show here a new version of our own class Line, from Section 10.2:

```
package extra;
import java.awt.*;
import java.io.*;
/**
 * The <code>Line</code> class represents a line between two
 * points in a two-dimensional coordinate space.
 * For example:
 * <pre>
 *    Line l = new Line(new Point(1,0), new Point(2,1));
 * </pre>
 * @version 1.0
 * @author   Jan Skansholm
 * @see      java.awt.Point
 */
public class Line implements Serializable {
   /**
    * The first end point.
    */
   public Point p1;

   /**
    * The second end point.
    */
   public Point p2;
```

```
/**
 * Constructs a line with start and end points at (0,0).
 */
public Line() {
  p1=new Point();
  p2=new Point();
}

/**
 * Constructs a line with the specified start and end points.
 * @param a the first end point.
 * @param b the second end point.
 */
public Line(Point a, Point b) {
  p1=new Point(a);
  p2=new Point(b);
}

/**
 * Draws a line between the end points.
 * @param g The graphics context to use for painting.
 */
public void draw(Graphics g) {
  g.drawLine(p1.x, p1.y, p2.x, p2.y);
}
}
```

15.2 More operators

We have already discussed most of the operators in Java earlier in the book. In this section, we shall examine the operators we have not met so far.

15.2.1 Bit operators and the binary storing of whole numbers

Most of the language constructs in Java have been inherited from the programming language C++, which in turn is a development of C. From the beginning, C was constructed to be used for writing machine-friendly programs, programs that worked closely with a computer's operating system and hardware. In this context, we often need to be able to handle individual bits in a memory cell. In C, C++ and Java, there are a number of operators with which we can handle whole number variables as though they contained groups of bits rather than whole numbers. In this section, we shall give a brief account of these operators. The reader will need to know more about how whole numbers are stored in binary form to understand everything in this section. So we shall begin with a short review of the principles involved.

A computer's memory consists of a number of memory cells. Each of these consists of a certain number of bits, and each bit can contain a binary digit (a zero or a one). It is therefore natural for numbers to be stored in binary form in the memory. Let us look then at the *binary number system*. The decimal number system is the dominating system in our culture (probably because we have 10 fingers). If, for example, we write the number 158.32, we automatically assume that it is expressed in the decimal number system, with a base of 10. This means that we interpret the number 158.32 as:

$$1 \times 10^2 + 5 \times 10^1 + 8 \times 10^0 + 3 \times 10^{-1} + 2 \times 10^{-2}$$

More generally, we can say that a decimal number:

$$a_n a_{n-1} \dots a_1 a_0.d_1 d_2 \dots d_m$$

(where the *a*s indicate whole number figures and the *d*s, decimals) really means:

$$a_n \times 10^n + a_{n-1} \times 10^{n-1} + \dots + a_1 \times 10^1 + a_0 \times 10^0 + d_1 \times 10^{-1} + d_2 \times 10^{-2} + \dots + d_m \times 10^{-m}$$

If we now use the base 2 instead of 10, we can similarly interpret the binary number:

$$b_n b_{n-1} \dots b_1 b_0.c_1 c_2 \dots c_m$$

as:

$$b_n \times 2^n + b_{n-1} \times 2^{n-1} + \dots + b_1 \times 2^1 + b_0 \times 2^0 + c_1 \times 2^{-1} + c_2 \times 2^{-2} + \dots + c_m \times 2^{-m}$$

The *b*s here indicate binary whole number digits and the *c*s, *binals*. The binary number 10111.101 can, for example, be interpreted as:

$$1 \times 2^4 + 0 \times 2^3 + 1 \times 2^2 + 1 \times 2^1 + 1 \times 2^0 + 1 \times 2^{-1} + 0 \times 2^{-2} + 1 \times 2^{-3}$$

or, if we wish:

$$16 + 0 + 4 + 2 + 1 + 0.5 + 0 + 0.125 = 23.625$$

A certain number of bits are used when a whole number is stored in a computer. The number of bits used will depend on the type. In Java, for example, 32 bits are used for type `int` and 16 bits for type `short`. If we want to store the number 23 with 16 bits, we will get the binary configuration:

```
0000000000010111
```

If we let each bit represent a binary digit, we will get an *unsigned* form. The largest number that can be stored in an unsigned form with N bits will then be $2^N - 1$. If we have 16 bits, the largest number we can store will then be $2^{16} - 1 = 65535$. The unsigned form cannot be used to store negative numbers.

Unsigned forms are not used in Java. Instead, we use another form for storing numbers called *two's complement*. With this form, we can store both positive and negative whole numbers. In the two's complement form, the bit furthest to the left will give the number's sign. A zero indicates that it is a positive number, and a one that it is negative. The largest positive number that can be stored in the two's complement form with 16 bits will then be:

```
0111111111111111
```

This turns out to be $2^{15} - 1 = 32767$. In the two's complement form, the number -1 is stored with 16 bits as:

```
1111111111111111
```

We get the number -2 by subtracting a binary 1 from this to give:

```
1111111111111110
```

The number -3 will then be:

```
1111111111111101
```

By continuing to subtract, we find that the smallest whole number (that is, the largest negative number) that can be stored in the two's complement form with 16 bits will be:

```
1000000000000000
```

This turns out to be the number $-2^{15} = -32768$. We can generally say that if a whole number is stored in the two's complement form with N bits, the smallest number that can be stored will be -2^{N-1} and the largest will be $2^{N-1} - 1$.

The values of the standard types **byte, short, int** and **long** are represented in the two's complement form but programmers do not normally have to know anything about the storing process. The compiler takes care of that.

Let us now turn to the operations of bit operators. Note that these are only defined for whole number types. The ~ operator is the simplest one. It only has one operand. As result it gives a bit configuration where all the zeros in the operand have been exchanged for ones, and vice versa. Let us look at an example. (In the following statements we will suppose that all the variables have type **int**.)

```
a = 7;       // a = 0000 0000 0000 0000 0000 0000 0000 0111
b = 20;      // b = 0000 0000 0000 0000 0000 0000 0001 0100
c = ~a;      // c = 1111 1111 1111 1111 1111 1111 1111 1000
```

The operators &, | and ^ carry out the operations *and, or* and *exclusive or*, bit by bit. 'Exclusive or' means that a particular bit in the result will be a one if exactly one of the operands contains a one in the corresponding position. If none or both of the operands contain a one, the result bit will be equal to 0.

```
d = a & b;   // d = 0000 0000 0000 0000 0000 0000 0000 0100
e = a | b;   // e = 0000 0000 0000 0000 0000 0000 0001 0111
f = a ^ b;   // f = 0000 0000 0000 0000 0000 0000 0001 0011
```

The operators `<<` and `>>` carry out *shift left* and *shift right*, respectively, that is, they move the bits to the right or the left. The left-hand operand contains the bit configuration to be moved, and the right-hand operand will indicate the number of places the bits are to be moved. Zeros are always moved in from the right when a left shift is carried out. If a number is shifted one place to the left, this means the number will be multiplied by 2. Similarly, a shift to the right will mean that the number is divided by 2. If we use the operator `>>` to perform a shift right and the value to be moved is positive, zeros are shifted in from the left. If, on the other hand, the value is negative, ones will be moved in from the left. So when we use the operator `>>`, the number shifted will keep its sign. We say, therefore, that the `>>` operator performs an *arithmetic shift*. There is another operator, `>>>`, which performs a *logic shift*. It will always move zeros in from the left, regardless of whether the number to be shifted is positive or negative. Here are some examples:

```
g = b <<  5;    // g = 0000 0000 0000 0000 0000 0010 1000 0000
h = c >>  2;    // h = 1111 1111 1111 1111 1111 1111 1111 1110
i = c >>> 2;    // i = 0011 1111 1111 1111 1111 1111 1111 1110
```

Bit operators			
Are only defined for whole number types. Carry out the operations bit by bit.			
~	changes 0 <-> 1	<<	shift left
&	*and*, bit by bit	>>	arithmetic shift right
|	*or*, bit by bit	>>>	logic shift right
^	*exclusive or*		

We often use the `&` operator to perform *masking*, that is, selecting certain bits. For example, the following statement will select eight bits in the bit configuration contained by the variable `i`:

```
j = i & 0xf00f; // j = 0000 0000 0000 0000 1111 0000 0000 1110
```

The `|` operator can be used to insert ones into certain bits. The following statement will ensure that there are ones in the eight bits furthest to the right:

```
k = j | 0x00ff; // k = 0000 0000 0000 0000 1111 0000 1111 1111
```

Note that none of the operators we have shown here will affect their operands. If we want operators that can do this, we can use the corresponding assignment operators, which also exist. We can write, for example:

```
a &= 0x000f;
```

which is the same thing as writing:

```
a = a & 0x000f;
```

In fact, the & and | operators can also be used with operands of type `boolean`, in which case they will not perform operations bit by bit. They are logic operators, exactly like the && and || operators. On page 45, we stated that the && and || operators were always computed from left to right and that the right-hand operand did not always need to be computed. The & and | operators do not necessarily work in this way. They *always* compute both operands. This can be useful when the right-hand operand has a side-effect of some kind.

15.2.2 The conditional operator

There is an operator which we can do without but which we should recognize and understand. This is the *conditional operator* we use to form *conditional expressions*. Let us suppose that we want to know which of the variables x and y is the larger, then to assign the larger value to the variable z. This is, of course, easily done with an `if` statement:

```
if (x>y)
    z = x;
else
    z = y;
```

but we can also use a conditional expression:

```
z = (x>y) ? x : y;
```

The conditional operator has three operands. The first is a test expression. If the test expression is true, the second operand, the one after the question mark ?, is computed, and the result of the whole conditional expression will be equal to this operand. However, if the test expression is false, the third operand is computed, the one after the colon :, and the result of the conditional expression will be equal to this operand. A conditional expression will therefore leave a value as result. The type the result has will be determined by the last two operands. These should have the same type (or at least be of types that can be assigned to each other).

The conditional operator

expression1 ? *expression2* : *expression3*

If *expression1* is `true`, the result will be equal to *expression2*, otherwise the result will be equal to *expression3*.
expression2 and *expression3* should have the same type.

As an example, we shall show some program lines that write out a text string s, with the aim that all the tab characters are translated into three blank characters. Other characters will be written out unchanged. (We will suppose that the variable `c` has type `char`.)

```
for (int i=0; i<s.length(); i++)
  Std.out.print(s.charAt(i) == '\t'
                  ? "    " : s.substring(i,i+1));
```

The result of the conditional expression is of class `string`. Note that we could not have written `s.charAt(i)` as the final operand, since the last two operands would have got different types, and a `string` cannot be assigned to a `char`.

15.3 More statements

Oddly enough, there are a number of statements in Java that we have not used. We shall describe them in this section.

15.3.1 The `switch` statement

A `switch` statement is one that can be used instead of an `if` statement when we are offered several options. As an example, we shall show part of a program that simulates a very simple calculator. The program reads in and computes expressions of the form x op y. Let us suppose that we have read in the two operands x and y and that the values are in two variables x and y of type `double`. Let us further suppose that the operator op has been read in to a variable of type `char`. The expression's value can then be computed and written out with the following `switch` statement.

```
switch(op) {
  case '+':
    Std.out.println(x+y);
    break;
  case '-':
    Std.out.println(x-y);
    break;
  case '*':
    Std.out.println(x*y);
    break;
  case '/':
    if (y != 0)
      Std.out.println(x/y);
    else
      Std.out.println("Division by zero");
    break;
  default:
    Std.out.println("Incorrect operator");
}
```

A `switch` statement is introduced by the reserved word `switch`. A *test expression* in brackets, which must be of an integer type, or of the type `char`, then follows this word. Every alternative in a `switch` statement is introduced by the word `case`. The expressions that come after `case`, the `case` expressions, must be constants, and two or more `case` expressions cannot have the same value. There may also be a `default` alternative. The test expression after the word `switch` is computed first, when a `switch` statement is executed. The value of the test expression is compared with the values of the different `case` expressions. If the test expression has the same value as a `case` expression, there will be a jump to the statement after this `case` expression. If none of the `case` expressions has the same value as the test expression, there is a jump to the statement after the word `default`. If the `default` alternative is missing and none of the `case` expressions is appropriate, nothing will be done in the `switch` statement. Note that there must be a `break` statement at the end of every alternative (excepting the last one). The `break` statement will terminate the alternative, and there will be a jump to the end of the `switch` statement. If there is no `break` statement in a particular alternative, a jump should not occur. Execution will instead continue with the statements in the next alternative!

We can make our example a little more complete by adding the lines that read in the values of the variables x, op and y. The simplest thing to do would be to read from `Std.in` and use the methods `readDouble` and `readChar` but this will not work very well in this example, as everything should be written on the same line. So we shall instead read a whole line at a time and then use the method `parse`, in class `NumberFormat`, to decode the numbers; see our discussion on page 82. This time we will use an alternative version of `parse`. Apart from the text to be decoded, this also has a parameter of class `ParsePosition`. We use this parameter to indicate where in the text decoding is to begin but we can also use it to discover where the previous decoding finished. The class `ParsePosition` has two methods, `getIndex` and `setIndex`, which are used for this purpose. Our example will look as follows:

```
NumberFormat   nf  = NumberFormat.getInstance();
ParsePosition pos = new ParsePosition(0);  // start position 0
String line;
while ((line=Std.in.readLine()) != null) {
  pos.setIndex(0);                    // indicate where x begins
  double x = nf.parse(line, pos).doubleValue();
  char op = line.charAt(pos.getIndex());
  pos.setIndex(pos.getIndex()+1); // indicate where y begins
  double y = nf.parse(line, pos).doubleValue();;
  switch(op) {
    as before
  }
}
```

We are allowed to have several `case` expressions for a particular alternative in a `switch` statement. Let us suppose, for example, that we want to calculate the number of characters of different kinds in a text. Then the following statement can be used. (We suppose that the variables `numberOfFigures`, `numberOfWhite` and `NumberOfOthers` are of type `int` and that c has type `char` and contains a character in the text read in.)

```
switch(c) {
    case '0': case '1': case '2': case '3': case '4':
    case '5': case '6': case '7': case '8': case '9':
        numberOfFigures++;
        break;

    case ' ': case '\t': case '\n':
        numberOfWhite++;
        break;
    default:
        numberOfOthers++;
}
```

Unfortunately, this is not very elegant, as the word `case` has to be repeated.

---

switch statement

```
switch(test_expression) {
    case constant_value1:
        statements
        break;
    case constant_value2:
        statements
        break;

    . . .

    default:
        statements
}
```

The expressions after `case` must have different values.

The `default` alternative can be left out.

Several `case` expressions can be found in front of a particular alternative.

There is a jump to the alternative for which *test_expression* is the same as *constant_value*.

If no alternative fits, there is a jump to the `default` alternative, if one exists.

15.3.2 The do statement

In this book, we have used `while` statements and `for` statements to produce repetition but there is a third repetition statement, the `do` statement. It has the form:

```
do
   statement
while (expression);
```

This statement is similar to the `while` statement, the difference being that the test expression is computed and tested *after* instead of before every loop. This means that the statement inside the `do` statement must always be performed at least once. We can use curly brackets if there are more than one statement to be performed at every loop. Then we usually write the `do` statement in the following way:

```
do {
   statements
} while (expression);
```

It is useful to write the right-hand curly bracket first, on the last line. Then, when we read the program, we will not be fooled into thinking that the word `while` is the beginning of a statement.

An example now follows of the type of program where it can be useful to use a `do` statement. Repeated computations are made in the program (in the method `res`) for different kinds of input data. The user is asked, after each computation, whether further computations are to be carried out:

```
String answer;
do {
   Std.out.print("Give input data: ");
   double x = Std.in.readDouble();
   Std.out.print("Result="); Std.out.println(res(x));
   Std.out.print("Continue? (y, n) ");
   answer = Std.in.readLine();
} while (answer.charAt(0) == 'y');
```

15.3.3   Statements with labels

Every statement (or declaration) in Java can be provided with a *label*. A label is a kind of name written in front of the statement. Here is an example:

```
start: int n = Std.in.readInt();
loop1: for (int i=0; i<n; i++)
```

Labels can be useful in connection with `break` and `continue` statements, which we shall deal with in the following sections.

15.3.4   The break statement

We have made use of `break` statements on several occasions. A break statement can be used to jump out of a repetition statement (`while`, `for` or `do`), or a `switch` statement. If we only write `break`, we will jump from the *nearest* surrounding statement. This jump always takes place to the first statement directly after the statement we jump from. Here is an example:

```
loop1: for (i=0; i<n; i++) {
  statement1
  loop2: for (j=0; j<n; j++) {
    if (a[i][j] == 0)
      break;    // there is a jump to statement3
    statement2
  }
  statement3
}
statement4
```

The nearest surrounding repetition statement around the **break** statement is the innermost **for** statement.

We can also indicate a label after the word **break**. We then make a jump from the statement that has this label. We will change our example:

```
loop1: for (i=0; i<n; i++) {
  statement1
  loop2: for (j=0; j<n; j++) {
    if (a[i][j] == 0)
      break loop1;    // there is a jump to statement4
    statement2
  }
  statement3
}
statement4
```

We now make a jump out of the **for** statement (the one with the label loop1).

15.3.5 The continue **statement**

This (rather strange) statement is also inherited from the programming language C. We can manage without it but it is important to recognize it and understand what it does if we happen to come across it in some program code. A **continue** statement can be found inside a repetition statement. We can either simply write **continue**, or indicate the label of a surrounding repetition statement:

```
continue;
continue label;
```

If we do not include a label, the **continue** statement will apply to the nearest surrounding repetition statement; otherwise it will apply to the repetition statement that has been indicated. A **continue** statement, like a **break** statement, will interrupt execution at the actual position and make a jump. However, there is no jump out of the repetition statement. Instead, the *actual loop* in the repetition statement is interrupted, whereupon execution continues immediately with the next loop. We shall first show an example where a label has not been indicated, when the actual loop in the inner `for` statement will be interrupted:

```
loop1: for (i=0; i<n; i++) {
   statement1
   loop2: for (j=0; j<n; j++) {
      if (a[i][j] == 0)
         continue; // continue immediately after statement2
      statement2
   }
   statement3
}
statement4
```

If we indicate the label `loop1` after `continue`, the actual loop in the outer `for` statement will be interrupted instead. This looks as follows:

```
loop1: for (i=0; i<n; i++) {
   statement1
   loop2: for (j=0; j<n; j++) {
      if (a[i][j] == 0)
         continue loop1; // continue immediately after statement3
      statement2
   }
   statement3
}
statement4
```

15.4 Recursion

We have seen how a method can call other methods. A method is even allowed to call itself; when this happens, it is called a *recursive method*. It is convenient to use recursive methods when we have to find solutions to certain kinds of problems. It is most appropriate to use recursion when we are faced with problems that are specified recursively from the very beginning; this is often the case with certain mathematical problems. The most common example of a recursive method (this one is found in most books on programming) is the one that will compute n factorial, *n!*, of a whole number *n*. The factorial of a number *n* can be defined in the following way:

$$n! = \begin{cases} 1 & \text{if } n = 0 \\ 1 \times 2 \times 3 \times \ldots \times n & \text{if } n > 0 \end{cases}$$

Naturally, we can easily calculate this product by means of a repetition statement. The following method will get a number n as parameter and will compute the factorial of the number.

```
static int nfac1(int n) {
   int prod = 1;
   for (int i=1; i<=n; i++)
     prod = prod * i;
   return prod;
}
```

Let us now see how we can make use of recursion instead. Another way of defining the factorial of a number is:

$$n! = \begin{cases} 1 & \text{if } n = 0 \\ n(n-1)! & \text{if } n > 0 \end{cases}$$

There is an obvious case (*n*=0) and one where we use induction to express the solution by means of values already defined. This way of writing the definition will lead naturally to the following method:

```
static int nfac(int n) {
   if (n <= 0)
     return 1;
   else
     return n * nfac(n-1);
}
```

Here it is the last but one line that interests us: it calls nfac itself.

Those of us unfamiliar with recursion usually find it a little strange but we should remember a basic rule: recursive method calls work in *exactly the same way* as other method calls. (See the Revision Table on page 58.) There are no special rules for recursion, so when a method is called (by itself or by another method) the arguments will be computed first. Memory space is then generated for the parameters of the method called, and the arguments are copied into this. New memory space is generated for the parameters and for the *local* variables with *every* new call. If a particular method is called several times, *every* edition of the method will have its *own edition* of parameters and local variables. The statements are then performed in the method called. When these statements have been finished, we return to the point from which the method was called. If a method calls itself, we hence return to a point within the method itself. Let us take a concrete example and look at exactly what happens. Let us suppose that the method nfac is defined in the class c and that we write the statement:

```
m = C.nfac(3);
```

The method `nfac` is called. It will generate space for the parameter `n`, and this will have the value 3. Since `n` is greater than 0, the statement after `else` will be performed. There is now a new call of the method `nfac`. The value of the argument `n-1` is 2. A new space is generated for the parameter `n`, and this space will get the value 2. From this moment, there will therefore be two different parameters, both with the name `n`. The first one, with the value 3, belongs to the first edition of `nfac`, and the second, with the value 2, belongs to the second edition of `nfac`.

In the second edition, `n` is also greater than zero, and the statement after `else` is performed. `nfac` is called here for a third time, and yet another parameter `n` is generated, this time with the value 1. The statement after `else` will also be performed in the third edition of `nfac`, as 1 is greater than 0. The method `nfac` is called for the fourth time, and a parameter with the name `n` is created once again. This one will have the value 0. Four different parameters with the name `n` will therefore be in existence at the same time.

The condition after `if` will be true in the fourth edition of `nfac`. So the statement:

```
return 1;
```

will be executed. Exactly as we would expect, the method is terminated, the result value is 1, and there is a jump to the point from which the call took place. Since the fourth call of `nfac` took place from the statement:

```
return n * nfac(n-1);
```

the jump will be to that statement. As the result value is `1`, the expression `n*1` will be computed. But what value does `n` have? In the fourth edition of `nfac`, `n` had the value 0 but the fourth edition is now finished. We have returned to the third edition and `n` had the value 1 there, so the expression `1*1` will be computed. Now we can finish executing the `return` statement and this means that the third edition of `nfac` will also be terminated. The result will be 1 and there is another jump to the point where the call took place. We therefore return again to the statement:

```
return n * nfac(n-1);
```

As we return to the second edition of `nfac`, `n` will have the value 2 this time, so the expression `2*1` will be computed. Edition number two is terminated with the return value 2, and once again there is a jump to the point of the call, that is, to the statement:

```
return n * nfac(n-1);
```

We have now returned to edition number one of `nfac`. In this edition, `n` had the value 3. As the result value of the expression `nfac(n-1)` was 2, the expression `3*2` will be computed. So edition number one of `nfac` will give a result value of 6. Edition number one is now terminated and there is another jump back. The first call of `nfac` took place from the statement:

```
m = C.nfac(3);
```

so the jump will be to this statement. The variable m will be assigned the value 6.

Recursive method
A method that directly or indirectly calls itself. When executed, there are as many editions of the method as the number of calls that have been made but not terminated. Every edition of the method has parameters and local variables with their own unique values.

Recursive solutions always follow the same idea. Faced with a problem, we first identify one (or more) simple, special cases, where the solution is self-evident ($n=0$, in nfac). We now try to formulate the problem so that it becomes simpler in some way (($n–1$)! is simpler than $n!$). We can then imagine that the method we are writing already exists and that it can solve the simpler problem.

As an example, we shall construct a recursive method that reads from an input stream and writes it out *backwards* to an output stream. We use the following recursive idea:

1. Try to read the input stream's first byte and save it.
   If it could be read, do the following:
   1.1   Read in the rest of the input stream and write it out backwards.
   1.2   Write out the input stream's first byte.

The obvious, special case is that the input stream is empty. So, we do nothing at all. In step 1.1, we suppose that there already is a method that can read in a stream and write it out backwards. We make use of this method to solve the simpler problem that arises when the input stream is one byte shorter than it was from the beginning. By means of this algorithm, we can construct the following Java program that reads a file and copies it backwards to another file. The names of the files are given as parameters of main. The copying of the files is done by the recursive method backwards.

```java
import java.io.*;
class CopyBack {
  static InputStream  in;
  static OutputStream out;

  static void backwards() throws IOException {
    int c;
    if ((c = in.read()) != -1) {
      backwards();
      out.write(c);
    }
  }
}
```

```
public static void main(String[] arg) throws IOException {
  in  = new FileInputStream (arg[0]);
  out = new FileOutputStream(arg[1]);
  backwards();
}
}
```

Reading takes place by means of the method read, which reads one byte at a time. When the file is finished, read returns the value −1. The method backwards will exist in as many editions (plus one) as the number of bytes in the stream. The first edition will read the first byte in the stream. This edition will not be terminated until all of the other editions have been terminated. The last thing that happens, therefore, is that the first byte is written out. Note that every edition of the method backwards has its own, unique edition of the local variable c. So, at most, there is the same number of cs as there are bytes in the file.

Note that the method backwards makes use of the *class* variables in and out. These only exist in one edition that is shared by all the other editions of the method backwards. We also could have given the streams in and out as parameters of the method backwards but this would have been unnecessary, as we would then have had as many copies of these parameters as the number of editions of the method backwards.

The recursive method has been a class method (static method) in the examples we have seen here. Naturally, we could also have used recursion in an ordinary instance method. Note, however, that the objects' *instance* variables only exist in one edition per object. It is only the recursive method's parameters and *local* variables that exist in as many editions as the number of calls.

Recursion will normally arise because a method calls itself. This is called *direct recursion*. We can also have *indirect recursion*. For example, a method m1 can call another method m2, which in turn calls m1. We then say that m1 and m2 are *mutually recursive*. Recursion can even arise over several stages (for example, m1 can call m2, which calls m3, which then calls m1).

In some cases, it can be useful to have recursive methods with arrays as parameters. To demonstrate this, we write a method sum, the task of which is to compute the sum of all the components in an array of whole numbers. This method has two parameters. The first is the array that will be summed and the second is an int that indicates where in the array summing is to begin. If we want to add up the entire array, we will give this second parameter the value 0. For example, the following statements will result in the value 69 being written out:

```
int a[] = {1, 3, 5, 2, 4, 7, 10, 20, 15, 2};
Std.out.println(sum(a, 0));  // 69 is written out
```

The method `sum` will look like this:

```
static int sum(int[] a, int startPos) {
  if (startPos>=a.length)
    return 0;
  else
    return a[startPos] + sum(a, startPos+1);
}
```

The recursive idea is a simple one. In the most obvious case the start position is greater than, or equal to, the length of the array. The chosen part of the array will therefore lack components and the sum will be equal to zero. If the start position is less than the length of the array, we can calculate the sum of the elements by adding the value in the start position to the sum of all the remaining components in the array. The method `sum` will call itself recursively in order to compute the sum of the remaining components.

15.5 Standard classes for collections

We use the word *collection* to denote a collection of objects; the objects that form a collection are called its *elements*. The class `Vector`, which we discussed in Section 7.7, is an example of a class that we use to construct collections. In Version 1.1 and earlier versions of Java, we only have the standard class `Vector` (and its subclass `Stack`) to describe collections but in J2SDK, a whole new group of classes and interfaces were introduced to deal with collections. We shall give an overview of these new classes and interfaces in this section. They can all be found in the package `java.util`.

There are two categories of collections: lists and sets. A *list* is an ordered sequence of elements. Each element can be found in a certain position in a list; this position can be indicated by an *index* (a whole number). An element is allowed to occur in several places in a list.

A *set* is a collection where an element may occur only once, at most. The elements of a set do not have to be in a special order. We do not use an index to access individual elements.

In Figure 15.1, we show the interfaces and classes that we use to describe collections. The interface is shown in the shaded area of the figure. The interface `Collection` describes properties that are common to all classes in a collection. This interface has two sub-interfaces: `List`, which describes lists and `Set`, which describes sets. The latter also has the sub-interface `SortedSet`, which describes sets where the elements are internally sorted. On the right in the figure are shown the standard classes that implement these interfaces. For example, we can see that the class `Vector` implements the interface `List`. We might think that it is unnecessary to have several standard

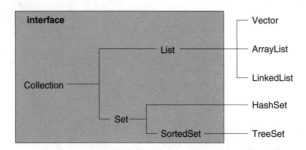

Figure 15.1 Interfaces and classes for collections

classes that implement the same interface. They have the same methods, which can be used in the same way. The reason is that there are often alternative technical solutions that can be used inside the classes. These classes will then have different properties. It is true that they all implement methods but they may do this with varying degrees of success. For example, the classes `Vector` and `ArrayList` are good at changing individual elements inside a list but they are ineffective when it comes to inserting new elements, for example, in the list's first position. The opposite is the case with the class `LinkedList`. The point is that we should make use of the class that is best suited for the operations we have to carry out most often.

15.5.1 Common properties of collections

All collections have (at least) two constructors, one without parameters and one that has another collection as parameter. We can create a copy of a collection by means of the second constructor. The copy does not have to be organized in the same way as the original. For example, we can write:

```
HashSet h = new HashSet();
... // place elements in the set h
LinkedList l = new LinkedList(h); // make a copy of h
```

In the Revision Table we list the methods defined in the interface `Collection` and which, therefore, all the collection classes must implement. Most of the methods do not need explanation. All the parameters that indicate objects are of the class `Object` to enable us to put any kind of object into a collection. For example, to insert a text last in the list `l`, we can write:

```
l.add(new String("a text"));
```

The method `iterator` corresponds to the old method `elements` in class `Vector` (see page 239) although it returns an iterator of the class `Iterator` instead of class `Enumeration`. The class `Iterator` has three methods: `hasNext`, which checks to see

The interface java.util.Collection	
add(o)	inserts the object o into the collection (In a list, o is inserted last. In the case of a set, o is only inserted if it does not already exist.)
addAll(s)	inserts all the objects in the collection s into the actual collection
clear()	removes all the elements from the collection
contains(o)	checks whether the object o is in the collection
containsAll(s)	checks whether all the objects in the collection s are in the collection
equals(s)	checks whether this collection is equal to the collection s. Two collections are equal if they are of the same category (list or set) and have the same elements (in the same order, for lists)
isEmpty()	checks whether this collection lacks elements
iterator()	returns an iterator of class Iterator that can be used to run through this collection
remove(o)	removes the object o from the collection if it is there
removeAll(s)	removes all the objects in the collection s from the collection
retainAll(s)	removes all the objects except those in the collection s
size()	gives the number of elements in the collection
toArray()	returns an array with all the elements in this collection
toArray(a)	a is an array. Returns an array with all the elements in this collection that have the same type as the elements in a

whether there is a next element, next, which gives the next element, and remove, which removes the element that the latest call of next gave as result. The method next returns a value of type Object, so that we generally have to make an explicit type conversion to the desired type. Let us suppose, for example, that we have put objects of class String into the list l. We can then run through the list and remove all elements containing the text "old".

```
for (Iterator i=l.iterator(); i.hasNext(); ) {
  String s = (String) i.next();
  if (s.indexOf("old") != -1)
    i.remove();
}
```

Apart from the interface Collection, there is also a *class* Collections (with an s at the end), which contains some class methods that can be of interest. For example, we can find here the methods min and max, which can be used to get the least or the greatest element in a collection. In order to find the greatest element in the list l, for example, we can write:

```
Object obj = Collections.max(l);
```

The objects in the collection must be *naturally comparable*, if this is to work. More precisely, they must implement the interface `Comparable`. The only method in the interface `Comparable` is the method `compareTo`. This has another object `obj` as parameter and compares the actual object with this one. The result value is a whole number. If the objects are equal, a value of 0 is returned; if the active object is smaller than the parameter `obj`, a negative value is returned, and if the active object is greater than the parameter `obj`, a positive value is returned. Many standard classes are naturally comparable. This applies, for example, to the classes `Date`, `File` and `URL`, as well as the wrapper classes `Integer`, `Double`, etc. The class `String` is also naturally comparable but the comparisons will not give the correct alphabetical order. If we want to compare texts, it is better to use a collator (see below).

The methods `min` and `max` can be found in alternative versions that can be used for objects that are not naturally comparable. We then have to give an extra parameter. To find the smallest element in the set h, we can write, for example:

```
Object obj = Collections.max(h, comp);
```

Here `comp` will be an object of a class that implements the interface `Comparator`. This interface only has the method `compare`, which will have two objects as parameters. The result value is (exactly as for the method `compareTo`, above) a whole number indicating which of the objects was the greater. The class `Collator`, which we used in Section 6.3, implements the interface `Comparator`. So we can use an object of this class as an extra parameter for the methods `min` and `max` when we want to search for the smallest and the largest element in a collection of texts.

The class `Collections` also contains two constants, `EMPTY_SET` and `EMPTY_LIST`, which we can use when we want to check whether a list or a set is empty.

When we construct programs with parallel threads, note that the collection classes `ArrayList`, `LinkedList`, `HashSet` and `TreeSet` are not synchronized (their methods have not been marked with the word **synchronized**). This means that errors can arise if several threads use a collection at the same time. To remedy this, we can use one of the class methods, `synchronizedList`, `synchronizedSet` and `synchronizedSortedSet`, in the class `Collections`. For example, to get a synchronized list that can be used in a program with parallel trees, we can write:

```
List list = Collections.synchronizedList(new LinkedList());
```

The standard classes that implement the interface `Collection`, that is, the classes `Vector`, `ArrayList`, `LinkedList`, `HashSet` and `TreeSet`, have another property that can be interesting to know. They all implement the interface `Serializable`. So we can output whole lists and sets to streams. We can therefore easily store a list or a set in a file; see Section 13.4.2 on page 420.

15.5.2 General properties of lists

Properties peculiar to lists are defined in the interface `List`. The new methods that have been added are shown in the next Revision Table. For example, we can find methods here to access individual elements by the use of indexing:

```
l.add(5,new String("Java"));  // insert the text "Java" in
                              // position 5
String s = (String) l.get(5); // retrieve the text in position 5
```

The interface java.util.List	
`add(k,o)`	interposes the object `o` in position number `k` in the list
`addAll(k,s)`	interposes all the objects in collection `s` in position number `k` in the list
`get(k)`	returns the object in position number `k`
`indexOf(o)`	gives the index for the object `o`, or −1 if `o` cannot be found in the list
`lastIndexOf(o)`	as `indexOf(o)`, but searches from the back
`listIterator()`	returns a `ListIterator` that begins in position number 0
`listIterator(k)`	returns a `ListIterator` that begins in position number `k`
`remove(k)`	removes the object in position number `k`
`set(k,o)`	replaces the element in position number `k` in the list with the object `o`
`subList(i,j)`	gives the part of the list that includes the elements `i` to `j-1`

In addition, all the methods in the interface `java.util.Collection` can be found here.

The method `subList` is useful when we want to change a part of a list. An example:

```
l.subList(3,8).clear();  // remove the elements 3-7
```

There is also a special iterator, `ListIterator`, for lists. The class `ListIterator` is a subclass of class `Iterator`, so it will inherit the methods `hasNext`, `next` and `remove`. There are also methods to run through a list backwards and to add or change list elements. A compilation is given in the following Revision Table.

The class `Collections` also contains some useful class methods for lists. The method `fill` will replace all the elements in a list by a certain value:

The interface java.util.ListIterator	
`next(k)`	gives the next element when we run forwards through the list
`previous()`	gives the next element when we run backwards through the list
`hasNext()`	indicates whether there are more elements (forwards)
`hasPrevious()`	indicates whether there are more elements (backwards)
`nextIndexOf()`	gives the index for the next element (forwards)
`previousIndexOf()`	gives the index for the next element (backwards)
`add(o)`	interposes the object o in the actual position in the list
`remove()`	removes the element in the actual position from the list
`set(o)`	replaces the element in the actual position with the object o

```
Collections.fill(l, "Java"); // puts "Java" in all elements in l
```

The method `nCopies` forms a list that consists of n similar objects:

```
List zeros = Collections.nCopies(100, new Integer(0));
```

The method `copy` copies all the elements in a list to another list. We can write:

```
Collections.copy(lTo, lFrom);
```

The list we copy to must be at least as long as the one we copy from. If it is longer, the extra elements will remain unchanged.

There are methods that will move elements in a list. The method `reverse` puts elements in reverse order, the method `shuffle` puts elements in an arbitrary order, while the method `sort` will sort elements. For example, we can write:

```
Collections.sort(l);
```

The method `binarySearch` searches for a particular element in a list:

```
int pos = Collections.binarySearch(l, searchedObj);
```

As we have shown here, the methods `sort` and `binarySearch`, in their simplest versions, require the elements in the list to implement the interface `Comparable`. In other words, they should have a `compareTo` method. If this is not the case, we can use alternative versions of `sort` and `binarySearch`, where we give an object that implements the interface `Comparator` as an extra parameter. If we want to sort a list with text alphabetically, we can use a collator of the type `Collator`; see Section 6.3. If the list l contains texts, we can sort it with the following statements:

```
Collator co = Collator.getInstance();
co.setStrength(Collator.PRIMARY);
Collections.sort(l,co);
```

15.5.3 Implementing lists

As we saw in Figure 15.1, there are in Java three standard classes that implement the interface `List`. These are the classes `Vector`, `ArrayList` and `LinkedList`. The first two make use internally of an array to describe the list. The class `Vector` is included for historical reasons. We described this in Section 7.7, and all the methods are shown in the Revision Table on page 242. The class `ArrayList` has roughly the same properties as the class `Vector`, the biggest difference being that it is not synchronized. Class `ArrayList` has all the methods in the Revision Table on page 242, although the methods `addElement`, `insertElementAt`, `setElementAt`, `ElementAt`, `removeElementAt` and `removeAllElements` have been replaced by equivalent methods with more modern names; see the interfaces `Collection` and `List`.

Implementing a list with an array is effective when we want to carry out operations that make use of indexing to read and change individual elements. This is not the case, however, when we want to interpose new elements in a list or remove elements, as we have to move the elements, which can take some time if the array is a large one. If we often have to carry out this type of operation, it is more convenient to use the class `LinkedList`. This makes use of a completely different technique, that of a doubly linked list, to make the implementation.

A *linked list* consists of a number of *nodes*. Each node contains both a reference to the next node and a reference to an element to be found in the list. There are therefore as many nodes in the list as there are elements. If every node in addition contains a reference to the previous node, then we have a *doubly linked list*. This can look as in Figure 15.2. The shaded boxes indicate the elements of the list themselves. There are also two references, called `first` and `last` in the figure, which refer to the first and last nodes. We make use of these references as starting-points whenever we want to perform an operation on the list. The value `null` has been used to indicate when the list has ended. There is also another technique, where we let the list be circular, that is, the last node refers forwards to the first and the first node refers backwards to the last one.

It lies outside the scope of this book to go into the details of how we implement a linked list. As luck would have it, we do not have to know this to make use of the standard class `LinkedList`. However, we should know that we can interpose new elements anywhere in a linked list without having to move the old elements. We simply create a new node that refers to the new element and link in this node at the required point in the list by changing references; neither do we have to move elements when we want to remove an element. As we have direct references to the beginning and end of the list, we can access the first and last elements very quickly. It is also particularly easy to insert or remove elements at the beginning and end of the list. On the other hand, it may take some time to access elements inside the list, as we will always have

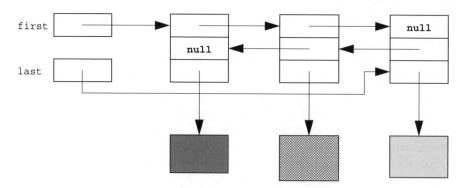

Figure 15.2 A doubly linked list

to run through it from the beginning or the end. So we can see that lists implemented as linked lists have quite different characteristics from lists implemented with arrays. This explains why there are standard classes that use both techniques.

As the class LinkedList is especially suitable in applications where we have to deal with the beginning and the end of a list, there is a set of extra methods for these operations in class LinkedList. These are called addFirst, addLast, etc. In addition, class LinkedList, like the classes Vector and ArrayList, has the method clone; see the Revision Table.

Extra methods in java.util.LinkedList	
addFirst(o)	inserts the object o first in the list
addLast(o)	inserts the object o last in the list
getFirst()	returns the first object in the list
getLast()	returns the last object in the list
removeFirst()	removes the first object from the list
removeLast()	removes the last object from the list
clone()	returns a copy of the list (the references to the objects in the list are copied, not the objects themselves)

15.5.4   General properties of sets

The properties applying to sets are defined in the interface Set. No new methods are defined in this interface, in addition to those that apply for all collections and that are shown in the Revision Table on page 495. What is particular to this interface is that the constructors and the method add must be designed in such a manner that no element can be added to the set more than once. If we try to add an element that is already there, nothing will happen.

Note also that there is a method `singleton` in the class `Collections` with which we can create a set that contains a single element:

```
Set  s = Collections.singleton(new String("Sole"));
```

Sorted sets have some unique properties. These are described in the interface `SortedSet`. We must be able to compare the elements of a set with one another in order to be able to sort it. We can do this if the elements are naturally comparable, that is, they implement the interface `Comparable` and have a method `compareTo`. If, when we create a sorted set, the elements are not naturally comparable, we will have to indicate that a special collator is to be used. This collator will be an object that implements the interface `Comparator`, that is, it will have a `compare` method. (We discussed the interfaces `Comparable` and `Comparator` on page 496.)

A class, for example the standard class `TreeSet` that implements the interface `SortedSet`, should have (at least) the following four constructors:

```
TreeSet()
TreeSet(Comparator comp)
TreeSet(Collection coll)
TreeSet(SortedSet ss)
```

The first creates an empty set. All the elements to be placed in the set must be naturally comparable. The second constructor also creates an empty set but does not require elements to be naturally comparable. Instead, we give a collator to be used as parameter. The third constructor creates a sorted set of the elements included in the collection that is given as parameter. These elements must be naturally comparable. The last constructor gets a sorted set as parameter and creates a copy of this set.

There are methods in the interface `SortedSet` that are typical for sorted sets. These are shown in the Revision Table. What distinguishes a sorted set from an ordinary one is, of course, that the elements of a sorted set are internally sorted. So we shall get the elements in sorted order when we use an iterator.

As an example of this, we shall show a program that reads a file containing a text and writes out all the words included in the text. The name of the file is given as parameter for `main`. The printout of the words will be sorted in alphabetical order and words that occur several times in the text will be found in only one place in the printout. All the words are written out in capitals. The program has the following appearance:

The interface java.util.SortedSet	
first()	returns the set's smallest element
last()	returns the set's largest element
headSet(toE)	returns a sorted subset with all the elements that are smaller than the element toE
tailSet(fromE)	returns a sorted subset with all the elements that are larger than, or equal to, the element fromE
subSet(fromE,toE)	returns a sorted subset with all the elements that are larger than, or equal to, the element fromE and smaller than the element toE
comparator()	returns the collator that is used, or null, if the elements are naturally comparable

In addition, all the methods in the interface java.util.Collection are included.

```java
import java.util.*;
import java.text.*;
import java.io.*;
import extra.*;
public class TextAnalysis {

  public static void main(String[] arg)  {
    String word;
    Collator co = Collator.getInstance();  // compare texts
    co.setStrength(Collator.PRIMARY);       // see page 182
    TreeSet wordSet = new TreeSet(co);
    // open the file
    ExtendedReader r = ExtendedReader.getFileReader(arg[0]);
    // read one word at a time and add to the set
    while((word = nextWord(r)) != null)
      wordSet.add(word.toUpperCase());
    // write out all the words
    for (Iterator i=wordSet.iterator(); i.hasNext(); )
      Std.out.println(i.next());
  }

  // The method nextWord reads a word, gives null at end of file
  public static String nextWord(ExtendedReader r) {
    String s ="";
    int c;
    // skip all the characters that are not letters
    while ((c=r.lookAhead()) != -1 &&
           !Character.isLetter((char) c))
      c = r.readChar(); // skip this character
```

```
    // form a word from the letters that follow
    while ((c=r.lookAhead()) != -1 &&
            Character.isLetter((char) c))
      s = s + (char)r.readChar();  // insert this letter into s
    if (s.length() == 0)
      return null;   // at end of file
    else
      return s;
  }
}
```

A sorted set, `wordSet`, is created in the method `main`. In order to get the correct alphabetical order, we give a collator of class `Collator` as parameter for the constructor; see Section 6.3. One word at a time is then read from the file and added to the set. When all the words have been read, an iterator is used to run through the set. Words are read in from the file in the method `nextWord`. In this method we first skip all the characters that are not letters. (We use the method `lookAhead` so that the algorithm will be as simple as possible. This method looks ahead to the next character, without taking it out of the stream.) Then we read in one letter at a time until a character comes that is not a letter. The letters that are read are put together to form a word, which is then returned from the method.

15.5.5 Implementing sets

In Java there are two standard classes for sets, `TreeSet` and `HashSet`. `TreeSet` forms sorted sets and `HashSet`, unsorted sets. The class `TreeSet` is implemented with the class `TreeMap`, and the class `HashSet` with the class `HashMap`. These classes will be discussed in the next section, which deals with maps. We shall not go into details now, therefore, but will confine ourselves to giving some general properties of the classes `TreeSet` and `HashSet`.

The class `TreeSet` sorts elements into a *binary search tree*. It allows us to search, add or remove elements relatively quickly. (The time it takes is proportional to the logarithm of the number of elements in the set.) Running through the set with an iterator is done in the fastest way possible. (The time this takes is proportional to the number of elements in the set.)

The class `HashSet` uses a *hash table* internally. If configured correctly, this can be an extremely fast way to search, add or remove elements. (The time it takes is constant and not proportional to the number of elements in the set.) On the other hand, a hash table can be inefficient if we want to run through all the elements in a set. There is also another disadvantage. For it to work correctly, we have to reserve a little more memory space for the hash table than there are elements in the set.

In conclusion, we can say: if we want to run through a set, it would be best to use the class `TreeSet`, certainly if we will perform the operation frequently. If we want to sort elements, we must use `TreeSet`, since `HashSet` does not sort elements. If we do not need to run through the set, we can find it more appropriate to use the class `HashSet`. It will then be much faster to search, add or remove elements.

15.6 Standard classes for maps

A *map* is a table where we use a *search key* to access information. An example of this is a motor-vehicle registration office. The search key in this case is a car's registration number. If we know the registration number, we can retrieve information about a car, the make and model, for instance. We say that the search key in a map is *mapped* onto a *value* (the information). So a search key and its accompanying value form a pair, called a *mapping*. The term *key–value pair* is often used. A search key can only be mapped onto *one* value. (One car cannot have several registration numbers.) A particular search key can, therefore, only be found a single time in a map. On the other hand, a particular value can occur several times. For example, if we have a map where the search keys are the names of people and the values are ages, it would be possible for several people to have the same age.

In Figure 15.3 are shown the standard interfaces and standard classes in Java for describing maps. The interfaces are shown in the shaded part of the figure. The interface `Map` describes properties that all maps have in common. The sub-interface `SortedMap` describes maps where the search keys are sorted internally. To the right in the figure are shown the three standard classes, `Hashtable`, `HashMap` and `TreeMap`, which implement these interfaces. The class `Hashtable` also has a subclass `Properties` which, among other things, is used to represent system properties.

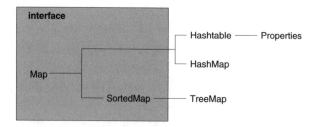

Figure 15.3 Interfaces and classes for mappings

15.6.1 Properties common to maps

All maps have (at least) two constructors, one without parameters and one that has another map as parameter. We can use the second of these if we want to create a copy of a map. For example, we can write:

```
TreeMap tab1 = new TreeMap();
... // insert mappings in tab1
HashMap tab2 = new HashMap(tab1);
```

The interface java.util.Map	
put(key,value)	inserts a mapping in the map. Any previous values of key are replaced. The old value is returned.
putAll(tab)	inserts all the mappings to be found in another map, tab, into this map
remove(key)	removes the mapping for key from the map
clear()	removes all the mappings from the map
get(key)	returns the value for key, or **null**, if key cannot be found
containsKey(n)	checks whether the key n can be found in the map
containsValue(v)	checks whether one or more keys are mapped onto the value v
isEmpty()	checks whether this map lacks mappings
size()	gives the number of mappings in the map
equals(tab)	checks whether the map has the same mappings as tab
keySet()	returns a set (Set) with all the keys in this map
values()	returns a collection (Collection) with all the values in the map
entrySet()	returns a set (Set) with all the mappings in the map. Every mapping has the type Map.Entry
Map.Entry	class that represents a mapping. Includes the methods getKey, getValue and setValue

The Revision Table lists the methods in the interface Map. These methods can be found in all the classes that implement the interface, that is, in the classes Hashtable, HashMap and TreeMap and which, therefore, must be implemented by all the map classes. The most important methods are put and get, which are used to insert mappings in the map and to look up the value of a particular search key. Both keys and values are of type Object, so that in a map, we can have any kind of object as key and value. For example, to insert a mapping that says that the person David is 12 years old, we can write:

```
tab1.add("David", new Integer(12));
```

If in a car registration `reg` we want to get information about the car with registration number ABC123, we can write:

```
MotorVehicle mv = (MotorVehicle) reg.get("ABC123");
```

The classes `HashMap` and `TreeMap` are, unlike class `Hashtable`, unsynchronized. (Their methods have not been marked with the word **synchronized**.) This is a point to ponder, if we are writing programs with several threads. To get a synchronized map, we can use the class method `synchronizedMap` in the class `Collections`. For example, we can write:

```
Map m = Collections.synchronizedMap(new TreeMap());
```

One point worth noting is that all the three standard classes `Hashtable`, `HashMap` and `TreeMap` also implement the interface `Serializable`, so we can write out a whole map to a file without difficulty; see Section 13.4.2.

15.6.2   The class `TreeMap`

With the class `TreeMap`, we can create *sorted* maps. The class `TreeMap` implements the interface `SortedMap`. What distinguishes a sorted map from an ordinary one is that we get *sorted* sets as result if we call one of the methods `keySet` and `entrySet`. Search keys are stored in sorted order in sorted maps. For search keys to be sorted, they must be naturally comparable. In other words, they must implement the interface `Comparable`. If they do, they will have a method `compareTo`. If the elements are not naturally comparable and we want to create a sorted map, we have to indicate that we will use a special collator. This will be an object that implements the interface `Comparator`, that is, it will have a method `compare`; see page 496.

The class `TreeMap`, which implements the interface `SortedMap`, has four constructors:

```
TreeMap()
TreeMap(Comparator comp)
TreeMap(Map m)
TreeMap(SortedMap sm)
```

The first creates an empty map and requires all the search keys that will be put into the map to be naturally comparable. We can use the second constructor when search keys are not naturally comparable. We then give as parameter a collator that we will use. The third constructor creates a sorted map of the mappings included in the table given as parameter. Search keys must be naturally comparable. The last constructor gets a sorted map as parameter and creates a copy of this table. The same sort order is used.

The methods characteristic of sorted maps have been defined in the interface `SortedMap`; see the Revision Table. The class `TreeMap` also has all the methods in the interface `Map`. There is also a method `clone` to enable us to create copies of a table.

The interface java.util.SortedMap	
firstKey()	returns the smallest search key
lastKey()	returns the largest search key
headMap(toK)	returns a map with all the mappings where the search key is smaller than toK
tailMap(fromK)	returns a map with all the mappings where the search key is larger than, or equal to, fromK
subMap(fromK,toK)	returns a map with all the mappings where the search key is larger than, or equal to, fromK and smaller than toK
comparator()	returns the collator that is used, or **null**, if the search keys are naturally comparable

In addition, there are all the methods in the interface java.util.Map.

We shall now write a new variant of our text analysis program on page 502 to show how the class TreeMap can be used. That program read a text from a file and wrote out all the words included in the text in alphabetical order. In the new variant of that program, we shall not only write out the words included in the text but also the number of times the word occurs. As before, the words will be written out in alphabetical order. We merely have to reconstruct the method main. The rest of the class TextAnalysis will remain as before. We will now use a sorted map, where the words are search keys. For each search key, we let the value be an object of class Integer. This object will contain the number of times the word in question occurs in the text. The program will look as follows:

```java
public static void main(String[] arg)  {
  String word;
  Collator co = Collator.getInstance();   // compare texts
  co.setStrength(Collator.PRIMARY);       // see page 182
  // create the map
  TreeMap wordTable = new TreeMap(co);
  // open the file
  ExtendedReader r = ExtendedReader.getFileReader(arg[0]);
  // read one word at a time
  while((word = nextWord(r)) != null) {
    word = word.toUpperCase(); // translate to capitals
    // look up the word in the table
    Integer number = (Integer) wordTable.get(word);
    if (number == null)
      number = new Integer(0); // the word did not exist before
    // insert the word into the table
    wordTable.put(word, new Integer(number.intValue()+1));
  }
```

```
    // create a sorted set with all the pairs of words and numbers
    Set mappings = wordTable.entrySet();
    // write out all the pairs
    for (Iterator i=mappings.iterator(); i.hasNext(); ) {
      Map.Entry e = (Map.Entry) i.next();
      Std.out.println(e.getKey() + "   " + e.getValue());
    }
  }
```

We look up a word in the table every time it has been read from the file. If the word can be found in the table, we will get as result an object of the class `Integer`. If the word is not found, we will get as result the value `null`. We then insert the word that has been read into the table and increase the number for this word by 1. When the whole text has been read, we use the method `entrySet` to form a set of all the mappings, that is, pairs of words and corresponding numbers. The mappings are of the class `Map.Entry`; see the Revision Table on page 505. We then use an iterator to run through these pairs and output the information.

The class `TreeMap` is implemented by means of a *binary search tree*. A *tree* is a programming construct that is built with a number of *nodes*. Unlike ordinary trees, the *root* comes at the top. Each node contains references to its nodes underneath, which are called its *children*. In a *binary* tree, each node has at most two children. Apart from the references to its children, each node contains information of some kind. In a tree used to create maps, there will be one node per mapping. So each node will contain a reference to a search key and a reference to the corresponding value. We do not have the space to go into more detail here but we can show the principles involved in a figure. If we had a map that was used to count the number of words in a text, it might look something like Figure 15.4 For example, from the figure we can see that the word "and" has occurred 5 times and the word "is" 8 times.

But how has this construct been sorted? If we look carefully in the tree, we shall see that the search keys have been ingeniously placed. For every node, the search key in the node is larger than all the search keys in the nodes that are in the node's left-hand children and all the children of these nodes, grandchildren, etc. For instance, the word "bad" is larger than both the word "ask" and the word "and". Similarly, the search key in every node is smaller than the search key in the node's right-hand children and all the children of these nodes, grandchildren, etc. The word "far", for example, is smaller than the words "is", "in" or "zoo".

We can make use of the fact that the search keys have been deployed in this way when we have to search for a particular key. The reference at the top of the figure is always used as a starting-point, and from there on we search downwards in the tree. For every node we search through, we compare the search key in this node with the one we are looking for. If the node contains a search key that is larger than the one we are looking

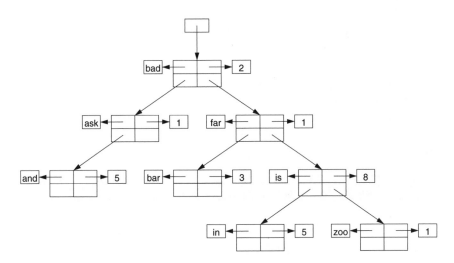

Figure 15.4 A binary search tree

for, we continue the search in the node's left-hand children, and if the node contains a search key that is smaller than the one we are looking for, we continue the search in the node's right-hand children. We continue in this way until either we come across the search key we are looking for, or we reach the end of the tree. If a tree is balanced, that is, if each level is filled out before a new one is started, a search can be quite fast, as the maximum number of comparisons that must be made to find a particular word is proportional to the number of *levels* in the tree, not the number of words.

If we wish to form a sorted list of words or mappings, we begin with an empty list and use the following recursive algorithm:

> If the tree lacks nodes, do nothing.
> Otherwise, do the following:
> > Call this algorithm for the sub-tree that has the root's left-hand child as root.
> > Place the root's search word (and value) last in the list.
> > Call this algorithm for the sub-tree that has the root's right-hand child as root.

By way of a summary, we can state the following in connection with maps that have been created with the class `TreeMap`: searches, insertions and removals of mappings can be done relatively quickly. (The time required is in proportion to the logarithm of the number of search keys.) We can easily form *sorted* lists of search words and mappings.

15.6.3   The classes `Hashtable` and `HashMap`

For fast searches where we are not interested in having sorted lists of search keys and mappings, we should use one of the classes `Hashtable` and `HashMap`. Both classes function in the same way. They both implement the interface `Map`, shown in the Revision Table on page 505. The only real difference between these classes is that `HashMap` is not synchronized, while `Hashtable` is. The class `Hashtable` has remained for historical reasons, having been in earlier versions of Java. Apart from the methods in the interface `Map`, it contains some methods that are shown in the Revision Table below. The method `clone` can also be found in the class `HashMap`:

Extra methods in java.util.Hashtable	
`contains(v)`	same as the method `containsValue`
`keys()`	gives an iterator of the class `Enumeration`, which runs through all the search keys in the table
`elements()`	gives an iterator of the class `Enumeration`, which runs through all the values in the table
`clone()`	returns a copy of the table (references to the objects in the table are copied and not the objects themselves)

The classes `Hashtable` and `HashMap` make use of something called a *hash table*, as we would expect, given their names. A hash table is constructed for fast searches. As we know, an array is the programming construct that produces the fastest searches. If we know the index of a particular element, we can immediately look it up in an array. Ideally, we would always use arrays for our searches but the search keys always have to be whole numbers, so that they can be used as indexes in the array. In addition, a search key has to lie within a limited interval, otherwise the array would have to be unacceptably large. Despite these limitations, we still make use of arrays in hash tables. One of these is shown in Figure 15.5, with the array at the top. All the ks indicate search keys, and all the vs their corresponding values.

To index with a search key in an array, we first have to translate the search key into a whole number. The translation of search keys into whole numbers is done by a *hash function*. For example, if the search key is a text, the hash function will compute a whole number on the basis of this text. (The whole number for a text can, for instance, be calculated as the sum of the LATIN_1 codes for the characters included in the text.) We then use the resulting whole number h to index in the array. We use the value $h\%m$ to index with to ensure indexing will not take place outside the array. Here m is the size of the array, and the operator $\%$ gives the remainder when h is divided by m. Of course, different hash functions are required for different types of search key. A method called

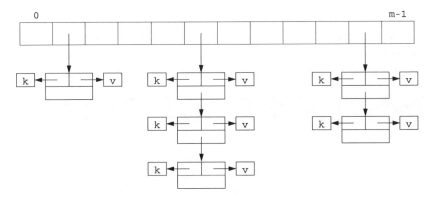

Figure 15.5 A hash table

hashCode, which corresponds to the hash function, is defined in the class Object. If objects of a certain class are to be used as search keys, the class must have defined its own version of the hashCode method. Several standard classes, for example the class String, have their own version of this method. For objects of a certain class to be used as search keys, the class must also have defined its own version of the method equals to ensure search keys can be compared with each other.

The problem with hash functions is that several values can be translated into the same whole number. (If, for example, we add the LATIN_1 codes for the texts "fat" and "gas", we will get the same total.) We then get a *collision*. Several different search keys can therefore get the same index in an array. To solve this problem, we do not let each element in an array contain a single value, but a list of search keys and corresponding values, that is, a list of mappings. In Figure 15.5, for example, we can see that collisions have arisen for two elements in the array. In one case, even three search keys have been translated into the same whole number.

Naturally, we would prefer it if there were no collisions at all. We would then find the search key immediately, without having to search through a list. We could avoid collisions if we had a perfect hash function that translated all the different search keys into different indices. In most cases, it is not possible to construct such a hash function but it is important that the hash function should be so designed that it will spread the different search keys as evenly as possible in an array. The risk of a collision will also decrease, of course, if the array is a large one, so we usually let the array be larger than the number of search keys. For hash tables we frequently use the word *capacity* to indicate the number of elements (= m) in the array. We also usually indicate a *load factor*, which is the ratio of the number of mappings (that is, the number of search keys) to the capacity. We usually have a low load factor in order to diminish the risk of

511

collisions but this requires more memory space. In practice, the risk of a collision is high if the load factor exceeds 0.75.

The classes Hashtable and HashMap have four constructors, the two that all maps have (see page 505) and two extra ones, where we can choose the capacity and load factor ourselves; see the Revision Table. If we choose the capacity ourselves, we should let it

Constructors in java.util.Hashtable and java.util.HashMap	
HashMap() and Hashtable()	create an empty hash table with default values for the capacity and load factor (101 and 0.75, respectively)
HashMap(map) and Hashtable(map)	create a hash table that contains all the mappings in the map map. The capacity will be 3 times the number of mappings in map, and the load factor will be 0.75
HashMap(m) and Hashtable(m)	create an empty hash table with capacity m and load factor 0.75
HashMap(m,f) and Hashtable(m,f)	create an empty hash table with capacity m and load factor f

be a prime number. If we insert so many mappings in a hash table that the load factor is exceeded, the hash table's capacity will be increased automatically (doubled). All of the old mappings in the table will then be moved around, which will naturally take a little time. If we know in advance roughly how many mappings the hash table is to hold, it would be best to use one of the constructors in which we can indicate the capacity ourselves.

As an example, we shall show one of our own classes, by means of which we can translate a text that contains the name of a colour to an object of the standard class Color. Our class will be called Colors. It will have a class method get that has a String as parameter and returns a Color object. The names of the colours that we will be able to give as parameters will be those that have been pre-defined, displayed in the Revision Table on page 25. For example, we will be able to write:

```
Color col = Colors.get("orange");
```

The method get will be designed such that it will not make any difference whether we indicate the name of a colour with a capital or small letter. The class Colors will have the appearance shown below. It makes use internally of a hash table that is initialized in a static initializer. There are 13 colours to be inserted into the table. The hash table's capacity has therefore been given as 19. This is a prime number and gives a load factor under 0.75. We look up colours in the hash table in the method get but before we do this, we translate the name of the colour to small letters. If the given name of a colour is missing from the table, the colour black will be returned.

```java
package extra;
import java.awt.*;
import java.util.*;

public class Colors {

  private static Hashtable tab = new Hashtable(19);

  // initialize the hash table
  static {
     tab.put("black",    Color.black);
     tab.put("blue",     Color.blue);
     tab.put("cyan",     Color.black);
     tab.put("darkgray", Color.darkGray);
     etc., for other pre-defined colours
  }

  public static Color get(String name) {
    Object c = tab.get(name.toLowerCase());
    if (c != null)
      return (Color) c;
    else
      return Color.black;
  }
}
```

15.6.4   The class Properties

The last class we shall be discussing in this survey is the standard class Properties. This class is a subclass of the class Hashtable. We use it to create maps, where both the search key and its corresponding value are of type String. We therefore use the class Properties to map *key words* onto texts. We call a map of class Properties a *property table*.

A unique property of class Properties is that we can connect, to a certain Properties object p1, another Properties object p2, which contains default values. So if we are searching for a particular key word in p1 and this key word cannot be found, the search will automatically continue in p2. If the search word is found in p2, we will get the value that is stored there. This takes place recursively. If the searched word cannot be found in p2 either, and if p2 in turn has a third Properties object with default values, the search will proceed to p3, and so on.

Another unique property of the class Properties is that we can store a map in a text file, a *property file*. We can also read in a property file and put the mappings indicated there into a property table. A property file will contain lines of the form:

java.util.Properties	
`Properties()`	creates an empty table without default values for search words
`Properties(pdef)`	creates an empty table and indicates that the `Properties` object `pdef` contains default values for the search words
`put(searchWord,txt)`	inserts a map in the table. Earlier values for `searchWord` are replaced. The old value is returned
`setProperty(searchWord,txt)`	the same as `put(searchWord,txt)`
`getProperty(searchWord)`	gives the text for `searchWord`
`getProperty(searchWord,txt)`	the same as `getProperty(searchWord,txt)`, but gives the result `txt` if `searchWord` is missing
`store(out,rubric)`	saves the table as a property file in the output stream `out`; `rubric` is inserted as comment in the first line
`load(in)`	reads a property file from the input stream `in` and inserts the mappings into the table
`propertyNames()`	gives an iterator of class `Enumeration` that runs through all the search words in the table
`list(out)`	outputs the table in `out` (an `OutputStream` or a `Writer`). Used for debugging

```
keyword=the text that applies for this keyword
```

A keyword will appear first on every line; then, after the equality sign (or a colon), will come the text that is to be the value for this keyword. The text to the right of the equality sign can contain blank characters. If we want special characters to be included in the text, we can make use of the escape sequences that are shown in the Revision Table on page 176. If a text is too long to be contained in a line, we can conclude the line with the character \ and continue on a new line. Lines introduced with the character # or ! are considered to be comments and are skipped when we read in the mappings. Property files often allow us to make programs exactly as we want them to be, without having to change the program code. Colours, fonts and sizes are examples of the things that we can change by using property files. We shall give an example of this shortly.

The Java interpreter makes use of a property table, that is, an object of the class `Properties`, to describe system properties. Some of the keywords that can be found in this table are `java.version`, `os.name`, `user.language` and `user.timezone`. In the standard class `java.lang.System` there is a method `getProperties` that we can use to get access to a system's property table. For example, we can make the following statement to get a printout of the actual system properties:

```
System.getProperties().list(System.out);
```

A system's property table is initialized automatically at the start of a program. If we use D parameters when we start our program (see page 284), the mappings we write there will also end up in the system's property table. The methods in the class System that have to do with the system's property table, are shown in the following Revision Table. Note that we can both read and change individual properties. We can even replace the system's property table with one of our own.

Some of the methods in java.lang.System	
`getProperties()`	returns the system's property table
`setProperties(p)`	replaces the system's property table with `p`
`getProperty(searchWord)`	gives the text for `searchWord` in the system's property table
`getProperty(searchWord,txt)`	the same as `setProperty(searchWord,txt)` but gives the result `txt` if `searchWord` is missing
`setProperty(searchWord,txt)`	inserts a mapping in the system's property table. Earlier values are replaced. The old value is returned.

We shall conclude by showing a new version of the program `Message4` on page 122, which showed a message in a window on the screen. In the new version, which we call `Message`, we use a property file called `Message.properties` to control the font, together with the foreground and background colours to be used. We shall also arrange for the message itself to be included in the property file. This can look as follows:

```
# Properties for the program Message
background=yellow
fontName=SansSerif
fontStyle=ITALIC
fontSize=18
message=Goodbye and Thank You!
```

The program uses a property table that is initialized from the property file. It then looks up the different properties that are required in the table. Default values have been indicated for each property. The class `Colors`, which we showed on page 513, is used to translate the names of the colours indicated in the property file to objects of the standard class `Color`. The class `Message` looks like this:

```
import java.awt.*;
import java.util.*;
import java.io.*;
import extra.*;
```

```
class Message extends Frame {
  public static void main (String[] arg) throws IOException  {
    // create and initialize the property table
    Properties p = new Properties();
    p.load(new FileInputStream("Message.properties"));
    Message m = new Message();

    // create a Label object with the message
    String mess  = p.getProperty("message",  "Hello");
    Label l = new Label(mess, Label.CENTER);
    // retrieve the font
    String fName  = p.getProperty("fontName",  "Serif");
    String fStyle = p.getProperty("fontStyle", "PLAIN");
    // translate the style to a whole number constant
    int ifStyle;
    if (fStyle.equals("BOLD") )
      ifStyle = Font.BOLD;
    else if (fStyle.equals("ITALIC"))
      ifStyle = Font.ITALIC;
    else
      ifStyle = Font.PLAIN;
    int fSize = Integer.parseInt
                (p.getProperty("fontSize", "24"));
    l.setFont(new Font(fName, ifStyle, fSize));
    // set the foreground colour
    String fColor = p.getProperty("foreground",  "black");
    l.setForeground(Colors.get(fColor));
    // set the background colour
    String bColor = p.getProperty("background",  "white");
    l.setBackground(Colors.get(bColor));
    m.setLayout(new GridLayout(1,1));
    m.add(l);
    m.pack();
    m.setVisible(true);
  }
}
```

If the property file has the content shown on the previous page, the program will look as in Figure 15.6 when it is run.

Figure 15.6 Using a property file

516

15.7 Swing components

Something called *Java Foundation Classes* (JFC) was introduced in J2SDK. JFC consists of a number of class libraries that can be used when we construct GUI programs. One of these libraries is AWT (Abstract Window Toolkit), which was described in Chapters 5 and 11 and which we have used consistently in this book. Another class library in JFC is *Swing*. Swing contains a set of GUI components, such as buttons, menus, etc. We could say that Swing is an extended and more advanced version of AWT. There are more components and these are more advanced than the ones in AWT; its components are also rather more elegant than those in AWT. In Swing, we can choose to have the appearance of the components modified to suit the platform we are using, so that they may adopt a "Windows look" or, independent of any platform, a "Java look".

All the classes in Swing that describe components are subclasses of a class with the name JComponent. The class JComponent is, in its turn, a subclass of the "ordinary" class Container, in java.awt. This means that all Swing components can contain other components, other Swing components as well as AWT components. In Swing, there are new, more advanced versions of the classes in AWT. Some examples are JButton, JLabel and JMenu. These are used in the same way as the corresponding classes in AWT but offer a number of new possibilities. For example, we can place small pictures, or *icons*, in the components. There are also new components that have no equivalent in AWT, the class JToolBar, for example, which makes it possible to put a toolbar into a window and the class JTree, which enables tree-like structures, such as files and maps, to be shown.

Swing uses layout managers, exactly like AWT, to arrange components in a window. The layout managers in AWT can be used; there are also some new ones, such as BoxLayout, where the components are arranged along an x- or y-axis. Swing also uses the same model as AWT for handling events, so we can make use of listeners. These listen to the different kinds of events that can be generated by the various components. There are a number of new events, in addition to the different event classes and events that we discussed in Section 10.1. TreeSelectionEvent is one of these, for example. There are also a number of new listener interfaces, such as TreeSelectionListener.

However, in Swing we can also make use of something called Model View Controller (MVC). This is a rather advanced technique involving GUI components, where we separate what is shown on the screen from what the component logically represents in the program (the model).

We cannot go into a description of the Swing classes in this book but since Swing components can be used in the same way as AWT components and the same layout and event models are used, the reader will be well equipped to go further and learn more about Swing. Everything we have learnt about GUIs and AWT in this book can then be put to immediate use.

15.8 Exercises

1. Insert documentation comments into one of your own classes, then use the `javadoc` program to document your class.

2. Let us suppose that the variable `c` of type **byte** contains two small whole numbers in the interval 0 to 15. One of the whole numbers is stored in the four left-hand bits in `c`, and the other in the four right-hand bits. Write a program to output the sum of the two small numbers.

3. Let us suppose that we use an array `a` of the element type **byte** to store an array of logic values. Every logic value is to be represented by only one bit. There will therefore be room for 8 logic values in every **byte**. Write part of a program to show how we can index in the array. In other words, given a variable `k`, we have to produce the logic value number `k`.

4. Write a program that reads a date in the format yyyy-mm-dd. The program should write out the day number of the date during the year, that is, a number between 1 and 365, or 366 if it is a leap year. (Leap years are years that are divisible by 4 but years exactly divisible by 100 are not leap years, except those divisible by 400, which are.) Use a **switch** statement with the different months as an alternative.

5. A trade union is offered an agreement over a number of years in accordance with the following model:
    In the first year (year 1), every employee will get a monthly wage of $2000.
    In the following years (year 2, 3, 4, etc.) employees will get an increase of 4% on the previous year's wages and, in addition, a general increment of $60.

    Write a recursive method that will compute a monthly wage in a particular year. The function will have the number of a year as its only parameter.

6. Write a recursive method `sgd` that will compute the greatest common divisor of two positive whole numbers m and n on the basis of the following definition:

$$\text{sgd}(m, n) = \begin{cases} m & \text{if } m = n \\ \text{sgd}(m - n, n) & \text{if } m > n \\ \text{sgd}(m, n - m) & \text{otherwise} \end{cases}$$

7. Write a recursive variant of the method `binarySearch` on page 203.

8. Change the program `TextAnalysis` on page 502, so that it will only write out words that are reserved words in Java. (See Appendix A.) Use a set that contains

the reserved words and check to see whether the words read in are present in this set.

9. Solve Exercise 9 on page 219 in a different way, using a map to map article designations onto objects of the class `Article`. Use the classes `ObjectInputStream` and `ObjectOutputStream` to read in and write out the map.

10. Instead of having several property tables in a program, it can be more useful to combine the mappings we read in from a particular property file of system properties, so that we only have one property table to search in. Write statements that will form a new property table of this kind and replace the system's property table with the new one.

Appendix A
Reserved words
and operators

The reserved words in Java are shown in Table A.1. The words written in brackets are reserved but are not used in the language at the moment, although they may be used in future versions of Java.

abstract	do	if	(outer)	this
boolean	double	implements	package	throw
break	else	import	private	throws
byte	extends	(inner)	protected	transient
(byvalue)	false	instanceof	public	trap
case	final	int	(rest)	true
(cast)	finally	interface	return	try
char	float	long	short	(var)
class	for	native	static	void
(const)	(future)	new	super	volatile
continue	(generic)	null	switch	while
default	(goto)	(operator)	synchronized	

Table A.1 Reserved words

A compilation of the operators in Java is given in Table A.2. Operators with only one operand, *unary* operators, have been placed in the first two boxes, while operators with two operands have been placed in the other boxes. (The exception is the conditional operator, which has three operands.) The operators have been listed in order of priority, with the operator in the first box having highest priority. Operators in the same box have the same priority. (In the table, the symbol a is used to indicate an arbitrary expression.)

postfix, increase and decrease	`a++` `a--`

prefix, increase and decrease
unary + and –
the bit operator NOT
logic NOT
	`++a` `--a`
	`+a` `-a`
	`~a`
	`!a`

multiplication, division, remainder	`*` `/` `%`
addition, subtraction	`+` `-`
shift	`<<` `>>` `>>>`
less than and greater than test of an object's class	`<` `>` `<=` `>=` **instanceof**
equality, inequality	`==` `!=`
the bit operator AND	`&`
the bit operator XOR	`^`
the bit operator OR	`|`
logic AND	`&&`
logic OR	`||`
the conditional operator	`?:`

assignment operators	`=` `+=` `-=` `*=` `/=` `%=`
	`&=` `^=` `|=`
	`<<=` `>>=` `>>>=`

Table A.2 Operators

Appendix B
LATIN_1 codes

\u0000	nul	\u0020	space	\u0040	@	\u0060	`
\u0001	soh	\u0021	!	\u0041	A	\u0061	a
\u0002	stx	\u0022	"	\u0042	B	\u0062	b
\u0003	etx	\u0023	#	\u0043	C	\u0063	c
\u0004	eot	\u0024	$	\u0044	D	\u0064	d
\u0005	enq	\u0025	%	\u0045	E	\u0065	e
\u0006	ack	\u0026	&	\u0046	F	\u0066	f
\u0007	bel	\u0027	'	\u0047	G	\u0067	g
\u0008	bs	\u0028	(	\u0048	H	\u0068	h
\u0009	ht	\u0029	)	\u0049	I	\u0069	i
\u000A	lf	\u002A	*	\u004A	J	\u006A	j
\u000B	vt	\u002B	+	\u004B	K	\u006B	k
\u000C	ff	\u002C	,	\u004C	L	\u006C	l
\u000D	cr	\u002D	-	\u004D	M	\u006D	m
\u000E	so	\u002E	.	\u004E	N	\u006E	n
\u000F	si	\u002F	/	\u004F	O	\u006F	o
\u0010	dle	\u0030	0	\u0050	P	\u0070	p
\u0011	dc1	\u0031	1	\u0051	Q	\u0071	q
\u0012	dc2	\u0032	2	\u0052	R	\u0072	r
\u0013	dc3	\u0033	3	\u0053	S	\u0073	s
\u0014	dc4	\u0034	4	\u0054	T	\u0074	t
\u0015	nak	\u0035	5	\u0055	U	\u0075	u
\u0016	syn	\u0036	6	\u0056	V	\u0076	v
\u0017	etb	\u0037	7	\u0057	W	\u0077	w
\u0018	can	\u0038	8	\u0058	X	\u0078	x
\u0019	em	\u0039	9	\u0059	Y	\u0079	y
\u001A	sub	\u003A	:	\u005A	Z	\u007A	z
\u001B	esc	\u003B	;	\u005B	[	\u007B	{
\u001C	fs	\u003C	<	\u005C	\	\u007C		
\u001D	gs	\u003D	=	\u005D	]	\u007D	}
\u001E	rs	\u003E	>	\u005E	^	\u007E	~
\u001F	us	\u003F	?	\u005F	_	\u007F	del

the table continues on the next page

\u0080		\u00A0	*nbsp*	\u00C0	À	\u00E0	à
\u0081		\u00A1	¡	\u00C1	Á	\u00E1	á
\u0082		\u00A2	¢	\u00C2	Â	\u00E2	â
\u0083		\u00A3	£	\u00C3	Ã	\u00E3	ã
\u0084	*ind*	\u00A4	¤	\u00C4	Ä	\u00E4	ä
\u0085	*nel*	\u00A5	¥	\u00C5	Å	\u00E5	å
\u0086	*ssa*	\u00A6	¦	\u00C6	Æ	\u00E6	æ
\u0087	*esa*	\u00A7	§	\u00C7	Ç	\u00E7	ç
\u0088	*hts*	\u00A8	¨	\u00C8	È	\u00E8	è
\u0089	*htj*	\u00A9	©	\u00C9	É	\u00E9	é
\u008A	*vts*	\u00AA	ª	\u00CA	Ê	\u00EA	ê
\u008B	*pld*	\u00AB	«	\u00CB	Ë	\u00EB	ë
\u008C	*plu*	\u00AC	¬	\u00CC	Ì	\u00EC	ì
\u008D	*ri*	\u00AD	-	\u00CD	Í	\u00ED	í
\u008E	*ss2*	\u00AE	®	\u00CE	Î	\u00EE	î
\u008F	*ss3*	\u00AF	¯	\u00CF	Ï	\u00EF	ï
\u0090	*dcs*	\u00B0	°	\u00D0	Ð	\u00F0	ð
\u0091	*pul*	\u00B1	±	\u00D1	Ñ	\u00F1	ñ
\u0092	*pu2*	\u00B2	²	\u00D2	Ò	\u00F2	ò
\u0093	*sts*	\u00B3	³	\u00D3	Ó	\u00F3	ó
\u0094	*cch*	\u00B4	´	\u00D4	Ô	\u00F4	ô
\u0095	*mw*	\u00B5	µ	\u00D5	Õ	\u00F5	õ
\u0096	*spa*	\u00B6	¶	\u00D6	Ö	\u00F6	ö
\u0097	*epa*	\u00B7	·	\u00D7	×	\u00F7	÷
\u0098		\u00B8	¸	\u00D8	Ø	\u00F8	ø
\u0099		\u00B9	¹	\u00D9	Ù	\u00F9	ù
\u009A		\u00BA	º	\u00DA	Ú	\u00FA	ú
\u009B	*csi*	\u00BB	»	\u00DB	Û	\u00FB	û
\u009C	*st*	\u00BC	¼	\u00DC	Ü	\u00FC	ü
\u009D	*osc*	\u00BD	½	\u00DD	Ý	\u00FD	ý
\u009E	*pm*	\u00BE	¾	\u00DE	Þ	\u00FE	þ
\u009F	*apc*	\u00BF	¿	\u00DF	ß	\u00FF	ÿ

Table B.1 LATIN_1 codes

The characters included in LATIN_1 are shown in Table B.1. These characters correspond to the first 256 characters in Unicode, so the Unicode sequences of the characters have also been shown. Some characters, such as *esc* and *del*, relate to system control and are not represented by graphic symbols. In the table, the symbolic names of these characters have been written in italics.

Index

Page numbers written in bold refer to facts tables.